T0381013

Reflections on the Gospel of John

A Daily Devotional Journey via Three-Minute Meditations

DR. RANDY L. JAMES

authorHOUSE

AuthorHouse™
1663 Liberty Drive
Bloomington, IN 47403
www.authorhouse.com
Phone: 833-262-8899

Published by AuthorHouse   05/26/2023

ISBN: 979-8-8230-0921-8 (sc)
ISBN: 979-8-8230-0920-1 (e)

ACKNOWLEDGEMENTS

This book would not be a finished product without the editing capabilities of my dear wife, Mary Jane. She continues to not only correct my mistakes as needed, but also honors me with her praise and continued support. I will forever be indebted to her for so many things, but especially for this labor of love.

I also want to thank the audience of my Daily Devotional Focus, who listened faithfully to these words as they were first broadcast audibly, and who have inspired me to continue in my journey through the Word of God.

INTRODUCTION

All the Bible is considered by most Christians to be inspired by God. However, there are certain books within the Holy Scriptures that are often loved more than others, since they speak to specific needs within the human heart.

Such is the Gospel of John. It has been treasured by countless souls over the centuries since its authorship, for it has been the source of inspiration that transforms the minds of thinking people, and truly transforms lives for the glory of God.

This book is intended to digested slowly, a page at a time, as the verses pour out messages of the author's own personal reflections to what God has already inspired. It could be considered a commentary for the average person who has no previous biblical experience or a springboard for deeper thought for those who have been in the Christian faith for a long time.

If these words are beneficial to the reader and draws the human heart closer to the heart of Almighty God, then the purpose of the writing has been achieved.

CONTENTS

IN THE BEGINNING...

John 1:1 *In the beginning was the Word, and the Word was with God, and the Word was God.*

As we open this account of the Gospel of John, we need to note that he was not writing from a historical account, but from a spiritual one. Many scholars feel that by the time this book was written, some fifty to sixty years had passed since the crucifixion and resurrection of Jesus, so John has had plenty of time to reflect on all those events and what they meant in his own life, and for the world. He would have been an old man, and the wisdom of his years, along with the anointing of the Holy Spirit, poured out through quill and ink.

John takes us back to the start of everything, to the beginning. Because this is a spiritual view and not a historical view, we can see with eyes of faith what it was like before anything existed that we see today. The beautiful and life-changing truth that comes from his view is that when nothing else was around, Jesus was there. He, the blessed Word of God, is everlasting in every sense. Before there was anything, He was there. After this world and the universe comes to an end, He will be there. He was alive in the time of Abraham, Noah, and Moses, as well as in the days of our great-grandparents, and is with us today.

Not only is Jesus the Son the eternal Word that John mentioned, but also is one with God the Father. They are inseparably linked as one everlasting being, but with separate functions and personalities. They are together as one might see any couple of figures, but also connected as the Divine Godhead with one essence, one purpose, and one substance. John doesn't make any equivocation here. He said it plainly for all to read, Jesus is God. The man who was born to Mary, who performed miracles throughout His life, who died on a Roman cross and was resurrected from the dead, is God Himself.

For us, that means when we read about Jesus, we are reading about God, for Jesus showed mankind what God looks like and how God acts. God truly became man and lived among us, but when doing so He gave up none of His divinity. Jesus the Lord was God in the flesh. He always has been and always will be our Creator, Redeemer, Savior, and King.

BEFORE THE BEGINNING...

John 1:2 *He was with God in the beginning.*

There can be little doubt here that John was remembering Genesis 1:1. Just compare the two scriptures together. Genesis 1:1 says, "In the beginning, God created the heavens and the earth." John was not squeamish in his declaration of the eternal nature of Jesus, because he was fully convinced of his own theology by this point in his life. John had walked with Jesus, talked with Jesus, eaten with Jesus, learned from Jesus, saw Jesus die on the cross, and was a witness to His resurrection. All doubt was removed from his mind. Jesus was and is, God.

The reference to the beginning brings out some more questions though. The beginning of what? The beginning of man? No, there is something before that. The beginning of the world? No, there was still something before the earth was created. By looking carefully at Genesis 1:2 we find, "Now the earth was formless and empty. Darkness was over the surface of the deep, and the Spirit of God was hovering over the waters." It seems like something is missing. Before the creation story begins, there was an empty and formless world. There was darkness and there was water, and apparently, deep water. And the Spirit of God, the third person of the Holy Trinity, was presiding over it all.

What John said in a few simple words screams out to us today, that the fullness of God rested on the person of Jesus. If we want to know someone well, we don't go to a distant acquaintance to find out information, rather, we go to an intimate friend. When we want to know about God, we go to Jesus, who reveals the divinity of the Father to us. Though the Spirit, the Son, and the Father are separately revealed to us, they are one in essence, and as one God He has presided over all there is in eternity of the past and will do so for eternity in the future.

The very concept of Jesus being "the Word," or in the Greek language, "the Logos," seems very strange to us in the twenty-first century. However, John was writing to the people of the first century, not particularly to us. But the Spirit of God inspired his words to be used for all time, so we also get the benefit it provides. We may not understand fully the Greek references that John uses, but the people of his day did.

WHO IS RESPONSIBLE?

John 1:3 *Through him all things were made; without him nothing was made that has been made.*

When John was writing these words, he was writing in part to combat the false doctrine of Gnosticism, which was plaguing the church of his day. In the simplest form, Gnostics believed that matter is evil and only the spirit is good. The teaching went on to say that since God is good and pure, He could not touch or create matter, which was evil. Therefore, He would have sent out emanations from His holy presence, which became less holy the farther away they got from the core of His divine presence. It was an emanation from God that turned evil and became hostile to God Himself. It created the material world and therefore the world itself became evil also.

John would not accept any of this. God is holy, Jesus is holy, and the Spirit is holy, and collectively as one He created this material world. Everything physical that exists came about because Jesus had a hand in it. The bare bones of Christianity states that this is God's world and that He is intimately involved in it. Since the Father, the Son, and the Spirit have been one since the beginning and the Trinity is holy, then the world created by the Godhead is also holy. Whatever is wrong with this world is due to nothing but man's rebellion and sin against God, and it is because of that sin that Jesus came to live among us and bring mankind back to the Father.

It can be a bit confusing when we start talking about the Holy Trinity, but it is a doctrine of faith that has been developed, debated, and decided upon over the course of time during these last two thousand years. God is one, but He is depicted to us in the persons of Father, Son, and Spirit. It was through God as one that the universe and all that there is, was created, and it has been governed by that Holy One since anything was created.

John focused on the part Jesus played in all of this. Our Lord didn't have to take a backseat or play a lesser part in the creative process. He was front and center, orchestrating all that happened. For us today, this is a foundation statement of our Christian faith. Jesus is not only our Redeemer, Sanctifier, Lord, and Friend, but He is also the Creator of all that has ever existed or ever will exist. He is the King, the Master Planner, and Divine Architect of the universe.

REAL LIFE

John 1:4 *In him was life, and that life was the light of men.*

As John goes through his basic doctrinal teaching about Jesus, he makes note of the personal experience he had with his Master. When John met Jesus, he found life. Before Jesus, everything else was just existence.

Life is the opposite of destruction, condemnation, and death. The person who lives a Christ-less life exists, but really doesn't know what true life is. Jesus is the bringer and giver of life because the source of all life is found in God, and Jesus is God in the flesh. We enter this life experience by putting our faith in Jesus for our salvation. We believe that everything He said was and is true, and we can base all our hopes and plans on Him.

We have all known of people who have lived in this world for many years, but have never met the source of life, the giver of real life. They wander from experience to experience, but along the way have had to just settle for getting by, or somehow surviving. Even those who have a more comfortable existence due to wealth and privilege usually find themselves feeling empty and questioning the meaning of it all, once they stop long enough to think.

John makes the sermon for us very clear, "In him was life." To put it even more succinctly we could say, "If we have Jesus, we have life. If we don't have Jesus, then we haven't even begun to live." It's really, just that simple. People will try to make excuses and offer other explanations as they try to get around the truth that is staring them in the face, but the joy of the Lord is only found in those who have experienced a personal relationship with the Christ Himself.

We can find extensive examples in the Bible concerning the difference meeting Jesus made in the lives of people wherever He went. Throughout history since that time, countless numbers of testimonies come from people who relate how their real life truly began when they met Jesus. He is the life producer who never leaves or forsakes those to whom He has imparted life. Others may seek pleasure for a season, but Jesus is where all real life begins. This light that comes from Jesus produces life, and life is what Jesus is all about, for without Him everything else is just a meaningless game. In Him, we have all that we ever need, for His light never goes away or goes out. It is with us always, for He is with us always.

LIGHT THAT OVERCOMES

John 1:5 *The light shines in the darkness, but the darkness has not understood it.*

Twenty-one times in the Gospel of John he uses this word for light. To be technical, he is echoing an ancient Persian thought known as Zoroastrianism, which basically puts life into a focus of living in the light or living in the dark. In other words, think Star Wars, and the light and dark side of the force.

What John proclaims is that the light of Jesus is on the offensive. It dispels darkness. If you have ever been in a room that is totally cut off from light and just light a match or a candle, it will quickly become apparent just how little light it takes to have an impact on darkness. Jesus is the light with a capital "L." He is the light that is the personal revelation of God to men because He is continually revealing Himself to us.

John reminds us that the light of Christ has been given to all who enter the world. Depending on our circumstances we receive it in greater of lesser degrees, but all people are exposed to His radiance at some point. The light of Christ becomes our source of guidance for the decisions we make. It helps us find our way to God because when we are left to our own devices, we always end up blind.

John even makes it clear that some people do their best to dim the light, or even try to put it out. They may refuse it, or curse it, but even if they can't grasp it, they are never able to extinguish it. The light that came from the Father, the light that transforms lives, the light that shows us the way to live, is eternal, and even though often misunderstood, it will never go out.

The light is the divine Word that John has been referencing. He is eternal, He is one with the Father. He is the Creator of all things. He is the source of all life as well as the light that shines on our dark world. Jesus is the revelation of God that we need for our own lives, our families, our communities, our nation, and our world. He is the one we must have if we are to be all we were created to be.

Of course, even though the sun may shine, the darkness of sin still has a strong hold on our world. Christ's light is our only hope to break free of it.

SENT FROM GOD

John 1:6 *There was a man who was sent from God, his name was John.*

After 400 years of relative silence, four centuries of no fresh word from the Lord, at least not recorded in the Bible, while there were generations of wars, conflicts and spiritual crises, God was still working. Old men would tell stories around the cooking fires about the glory days when God still spoke to His people, and they would tell of a promised deliverer, a Messiah. But for four hundred years, nothing. Then there came a man sent from God.

When John, whom we know as "the Baptist," or "the baptizer," made himself known in Israel, he created quite a splash (pardon the pun). Through him the Lord spoke about revival, repentance, restitution, and the coming fulfillment of the messianic promise. He was certainly no ordinary preacher.

John was sent by God, and being sent by God always requires two things at least. First, being sent by God always requires surrender. He surrendered everything that would not propel him in the work he was called to do. He lived in the wilderness, he survived on a diet of meager rations, and he took people to task instructing, correcting, and even sometimes scolding. Being sent also required paying a price. John's forceful ministry would be met with force and eventually he would be arrested by King Herod and lose his freedom entirely. His end would come as a political prisoner who would be beheaded at the word of that despotic ruler.

From a human perspective it might seem that John's life was lived almost in vain. Apparently, he never married, left no offspring, and his followers would eventually go back to their usual way of life, and forget about him for the most part. However, the Bible records that is not the case.

God sent him to do a job, he did it, and was then released from his responsibility, and now reaps the rewards for his faithfulness throughout eternity. After all, Jesus would eventually say, "I tell you, among those born of women, there is no one greater than John" (Luke 7:28). That's high praise from a very high source. There may be times in our lives when we may feel that we are not accomplishing all that we think we should, but if we follow God's call on our life, we will never be failures. Fitting into His divine plan will turn out to be the best choice we could ever make, for our Lord never makes a mistake.

Preparing For The Light

John 1:7 *He came as a witness to testify concerning that light, so that through him all men might believe.*

Witnesses are important to any court proceeding where truth is not readily evident. Over the course of history many determinations have been made based on the testimony of witnesses who would come forward for either the prosecution or the defense of a person on trial.

In this case, John was born into the world just for this purpose. We aren't told anything about his childhood after the announcement of his birth to Zacharias and Elizabeth (Luke 1:57), but we know from other readings that his birth and life were given as primary evidence of his role as the forerunner of the Messiah. John was an important part of God's plan to save the world He had created.

His testimony concerning Jesus was to announce that Jesus was the light of the world. Though they were cousins and though their mothers were close, we have no record of their interaction as youngsters or teens, though that is possible. What we do have though, is a declaration by John, the writer of this gospel account, that John was from God on a mission to declare the Lordship of Jesus to the world.

It's important to note here why it was so necessary for John to make this testimony about Jesus. The reason behind John's declaration was that everyone would have an opportunity to believe the plan of God that was being put in place in the world through His beloved Son. God cares enough for this world that He put a plan in place not only concerning Jesus, but also by giving messages to the Old Testament prophets concerning His coming and to John so that the way for the divine plan could be possible. John's role would be to gain a following of considerable size and then turn that following over to the one who would take center stage. John was the opening act. Jesus was the main event that would change history and the world by being the Lamb of God that would take away the sins of man.

This is why Jesus would later say that no one was greater in the Kingdom of God than John (Matthew 11:11). From birth he was filled with the Spirit, and the Spirit led him to prepare for Jesus, so that you and I could be saved. I think that makes him a pretty important character.

Pointing To The Light

John 1:8–9 *He himself was not the light; he came only as a witness to the light. The true light that gives light to every man was coming into the world.*

"This little light of mine, I'm going to let it shine." That's the way the song we learn as children begins. It's all about not being bashful when we tell the story of Jesus, and hopefully it's a lesson that Christians of all ages put into practice in every aspect of their daily lives.

John never claimed to have any light within himself. He was only going to prepare an atmosphere and provide a place for the True Light to shine. The best he could hope for was to be able to reflect the light of Jesus to someone else, but he, like us, was totally powerless on his own when it came to generating any ability to bring light into this world. Jesus alone is the light, and everything else is only a cheap imitation of His glory.

What John did was to set a pretty good pattern for the church to follow. The task for our local churches is to produce a place where the atmosphere of our gathering makes it easier for people to see the light of Jesus and hear His voice. We have nothing to offer anyone, anywhere, beyond being a place where God meets with His people and blesses them by such an interaction. Making the environment "Jesus friendly" is not as easy as it sounds, but it's something that every congregation should attempt to do.

I remember a time in my first pastorate when a fairly new convert to the faith related to me, "I don't know what there is about this place, but I feel Jesus here when I come in the building." That was one of the highest compliments I ever received as a pastor. I never want people to say that when they come into my church they are impressed by the music or awed by the preaching; I want them to be impassioned by the Christ. If we can create the setting where people sense the presence of Jesus, then whatever else we have done in the liturgy, the music, the preaching, or anything else that happens for good, is just icing on the cake. Making God look good to those who need to see Him is the best job we could ever have.

John knew that and he was content to be just a pointer to the light. He wasn't looking to be famous. He was striving to be faithful. Because of such an attitude Jesus was able to break out from the ministry John started and begin His plan to change the world. John certainly did let his little light shine.

A Missed Opportunity

John 1:10–11 *He was in the world, and though the world was made through him, the world did not recognize him. He came to that which was his own, but his own did not receive him.*

"Haters gonna hate!" That's a phrase that has become popular in our American society lately, but there's a lot of truth in it. This certainly describes the world in which Jesus made His debut. Jesus came to live among His creation, and though He had made the world, and though He only wanted the best for the people of this world, He was rejected by the majority of the population in it. This part of the Gospel story is very sad.

It's not as if Jews, or even the Samaritans, had not been told about Him. The prophets of the Old Testament made continual announcements about a messiah who was to come, but when He arrived, they didn't see Him for who He was. Again, that's a sad part of the Gospel story.

What makes it especially sad is that Jesus loved, and loves, this world so very much. We feel the agony in His voice as He would say, "O Jerusalem, Jerusalem, you who kill the prophets and stone those sent to you. How often I have longed to gather your children together as a hen gathers her chicks under her wings, but you were not willing" (Matthew 23:37).

Many pastors, parents, and spiritual leaders have felt the weight and pain of rejection when their attempts to share the good news about Jesus have been rebuffed. It shouldn't come as a surprise though. If they rejected Jesus in John's day, it's not unexpected that they would reject Him now.

So, do we just throw up our hands and just consider that people have had their chance and let it go? No, I think the route that Jesus gave us is a better plan. As this writer would later record, "Having loved his own, which were in the world, he loved them to the end" (John 13:1). Though rejected, Jesus just kept on loving. Though they crucified Him, He never stopped loving and forgiving them.

Christ is the role model for all who would walk the holy way. His attitude, action, and message has changed the world forever. We will do well if we will follow His example and continue loving others, the good and the bad, for as long as breath remains in us.

THE MOST IMPORTANT
RIGHT OF ALL

John 1:12–13 *Yet to all who received him, to those who believed in his name, he gave the right to become children of God—children not born of natural descent, nor of human decision or a husband's will, but born of God.*

It may have been the minority of the nation's population, but from the very beginning of Jesus' ministry, there were those who followed after Him. Those who would not receive Him world reject Him, but those who would receive Him received more than they could ever have imagined. They became new creations and were adopted into, the family of God. Being born of God is in every sense, a do-over for our life.

It must have seemed strange for Jewish people to have a new start with God. After all, they were the ones who had grown up on the stories of Abraham, Moses, David, and Elijah. They had participated in the Feasts, Festivals, and Holy Days of the people of Israel. If anyone belonged to God, they surely did. But when Jesus came on the scene, they found truth like they had never seen it before.

The gift of faith that Jesus provided them gave them a new awareness of their standing before God. From that point on they found that salvation wasn't found in a bloodline or a religious heritage, but in a living relationship with Almighty God. They realize that they were no longer just children of Abraham, for they were spawned by the immovable Spirit of their Divine Father. Those who received Jesus, those who had faith in Him for their salvation, those who would follow after Him, would find reality on a scale that others would only dream about.

Down through the centuries that story has remained the same. God has been redeeming His creation since the story of the Garden of Eden, but in the person of Jesus that redemption has been put into overdrive. What man, with all of his religiosity, his focus on sacrificial details, and his determination could not do, namely establish a relationship with God, Jesus did by becoming man and living among us.

Being born of God is the greatest experience we could ever hope to have in this world, and even that is just the start. After birth, there is growth. And after growth in this world there is life eternal. Thanks be to God through Jesus Christ our Lord.

WHEN GOD BECAME MAN...

John 1:14 *The Word became flesh and made his dwelling among us. We have seen his glory, the glory of the One and Only, who came from the Father, full of grace and truth.*

The idea of God becoming man is mind-blowing. Our thoughts drift to the old Greek and Roman legends of gods like Zeus, Hera, Jupiter, Hercules, and Mars. Man has had a tendency to create his gods in his own image for as long as man has had an imagination. Whenever we have not been able to explain something, someone has come up with a god-like idea to try and provide sense out of this life.

John is telling us that Jesus is so much more than these old stories however. Not only did God become flesh and blood so that He could live as we live and experience what we experience, but He also developed a relationship with men, and John was bearing witness to that fact. John saw Jesus, talked with Jesus, ate with Jesus, heard the teachings of Jesus, and saw the miracles of Jesus. He saw Him glorified on the mountain of transfiguration, and fully understood that this was no ordinary man.

We are told here that Jesus, this God-man, was unique. He was not just *a god*, one that people could line up on the shelves of their beliefs along with all their other gods of antiquity. He was *THE GOD*. He was, and is, in a class all by Himself. As part of the Divine Trinity, He was fully wrapped up in the person of the Father and in the Holy Spirit. He came from the Father, but He was one with Him. There was, and is, no way to separate the collectiveness of the Trinity of God.

Because Jesus was God in the flesh, He was the epitome of God's love and God's truth. His love was for all of the creation He had brought into being, and His truth was timeless and is timeless. He is the definition of the perfect man because He is in reality, the perfect God.

All of this is more than our finite minds can begin to comprehend. We want to understand, but our brains can't handle all the information and data that is required to grasp this miracle of grace. We find ourselves in overload mode whenever we try. What we can grasp though, is that Jesus loves us. He wants the best for us, and He can provide a way for us. Maybe that's all we really need to know anyway.

THE POWER OF A WITNESS

John 1:15 *John testifies concerning him. He cries out, saying, "This was he of whom I said, 'He who comes after me has surpassed me because he was before me.'"*

The John that was testifying here is the person we know as John the Baptist, or John the Baptizer. He was the cousin of Jesus, the son of Zacharias and Elizabeth, and we can read the story of his background in the first chapter of the Gospel of Luke. Because this testimony is recorded before the actual account of Jesus' baptism, it's hard to know how this declaration fits into the overall account. Was it something John knew before he actually baptized Jesus, or is this passage just an addendum to the overall story? It's really hard to tell.

What is certain, however, is that John has no doubt as to the authority that Jesus brings on the scene. Though John may have been older and had the more established preaching ministry, Jesus surpassed him on every level, for Jesus was from the beginning. John bowed to Jesus' authority, saying that the one who came after him was actually before him.

If nothing else, this verse should be a shining example for all of us to emulate. We too need to recognize the order of ranking when it comes to who is more important in our relationship with God. Either Jesus gets top billing in our lives, and gets to make the calls concerning the direction of our path, or we make those calls. If we do, then we are telling Jesus that His authority is of less value than ours. When Jesus is in charge, He is in charge of everything. Our submission to Him is paramount if our relationship with Him is going to grow and be productive.

John certainly knew his place and that place was in submission to his younger cousin. Jesus was the one who would take the center stage in the coming days, and John's role was to do everything in his power to make sure that everyone else knew that that's the way it was supposed to be.

It's a pretty good lesson for us too. Shouldn't our role be to let other people know that Jesus takes center stage in our lives? Shouldn't we be the people who live before the world in such a way that God is glorified by how we lift up the name of Jesus? In fact, this seems the be a good definition of the way of holiness.

FULLNESS OF GRACE

John 1:16 *From the fullness of his grace we have all received one blessing after another.*

Sometimes when I am in my time of prayer, I begin going through a list before the Lord of all the blessings I have received in my life. I think about my wife, my children, and my grandson. I think about other relatives like siblings, cousins, aunts, and uncles. I think about the heritage I have been given from my parents, my grandparents, and my ancestors before them. The list of people that are precious to me goes on and on.

I sometimes also recall the blessings I have received in the faith. I was raised as a part of a loving church family. I have had godly men for pastors and teachers. I was trained in various Bible-based schools that provided me with an education that I can pass on to others. I know of the blessings of spiritually-minded co-workers and denominational networking leaders. These people are also intricately interwoven into my being of who I am.

While I am counting my blessing, I can list all the material things that I have, and all the material things that I have lost, showing me the real value of things over the course of time. Material possessions are to be appreciated, used as tools, and loved as gifts that came from someone else's generosity. But they remain just things that can be lost, burned, and worn out over the course of time. They are blessings, nonetheless, and I am grateful to have use of them.

John really nails a picture of the life in Christ with this verse. We who are members of the Jesus team have had a marvelous amount of grace poured out on us, and as a result we have received one blessing after another. The way is not always easy, and the price that some may have to pay to walk with the Master may be high indeed, but at any cost, God's grace is always sufficient. The trip is truly worth the admission fee.

This is one reason why I find it so important for us to tell as many people as possible about what Jesus has done in us. It's not just bragging on Jesus, though that's a pretty good thing to do, it is so that others who don't know Jesus can get to know Him and get in on the grace and blessings. We in Christ have received the gift of life abundant and so much more. It would be a shame, a real selfish shame, to keep it all to ourselves. Jesus is the gift that keeps on giving, so we need to keep spreading the word about Him!

BREAKING THE LAW

John 1:17 *For the law was given through Moses;*
grace and truth came through Jesus Christ.

We first read about the Law in the book of Exodus. It was given to Moses when he led the people of Israel from a life of slavery and being prisoners in the land of Egypt, to a life of freedom and self-determination in the promised land of Canaan. To this day scholars still argue about who actually recorded the words and works of Moses, and there is still a huge discussion as to the place those words and works have in our present-day Christian family. Obviously, we are not going to settle those questions here.

We can speak with authority, however, concerning the reality of what John tells us about Jesus. He is the author and distributer of grace and truth. No life has ever been lived that contained more grace than did the person of Jesus. No one has ever borne witness to the truth in greater measure than Jesus did. In our world of gracelessness and fake news, these commodities are certainly things we need for every person.

The Good News of the Gospel is not only that Jesus is the embodiment of grace and truth, He is the one who spreads these blessings around to all who would receive them. Grace is God's love that we don't deserve, and truth is the absence of all falsehood. Jesus brings both of these gifts to those who will by faith accept Him and the life that He wants to provide for us.

Mankind has proven over the years that he is not capable of living up to any kind of stationary law or standard. In fact, the Law was put into place to show us just how limited we are when we try to live up to God's values in our own power. We always fall short as we try to keep up with all the rules. However, grace and truth are given to us so that we will have the opportunity to enjoy fellowship with God on a scale we could not even imagine through human trial and error.

God gives us, through the Spirit of Jesus, exactly what we need to live in harmony with holiness in heart and life. Today we can try to keep the Law and obey all the rules, or we can bow before Jesus and admit that we can't do it. When that happens, He reaches out to us and shows us a path upon which we can walk with Him and find the way to God, the way of joy and fellowship.

SEEING GOD

John 1:18 *No one has ever seen God, but God the One and Only, who is at the Father's side, has made him known.*

There are various places in the story of the Jewish exodus from Egypt where the Bible records that Moses saw God. In Exodus 33:11 it says, "The LORD would speak to Moses face to face as a man speaks with his friend." Then in Exodus 33:20 it is recorded as God who is speaking, "But," he said, "You cannot see my face, for there is no one may see me and live." In Numbers 14:14, Moses says, when speaking about the Egyptians, "They have already heard that you, O LORD, have been seen face to face." In Deuteronomy 4:4–5 it says, "The LORD spoke to you face to face out of the fire on the mountain." So, which is it? Did Moses see God, or not?

It's important to always keep each scripture passage in context. In these Old Testament scripture references, it does not say that God was a literal anthropomorphic being that Moses got to witness personally. In each case God is represented in a fire, a cloud, or a burning bush. Moses certainly was aware of the Lord's presence and His voice, but the holiness of God is too majestic and overwhelming for any human being to endure and survive.

John is making the point here that this is not the case with Jesus. Our Lord, who is truly and wholly God, came to earth so that lowly mortals could communicate with Him, and He with them. In His human form, Jesus, the God-man, lived as all men live and had interactions with His creation so that they could experience His love first-hand.

The greatest gift from the Father to us is that He sent His Son to live with us and experience all that we experience. Though we can't see God, those who lived in Galilee in the first century did get to experience the divine presence of Jesus, and that has made all the difference we need.

Jesus ushered in the Kingdom of God, and ever since that time the Kingdom has been growing and gaining ground for the Father. We have a long way to go before the fullness of the Kingdom is realized, but we are a lot closer than we were before men met God in the flesh. Every day we should give thanks to God for the gift of His Son to us. Our world will never be the same, for we now have hope that will last us into eternity. Thanks be to God, the King of kings!

THIS IS WHO I AM

John 1:19–20 *Now this was John's testimony when the Jews of Jerusalem sent priests and Levites to ask him who he was. He did not fail to confess, but confessed freely, "I am not the Christ."*

Every Christian has a testimony about who they are in the plan of the Father. We may not articulate it as well as we should, but we ought to think about it and practice it until we can state our place in Christ clearly. After all, we are instructed in I Peter 3:15 "But in your hearts set apart Christ as Lord. Always be prepared to give an answer to everyone who asks you to give the reason for the hope that you have."

Certainly, John was ready for the Jews who came out to the water's edge to witness what he was doing there. Apparently, the priests and Levites had heard the news about him, and they were anxious about what He was up to. At least somebody in Jerusalem had enough curiosity concerning the rumors to send them on a mission to investigate.

John didn't disappoint them. He made known who he was not, crystal clear, as he stated, "I am not the Christ." He would have more to say about that later in the chapter, but he was addressing here the thing that was foremost on the minds of those questioning him. "Christos," is the English transliteration of the Greek word that we translate as Christ. The term means, "Messiah," or "the anointed one." The people of Israel had been looking for the Messiah to come for centuries, and every once in a while, someone popped up that took on that title for himself, and the authorities needed to clarify whether the claim was true or not. Of course, all had been false prophets to this point. But since John was drawing a lot of attention, they had to know what claims he was making about himself.

We are in good company with John and his testimony. No, we are not the Messiah either, but as we are born again by the power of His Spirit, we walk in newness of life, and that is the testimony that we need to be sharing with people. We in Christ are people who have been born in sin, but we have been transformed, redeemed, delivered, saved, sanctified, or whatever term you would like to use. The point is that Jesus has changed us. He is making us into new creations, fit for whatever He wants to do with us, and when that happens we find that His remaking of us is the best thing that could happen.

WHO DO YOU THINK I AM?

John 1:21 *They asked him, "Who are you? Are you Elijah? He said, "I am not." "Are you the Prophet?" He answered, "No."*

Since John stated clearly that he was not the Christ, the people wondered about his actions along the Jordan River. If he was not the Christ, then why was he preaching and why was he baptizing people for the remission of their sins? What were his credentials to do such things?

Maybe he was Elijah. After all, the prophet Malachi had prophesied, "See, I will send you the prophet Elijah before that great and dreadful day of the LORD comes" (Malachi 4:5). Though Jesus would later tell people that John truly was fulfilling the role of Elijah (Matthew 11:14), John didn't see himself in that light. Elijah the prophet had been gone for 900 years and stories of his legendary life had been making the rounds of Jewish homes ever since. Elijah was a bigger than life figure, and even though John didn't see himself in that way, Jesus affirmed that he certainly was cut from the same mold as Elijah.

When the priests and Levites asked as to whether John was "The Prophet," he again denied it. They were thinking back to the words of Moses in Deuteronomy 8:15, "The LORD your God will raise up for you a prophet like me from among your own brothers." On the day of Pentecost, as recorded in Acts 3:22, Simon Peter recognized "The Prophet" as being Jesus, who also filled the role of Messiah, or Christ. Jesus was the one the folks from Jerusalem were really looking for, but they didn't know it.

It's important to know who we are and who we are not. In this age, so full of egomaniacs, there are plenty of people who love to toot their own horns and tell others just how wonderful they are. Jesus was not like that, nor should any follower of Jesus be like that. The service the gospel writer does for us here, is that he helps us to clarify who we are not before we declare who we are. We are nothing without Jesus, but we are somebody with Him. That's probably a good place to start any testimony.

Eventually John will get around to telling the people sent to him what they needed to know, but the problem was that they weren't satisfied even then. The same may be true for us because the world is not going to receive the answer they want. However, Jesus is what they need, then and now.

WHY?

John 1:22 *Finally they said, "Then who are you?
Give us an answer to take back to those who sent
us. What do you say about yourself?"*

I love how John strings the priests and the Levites along until they are nearly begging him to tell them about what he is doing and why. He shows his wisdom here in that he doesn't tell them too much too soon. When it comes to sharing the Good News about Jesus, timing is everything.

I believe that the best witness we could ever have for the Master is for us to live in such a way that people have to ask us, "Why?" "Why do you do what you do? Why don't you do what you don't do? Why are you so wrapped up in this Jesus thing? Why does it even matter?"

Our walk in holiness is all about our witness. The places we go and the things we do when we get there speak louder, much louder, than our words ever will. When people see us go to church on Sunday, when they catch us praying over our food in a restaurant, when they watch us as we sit on a park bench reading our Bible, they have to wonder at some point, "Why?"

Being a witness for Christ isn't nearly as much about what we say as what we do. Do we remind people of Jesus? Do we act in such a way that people say about us, "Now, that's what a real Christian is like!"? If someone asked us what they asked of John, we could say, "I was lost, but Jesus found me. I was without hope until Jesus gave hope to me. I was once bound by sin and the pain that it brought me, but Jesus freed me from it and now I have joy where the pain used to be." There are many ways to phrase it, but the bottom line is that once we didn't have a relationship with God, and now we do, and it's all because of Jesus.

If someone wanted to get an answer from you to take back to others who wanted to know about you, what would you tell them? We have all kinds of identification credentials from driver's licenses, to passports, to credit cards, and business cards, but those things are not what matter. What matters about our lives is whether or not we have entered into a personal relationship with Jesus, the King of kings. Do we have a walk with Him that we can tell others about? If we do, then we have plenty of information to pass along, because He has done so much for us. If we don't, then perhaps we should ask ourselves why we don't.

MAKING THE WAY STRAIGHT

John 1:23 *John replied in the words of Isaiah the prophet, "I am the voice of one calling in the desert, "Make straight the way for the LORD."*

When John makes this statement, he is quoting directly from Isaiah 40:3. It is a passage where the prophet is changing direction from the previous writings by his name. Chapter 39 of Isaiah closes with a cloud of impending doom that has fallen across the people of Judah, but as chapter 40 opens we see a message of comfort coming through loud and clear.

John the Baptist is not the person we think about when we think of comfort. After all, according to the Gospel of Matthew, he was the guy who lived down by the Jordan River, wore clothes made of camel's hair that was held in place with a leather belt. He lived on a diet of locusts and wild honey, preached a rugged message of repentance, and was not at all a pastoral figure that would bring one a sense of comfort. Still, he was God's man for the hour, and his purpose was being fulfilled daily as he prepared people to receive the Prince of Peace, Jesus, the Messiah.

John called people to do then, what we are called to do even now. We are to do our best to prepare the way for the Lord. We do this first of all, by making sure that Jesus has a direct path into our lives and has the freedom to make whatever rearrangements in us that He wants to make. When we clear the way for Him, then He begins to clear the way for us to live our lives as God intended us to live. Once we have prepared the way for the Lord in our own lives, then it's time for us to make way for others to know about Jesus like we have gotten to know about Him. Lots of people have heard the name, and lots of people even lend a sympathetic ear to His call for people to love each other and God. However, it is only when He is given a clear path into a person's life, that they can ever begin to understand and appreciate the blessing of His presence.

So many people have worked to clear the way for Jesus to speak with me and connect with me. My parents, my pastors, my Sunday School teachers, faithful laypeople at church, youth leaders, college professors, co-workers, and so many others have blessed me with a clear path to Jesus. My highest goal these days is to clear the way for others. Showing people a straight path to Jesus is the best business I could ever be about.

WHY DO YOU DO WHAT YOU DO?

John 1:24–25 *Now some Pharisees who had been sent questioned him, "Why then do you baptize if you are not the Christ, nor Elijah, nor the Prophet?"*

I wish I could have been there that day when the Pharisees questioned John. Though the Bible gives us the basic information needed to understand the message God wants us to get, I would love to have seen John's face, heard the words he spoke, and watched the reaction of those who had been sent from Jerusalem to check this unusual preacher out. I'm sure John caused many more questions than the answers they were looking for.

I guess the same question that the Pharisees asked John, could be asked of us as well. Why do you do what you do when you are neither the Christ, Elijah, nor the Prophet? This then, would lead to us quantifying all we do as they qualify the reasons we have for doing those things.

Let's make it up to date and personal. Why do you read your Bible? Why do you pray? Why do you go to church? Why do you do acts of kindness for the people who are around you? Why do you give offerings to various types of ministries? The questions could go on and on as we reflect on the what's and whys of our daily actions.

For me, like John, I could only say I do what I do because of Jesus. The reason I don't do what I don't do is also because of Jesus. Because Jesus has called me, cleansed me, filled me, and challenged me to see the world through His eyes, I realize that everything begins and ends with Him. He is the reason for my being and the source for the direction my life takes.

Well, John didn't phrase it quite like that, but in the following verses he would make clear that his whole life's focus also was because of Jesus. Jesus was the Father's plan for our world so it could be redeemed. He is more important than anyone else we will ever meet, and meeting Him is more life transforming than any experience we will ever have.

Why do we do what we do? Because at our deepest level we want to do the will of God and be pleasing in His sight. Because God is in the business of redeeming the world, we want to get in on that action and do so by being the servants He can count on always.

MY BAPTISM

John 1:26–28 *"I baptize with water," John replied, "but among you stands one you do not know. He is the one who comes after me, the thongs of whose sandals I am not worthy to untie." This all happened at Bethany on the other side of the Jordan, where John was baptizing.*

Baptism has been the standard for the public announcement of a person's beginning in the Christian walk since the first century. Here John is doing a pre-Christian baptism, because he is doing it before Jesus had even begun His public ministry. In fact, Jesus continued the practice that John was doing and made it the public statement of faith that it is now.

John's baptism was a declaration of the end of a life of sin. After repentance for doing things that displeased God, baptism was the sign before the world that one had changed his or her ways. Without repentance, John wouldn't even consider doing the ritual.

Baptism has taken many forms since that time. Sometimes babies are baptized, sometimes it is done as a part of entrance into church membership. Sometimes it is done with great sincerity and sometimes people are baptized just because they think by doing so their entrance into heaven is guaranteed.

For John, this was just a precursor to what was to come in the reality of Jesus' ministry. He knew that his own ministry was going to be temporary, and that it was merely setting the stage for what Jesus was bringing to pass. He laid the groundwork, and Jesus built upon what John started.

John recognized Jesus as being among the group, but others were oblivious to His presence. There's something telling in that statement, for the same thing has happened countless times down through the centuries. We find that it is possible to know and observe the rituals but miss out on the meaning and the person behind the rituals. Jesus needs to be kept at the center of the baptism focus, for Jesus, not the water, not the ritual, makes all the difference as to one's salvation.

John also knew his place. Jesus was and is Lord. John and the rest of us are just "also ran" players in God's plan of personal salvation. With Christ we have all we need. Without Christ, nothing will ever be enough. Baptism is our declaration of that fact.

ENTER THE LAMB

When John saw Jesus and realized who He was, and what He was about, it must have taken a great load off his shoulders. His task was to prepare the way for the King, but once the King arrived his job was over and he could leave the place of public prominence.

We are to be like that in our work for the Lord. We receive a calling from God and work to fulfill it to the best of our ability. Once we have finished what God has designed for us to do, we are relieved of our responsibilities and allowed to move on to our eternal reward. It's a wonderful retirement plan with benefits that are out of this world. While we are on the job though, our task is to point to Jesus, who takes away the sins of the world.

Sometimes people ask, "Just what is sin?" One of the best definitions I have heard concerning sin is this: "Sin is when I decide that what I think, can take priority over what God thinks." It was the problem with Adam and Eve in the Garden of Eden. It was the problem with Jonah as he tried to run away from God's call. It was the problem with David when he took the wife of Uriah for himself, and it was even the problem of Judas when he chose to enrich himself rather than to be faithful to follow the Master, who had offered him everything.

How do we know what God thinks? It's in the book that He gave us, the Bible. There are places in the Bible where it is sometimes difficult to discern exactly what God is saying to us, and such passages require deeper study and investigation to make the meaning clear. But there are other places in God's book where the message is crystal clear and all we have to do is obey. Sometimes it's as simple as, "Don't eat the fruit," or "Forsake all and follow Jesus," or "Do unto others as you would have them do unto you." However clear or vague the Bible may seem to us, it is God's Word, and the Holy Spirit of God will explain it to us if we will take the time and effort to search for the truth.

Jesus came to take away our sins. He came to take away what keeps us away from God, so that we could be one with Him. Either Jesus delivers us, or we are not delivered. John knew what he was talking about.

BEING SECOND BEST

John 1:30 *This is the one I meant when I said, 'A man who comes after me has surpassed me because he was before me.'*

Some people work all their lives to be the best. Athletes pride themselves on going for the gold medal or the blue ribbon, so that they and others can say that they are the best there is in their particular sport or class. Scholars apply themselves to years of intensive study to become more knowledgeable than anyone else in their field. Even commercial advertising challenges people to buy the products that a particular company is selling so that they can be the best, or have the best.

John turned this popular trend of mankind on its head as he realized that he was never going to be the best. He was born and brought into his public position for the expressed purpose of not being the best. He would play second-fiddle to Jesus, because after Jesus came on the scene, John rapidly retreated and was relegation to a much lesser spot in history.

However, this was okay with John. He knew his place, and that place was to be the one who prepared the way for, and pointed others to Jesus, the Messiah of Israel and Savior of the world. He was right in line with God's plan and John freely acknowledged, "He must become greater; I must become less" (John 3:30).

Some people have a hard time taking a backseat to Jesus. It's so tempting to love the spotlight, hold a microphone in one's hand, and amaze the masses when the opportunity to do so falls on us. John was once there, but he knew that his influence was nothing compared to the person of Jesus. So much more would be accomplished because of the appearance of Jesus than John could hope to bring about in a dozen lifetimes. Submission to Jesus was the best example he could ever give his followers, and the wisest thing he could show to all who would come after him.

Jesus is eternal. He always has been, and He always will be. He made all that there is and controls the destinies of men, nations, and nature. He is God, and our place is to worship Him, serve Him, and point others to Him. We may do it in various ways, but that's what our role boils down to. John knew that. He was the best at that, so I guess He was the best at something after all.

REVEALING JESUS

John 1:31 *"I myself did not know him, but the reason I came baptizing with water was that he might be revealed to Israel."*

This statement from John seems a little perplexing. We have the first interaction between John and Jesus in Luke 1:41, while both these men were still in their mother's wombs. "When Elizabeth heard Mary's greeting, the baby leaped in her womb, and Elizabeth was filled with the Holy Spirit." From that point on the Spirit of God moved mightily in John's life.

We don't have any record in the Bible of any contact between John and Jesus as children, or as teenagers, or even in their early years of adulthood. But because they were cousins, because it was mandatory for Jewish families to attend the three main Jewish Festivals each year in Jerusalem, and because Palestine isn't that large of an area, then it would seem unlikely that they would not have connected somewhere.

It could be that John knew Jesus as a cousin but didn't know Him as the Savior of the world until they met along the river's edge. We may not be able to discern exactly what John means by this statement here on this side of eternity. What we can know for sure though, is that John knew the role he was to play in God's plan very clearly. His public ministry of preaching and baptizing was to get people ready for what was to come. In the vernacular of our modern concerts, John was the opening act for the main event that would headline the show. The group, or person of lesser importance, always comes out first to warm up the crowd for the star. John was the opening act; Jesus was the headliner, and John was okay with it.

Again, this is explained in Luke 1:41, which was quoted earlier. Being filled with the Spirit of God while in his mother's womb caused John to be about the Father's business from the start. Being filled with the Spirit of God caused him to be able to put the Father's business before his own. From the start, John knew his role was to get folks ready for Jesus.

I wish we could all do as well today. If we could just remember that our highest purpose in life is to point people to Jesus, then much more for God could be accomplished. Such a life begins with the Spirit's filling. After that God directs as He wishes, and we gladly comply. The reason we do what we do is so that Jesus might be revealed. What a wonderful job!

CAN I GET A TESTIMONY?

John 1:32–33 *Then John gave this testimony: "I saw the Spirit come down from heaven as a dove and remain on him. I would not have known him, except that the one who sent me to baptize with water told me, 'The man on whom you see the Spirit come down and remain is he who will baptize with the Holy Spirit.'*

This scene is often seen in movies and in our imagination as a literal image of a dove dropping from the sky and landing on Jesus. That may or may not be the case. There may have been an actual bird present, or it may be that John is speaking figuratively here, but the important thing is that when this happened it confirmed in John's mind who Jesus really was. This mark on his ministry was a moment that would never leave him.

The fact that John tells us he was tipped off in advance about what the Spirit would do, tells us at least two things. First, we see here that God and John were on speaking terms. Because of the austere lifestyle John had taken on, he was left with many hours in the presence of the Almighty, and the two of them had come to communicate with each other. John was able to discern in some way just what it was that the Father was going to do, so when it happened, John knew that this is what he had been told about.

The second thing that we see her is that God worked in such a way that there was no doubt about what was happening. As soon as John saw the Spirit settle upon Jesus, he was fully assured that God was fulfilling what had been promised. With his own ears he heard the words of God, and with his own eyes he saw God bring to pass just what He said He would do. These things resulted in a testimony that has transcended the ages. John, the writer of this book, made it very, very clear, "Then John gave this testimony." That would be his role for the remainder of his days, giving testimony to the person and presence of Jesus, the Messiah.

Don't you long to hear from God and see God's hand at work? I know I do. I long to make sure I am on the right track in every aspect of my life, so that I too can testify in some way concerning Jesus and His impact on the world. Like John, I need to take steps to be where I can hear from God and be ready to see how God will show that Jesus is always the answer for His church and for the world He created.

KNOWING FOR SURE

John 1:34 *"I have seen and I testify that this is the Son of God."*

The Son of God. We have gotten so used to that phrase. In our Western societies, the very term is often scorned and derided as something that comes out of ancient literature but has no impact on our real lives. Some people just lump all the so-called gods of the ancient and modern religions together and consider them equals, or valueless, for our current age.

The difference that we find in this verse is that something actually happened to John to prove to him that this person, Jesus, was more than just another Jew with a named derived from their ancestor, Joshua. As mentioned in the previous verses, John heard from God, and John saw the promise of God fulfilled before his very eyes. That was all he needed to move beyond skepticism to a confirmed faith in who Jesus really was.

Our testimony, like John's, is only as good as the reality that backs it up. We can only truly testify to what we have experienced or seen. Others may have different stories or belief systems, but our testimony is what we know, and what we can rely on regardless of what others say.

This points back to the reality that Christianity is totally based on our having a personal relationship with Jesus right now. We can talk about what preachers say, what critics say, and what others hope for, but we can only really testify about what we have personally experienced.

I have heard stories and read stories about events great and small all my life. I believe in history and the lessons we can learn from it. However, I can't testify to anything of historical value unless I was actually there to experience it. Book knowledge and folklore may produce some interesting discussions, but unless we were there to see an event first-hand, all we have is opinions about what we have heard.

This is why our belief needs to be grounded in our daily walk with Jesus. As we talk with Him, listen for His voice, read His word and meditate on His teachings, then what He shares with us becomes our testimony. When He speaks to our hearts, we can authoritatively share our message with others. If we don't experience Him as the living God, then we just have an opinion about Him, like others have about a variety of truly dead religious leaders.

FULFILLING THE MISSION

John 1:35–36 *The next day John was there again with two of his disciples. When he saw Jesus passing by, he said, "Look, the Lamb of God."*

I really can't grasp the concept behind being someone's disciple in the first century world. It seems that they left all of life's responsibilities to follow after someone, and be totally devoted to them. It's almost like a marriage between leadership and followers. That's a lot of devotion for sure.

It also goes without saying then, that it is strange that John's disciples, who were truly devoted to him, would be influenced to follow someone else. However, because John knew his role as the forerunner to the Messiah, he had no problem pointing his fans toward Jesus when He came on the scene.

There was no glory-seeking from John. He was simply a man on a mission, and that mission was about making the transition from his work to the work Jesus would do, as smoothly as possible. By pointing out Jesus as the Lamb of God, John was in essence telling his crew that it was not only okay to follow after Jesus, but that he encouraged them to do so. John's work was coming to an end. The work of the Messiah was just beginning.

Perhaps it is a poor analogy, but I know what it's like as a pastor to leave a church, and to encourage people who have been devoted to you as co-workers with Jesus, to follow the leadership of the next person who would have your job. After all, they were "your people," "your flock," and the focus of "your ministry." Handing them over to someone else is often painful, even if that person is of the highest quality. There is something about the human ego that has a temptation to hold on.

John doesn't seem to have a problem with this. He is so convinced of God's plan for his life that he remembers "his work" is not "his work." It's God's work, and as long as God's work is getting done, everything will be fine. There is no room or place for jealousy in God's plan, for we all need to remember that they are not "our people," "our flock," or the focus of "our ministry." They are God's people, God's flock, and the focus of His ministry.

As with John, our role is to point to the Lamb of God who takes away the sins of the world. When we do that, it doesn't matter who gets the credit. All we have belongs to the King anyway. Let's be satisfied with that.

WHAT DO YOU WANT?

John 1:37–39 *When the two disciples heard him say this, they followed Jesus. Turning around, Jesus saw them following and asked, "What do you want?" They said, "Rabbi," (which means Teacher), "where are you staying?" "Come," he replied, "and you will see." So they went and saw where he was staying, and spent that day with him. It was about the tenth hour.*

Once John had made clear to his disciples just who Jesus was, it was fully understandable that they would follow after this new voice who had come on the scene. Apparently, they followed closely enough that Jesus noticed them and asked them a very important question. The question that He asked them is a question that He asks of all of us, "What do you want?"

The disciples of John missed the significance and turned it into an inquiry as to Jesus' address, but I'm sure that Jesus had more information to share with them than that. He was so interested in what it was that they wanted, that He invited them to spend the day with Him. Is that cool, or what?

Can you imagine being able to sit down with Jesus in the flesh and just spend a day with Him? The tenth hour would be 4:00 p.m., but we aren't told whether that's when they left Jesus, or when they first started visiting with Him. Either way, it was a day that these disciples would never forget.

Maybe it's time that we applied that question from Jesus to our lives. "What do you want?" What do you want out of life? What do you see as the thing that matters most to you? What kind of priority system do you have in place? For many people the answer to that question would be tied to material things like money, fame, health, power, pleasure, or knowledge. While those things are not bad in themselves, the degree of our desire for them tells Jesus everything He needs to know about us. I would hope to think that once we discover that Jesus truly is the Lamb of God, we would be able to answer such a question with, "Lord, I want what You want, and I will do anything and everything in my power to see Your will accomplished." That's the answer I believe would be the most pleasing to our Master.

Spend some time with Jesus today and hear the question anew. When He asks you what you want, what will you say? It's certainly something to think about.

FINDING THE MESSIAH

John 1:40–41 *Andrew, Simon Peter's brother, was one of the two who heard what John had said and had followed Jesus. The first thing Andrew did was find his brother Simon and tell him, "We have found the Messiah" (that is, the Christ).*

Here we have the first of Jesus' disciples identified. Apparently, Andrew had been a follower of John, but after spending a day with Jesus he had completely transferred his loyalty to Him. That's what spending time with Jesus does. It either pulls us in close or drives us away, for there is no middle ground. Andrew heard the words he had been waiting to hear all of his life. His search for light, life, and meaning had come to a close. He had found Jesus, the Lamb of God and nothing else in his life would ever be the same again.

Isn't it interesting that after Andrew left Jesus, that the first thing he did was to find his brother and tell him about his discovery? We will see later on in this book that telling people about Jesus and bringing people to Jesus became a way of life for Andrew. It's a practice that needs to be imitated by a whole lot more people.

Finding Jesus is the most important find we will ever make in life. There is nothing else that even comes close. As wonderful as it to find the right person to marry, the right career move, or the right school to attend, finding Jesus casts a huge net over all these things. As we become followers of Christ, we come quickly to realize that all other decisions are secondary in importance because His plan for us is better than we could ever come up with on our own.

Simon Peter would later have his own encounter with Jesus and would go on to be one of the most influential disciples that Jesus would choose. However, Andrew was the one who broke the ice and cleared the path for Jesus and Simon to come together. Without Andrew, Peter might just have stayed with his boats and nets. But Andrew made sure that Peter came to know about the Messiah.

Maybe your role is to be like Andrew, just telling people about Jesus. It may not make you famous, but it could very well be the most important job you will ever have. Someone's eternal destiny may depend on it.

YOU WILL BE CALLED...

John 1:42 *And he brought him to Jesus. Jesus looked at him and said, "You are Simon, son of John. You will be called Cephas," which when translated is, Peter.*

Peter, the Rock. The tales of his deeds would become legendary down through the years of church history. Peter would become the one that many people considered to be the most important and influential of all the disciples. Though at times he talked too much, and at times he acted in haste without thinking, Jesus saw something in Peter that He could mold and use to accomplish the plan of the Father here on earth.

As we have said, Peter came to know Jesus because of his brother, Andrew. After telling Peter about the person that John the Baptist proclaimed to be the Lamb of God, he took it a step further and actually made the introduction to bring them together. It was a moment that changed history.

This encounter bears a second look, and it brings with it a very important question. Who have you brought to Jesus? This is not a trick question, nor one that is intended to put people under a load of guilt, but it is a vital question. Who have you brought to Jesus? If you are a parent, have you told your children about Jesus and brought them to Him? If you are a married person, have you introduced your mate to Christ? If you are involved in any kind of public arena, have you made your connection to Christ known to those around you, so that they too could have the opportunity to know Him for themselves?

Evangelism is at the core of who we are as Christians. It doesn't have to happen in church, in fact, it probably shouldn't happen there as much as it would happen outside the sanctuary. When God's people are doing naturally what Andrew did with his brother, Simon Peter, then the good news spreads and cannot be contained. If someone has to come to church to hear about and meet Jesus, then most likely there are disciples of Christ who have forgotten the importance of bringing people to meet their King.

The people who are closest to you need to know Jesus. They need to hear how you met Him, and how they can meet Him. It's not the job of the preacher or the professional evangelist alone. It's the task of the person who has found Jesus and knows Him to be the Lamb of God.

FOLLOW ME!

John 1:43 *The next day Jesus decided to leave for Galilee. Finding Philip, he said to him, "Follow me."*

Those two little words, "Follow me," are so easy to say, but often so hard to do. As difficult as the journey may be sometimes, just think how special the opportunity given to us is when Jesus calls. Philip was invited to walk with Jesus and fellowship with Him as they made their way over the many miles from Bethany, beyond the Jordan River, to Galilee. Those days would be remembered by Philip for the rest of his life. They would be special for anyone to experience.

We too have been invited to make the journey with Jesus. Though we can't walk with Him physically as Philip did, we can be aware of His continued presence every day of our lives. We can talk to Him, listen to Him, ask Him questions, and wait for His responses to us. The issue boils down to whether or not we want to take Him up on His invitation for us to follow Him.

I have found that walking with Jesus is the most precious gift I could ever receive. As wonderful as it is to be married, to be a parent, to be a minister of the Gospel, and to experience all the other joys of life, there is nothing that matches walking with our Lord. All these other things will eventually be taken from us, but our walk with Jesus goes on throughout all of our days here, and then on throughout eternity.

Because Philip was from Bethsaida, he had to opportunity to walk with Jesus approximately seventy miles on this journey. One can only imagine the conversations that were held over the miles, and around the campfires at night. Jesus was already preparing Philip for days of ministry that would come, and I'm sure that Philip was soaking up every word that Jesus spoke as if he were a sponge.

Today would be a good time to listen for the Master's voice concerning His call for us to follow Him. Today would be a wonderful opportunity for each of us to decide that walking and fellowshipping with Him would become the most important thing we would ever do. Today, walking with Jesus could just change our life forever. We may envy Philip for this special and rare invitation, but don't forget that He is calling each of us to join the journey with Him as well.

WE HAVE FOUND HIM!

John 1:44–45 *Philip, like Andrew and Peter, was from the town of Bethsaida. Philip found Nathanael and told him, "We have found the one Moses wrote about in the Law, and about whom the prophets also wrote—Jesus of Nazareth, the son of Joseph."*

The Hebrew and Aramaic definition of Bethsaida literally means, "House of hunting," or "House of fishing." One can imagine that in previous days even before this scripture was written, that it was a wilderness area where wild game, as well as fishing boats were plentiful. By the time Jesus traveled there with Philip, it was a community of people who lived on both sides of the Jordan River at the point where it entered the northern part of the Sea of Galilee. It's also the place where the feeding of the 5000 would happen, so apparently there was quite a population where Jesus could find a place to minister. Since Philip, Andrew, Peter, and Nathanael were from there, Jesus was able to connect with them as the first of His disciples. They had no idea at this point in the story as to all that was in store for them, but Jesus apparently saw in them something that was special.

It is most likely that the group who had been around John's baptizing area, would have traveled together along the journey north. Jesus not only got to connect with Philip, but probably Andrew and Peter walked with Him also. Just as Andrew had been excited to share what he knew about Jesus with his brother, Simon Peter, Philip was keen to relate the news to Nathanael.

I have to think that what got Philip all stirred up about Jesus came from what took place on the journey from Bethany to Bethsaida. Philip had become convinced that Jesus was the one Moses had written about, and the one to whom the prophets referred. He was sold on the legitimacy of this guy named Jesus.

The pattern that Philip presented would be repeated countless times down through the centuries to come. When people meet Jesus and spent time with Him, they are not the same afterwards. They want to tell His story, they want their friends to know about Him, and they become convinced that He is what they had been looking for and waiting for their whole lives. Jesus still affects us like that. Philip told others and so should we. It's the best news we will ever discover, and the best news we will ever pass on.

DON'T DESPISE HUMBLE BEGINNINGS

John 1:46 *"Nazareth! Can anything good come from there?" Nathanael asked. "Come and see," said Philip.*

According to the online data source, "Wikipedia," Nazareth is known as the Arab capital of Israel. In 2019 its population was 77,445. The inhabitants are predominantly Arab citizens of Israel, of whom 69% are Muslim, and 31% Christian. The Jews are certainly in the minority.

Of course, this was not the case in the first century. Nazareth was a Jewish community and more of a backwater town of less than 200 people instead of being a bustling city. It was because it had such little significance that Nathanael scoffingly asked if anything good could come out of there. A little village like Nazareth would hardly be expected to produce any person of importance or quality at a time when Jesus was a part of that community.

Nathanael's doubting attitude can certainly be understood, but Philip seemed to ignore this snide remark and demonstrated a good plan for anyone who has questions about Jesus. His advice to Nathanael, "Come and see!" It's a pretty good plan for evangelism to this day.

Today we can invite people who may not believe in Jesus, to come and see all that He has accomplished, and is accomplishing in our world. The very age in which we live marks His birth with the before and after initials of "B.C." and "A.D." Even when secularists try to get rid of the "Before Christ" or "anno domini" (Latin for "in the year of our Lord) references, and replace them with "Before Common Era" (B.C.E.) and "Common Era (C.E.), they still have the centuries of time divided around when Jesus lived.

Certainly, we can point to the billions of lives that have been transformed by the grace given by Jesus. His legacy is more than churches, cathedrals, hospitals, and cemeteries, however. The legacy of Jesus is one that is ongoing, and it is continuing to change people for the glory of God the Father and to the glory of the Son as well. "Come and see!" is a wonderful way to point people to Jesus. If we can help people to get past all the political and angry arguments to see the Savior of the world, they will find that all their heart's needs will be satisfied in Him. Nathanael may not have expected much, but when He met Jesus, all that changed, and Jesus still has that same effect on people to this very day.

AN HONEST MAN

John 1:47 *When Jesus saw Nathanael approaching, he said of him, "Here is a true Israelite, in whom there is nothing false.*

Technically, to be an Israelite during the time of this conversation between Jesus and Nathanael, was to an heir to the covenants that God had made with a particular people. There was a covenant of God with Abraham (Genesis 12:1–3), with Moses (Exodus 19–24), for the Palestinian land (Deuteronomy 29:1–29), with David (I Chronicles 17:11–14), and finally a new covenant in the time of Jeremiah (Jeremiah 31:31, 33). This was common knowledge among all the Jewish people. This is what made them the chosen people of God.

For the Apostle Paul, who also claimed to be an Israelite (Romans 11:1), being a true Jew meant something even more. Being a part of Israel meant that a person didn't necessarily have to born into the bloodline, but by faith in Jesus Christ a person became a part of the chosen people of God (Romans 8:16–17)

However, Jesus saw in Nathanael something even more. He saw him as an honest man. He saw him as someone who could be trusted with the words of life that He was going to impart to the world. I don't think any of us would mind if Jesus said something similar about us.

Nathanael's first reaction to the words about Jesus was one of skepticism. Because after all, how could anyone of any value come out of a little hamlet like Nazareth? This out of touch village certainly had no claim to fame about anything, but Jesus was about to change all that.

It is interesting to me that Nathanael came to Jesus at all. Though he first scoffed, he did make the effort to prove Philip's words true. He wanted to meet this carpenter/prophet, and because that meeting did take place, his life would be changed.

Jesus is still in the business of changing skeptics into believers. He is able to take the least of us and make us into more than we could ever be on our own, for He recognizes our strengths and our weaknesses, and knows just where to place us in the overall plan that would be best for us, and will glorify the Father. What He needs from us is, like Nathanael, for us to come to Him.

HE KNOWS WHAT WE DON'T

John 1:48–49 *"How do you know me?" Nathanael asked. Jesus answered, "I saw you while you were still under the fig tree before Philip called you." Then Nathanael declared, "Rabbi, you are the Son of God; you are the King of Israel."*

Anytime we try to put into words what we know about God, we usually find ourselves clumsily falling short. We do so because there is no way that our limited and finite minds can fully grasp the majesty and magnitude of the divine Godhead. We use terms to describe Him like omniscience—meaning that He knows everything, omnipresent—meaning that He is everywhere, and omnipotent—signifying that God is all-powerful. These words are a good start, but even they ultimately fall short of who God is.

We see an example of this divine power at work in Jesus as he was able to hear and see a conversation between Nathanael and Philip that happened a day earlier at a distant location. Jesus didn't have to be present to know what was being said and what was going on, because through the Holy Spirit He was being made aware of every part of the conversation.

Throughout the Bible we see examples of how God knows what other people don't know, and even throughout the ministry of Jesus we find repeated passages that He knew men's thoughts and motives. I don't know how it happened, but the Bible relates that it did, just as it happened to the Apostles after Jesus left them bodily and returned to the Father. Peter knew about the sin of Ananias and Saphira even before anyone told him about them (Acts 5:1–11).

Nathanael comes up with the best explanation as to how Jesus can know what He knows and do what He does. He says clearly, "You are the Son of God, you are the King of Israel." He had just met Jesus, but he summed up the situation pretty quickly and clearly. He was not just dealing with another Jewish rabbi.

We may never have a sixth sense to understand the thoughts of someone else, but we can know that Jesus is Lord. Knowing that fact and putting our faith in Him is all that we will ever need to be all that He wants us to be. Nathanael and Philip were convinced. I am too. I hope that all who hear the voice of the Spirit will be equally persuaded as to the Lordship of the Christ.

WHERE WILL YOUR FAITH TAKE YOU?

John 1:50–51 *Jesus said, "You believe because I told you I saw you under the fig tree. You shall see greater things than that." He then added, "I tell you the truth, you shall see heaven open, and the angels of God ascending and descending on the Son of Man."*

Nathanael was in for some days of real awakening that were just ahead of him. He may have spoken the words that Jesus really was the Son of God, the King of Israel, but at this point in time he had no idea what that truth would mean to his own life, and to the world.

In many respects, we are like Nathanael. We acknowledge who Jesus is and declare His majesty to the world, but we are really clueless about what that is going to mean for us in the days ahead. Whether we will see heaven opened and the angels of God ascending and descending on the Son of Man with our naked eyes during our lifetime or not, remains to be seen. What we do know is coming to pass, is that we are going to continue to see greater things done in the name of Jesus than Nathanael could ever have envisioned at that point in time.

So much has been accomplished through the power of Jesus's Spirit in our world. Our lifestyles have improved, our medicines have been enhanced by Christian-led hospitals, our churches have become sources for food, clothing, and care for our communities. Most important of all, billions of lives have been transformed by the regenerating power of the Holy Spirit, and families have been changed as a result. As I once heard someone say, "I don't know whether Jesus turned water into wine or not, but in my home, Jesus turned beer into furniture and groceries." Jesus definitely has had an impact for good on all those who have put their trust in Him.

Of course, there is still the matter of the cross that is in the life of anyone who is involved in the life of Jesus. The greater things that may come to pass could be increased persecution, societal pressures, and even explicit danger to life and limb. Following Jesus changes people and following Jesus often causes others to react strongly against the change that Jesus brings. History has proven this to be true on countless levels.

No, Nathanael had no real idea as to what his declaration of faith would bring to pass. We don't either, but whatever it is, it's sure worth the trip.

THE TIMING IS IMPORTANT

John 2:1–4 *On the third day a wedding took place in Cana in Galilee. Jesus' mother was there, and Jesus and his disciples had also been invited to the wedding. When the wine was gone, Jesus' mother said to him, "They have no more wine." "Dear woman, why do you involve me?" Jesus replied. "My time has not yet come."*

There is so much to unpack in these few verses. We could focus on weddings and the fact that Jesus felt they were legitimate to have, and important enough to attend. We could focus on Cana in Galilee, recognizing that it was the home of Nathanael (John 21:2), the person with whom Jesus had just been recorded as having a conversation. We could consider that by this time people were already considering those who followed after Jesus to be His disciples, as they were all invited to the wedding. We could notice that wine was the celebration beverage of choice, opening the door for discussion about the validity of the temperance movement. We could spend some time reflecting on the relationship Jesus had with His mother, seeing that the other children of Mary are not mentioned. We could even talk a bit about the announcement Mary made to Jesus, and what seems to be His sharp response to it. There is certainly plenty of food for thought here.

Perhaps a more important focus should be on the last statement that Jesus made, "My time has not yet come." As we have heard said, timing is everything. It's true for comedy, for drama, and it was certainly true for Jesus. He was, and is, the Master of perfect timing.

This tells me that all the events of Jesus' life were orchestrated by the Father. He didn't choose His disciples at random, for there was a plan behind each choice. He didn't just happen to be at this wedding that day, for it was all part of a divine idea to redeem the world. He wasn't ready yet to reveal His majesty to the world, so to do something that would draw attention to His authority and power would not fit the heavenly scenario. All things worked according to the planning and timetable of the Father.

That much hasn't changed in our relationship with Jesus. He is still the Master of time when it comes to the needs of our life. He knows what we need and He knows when we need it. He is never late, and never early. He is always right on time. Then like now, we can count on it.

Do What He Tells You

John 2:5 *His mother said to the servants,*
"Do whatever he tells you."

Sometimes I get really frustrated with people who take scripture verses out of the context in which they were written and apply them to fit whatever theme they are trying to illuminate. In some instances, this practice is so blatant that is embarrassing to equate them with any sense of biblical interpretation, because words are sometimes changed around, or a partial sentence is used, and the original meaning of the text is lost, or perverted.

However, the words spoken by the mother of Jesus here are few, but they apply to this situation in the passage, and to every other situation in which we may find ourselves throughout life. This verse instructs the hearer to be obedient to Jesus. In saying this, Mary gave the best advice that anyone could ever give, and we are the benefactors of such great wisdom, along with those who were servants at the wedding in Cana so many years ago. "Do whatever he tells you," is the best guidance we could ever receive.

For this to play out in our world, there are a couple of things that have to happen. First, we must hear when Jesus speaks. In order for us to hear Jesus, we must get into the regular habit of being with Him, listening to Him, and allowing our minds time to meditate on what exactly He is saying, so that we fully understand His words and direction. Second, we must act on the commands that Jesus gives us. They may be minor or major. They may be easy to do, as in this situation with the filling of the jars with water, or the commands that Jesus gives us may change our life's pattern and upend our world as we know it. But whatever the words from Jesus to us may be, to hear them and follow through on them is crucial for us if we ever hope to please God.

Jesus often asked people to do things they thought were unreasonable. But whether the goal behind His command was to produce a miracle, or just to test our obedience, there is always a purpose behind His revelations to us. Our challenge is whether or not we will hear what He has to say, and then be willing to carry out His instructions. We don't know where our obedience will lead us. But we do know, however, that disobedience will cause a break in our relationship with Christ, and what He wants to do in us and through us. It's all really our choice.

OBEYING EVEN WHEN IT DOESN'T ADD UP

John 2:6–8a *Nearby stood six stone water jars, the kind used by the Jews for ceremonial washing, each holding from twenty to thirty gallons. Jesus said to the servants, "Fill the jars with water"; so they filled them to the brim. Then he told them, "Now draw some out and take it to the master of the banquet."*

This story is about how 120 to 180 gallons of water got changed by the mere desire of Jesus. Because the servants were obedient to do as Mary instructed them, namely obey what Jesus told them to do, they were able to witness something that would be talked about down through the centuries of time to come. To this very day people are still making references in all circles of life to what Jesus did to jars filled with water that day.

Obedience is at the heart of this story. It happens to be the first time recorded in His New Testament ministry that Jesus would do the impossible, but in this situation where He didn't lift a finger to cause an impact, He depended on others to make the power of God evident for all to see.

Jesus seemed to have a particular knack for doing this. When He created the world, it wasn't through the sweat of His brow, but through the spoken word. Later, when He wanted the stone taken away from the tomb of Lazarus, He didn't lift a finger, but instead instructed others to do His bidding. When He wanted to train disciples, He sent out twelve, and then the seventy-two. Each time when these disciples came back, they were overjoyed at the results from the mission He had instructed them to carry out. He works continually through the actions of others.

To this very day, Jesus depends on the obedience of those who will hear His voice. Just as He commanded the servants here to fill the water jars with water and to take a sampling of the water to the master of the banquet, He was able to bring about the impossible and the amazing as a result. Yes, Jesus does some of His best work through those He calls into action.

How does this apply to you today? Do you hear the voice of the Master on a regular basis? Do you find it easy to not only say, "Yes," but also to follow through on what Jesus is telling you? If you answer these questions in the affirmative, then wonders await you. If not, well then, you will never fully understand what you are missing. "O Lord, give us ears to hear!"

THE GOOD STUFF

John 2:8b–10 *They did so, and the master of the banquet tasted the water that had been turned into wine. He did not realize where it had come from, though the servants who had drawn the water knew. Then he called the bridegroom and said, "Everyone brings out the choice wine first and then the cheaper wine after the guests have had too much to drink; but you have saved the best till now."*

Wouldn't you love to have a video recording of the events at this wedding feast? Wouldn't you love to have seen the eyes of the servants as they witnessed what had happened to the water that they had just put in the stone jars. To see the eyes of the master of the banquet light up when he got a taste of "the good stuff," would be worth all one could offer. A miracle had happened right there at an ordinary wedding in a place called Cana of Galilee.

The backstory here is that the servants knew about the source of the new wine, but the master of the banquet did not. They were only carrying out the order of this son of Mary's, who was merely a guest at the wedding, but they got so much more than they anticipated. We are not told here whether they got to sample some of this new wine, but they certainly got the message that something had happened to it between the well and the table.

It was announced that the latest wine to be brought out was better than the wine that was used to begin the feast. This was strange because it only makes sense to give people enough to dull their senses before a lesser quality drink was distributed. Once they had satisfied their thirst with the first batch, the second round of lesser quality wouldn't have been noticed much.

However, Jesus never does anything halfway or second-rate. Whatever He proposes, commands, or does always results in a vast improvement over anything man could ever do on his own. Just as He was able to use ordinary water to make a high-quality wine without even touching it, He is able to use the plain things of our lives to make the miraculous things happen.

To this very day, Jesus is still able to do as the Apostle Paul would later say, "immeasurably more than all we could ask or imagine, according to the power that is at work within us" (Ephesians 3:20). May God have His way in our hearts and lives today, through the power of Jesus Christ within us.

THE BLESSING OF FAITH

John 2:11 *This, the first of his miraculous signs, Jesus performed at Cana in Galilee. He thus revealed his glory, and his disciples put their faith in him.*

Growth in grace is such an amazing thing. Jesus would later say that the Kingdom would grow at a speed that was almost imperceivable, and yet it would stand the test of time. It is recorded that the first disciples, Andrew, Peter, Philip, and Nathanael were there at the wedding to see this miracle, and no doubt their faith jumped to a higher level when they realized fully what had been done.

Our lives are also surrounded by the workings of God on a regular basis. Though it's true that for something to be considered a miracle, we have to see the moving of God in a way that breaks in upon the natural order of life and history, God is continually working in ways to help our faith to grow.

As we age, our bodies are continually being renewed. Approximately every seven years, all our cells reproduce themselves and replace the old ones. A good illustration of this is to consider our fingernails and hair. They grow, are clipped, and then new cells grow them back. It's an amazing thing that happens in accordance with God's design for our bodies.

The miracles of our senses should make us more aware of God's working in our world. Who else could design such intricate organs as the eye, the ear, the skin, the taste buds, and smelling functions? We are fearfully and wonderfully made by our Master Designer, who is responsible for them all.

The wedding feast, and the turning of water into wine, was a big event for those who were there, and the rumors of it spread throughout the land, and down through the centuries of time. However, the focus of this section in scripture should be on the fact of what it caused the disciples to do. They became people of faith. Seeing is believing, and for them this was a sight too magnificent to be explained away.

While we may not see the specific miracles recorded in the Bible come to pass in front of our eyes, Jesus also said, "Blessed are those who have not seen, and yet have believed" (John 20:29). Faith is a gift from God, and whether we experience something defined as a miracle or not, our King is always at work. May faith increase as He continues to work in our lives.

HOME, SWEET, HOME!

John 2:12 *After this he went down to Capernaum with his mother and brothers and his disciples. There they stayed for a few days.*

It was only about sixteen or seventeen miles from Cana in Galilee to the city of Capernaum, which was on the north shore of the Sea of Galilee. We aren't told anything about the journey that took Jesus' family and His disciples to that waterfront community, but we can only assume that they made the journey on foot. Like so many of the events of Jesus' life, I wish I could have been a little bird nearby to overhear what Jesus told this group of travelers along the way.

It was the spring of the year, the time when new life was popping out from the ground and the trees, as warmer weather would begin to have its effect on the landscape. It would have been so great to hear Jesus expound on how the Father's plan for flowers, budding trees, and chirping birds, were all being worked out to perfection.

If this short verse shows us anything, it shows us the humanity of Jesus. We see Him with His mother, His siblings, and with these new believers who were still in the process of trying to figure Him out. They had been to a wedding together and enjoyed a time of partying and feasting. Now it was time for the journey home, walking, just taking part in a natural event in a human life.

I hope this reminds us that Jesus is actively at work in the normal things of life. We don't have to see Him doing miracles like changing water into wine, healing the sick, or raising the dead. We can witness His greatness as the grass grows, as the wind blows, and as the seasons come and go upon this planet. God's majesty is apparent for all who will merely open their eyes.

Jesus is also at work in our homes. He stayed with this group in Capernaum for a few days, and I'm sure that though the surroundings were mundane, the company was not. Christ's ministry had been launched through His collecting of His first disciples and the actions involving His first miracle. School was now open and on-the-job training had begun. His family probably didn't know what to make of it, but the Kingdom was being launched, just as it continues to grow in our present age. Jesus the King is always in the business of changing the normal into the magnificent.

RIGHTEOUS ANGER

John 2:13–16 When it was almost time for the Jewish Passover, Jesus went up to Jerusalem. In the temple courts he found men selling cattle, sheep and doves, and others sitting at tables exchanging money. So he made a whip out of cords, and drove all from the temple area, both sheep and cattle; he scattered the coins of the money changers and overturned their tables. To those who sold doves he said, "Get these out of here! How dare you turn my Father's house into a market!"

This is one passage of scripture that has been pointed to down through the centuries to show Jesus as anything but a cool, calm, collected guy, at least in this one example. Perhaps we should look at it a little more closely.

First, Passover was a very special time for the Jewish community. As the holiday, or "Holy Day," approached, it was natural for crowds to be gathered at the temple and in the temple courts to offer sacrifices in accordance with the Jewish tradition and law. The animals were there to be purchased so that sacrifices could be made by pilgrims who had traveled too far to bring their own livestock. Because the temple tax could only be paid with temple approved currency, money-changers were available to help people make the transition from secular currency to the accepted coins.

What upset Jesus was the fact that these transactions were taking place in the outer court of the temple, the only place where Gentiles were allowed to enter, should they wish to access God. Imagine trying to focus on spiritual matters amid animal noises and smells, the bartering of dealers and buyers, and the clanging of coins being exchanged. Jesus saw it as disrespectful and disgraceful. Who could pray with all this going on?

When Jesus made His whip of cords, it should be noticed that He didn't beat the offenders with the whip, but that He used it to drive the animals from the temple courts. He did overturn the money tables and kick out the dove merchants though, for He was incensed that people would treat God's house in such a manner.

We may not be Jews, and we probably don't worship in a temple, but we really do need to rethink just how we treat the place where people come to worship God. Are we helping, or hurting access to the King in our churches? It really is something to think about.

PUT GOD FIRST!

John 2:17 *His disciples remembered that it is written: "Zeal for your house will consume me."*

The original statement that the disciples remembered concerning the situation of Jesus in the temple, comes from Psalm 69:8. The full sentence is, "I am a foreigner to my own family, a stranger to my own mother's sons; for zeal for your house consumes me, and the insults of those who insult you fall on me." This is a psalm attributed to David, the former king of Israel.

Though we don't know at what point in his life David wrote these words, he appeared to be a person who was so focused on the house of the Lord that even his own family didn't understand his zeal, and he received criticism as a result of it. David, in this passage, truly does seem like a man after God's own heart (I Samuel 13:14).

Jesus took David's dedication to an even higher level. Where David was dedicated to the Lord, Jesus put the glory of God as the greatest focus of His life. He was willing to take action, to scold, to chastise, to disrupt, and to endure criticism to do so. In the eyes of Jesus, nothing came before the Father, and the temple was the place that the Jews of that time equated with the presence of God. What had been going on there was blasphemous, self-serving, and disgraceful.

To put it in more human terms, what was going on in the temple was like someone coming to your mother, spitting in her face, and slapping her to the ground. To allow such a thing to go unchecked is not Christian or even humane. Action was required, and Jesus didn't disappoint.

How far have we come from that time to the present! To disrespect God is the fad of the ages as comedians mock Him, sinners flaunt their sins before Him, and much of society totally ignores Him. In the face of such paganism, Christians are called to imitate Jesus.

How do we do that? By making sure that God is the highest priority of our lives before we do anything. We are to live for Him, talk about Him reverently, and respect every aspect of His creation and majesty. He is deserving of all our praise and worthy of our life's highest dedication. If that is the case, then our actions will reflect our commitment to Him in all that we do.

THE AUTHORITY BASE

John 2:18 *Then the Jews demanded of him, "What miraculous sign can you show us to prove your authority to do all this?"*

Everybody always wanted to see Jesus do a miracle. I guess people haven't changed very much because people still often refuse to believe in who Christ is and what He can do for their lives unless they see something spectacular that will take their breath away. The people at the temple that day, when Jesus disrupted their regular order of usury, marketing, and taking the things of God for granted, didn't like what they saw and wanted to see some proof of Christ's authority to do what He did. I think the anger that was pointed at Jesus was because He caught them in their sin, and sin never likes to be confronted.

We all like doing what we think is best, especially when it profits us financially. All that was happening that day in the temple, the selling of animals, the exchanging of common currency for the temple money, and all the other profiteering that took place was making people money, and we don't like it when someone stops us from making money. We really don't like it when someone calls what we are doing, sin, and demands that we be stopped. No, sin never likes to be confronted as being wrong.

The fact of the matter is that if those people who objected had had any idea who Jesus was, they would have understood that He was well within His authority to defend His Father's honor. They would have realized that putting God first is more important than making money, doing business as usual, or having our own wants satisfied. They certainly would have understood that worship in God's house was more important than anything else that was going on there, or at least they would have if they had not been so focused on doing what they wanted instead of doing what God wanted.

These words are aimed squarely at all of us. Who is this Jesus who wants to disrupt the way we do things? Who does He think He is that He can barge right into the middle of our affairs and demand that we stop putting our desires before God's desires? What authority does He have to tell us what to do?

Well, He is God's only begotten Son, and always the expert witness of His Father. He is God, and we are not. That's His authority.

WORDS MATTER

John 2:19 *Jesus answered them, "Destroy this temple, and I will raise it again in three days."*

One of the things that got Jesus in trouble with the Jews on several occasions was His use of parables. It seemed like He was always telling a story about something that had a deeper meaning than what it appeared on the surface. The parable might be about a lost sheep, a lost coin, or a lost son (Luke 15), or even in this case, a temple. But there was always an underlying message for people who would take His words to heart.

This scripture records the early days of Jesus' ministry, and at this point the only miracle He had performed was the changing of the water into wine. Nobody seemed upset about that. But the disruption of money making in the temple, well that was just pushing things a bit too far. Even though this was early in the ministry days of Jesus, we can see from these words that His mission was clear in His mind, and He was already focused on the cross that was before Him. The onlookers thought that He was talking about the physical buildings, but Jesus was dealing with the breaking and destructing of sin's power on a rugged Roman torture device. The cross was the reason He came into the world, and He didn't shy away from it.

O, that we would have such a focus for our lives. If only we could be so connected to the Father that we could have that kind of laser-fixed emphasis on God's plan being fulfilled in our lives. Maybe then we could understand the impact of these words more completely.

The world would try to destroy Jesus, and He knew it from the start. He didn't enter into His Father's plan so He could draw a crowd and be popular, or to gain money and prestige. He came to fulfill God's will at all costs, and that meant that there was going to be a cross involved for Him to do it.

We would do well to ask God to give us such a desire to be what He wants us to be. These years will pass so quickly, and we will find ourselves with so little to show for them unless we allow the Father's full right-of-way in our lives. When we do that, it's going to cost us something, but it's also going to accomplish something great with eternal value. Putting God first will always be the best decision we will ever make and when we get to the next world, we are going to see just how important that choice was.

A MATTER OF RESURRECTION

John 2:20–22 *The Jews replied, "It has taken forty-six years to build this temple, and you are going to raise it in three days?" But the temple he had spoken of was his body. After he was raised from the dead, his disciples recalled what he had said. Then they believed the Scripture and the words that Jesus had spoken.*

Isn't it amazing how well hindsight works? It wasn't until after Jesus was raised from the dead that the disciples of Jesus recalled and understood what He had done in the temple. It's hardly a wonder that some recalled it happening at the end of Jesus' ministry, while John remembered it happening at the start of Christ's journey through Galilee. Our recall teaches us much about the meaning of special events.

It would seem that the timing of this temple cleansing event wasn't nearly as important as the message that came from it. The forty-six years of temple building wasn't the issue; the three days before the resurrection was. It wasn't about raising the temple; it was about the resurrection from the dead.

The Holy Spirit of God seems to make a habit of teaching us things continually from past events. We gain information, but we don't always understand it. However, over time, as we ruminate on that information, we begin to see the layers of meaning and come to understand that when God is doing something, it may take a lot of time to decipher and glean the full impact. It has been nearly two-thousand years and we are still stretching to understand the work of Jesus at the temple that day.

It is for this reason that we need to continually be mindful of the voice of the Lord as He speaks to us. The Sunday sermon may be over in less than a half-hour, but hopefully its impact will carry much longer. The reading of the Bible can be finished in a cover-to-cover marathon, but to point out all the nuances of the Spirit's teaching takes a lifetime. As we read, recall, and reflect, the Holy Spirit continues to unfold and reveal His truth to us.

The disciples were not always the quickest of learners, and sometimes we identify with them in this regard. We need time to remember, time to ponder, time to meditate, and time to discern God's Word for our lives. We will find it, and it will be worth the effort if we stay true to it. God is continually teaching, and we are the blessed students to who are privy to His lessons.

HE REALLY KNOWS

John 2:23–25 *Now when he was in Jerusalem at the Passover Feast, many people saw the miraculous signs he was doing and believed in his name. But Jesus would not entrust himself to them, for he knew all men. He did not need man's testimony about man, for he knew what was in a man.*

It was becoming apparent as the days rolled by, that Jesus was more than just an ordinary carpenter from the village of Nazareth. In these particular verses we aren't told just what it was that Jesus did, but certainly He was causing a stir among those who came to Jerusalem for the Passover Feast.

Some may ask when reading this, "Why didn't Jesus just come right out and tell the people who He was?" That might have been what some of us would have done, but no doubt Jesus was wise enough to realize that too many people are attracted only by sensationalism, and they would be too fickle to follow Him when the signs and wonders weren't on display.

Jesus doesn't play games with us. He wants us to know what He expects of us right up front. When the lights are turned off and the crowds go away, and real life starts happening, too many people lose interest too quickly. The fact of the matter is, Jesus didn't trust the crowds. He loved everyone, but He didn't trust everyone. He knows our human nature and knows that unless we are serious about serving God, our interests will come and go like the seasons on the calendar.

Though some people can do nothing without positive feedback, Jesus didn't need the approval of men. He knew, and knows man's heart all too well, and He decided that the mission of the Father for His life was much too valuable for Him to just draw a crowd for the sake of popularity and numbers.

I don't know of any place in the Bible where we are told to trust people. We are to be trustworthy ourselves, and we are to love all people regardless of the circumstances of life, but we are always encouraged to put our trust in the Lord. We find a splendid example here of Jesus doing just that. People will change. People will often break confidences. People sometimes let us down and lead us astray. God, however, is always there, always true, and always trustworthy. Love is required, but trust is gradually and carefully earned over time and experience. That's what Jesus taught, and His example is good enough for me.

"I TELL YOU THE TRUTH!"

> **John 3:1–3** *Now there was a man of the Pharisees named Nicodemus, a member of the Jewish ruling council. He came to Jesus at night and said, "Rabbi, we know you are a teacher who has come from God. For no one could perform the miraculous signs you are doing if God were not with him." In reply Jesus declared, "I tell you the truth, no one can see the kingdom of God unless he is born again."*

It's important for us to remember that this takes place very early in the ministry of Jesus. We only have the one detailed miracle that has been recorded by John at this point, although he has made references to other signs that have occurred without providing details. Nicodemus appears to be curious, yet complimentary of this young Galilean, but in his effort to pay a compliment, he received much more than he no doubt expected.

A lot has been said as to why this "Nic-at-night" event happened when it did. It could have been that this was the first time for Nicodemus and Jesus to meet. It could have been what worked best for this busy Pharisee's schedule. They might have met at night because Jesus was surrounded by people every day and this was the only time that worked out for them to be together. Regardless of the reason, the timing here is not the issue. Though Nicodemus does appear to be kind, Jesus sidesteped the compliment and went directly to the heart of the matter. Nicodemus, like all of mankind, needed to be born again.

Jesus always has a way of cutting right through the fog and pointing the way to what is more vital in our lives. It's nice to be appreciated, even lauded, but that was for another time. On this night, Jesus needed Nicodemus to understand a new truth that would transform his own life, and the lives of countless generations yet unborn.

Being born again was a strange concept to this Pharisee and he would ask questions about it. It's strange to many people still, but then so are a lot of things that are complex. What matters most is that we understand a life change is vital if we are to be a part of the Kingdom of God. We will never be a member of that eternal family unless God provides us with a new birth. We may be confused by what it means and even surprise at how it all plays out, but the truth is still the same. Like old "Nic," we must be born again.

FROM CONFUSION TO CLARITY

John 3:4–8 "How can a man be born when he is old?" Nicodemus asked. "Surely he cannot enter a second time into his mother's womb to be born!" Jesus answered, "I tell you the truth, no one can enter the kingdom of God unless he is born of water and the Spirit. Flesh gives birth to flesh, but the Spirit gives birth to spirit. You should not be surprised at my saying, 'You must be born again.' The wind blows wherever it pleases. You hear its sound, but you cannot tell where it comes from or where it is going. So it is with everyone born of the Spirit.

I think the word "confusion" best describes what is happening in Nicodemus over the course of this conversation. The concept of being born again has confused a lot of people over the years, so I think we need to cut him some slack since he is hearing about this for the first time.

It's important to take the whole of these verses together so we see that Jesus is tying a biology lesson with a spiritual truth. When Nicodemus thought about birth, he was thinking biology. Jesus was speaking spiritually, but He had to meet Nicodemus where he was.

Of course, it is impossible for an adult to reenter a mother's womb for a rebirth, but not impossible for that same adult to be born from above. Jesus explained, that just as a baby is born in water, i.e., embryotic fluid, so also the spiritual birth must come about through the wind of the Spirit. He wasn't speaking of baptism here, though He later did instruct His disciples to follow the practice of baptism. No, here Jesus was using a physical reality to compare to spiritual renewal. Just as one is born physically, that person must also be born spiritually if membership in the Kingdom of God is achieved.

Seeing the Kingdom of God requires membership in it. So many people of the world see what takes place and are convinced that things are getting continually worse. This is the feeling that brought about the pre-millennial/pre-tribulation views of the end times. However, Jesus was not just preparing His followers for a heavenly home, but also about renewing this world through the power of the Spirit so that someday, at the trumpet call of God, a new heaven and a new earth will be joined as one. God is moving steadily, quietly, and surely as our lives are renewed in Him, and our world is being changed for His glory. The best is yet to come. Praise the Lord!

"YOU DON'T UNDERSTAND?"

John 3:9–10 *"How can this be?" Nicodemus asked. "You are Israel's teacher," said Jesus, "and do you not understand these things?"*

If these verses say nothing else, they should speak volumes about the necessity of spiritual leaders being at their best in their field. Jesus seemed surprised at the idea that someone who taught the people of Israel about the truths of God, didn't understand anything about having a spiritual birth. It seemed like a sad state of affairs.

I'm afraid we haven't learned much from that time to this in many church circles. A call from God to preach, to pastor, to be a spiritual leader is a call to study to show ourselves able to rightly handle theological issues and be at our best in the matters basic to salvation. Of course, not everyone can have the same educational levels of training, and the more experience we have should teach us things we didn't know when we were younger. However, there is no excuse for ministers who don't apply themselves to read, study, and master the Bible. That book is our main tool of our trade.

I remember being in a public service years ago when a young pastor was asked a question about a Bible truth, and his response was, "I don't do too well with the Old Testament." That was a disgraceful answer to me, for this man was university trained and an ordained elder in the church with several years of experience. He should have known better, and I hope he has changed his ways since that time.

Nicodemus was befuddled. He wasn't catching on to what Jesus was trying to teach, so further explanation from Jesus was going to be necessary. In the following verses we are blessed with timeless truths that have guided sinners to God and saints to a deeper walk down through the centuries. Perhaps in that sense, Nicodemus's lack proves to be to our benefit.

Still, we who are walking with Christ need to keep learning. Reading the Bible through each year, reading whole books with an intense focus, memorizing scriptures, and reading theology, church history, and books on scriptural interpretation, are avenues we need to travel if we are to lead others in the way of abundant living. Whether clergy or laity, we can all strive to be better informed than we are, and better equipped to serve. All it takes is devotion and effort on our part. Jesus will supply anything else we need.

SEEING WITH NEW EYES

John 3:11–12 *"I tell you the truth, we speak of what we know, and we testify to what we have seen, but still you people do not accept our testimony. I have spoken to you of earthly things and you do not believe; how then will you believe if I speak of heavenly things?"*

It appears to me that this section of scripture boils down to an issue that centers on earthly understanding and heavenly understanding. The premise is that if a person can't understand human things, then that person will certainly never be able to understand divine things. So what is the heavenly truth that needs to be grasped here? What can it possibly mean to us today?

We need to understand a new paradigm. A paradigm change means to move to a new way of looking at things. Jesus was talking about seeing the new Kingdom, and Nicodemus was struggling to keep up. The present-day world in its present state is temporary and of less importance than the eternal Kingdom, but society has missed this altogether.

Jesus reminded us that flesh gives birth to flesh, and we know that flesh eventually deteriorates and ends. We need to focus on something more important to us. The world in its renewed state will be the world that will last and calls for our highest priority. In the church we certainly give lip service to this, but too often not much more. Nicodemus had a hard time grasping this concept as well.

We begin correctly by understanding a primary truth. Jesus is not a way to the spiritual life, but *THE* way. He is where our journey to eternal life, to right understanding, and the ability to change our world into the Kingdom that He wants it to be, begins. We can try as many avenues and methods as possible to achieve peace on earth, the betterment of mankind, national equality and equity, and overall fairness and justice, but all of man's best efforts will fall short eventually. Only through Jesus can abundant life be realized in this world or the next.

Convincing people of this is our lifetime challenge. Every generation needs to raise up ambassadors of the cross to tell the gospel story to the world around it. We need to start with people that don't understand and lead them, as Jesus did with Nicodemus, to a place of personal renewal. We have a huge task ahead of us, but we also have a great God to help us do it.

HEAVENLY TRUTH

John 3:13 *"No one has ever gone into heaven except the one who came from heaven—the Son of Man."*

I n my work as a pastor over the years, I have had many conversations about death, heaven, and what life will be like when we get there. Though the Bible does give us some ideas concerning life after this life, it is not as clear as we wish it would be. The very reason for that is because no one has been there and come back to tell us about it. That is, no one but Jesus.

This one verse shouts out to us that there is life after this life, and that it is in an environment where we can be with Jesus. I know that the Bible is often full of imagery and apocalyptic language that paints general pictures for us, but the words used often leave us with more questions than we have answers. What we know for sure though, is that Jesus will be there. We will finally, someday, see Him face to face, and we will know as we are known.

We have to keep in mind that all Jesus is saying here is taking place in the midst of a conversation with Nicodemus. "Nic" had been confused over the idea of being born again, but now Jesus was taking the discussion to a whole new level. Nicodemus had acknowledged that Jesus was a teacher that had come from God, but probably didn't grasp the full meaning of what that entailed. When Jesus told him here that He had been to heaven, I'm sure that he was at a loss for words. In fact, there is not another word spoken by Nicodemus in the rest of the setting. The Son of Man had something to say and it was time to listen to the words that He would present.

How long has it been since you were left speechless by Jesus? How long since a big truth washed over you and you needed some time to process it before you could respond? I think Nicodemus was there.

Personally, I love it when I am challenged with new ideas that I have to work through. I picture heaven like this. I hope for conversations with Jesus that will stagger me in my tracks and cause me to revamp my thinking in ways I have never considered. I hope to be learning all throughout eternity.

Jesus has been there and Jesus has been here. He is the source of all knowledge and all inspiration. If we will just seek Him in all His fullness, that should be more than enough until we see Him inside heaven's gates.

LOOK AND LIVE

John 3:14–15 *"Just as Moses lifted up the snake in the desert, so the Son of Man must be lifted, that everyone who believes in him may have eternal life."*

The story to which Jesus was referring in verse fourteen, comes from the Old Testament book of Numbers, chapter twenty-one. As the story goes, when the people of Israel became impatient with God and Moses and complained against them, the Lord sent poisonous snakes to punish the rebellious mob. As a result of their sin, many died from the snakebites.

When the people repented, God instructed Moses to make a bronze snake and put it up on a pole, so that when someone was bitten by a snake, they could look at that image and not die. It sounds like a strange way to provide an anti-venom, but apparently it worked.

This Old Testament story was foreshadowing a day to come when God's own Son, Jesus, would be lifted up on a pole that we call a cross. Just as anyone during Moses's time could find life when they look on the bronze snake, all who truly look to Jesus for their salvation will also be saved.

No doubt Nicodemus was familiar with this old story. It had been passed down through the Jewish community for many centuries and few true Jewish believers doubted its authenticity. Though at this point he couldn't understand how Jesus tied Himself to the old story, in the days to come the comparison would become crystal clear. Looking to Jesus produces life, just like God's earlier command about the snake did.

Jesus had a wonderful way of taking the scenes of the Old Testament and applying them to His life. He used things with which the people He spoke were familiar to provide them with new insights in the path to salvation. Whether it was a snake, a farmer sowing seed, a lamb, a door, or a story, He reached people where they lived.

Such also is the job of Christ's church always. We take the Gospel message to people where they are. They usually don't come to us readily equipped with spiritual insights that will show them the way they should go, so we are to go where they are and find a way to connect God's truth with their situation. When we do that, then new life in the Spirit is possible.

THE GOSPEL IN A NUTSHELL

John 3:16 *"For God so love the world that he gave his one and only Son, that whoever believes in him shall not perish but have eternal life."*

This is one verse of scripture that seems much larger than it actually is. Though the words are brief, they are foundational to the whole Christian message. It is probably the one verse that is memorized by more people than any other single passage in the Bible. Its truth is simple, yet profound, and we will never get over the impact it has made on our world.

We again must remember that this verse comes in the midst of Jesus' words to Nicodemus, the Pharisee, who was a member of the Jewish ruling council, the Sanhedrin. He was an important man in the Jewish community, and Jesus was only considered to be an itinerant preacher, yet the teaching that flowed from Jesus had more of an impact than any words that had ever been spoken. This passage is an example of the insight that Jesus possessed, but also what the religious scholars of the day missed altogether.

The message is clear: God loves. He not only loves, but He loves so much that even His own divine being was not more precious than the creation that He had brought into existence. Seeing that mankind was going the wrong direction after his rebellion in the Garden of Eden, God put into play a plan that would eventually redeem what had been lost to the enemy's deception.

God doesn't want anyone to perish or be left out of the redemptive plan that He put into place. He was and is so concerned that mankind should live eternally with Him, for He showed that no price was too high to pay for our eyes to be opened to that truth. We can now be adopted into the family of God, and it is all because God loves us enough to make it possible.

Our finite minds can't really grasp eternal life. We think in seconds, minutes, hours, days, weeks, months, years, decades, centuries, and millennia. We hang around this life around 100 years, or less on average, and all that we know we have to figure out in that short amount of time. God has a better plan. He wants us to live forever with Him, and have time to explore the mysteries of the eternities. This however, is only possible through faith in Jesus. The sacrifice of Christ on the cross opened our eyes to just how much God cares, and the lengths He will go to prove that care for you and for me. Thanks be to God for ever and ever!

NO CONDEMNATION

John 3:17 *"For God did not send his Son into the world to condemn the world, but to save the world through him."*

It seems like in these days, that everyone is ready to jump on the condemnation bandwagon. Democrats condemn Republicans, Republicans condemn Democrats, and Independents condemn them both. Liberals look down on Conservatives and Conservatives distain Liberals, good is bad, and bad is good. What a confusing and frustrating time politically and socially!

Other groups that cast dispersions and often claims false information about each other are the religious and non-religious camps. Each side in all of these categories is having a field day in the public arena and on social media sites, as they tout their virtues and castigate the opposing views of others.

The words of John concerning God comes to us like cool water on a dry and thirsty situation. God is not about condemnation, but redemption. He doesn't want to destroy, but to build up. He doesn't hate anyone, but loves everyone equally. In fact, He is so bent on saving this world and everyone in it, that He put forth the ultimate sacrifice, the life of His Son, so that we could see that He is all about love and renewal, and not about hate.

God didn't create this world so that He could trash it, mistreat it, or make life hard for its inhabitants. He wants the best for each individual ever conceived, and puts the salvation of everyone as His top priority. No one could love more, do more, or be more proactive to make life better for us.

So when people say otherwise about our heavenly Father, they are just espousing "fake news." The God who created us, sustains us, redeems us, and is preparing an eternal place for us, has no ulterior motive for doing what He does. He acts out of that nature and that nature is always pure love.

People may not understand this fact, but the Bible and personal experience proves this to be true always. Jesus was doing His best to explain these things to Nicodemus that dark night so long ago, but the fact that these words are passed down to us, provides us with hope that perhaps Nicodemus didn't quite grasp. God is not about revenge and wrath, though He is always just. He is about doing what provides the best for His creation, and that best is found in Jesus.

BELIEF THAT MAKES A DIFFERENCE

John 3:18 *"Whoever believes in him in not condemned, but whoever does not believe stands condemned already because he has not believed in the name of God's one and only Son."*

It's a wonderful thing when one is deemed to be not guilty. There are so many forces in the world that try to impose guilt on others because of race, skin-color, heritage, income bracket, and a host of other things. We are sometimes accused of things that our ancestors may or may not have done, over which we have no control or responsibility. It can really be confusing and bewildering after a while.

God doesn't want us to feel guilty, or to be guilty. In fact, He wants so much for us to be free of guilt that He sent His Son to bear our guilt burden for us, and allow us to live free of that pain. All we have to do is believe on what Christ did on our behalf and follow after Him with our whole heart. That a pretty wonderful bit of good news!

Of course, not everyone will accept this fact, and when they do not, their belief will put them in the arena of the condemned. This is not what God wants, or what He planned for any part of His creation, but He has given us a free will and we can do whatever we want. If we reject Christ and His claims on our life, then God will always honor that choice. However, no choice is without consequences.

I know what guilt feels like. I know about the burden it brings to our minds and how it affects our relationship with God. That's why I am so thankful that God has released me from that condemnation, and why I am so amazed that anyone would want to stay in such a state of gracelessness. It's like hitting our hand with a hammer and then complaining about the pain. It doesn't make sense, but then sin puts blinders on its victims in a big way.

The point of this verse is that we can be free. We can be forgiven and we can stand before God without condemnation. We can make the choice to follow Jesus in true faith and be counted as sinless before God, or we can choose to not trust in Jesus and be responsible for our own guilt. We have the power to choose life or choose death. God loves us enough for it to be possible for us to be safe in His arms. For us to choose otherwise is our right, but it's certainly one of the most foolish decisions one can ever make.

PENATRATING LIGHT

John 3:19 *"This is the verdict: Light has come into the world, but men loved darkness instead of light because their deeds were evil."*

Ain't it the truth! People seem to naturally gravitate to the dark side when pressed with choices in life. The old instinct of self-preservation kicks in and most civilized societies seem to turn uncivilized if it means that they will benefit personally.

One could pass this off as a skeptical view of the world except for the fact that Jeremiah 17:9 tells us, "The heart is deceitful above all things and beyond cure. Who can understand it?" Romans 3:23 reminds us that we have all sinned at some point in our lives. The darkness that shrouds our selfish behavior has a tendency to be seen at some of the most inopportune times.

Because of this inbred tendency of mankind, light has come into the world. Though Jesus did not come to condemn us, He did come to shine His glorious light on our problem of sin so that it could be fixed. He came to point out where we offend God and turn away from Him, so that we could be brought into the light, and enter into fellowship with the Almighty. The Light of the world is doing us a great favor.

If you've ever walked into a dark room and quickly turned on the lights, only to see roaches scurrying to their hiding places, then you have a good analogy of how people try to hide from God. We don't want our sins known or exposed so we run to the darkness to hide, or try to hide, the wickedness that lies within us. We think that if we can run far enough from the light, we will be able to ignore its effect, but Jesus is not so easily put off. He has gone to the greatest lengths possible to free us from the powers of darkness, and He will never be satisfied until we are all walking in the light.

The reason for His persistence is given is I John 1:7, where it says, "But if we walk in the light, as he is in the light, we have fellowship with one another, and the blood of Jesus, his Son, purifies us from all sin." He wants the best for us, for us to get along with each other, and for us to have fellowship with God. This is all possible because of the cleansing light of Jesus Christ. The verdict is true, for His light has come. We can refuse it, but we can never get away from the loving light of God, and I'm so glad we can't.

FEAR FACTOR

John 3:20–21 *"Everyone who does evil hates the light, and will not come into the light for fear that his deeds will be exposed. But whoever lives by the truth comes into the light, so that it may be seen plainly that what he has done has been done through God."*

Fear is a great motivating factor, but the only problem with it as a motivating factor is that it causes people to do things they would not normally do for the wrong reasons. Light is the way of life. Darkness is the way of death.

The thing that would seem the most natural is that people would do whatever is needed to live, namely the way of light, rather than go a direction that will eventually lead to pain and destruction, namely the way of darkness. Though it would seem to make sense to avoid pain and sorrow, that is not the way people choose so very often. The darkness has a very strong pull.

Why is that? It's because part of the dark secret is that the repercussions for sin are not always seen immediately. Often the wages of sin, i.e., pain, sorrow, misery, and death, are delayed for a time, and people too many times have a very limited sense of foresight.

The light has more immediate rewards like love, joy, peace, patience, kindness and the rest of the fruit of the Spirit, but to get these benefits there has to be a commitment to the light, which is found in the person of Jesus.

Again, the problem that arises is that we like to be our own god, to make our own decisions, and to rule our own destinies. We want to eat of the fruit even when God says no, we want to not be our brother's keeper, and we want to determine our own rules and laws even when God makes His way explicit for us.

Yes, evil hates the light. That's why the name of Jesus is so often despised, hated, and forbidden in the public arena while other non-gods and religions are allowed to flourish. Counterfeit deities are plentiful and popular, but there is only one begotten Son of God.

Evil will never accept the light, but the person blinded by evil can be brought out of the darkness when the true light is presented. It remains the job of Christ's church to reflect the light of Jesus to a darkened world, so that it can be saved.

BAPTISM: A NEW START

John 3:22 *After this, Jesus and his disciples went out into the Judean countryside, where he spent some time with them, and baptized.*

In this verse the scene changes and we leave the discussion between Jesus and Nicodemus behind. We go back to the water's edge as baptisms are taking place, and apparently Jesus was the one doing the baptizing. That had to be a wonderful memory for those disciples as the years of their ministry would unfold.

Though I was just an elementary school student, I remember clearly when I was baptized, and I remember the person who baptized me, along with the people who were baptized when I was. Of that group of four, plus the pastor, I am the only one that is still alive. I remember that it was in the spring and that the water of White River at Kilbuck Park in Anderson, Indiana was really, really cold. Maybe it was my youth, or my limited understanding of all that was happening, but the cold stands out to me more than anything.

I wonder what these men would regard as the most significant thing regarding their baptism. First of all, the fact that Jesus was the one who baptized them, would be the most important thing of all. I mean, you can't go closer to the source of new life than that, can you? Perhaps they heard words that impacted their thinking. Perhaps they took note of their surroundings, far from Jerusalem, far from Capernaum, far from Nazareth, or anything that would have been familiar to them. This was a wilderness area. Perhaps Jesus was taking them on a kind of wilderness experience like He had previously gone through at the start of His ministry.

At this point in the record of John, the only disciples that were following after Jesus were Andrew, Simon Peter, Philip, and Nathanael. If others had joined them, John didn't record it. But regardless of the number, spending time with Jesus and learning from Him about the Kingdom of God would have been priceless.

How's it going in your life? Are you finding time to spend with Jesus, and are you finding it fulfilling? Do you know that He wants to share with you and bless your life? If we meet Him at that quiet place, He will meet us there and provide us with companionship and insights for living. Don't miss it for the world!

COMING TO BE BAPTIZED...

John 3:23–24 *Now John also was baptizing at Aenon near Salim, because there was plenty of water, and people were constantly coming to be baptized. (This was before John was put in prison.)*

I am captivated by the phrase, "people were constantly coming to be baptized." It sounds like what John was doing truly was striking a chord among the people of Israel at that time.

Having been a part of a church family since birth, I have witnessed many baptism services, most of which I was the officiating minister. However, though I have baptized many, the idea of people constantly coming to me for baptism is beyond my experience. We usually had baptism services once or twice a year for new converts, but John seems to be more active than that. This makes me ask the question, "What does it take for people to realize their need for baptism?"

Well, first I think it involves the prodding of the Holy Spirit into one's life. There are none of us who have the ability to cause people to seek a real baptism without God's involvement.

Second, I think it requires a real explanation from scripture as to the reasons for being baptized. After all, this practice didn't begin with this generation, and folks need to be shown where Jesus participated in and commanded this sacrament.

Third, I believe there is a tremendous need of people to witness other folks being baptized. We are social creatures, and being able to connect with other people who have already have been baptized, or are being baptized at the same time, makes it easier for people to take this step of faith.

Finally, it seems that an atmosphere of celebration and thanksgiving is necessary for baptism to be remembered and copied by others. Everyone loves a party, and what better thing to celebrate than the announcement of one's new faith-walk with Jesus.

Churches can help in three of the areas mentioned. Perhaps if we do a better job at promoting, preaching about it, demonstrating the sacrament, and partying with those who are baptized, we too could have people constantly coming to be baptized. It's certainly something to think about.

DIFFERING OPINIONS

John 3:25-26 *An argument developed between some of John's disciples and a certain Jew over the matter of ceremonial washing. They came to John and said to him, "Rabbi, that man who was with you on the other side of the Jordan—the one you testified about—well, he is baptizing, and everyone is going to him."*

It appears that we have two different things going on in these two verses. There is an argument with a fellow Jew, and then there are people complaining about too other people leaving John and following after Jesus. The nuances that come out of these two events feel a bit too close to home.

How many times have we in the church experienced certain disciples arguing over procedures and rituals? Too many times disagreements have started over modes of baptism, or how to do communion. Some people want chairs in the sanctuary and other want pews. Some pastors like pulpits to preach from, and others despise the idea of being bound to that piece of furniture. Whether it is the number of services each week that a church has, or how long they last, or a thousand other topics, we who claim to be disciples often get sidetracked from the "what" and the "why" of what we are doing, and ministry and witness can suffer as a result.

Or how about the second scenario? People are leaving our group and going to another group. I realize that this passage has to do with the Jewish community, but it is a real issue for the church today when someone from our particular church fellowship decides to leave our number start attending some other church. The reasons are as numerous as the people who make such transfers of loyalty, but there is hardly a church anywhere that hasn't had to deal with the problem of people leaving our church for another church, and feeling the fallout and blowback that such changes cause.

Someday, I hope that we who claim to be the followers of Jesus Christ can finally understand that we are not in competition with each other. We want people to follow after Jesus. Whether the ministry style of the church is loud and young, or old and traditional, we should be grateful for the Gospel being preached, and where people are being drawn to where they can best learn about and serve the Master. We must remember that it's all about Jesus. When we forget that, we have forgotten what our mission is all about.

LESS IS MORE

John 3:27–30 *To this John replied, "A man can receive only what is given him from heaven. You yourselves can testify that I said, 'I am not the Christ but am sent ahead of him.' The bride belongs to the bridegroom. The friend who attends to the bridegroom waits and listens for him, and is full of joy when he hears the bridegroom's voice. That joy is mine, and it is now complete. He must become greater; I must become less.*

It is so very true that we only have what God gives us. John knew that, and his words here shine like pearls of wisdom. Because he knew who he was and who he was not, he could rest in the divine plan of God to work out all the details for his life, his work, and his future.

I wish that we could all learn such a lesson. John knew that it was the plan of the Father for Jesus to increase in stature and popularity, just as it was his place to be relegated to a lower rank. It was okay with John because he saw himself as the friend of the bridegroom, ready to meet the needs of the bridegroom, but never to overstep his place in the pecking order.

Our churches and church leaders could learn much from this attitude. As so many of them scramble to be the biggest, the most attractive, the wealthiest, have the greatest number of ministries, and the greatest following of people, John would certainly be displeased with them.

Being jealous of another's place in Kingdom work shows that we really haven't understood the Kingdom of God at all. It's the lowest servant that is ranks the highest, and the one who sees himself as the greatest to be ranked the lowest. One who sees with Kingdom eyes truly sees the world with a whole different perspective than the one who patterns himself after this world. There will a rude awakening for such religiosity sooner or later.

Let's seek to find joy in the thought that while we must do all we can to promote Jesus, we can do that in the way God prescribes. The old saying is that when people begin to itch for power and position, they soon start to scratch. That's not the way of the Christian faith. Instead, may this be our prayer: "Lord, make us humble enough to know our place and trust You to move us around to anything else You have for us. Let us rejoice in glorifying Your Son and do all we can to make sure He always gets top billing. Make us like John here, so that we also may be like Jesus."

HE IS FROM ABOVE

John 3:31–33 *"The one who comes from above is above us all; the one who is from the earth belongs to the earth, and speaks as one from the earth. The one who comes from heaven is above all. He testifies to what he has seen and heard, but no one accepts his testimony. The man who has accepted it has certified that God is truth."*

John knew the facts. Jesus was from above and he was from the earth. There was no way that he would have the insights or knowledge that Jesus would have because his perspective was so limited when compared to that which Jesus possessed. This whole conversation began because some of John's followers were complaining that he was losing ground to Jesus. But John set the record straight as to how this was the proper thing to happen. Jesus needed to be exalted and John needed to be humbled.

When John spoke about the testimony that was not being received, he was making reference to the words of Jesus. The parables that He spoke and the truths that He imparted had great power and insight, but often people were not able to grasp their full impact. Jesus spoke of heavenly things and people with earthly minds just couldn't understand what He was talking about. John knew though, and he certified that God was doing a great thing.

There will be times in our own lives that we will try to share heavenly truths that haven been imparted to us by the Holy Spirit, and people will not understand what we are talking about. People sometimes read the Bible and their understanding is clouded because they have not yet met the Author and had the Holy Spirit reveal its truth to their hearts and minds. One could do a scholarly study over the whole Bible, but miss the messages that they need to receive if the Spirit of truth doesn't guide them. A child, however, full of the Spirit of God, can understand things that the secular experts never will.

This calls for wisdom on the part of we who would follow Jesus. He is from above and we are from below. We need His wisdom to understand and to make relevant to our society, the message of the Gospel. The Kingdom news is hard to grasp, but it is our job to share what the Spirit shares with us. For this task, much prayer is needed, much study is required, and a humble and teachable spirit within us is a must, because God has a message for our world, but it will never take hold without people like us to certify it.

THE LOVE OF GOD IN ACTION

John 3:34-35 *"For the one who God has sent speaks the words of God, for God gives the Spirit without limit. The Father loves the Son and has placed everything in his hands."*

There is some wonderful news in these final words of John the Baptist. He had been reflecting the increasing greatness of Jesus in the overall plan of God, to his disciples, and here he drops some precious nuggets of truth that will guide them in the coming days.

First, he told them that God sent Jesus and that Jesus would only speak what God told Him to say. In the fourteenth chapter of this book, Jesus would echo that same thought as He confirmed in His disciples the working of the Father in His life. Jesus and the Father are one, and they speak as one.

Another gem that is revealed by John is that God gives the Spirit without limit. Not only was this true for Jesus because He, the Spirit, and the Father were one, but it was also true for the people of John's time, and it is true for us today. God doesn't put a gauge on how much of His Spirit He is willing to pour out on those of us who seek after Him. God is willing to drench us in His love and with the anointing of His Holy Spirit. We who are finite creatures with no goodness in ourselves, can receive the fullness of God's Spirit for our lives in every area that we will open ourselves up to receive Him. We can't do it through the working up of our emotions, or by sacrificing ourselves through the disciplines of the body, but we can receive the gift God offers to us by allowing God to do what He wants to do in us.

This reminds me of an Old Testament verse that says, "For the eyes of the LORD range throughout the earth to strengthen those whose hearts are fully committed to him" (II Chronicles 16:9). If we will fully commit ourselves to the Lord, He will pour out His Spirit on us in equal measure. What a wonderful promise!

Finally, John reveals how much the Father loves the Son. He loves Him so much that He has placed everything under His command. In Matthew 28:18, Jesus said, "All authority in heaven and on earth has been given to me." That's how much God loves His Son. That love is also passed on to us. We have the opportunity to walk with God and experience His love today. May we never be accused of not taking advantage of this wonderful gift.

LAST WORDS; IMPORTANT WORDS

John 3:36 *"Whoever believes in the Son has eternal life, but whoever rejects the Son will not see life, for God's wrath remains on him."*

These are the last words from John the Baptist that are recorded in the Gospel of John. Perhaps because they are the final words, they are a perfect summary of the Gospel itself, for if we believe on Jesus Christ for salvation, we have eternal life. But if we do not believe we will never see life, and that person will face God's wrath. That's about as simple and clear as it gets.

Believing in the Son, Jesus Christ, as the pathway to our salvation is more than just an intellectual assent. Anyone can believe that Jesus was a historical figure, or even believe that He was a good man that we should try to emulate, but that is not what John was talking about. Believing in Jesus as Savior and Lord requires us to acknowledge His deity, His authority, and His right to rule over all areas of our lives. It is taking a leap of faith and knowing we will land safely in the arms of the Almighty, who is waiting for us to make a transition from a focus on the pleasures of this world to the way of the cross. It is giving up anything and everything to follow our risen Messiah.

It really shouldn't be a hard choice however, when we consider the alternative. Choosing Jesus is choosing eternal life, and rejecting Him is choosing to put all of our eggs in the one basket of this present age and hoping for the best. By doing so, we not only miss out on the best God has for us during these approximately seventy to eight years of living here, but missing out on an eternity of joy in the presence of the Father in His new earth. It's like choosing pennies over tons of gold, or choosing to live in a shack next to a mud puddle, when we could have an ocean front mansion. Some choices really aren't that hard.

The part about facing God's wrath shows us the seriousness of our choice. I don't see God's wrath as God being mad at us, or being out to get us. I see it as our poor choice resulting in forfeiting all He has for us in order to get nothing but pain and darkness in our daily walk. I can't fully envision what the next world will be like for those who reject Christ, but I can clearly see the misfortune that comes to the faithless in this world. God's wrath is living without hope, and living in fear of the future. He wants so much more for all of us than that, and we can find it through His Son, Jesus Christ.

REAL SUCCESS

John 4:1–3 *The Pharisees heard that Jesus was gaining and baptizing more disciples than John, although in fact, it was not Jesus who baptized, but his disciples. When the Lord learned of this, he left Judea and went back once more to Galilee.*

It must have been a mind-boggling time for the Pharisees of Israel during the early days of Jesus' ministry. They didn't know what to do with John, the renegade preacher who had been drawing huge crowds down by the Jordan River. And now they had no answer for Jesus, who was drawing people in greater numbers than John ever did. In fact, many who had once walked with John were then walking with Jesus, and that had to make the Pharisees nervous.

For a Jew to be baptized was radical enough because, after all, they were already the chosen people of God. The Pharisees could have passed it off at first as just the remnants of a great hoard of the unwashed masses, but as the numbers continued to climb, and the popularity of Jesus continued to increase, it would only be a matter of time before something would have to be done with this upstart from Nazareth.

It's not that Jesus was afraid of confrontation from the Pharisees. In fact, much of the gospel story is about His encounters with them. However, timing was vital in the plan of the Father and these were the early days of Jesus' ministry; far too early for events to come to a head, so He chose to withdraw.

To this day there are people who are having success in ministry to the degree that others are curious or even jealous. Certainly, every ministry has to stand on its own merits, but if God is in it then it will be vindicated eventually. But just as Jesus had to wait for the right time to move to the next stage of His ministry, we too have to wait on the plan of the Father before we can accomplish what He wants. If we are too early or too late, the plan will not bear fruit as God wishes.

Today may be a waiting time for us. God knows what we need to be doing and when we need to be doing it. We need to just wait for His direction before we plow ahead in our own strength. As Jesus waited, there were other things that called for His attention. We too can only be used according to God's timetable.

HE HAD TO GO...

John 4:4–6 *Now he had to go through Samaria. So he came to a town in Samaria called Sychar, near the plot of ground Jacob had given his son Joseph. Jacob's well was there, and Jesus, tired as he was from the journey, sat down by the well. It was about the sixth hour.*

I don't think the words here are written by accident, but by the directing of the Spirit. Jesus *had* to go through Samaria. Because He was on His way back to Cana of Galilee from Jerusalem, the most direct path was to go around Mount Gerizim and through the Samaritan village of Sychar. But I don't think that the travel route was the main concern. I believe He had to go through Samaria because there was a pressing spiritual need there, and He wanted to take care of it.

We will find out more about this particular need in the coming days, but I think it's safe to say, without doing injustice to this text, that Jesus is always on the lookout for people in need. He longs to save, and He longs to help us right up to this very day. This earthly example is given to us as a reminder as to just how much He cares for us.

We also see in this passage of scripture, the humanity of Jesus. We could easily envision Him walking, and then being tired after the approximate distance of thirty-five miles from Jerusalem to Sychar. It has probably taken He and His disciples a couple of days to get there since it was noontime when this event takes place. The hot sun, the miles of the journey, the physical need for food and water were taking their toll on Jesus as He took time to relax by the well. It was a well that His forefather, Jacob, had dug centuries before, but it was still producing water for the community.

Because Jesus has experienced the fatigue and frailties of man, He knows how we feel when we are ready to collapse from weariness. He is ever faithful to seek us when we need refreshing because He knew what it was like to have those needs Himself.

This lunchtime story has been told and retold countless times over the last two thousand years, and today we benefit from it still. From it we learn that Jesus knows where our need is and how great our need is. He will do whatever it takes to see that relief for our life is found. He was, and is, the most loving advocate we could ever have.

JUST A CUP OF WATER

John 4:7–8 *When a Samaritan woman came to draw water, Jesus said to her, "Will you give me a drink?" (His disciples had gone into the town to buy food.)*

Samaritans were a race of people that were offshoots from Israel. They had once been a part of the Jewish family, but because of generations of intermarriage with people from other groups, they were considered "unclean" by the populace of Israel. Prejudice comes from many places and takes many forms and this is one more example of how blind people can be in their judgments of others.

Our society is continually being afflicted by those who choose to divide us by race, by sex, by political affiliation, by age, and a myriad of other distortions. Instead of realizing that we are all people made by the same God to be brothers and sisters working for the good of all, we let ourselves be offended by what others say, what others do, and what others believe. Blame is cast by those who were never violated on those who never violated them. It's a vicious cycle that can only lead to destruction.

Jesus gives us a wonderful example for our actions as we move forward. He interacts with a person from a different race and different gender. He puts Himself in a position of need as He asks help from this person who many of His time would say that He should have no contact. He broke down barriers by His proactive movements that would lead to future ministry.

It will be a wonderful day when we can all look at God's creation with the eyes of Jesus. To see everyone as part of our family, part of God's family, and part of His interactive plan for us is a hope that will be truly fulfilled when the Kingdom of God has reached its climax. Until then, we need to work in that direction and trust that God is making all things new day by day. The movement may be slow, but we are headed for a day of great rejoicing.

The disciples of Jesus would miss out on the opening part of this conversation because they were off to the market to do the grocery shopping. By the time they would return, Jesus would have an object lesson of love waiting for them. Again, it would take time for them to know what He knew, but in the end, love conquers prejudice, fear, and diversity. May God open our eyes and ears to learn what they would learn in the following verses.

DARE TO SHARE?

John 4:9 *The Samaritan woman said to him, "You are a Jew and I am a Samaritan woman. How can you ask me for a drink?" (For Jews do not associate with Samaritans.)*

Have you ever gone up to a person who was a total stranger and asked them for a drink? How about a person who was not only a total stranger, but one who was of a different race, and a different gender?

I remember a time while a young boy when I witnessed such an occasion. Our family was renting a house in the country that was surrounded by many acres of crops. One year the fields were planted with tomatoes and when harvesting time came, the landowner brought in Mexican migrant workers to pick the tomatoes. On a certain day when my mom was out in the yard with my brother, sister, and me, a Mexican woman with several of her kids came up to the fence of our property and began speaking to us in Spanish. None of us spoke the language, but mom had taken some Spanish in high school, so she was eventually able to understand that the woman was asking if she and her children could get some water from the barnyard pump that we used to water our animals. Of course, mom told her that she could, and the little band of people who seemed so different from us got their water, and then went back to the fields to work.

It was such a long time ago and such a brief event, but that memory came back to me when I was reading this account of a thirsty Jesus. My mom was actually taking the role of the woman in the story and offering our water to our new acquaintances from the field. We had different colored skin and spoke different languages, but we all shared the basic need of water, and what we had we shared.

I saw my mom that day doing a Christian thing. She didn't allow the differences of our races discouraged her from being humane, and doing what she could to help someone who was in need.

Is there someone with whom you are afraid to share what you have? Jesus needed water and this woman had the capability of meeting that need. Those migrants needed what we had, and we had the ability meet that need and were glad to do so. Wouldn't our world be better off if we just put our differences aside and helped each other for the glory of God?

LIVING WATER

John 4:10 *Jesus answered her, "If you knew the gift of God and who it is who asked you for a drink, you would have asked him and he would have given you living water."*

S uch true words here. "If we only knew the gift of God." Those who are continually driven to thirst by the rush of society and the madness of power-grabbing, could benefit so much by getting to know the gift God has for them. And beyond the gift of life itself, there is the opportunity to know the Giver, the Source of all life and of our entire world. It's all for the asking. All one has to do to make contact with the divine Godhead is to ask.

There are so many people in our world who are like the woman at the well. The answer to all the hopes and dreams of her life was standing right in front of her, but she didn't have a clue with whom she was dealing.

People pass churches by the dozens as they drive to work, go to meetings, speed off to athletic events, and chat on their cell phones. But all the while, so many of them haven't got the foggiest notion that these buildings of various shapes and sizes, proclaim a message, or at least should proclaim a message, that can change the world. Someone once said that ignorance is bliss, but there is certainly nothing blissful about living in darkness, coping with pain, and facing continual disappointment with life. Jesus wanted so much more than that for this woman, and He wants so much more than that for us. He's waiting patiently for someone to take time to notice, and then ask Him for the living water that never runs dry, and takes away our thirst for things that don't matter forever.

Jesus sidestepped the woman's rejection to His request, and turned the situation into an opportunity to bring a new future to pass for her. He teaches us all the value of being ever on the watch for another way to reach out to the needs of mankind that are continually around us.

Today we will most likely pass people in the midst of our daily activities who are in great need of this life-changing, thirst-quenching touch from Jesus. So why don't we be on the lookout for opportunities as we move through life, to share this gift with others. Let's build bridges of connection that puts us in the path of the thirsty, so we can point them to the source of living water. This gift from God is available for the asking.

OVERCOMING OBJECTIONS

John 4:11–12 *"Sir," the woman said, "You have nothing to draw with and the well is deep. Where can you get this living water? Are you greater than our father, Jacob, who gave us the well and drank from it himself, as did also his sons and his flocks and his herds?"*

I think that a lot of people look at church, and at church folks, with the same attitude that this woman at the well had. We tell them that there is a source of living water that will cause them to never thirst again, and immediately they question and go on the defensive over our announcement. It probably goes like this: "Who do you think you are? You are nothing special, and my problems are huge! I don't see you carrying any bags of tricks that can solve the problems of my life!"

They might even compare us to the latest celebrity or social guru who has prescribed their own antidotes to life's big problems. "Do we think we are wiser than them? Do we claim to have more knowledge than what they can find on TV or the internet?" The objections to the offer of the water of life are endless.

Because, like the woman in this story, they have seen and heard too much, been disappointed too many times, and have experienced too many others with religious jargon, to give them hope in a simple cure. Religion itself is distasteful to more and more people because they have seen so many false representations of "righteousness," and they come to want no part of it.

We should be prepared for the objections to come. But in our preparation, we can remember what Jesus did. He didn't take offence. He wasn't put off. He didn't give up and just tell the woman to forget that He had said anything, and let her be off to her own business. He knew He had what she needed, and He was going to do whatever it would take to convince her to hear what He had to say.

Of course, it requires wisdom and careful preparation to handle objections from others. We most likely have the best approach we will ever have by just relating how we found the fountain of life, and how Jesus took away our thirst for things that just don't matter. They may, or may not believe, but then we have to trust in the Holy Spirit to do the convicting and convincing. Our job is to just spread the Word. Jesus will take it from there.

NEVER TO THIRST AGAIN

John 4:13–14 *Jesus answered, "Everyone who drinks this water will be thirsty again, but whoever drinks the water I give him will never thirst. Indeed, the water I give him will become in him a spring of water welling up to eternal life."*

I'm sad to admit that I am not much of a water drinker. I know that medical people don't like to hear about people like me, but it is actually a rare day when I drink a class of water. I drink coffee, tea, lemonade, soda, fruit juices, and milk, but unless there is no other option, I rarely consume water, regardless of how hot it might be. I've been to too many countries where drinking the local water could bring about some serious health issues, so I've learned to be very careful about where my water comes from. It's probably one of my greatest flaws, but I'm just not a water fan.

However, I am a big consumer and fan of living water. I have been dipping into the gospel well for this taste of refreshment since I was a child, and I have never been disappointed by its taste or content. I come back to it repeatedly, for it satisfies completely, and there is never a lack of its supply.

The great thing about living water is that I don't have to go anywhere to get it. The Master always has plenty on hand whenever I need it or want it, and never tells me that I've had too much. The living water from the throne of God satisfies my thirst more than anything this world has to offer.

The woman at the well was probably pretty confused by the play on words that Jesus was using. She knew what came up out of the well, for she drew from it every day. She knew about the hot sun and the human thirst that came about because of it. She knew that cool water from the well was a delight and a necessity for human life. What she didn't know is that spiritual water is so much more vital than physical water. Life lived only by what can be supported by physical means will eventually come to an end. Death comes to all who depend on physical water to satisfy their thirst, but eternal life springs from the well that Jesus offers. Once a person has a genuine and full taste of the "good stuff," from Jesus, then he or she never has a reason to get their thirst slaked from anywhere else. His provision, made possible by His connection to the Father, was, and is, transformative for all who drink. So, when Jesus offers, drink deeply, and often.

"GIVE ME THIS WATER"

John 4:15 *The woman said to him, "Sir, give me this water so that I won't get thirsty and have to keep coming here to draw water."*

One of my vivid memories comes from the land of Kenya, where we had the privilege of serving for a few years as missionaries. The image of which I speak is one of women and children carrying water from the local source, in various sized containers, back to their homes for their daily use. They would use it for drinking, for bathing, for washing clothes, and watering plants in their gardens, because few places out in the bush had access to a tap on their own property. Water had to be carried from the source to the home, and though it was done daily, it was never an easy job.

This woman was in the same situation. The village well was a source of life for the community, and she had come once again to receive what the underground source had to offer. We are told that she came a noontime to get her water, but that would be unusual. At noon it was hot. At noon water gathering would interrupt regular activities in the home. Morning or evening was the time when people would normally draw water, when the sun wasn't burning overhead, and people could collect it at their leisure. The watering hole was also a social place, giving way to the nicknames of those special places of refreshment that entice people even to this very day in our communities.

Perhaps the reason that this woman came for water at noon was because she was a scandal-laden woman. She had had five husbands and she wasn't married to the man with whom she then lived. She no doubt had a reputation for sinful living that would cause more respectable people to not care to share even a conversation with her, let alone hang out with her.

Jesus didn't mind though. Though He knew of her past and her current situation, He asked for water from her and then offered living water to her. His physical thirst brought about a spiritual thirst in her that was longing to be satisfied. If she could just taste this eternal water, it would be enough.

The same story is true for us today. Regardless of who we are or what we have done, Jesus offers us water that satisfies and frees us. One drink and we are not thirsty anymore. Our lives are changed forever because Jesus gives us what we need when we ask for it.

WATER THAT EXPOSES

John 4:16–18 *He told her, "Go, call your husband and come back." "I have no husband," she replied. Jesus said to her, "You are right when you say you have no husband. The fact is, you have had five husbands, and the man you now have is not your husband. What you have just said is quite true."*

Isn't it interesting that Jesus tells the woman to do something that He knows she can't do? Without her telling Him anything, He knows her heart, and knows that that she has been looking for something that she can't find on her own. She had gone from man to man, from one situation to another, but always ended up empty and alone, so she went on to the next offer. This day would be different though. This day would change her life forever.

Living water has some interesting properties. One is that it brings our darkness out into the light. There's not a person among us who doesn't have something in our past that we would not want uncovered. We sometimes avoid things that might benefit us just because we don't want to be discovered for who we are. But when a person takes a taste of living water, there is an awakening and an awareness that doesn't leave us the same anymore. That can be very revealing, and sometimes embarrassing.

I would imagine that the woman's jaw dropped when Jesus revealed He knew all about her. Who was this guy? Did He know her family? Had He been talking about her with the people of the village? Where did He get this information? She had to have been baffled by His comments. We don't see Jesus condemning her, but instead we see Him qualifying her. He was letting her know that though He was aware of her past, He had something to give her that would satisfy her needs. She only had to ask.

People sometimes hesitate to ask for what they need because they are in denial. They don't see themselves the way Jesus sees them. But the fact of the matter is, unless the problem of our soul is brought into the light, the problem will never be solved, the sin will never be dealt with, and the thirst will never be satisfied.

Coming to Jesus causes us to be laid bare before Him. There are no secrets in the Kingdom of God. Today He knows us intimately and calls us still. That's pretty amazing. Yes, that's grace that comes only from the Master.

WHERE DO WE WORSHIP?

John 4:19–20 *"Sir," the woman said, "I can see that you are a prophet. Our father worshiped on this mountain, but you Jews claim that the place we must worship is in Jerusalem."*

We are hung up a lot on where it is we worship. My, how we Christians love to scatter! We divide up by denominations and as we drive down the streets of our land we see Independents, Pentecostals, Baptist, Methodists, Friends, Nazarenes, Lutherans, Wesleyans, and a whole host of other groups that meet regularly for worship. We divide ourselves by worship styles, by size, by liturgy, by race, and by age. Sometimes these divisions are done unintentionally, and sometimes they are done deliberately, but we do have a tendency to sprinkle ourselves across the landscape.

The woman in this story was part of a diverse group that was divided from its Jewish background because of mixed marriages that changed the makeup of their common heritage. It was openly and widely known that Jews and Samaritans didn't mix in polite company, but still they worshiped the same God, even if they didn't get to do it in the same place.

The older I get, the more ecumenical I become. Don't get me wrong, I love my denomination, and it has been my choice to be a part of it since I was a child. However, I do not think that we are it; we are just a part of it—it being the real body of Christ in our world today. We are not competitors with other Christians, and we certainly do not want them to fail so we can succeed in rounding up their sheep into our corral.

Week by week pastors prepare sermons, laymen do various ministries, and the Kingdom of God is enriched by the common good that we provide for our communities. Certainly, there are always going to be theological differences of varying degrees, but anyone who says that Jesus is Lord and means it from the depths of their being, is my brother or my sister.

Buildings are just that; buildings. They may be humble in size or a massive cathedral, but the body of Christ is made up of the people that worship there, wherever they may be. God has no particular flavor for His children. We are created in His image, and we worship Him to the best of our abilities. It's time that we stand for Christ and not against each other. Otherwise, people like this woman are always going to be confused by our religion.

THE REAL WAY TO WORSHIP

John 4:21–23 *Jesus declared, "Believe me, woman, a time is coming when you will worship neither on this mountain nor in Jerusalem. You Samaritans worship what you do not know, we worship what we do know, for salvation is from the Jews. Yet a time is coming and has now come when the true worshipers will worship the Father in spirit and in truth, for they are the kind of worshipers the Father seeks."*

We will never be able to honestly deny the fact that salvation comes from the Jews. First of all, these are the words of Jesus, and no true Christian would take seriously the idea that Jesus would mislead us. Second, the whole of the Old Testament bears witness to the nation of Israel's struggle in their walk with God. Their very existence is proof of God's grace and mercy in light of their continual history of backsliding and idolatry. But even though the Jews were the initial instrument that God used to bring about salvation for the world, they often didn't understand it then, or even now. They may know who it is that they worship, but they don't always do it in such a way that meets with God's approval.

The problem is that so many people try to worship a God who is Spirit, in the power of the flesh. We have a tendency to create God in our own image, with preferences for the things we like. We make God out to favor our race, our denomination, our style of worship, our cathedrals, our buildings, and our traditions. Like this woman at the well, we try to do godly things, but based on human reasoning and information.

Jesus said that true worshipers worship the Father in spirit and in truth. What does that mean? It means that we don't always have all the answers when it comes to being what God wants us to be. We are doers, but it is always better to just wait and see what it is that God is leading us to do before we act. Worshiping in truth is seeking God wholeheartedly in our approach to Him and humbling ourselves before His majesty. Worshiping in the spirit is entering into a world where the material pales before the presence of God. We see God for who He is rather than for what He can do for us. We seek His presence first, and then allow Him to direct us from that point.

It will take us a lifetime to learn the all the lessons about seeking God, but since that's what He wants from us, it's worth whatever it takes to get there.

GOD IS SPIRIT

John 4:24 *God is spirit, and his worshipers*
must worship in spirit and in truth.

There have been times when I have entered into discussions with individuals and groups about the nature of God. People always want to know what is beyond our level of understanding, and because we have a Bible, some folks think that the answer to every question is in there.

I have learned, however, that the Bible is true and can be trusted, but not all information is recorded in it. I mean, the Bible won't teach me how to play the piano, or how to work on a car. There are some things that it just doesn't talk about.

Such is the explanation concerning exactly what God is like. We hear from the lips of Jesus that God is a Spirit, but what exactly does that mean? Does that mean that He doesn't have a physical body? Does that mean that He has an ethereal presence without a physical substance? After all, Genesis 1:27 says, "So God created man in his own image, in the image of God he created him; male and female he created them." Does our physical presence look like God's physical presence?

These and many more questions about the substance of God may have to wait until we meet Him face to face to be answered. However, Jesus had a purpose in saying what He did to the woman at the well. I believe He was trying to get across to the woman that God cannot be contained. He can't be housed in a temple, or on a mountain, or in any one church or denomination. God abides where He wishes, when He wishes, for He is in all things at all times. We don't have to go searching for Him, for He is closer than our next breath.

Worshiping Him in spirit and in truth requires sincerity on our part, and a focus on Him that goes beyond the trappings of what we can "work up" in our public services or private devotions. God, who is spirit, doesn't need anything we can offer Him. God, who is truth, isn't fooled by half-hearted allegiances to holiness. Worshiping Him in spirit and in truth requires us to be open, honest, dedicated, and willing to put Him first in every area of our lives. He is beyond understanding, but never beyond our reach. Today, as we look to draw near to Him, let us approach Him in humility, honesty, and sincerity. His Spirit, will mix with our spirit when we do.

LOOKING FOR THE MESSIAH

John 4:25–26 *The woman said, "I know that Messiah" (called Christ) "is coming. When he comes, he will explain everything to us." Then Jesus declared, "I who speak to you am he."*

There are those who say that Jesus never claimed to be the Messiah. Whoever thinks that has not read this passage, or the account that He gave before the Sanhedrin trial before His crucifixion (Matthew 26:64; Mark 14:62; Luke 22:67–70), and His confession before Pilate (John 18:36-37).

No doubt this proclamation from Jesus startled the woman at the well, but since He had already demonstrated that He knew all about her, she was convinced by His authority.

The people throughout Israel and their Samaritan cousins had built great hopes in the coming Messiah, and what it would mean for their lives. They used terms, "Messiah," or "Christ," to give us a bit of insight into their understanding. "Messiah" comes from the Hebrew word, "Masiah," and means, "Anointed One," or "Chosen One." The Greek equivalent is "Christos," or in English, "Christ." As the people of the Old Testament days waited for God to send His chosen one to free them once again, the reality was found in the person of Jesus, who is known as, "The Christ."

The Messiah was to be the answer for the problems that had plagued the people of God for centuries. Moses spoke of Him first when he said, "The Lord your God will raise up for you a prophet like me from among your own brothers. You must listen to him" (Deuteronomy 18:15). Other prophets like Isaiah and Jeremiah would endorse this idea and push its significance until all Israel stood waiting for God to bring about this man of deliverance. Even this Samaritan woman had heard the story and had the hope that the Messiah would reveal all that she needed to know, and now He stood right in front of her.

We who have come to know this Messiah as Lord can look back over the centuries and see how this woman was right. Jesus does explain everything to us. He is all that we need to be free. He is the answer to the longings of every seeking heart. He is our Redeemer, Counselor, Hope, and Friend. In Jesus we have the answer for this world's problems, and we know He is the King of the next world. Thank God! The Messiah has come!

DOES JESUS HAVE TO
EXPLAIN HIMSELF?

John 4:27 *Just then his disciples returned and were surprised to find him talking with a woman. But no one asked, "What do you want?" or "Why are you talking with her?"*

Men are from Mars and women are from Venus. That's how John Gray, the American author penned it. Regardless of how our post-modern society tries to blur the issue, men and women have been different since their creation in the beginning of time, and those differences show up in all walks of life.

In this story we have a group of Jesus' disciples, men, who come upon the conversation that Jesus, a man, is having with this woman at Jacob's well, just outside the Samaritan village of Sychar. The disciples were taken aback at the thought of their teacher talking to a woman, and a Samaritan woman at that. She was so far below a Jewish male in their concept of society's rank the He should not have even noticed her, at least in their thinking. Still, Jesus was the teacher and they were the disciples. He no doubt had some reason for doing what He was doing, and they knew enough about Him by this time to not interrupt what He was saying to this woman.

This caused me to ask a question. "Do we trust Jesus enough to allow Him to do what He wants to do without Him having to explain His actions to us?" Just as the disciples thought it was unseemly for Him to have a conversation with this foreigner, we sometimes question the working of the Lord when we can't see the purpose behind His actions.

Why does God allow sicknesses, injuries, job losses, and financial hardship? Why does He take us through valleys so low that we can't see the sun coming over the mountains? Why would He allow pain to happen when what we really think we need is relief?

For the disciples and us, here is something for us to understand and remember: Jesus knows what He is doing. The route that He takes us in our journey has a purpose even when we can't see it. He knows that we need our faith tested so it will strong, and He urges us to stop, wait, and listen to His voice so that we will be wiser in the days to come. We may go through times of silence, having nothing to hold on to except our faith, but later on as we look back, we will see that those were the times that Jesus was in control.

THE POWER OF OUR STORY

John 4:28–30 *Then, leaving her water jar, the woman went back to the town and said to the people, "Come, see a man who told me everything I ever did. Could this be the Christ?" They came out of the town and made their way toward him.*

People who are really changed just can't keep the news of their change to themselves. If we are successful losing weight, we want to tell people about it. If we get a new car, we want to show it off. If we go on vacation to some exotic place, we want to show pictures and tell stories of our adventures there. The same is true for the person who has met Jesus and has had their life transformed by Him. The news is just too good to keep to ourselves.

We are never told the name of the woman at the well, but she seems to be very well known by the people of the village called Sychar. We don't know if they were not used to getting visitors and if having a stranger in the midst would normally generate curiosity, but on this occasion the turnout to meet Jesus seems to be in great number.

John was not present when the conversation between the woman and Jesus began because he had gone into town with the other disciples to buy food. But when he returned and saw Jesus engaged in discourse with this Samaritan, he soon realized that His Master never stopped working for the Father, even when He was tired and thirsty. The fact that the village came out to see Jesus provides a backdrop for what He would do later in their midst. He would eventually not only convince His disciples about His mission, and confirm in the woman's mind the reality of His identity, but He would also help the villagers to see things they had never seen before. They would discover that He truly was the Savior of the world.

Our testimony has a far greater impact on people than we usually imagine. We may think that our story isn't worth hearing and that people won't be interested in what we have to say, but when we tell people about Jesus and what He has done in our lives, the Holy Spirit enables our speech to impact those that hear. This woman was convinced concerning Jesus, and others were influenced by her zeal. The big difference was when they would meet Jesus for themselves and change would happen in their lives. That much hasn't changed; we just need to tell the story.

FULLY SATIATED

John 4:31–34 *Meanwhile his disciples urged him, "Rabbi, eat something." But he said to them, "I have food to eat that you know nothing about." Then his disciples said to each other, "Could someone have brought him food?" "My food," said Jesus, "is to do the will of him who sent me and to finish his work.*

Jesus was human and Jesus got hungry. He was thirsty because it was around noon. He had been walking and no doubt the sun was hot. Because of His thirst, it was natural for His to ask water from the woman, and because it was lunchtime it was natural for Him to be hungry. The disciples understood this. After all, they had taken the time and effort to go into the village to buy food for Him to eat. So why wouldn't Jesus eat?

I picture Jesus here like a child on Christmas morning, who would be willing to skip breakfast in order to get at the presents. I see Him with the enthusiasm of a teenager who skips his lunch so he can go to the Department of Motor Vehicles and take his test for his first driver's license. Maybe He was like the newlywed couple who just want to get the reception over so they can get on with their honeymoon. I think you get the idea. Jesus was focused on something more important than food. He has just shared living water and the words of life with a young woman who was in great need. That experience satisfied Him more than any lunch ever could.

What we see in Jesus here could be summed up in the word, "focus." He was focused on the plan of the Father, focused on fulfilling the mission that was given to Him, and focused on meeting the need of this woman. His concentration on what mattered most put the thought and need of food out of His mind. He would eat later. Right now, what was happening in front of Him was much more satisfying.

This is such an example for the church today. Sometimes it is so hard to keep the main thing the main thing because we get distracted by so many other legitimate things in church life. We worry about the music, the facilities, the lighting, and the order of service. We are tempted to focus on the potlucks, the offerings, and the numbers we have in attendance for our services. Jesus shows us a better way. Just focus on people and focus on the plan of the Father. Everything else will happen in its own good time.

THE CLOCK IS TICKING

John 4:35 *"Do you not say, 'Four months more and then the harvest'? I tell you, open your eyes and look at the fields! They are ripe for harvest."*

In several of my pastorates I have had parishioners who were farmers. Though their number seems to diminish with the changing of our world to a more technological based way of making a living, there is still a great need for, and much we could learn from, those who farm the lands of our world. The practice was very common when Jesus walked throughout Galilee, and it would not have been a stretch for Him to point at a nearby field and instruct His listeners to focus their attention on His message. He started with the literal field, a point of reference with which they could all identify, but then He brought it around to a spiritual truth. Just as fields mature and produce certain times of the year, the need for laborers to bring in a spiritual harvest is great all the time.

When we were young, we thought we had all the time in the world. We couldn't wait to get our driver's license, get our first car, have our first date, go to college, get a good job, get married, have a family, and then someday retire comfortably. We wish our lives away and then wonder why they seem so futile and empty at times. We long for our lives to have real meaning and purpose.

We all have 168 hours in each week and twenty-four hours in each day, and we get to decide how we are going to use those hours. We can't save them or store them away. We have to take then as they come and once they are gone, they are gone forever.

This is why it is so vital for believers in Jesus Christ to follow in His mission and be about bringing in a harvest that will last for eternity. In our families, our schools, our communities, and often even in our churches there are good people whose lives need to be transformed and harvested for their good and for the glory of God. We can't say that we will wait until there is a better time, for there is no better time than the present for us to be bathing people in prayer, building bridges, and laying groundwork for ministry on their behalf. The harvest truly is plentiful and comparatively, the laborers are few. My prayer is like that of Jesus, we will open our eyes and see the harvest that is before us. Time is marching on and there isn't a day to lose.

THE DEBT WE OWE

John 4:36–38 *"Even now the reaper draws his wages, even now he harvests the crop for eternal life, so that the sower and the reaper may be glad together. Thus the saying, 'One sows and another reaps' is true. I sent you to reap for what you have not worked for. Others have done the hard work, and you have reaped the benefits of their labors."*

I am the result of those who have gone before me. In fact, we all are. We are the collective product of our parents, our teachers, our pastors, our schoolmates, our co-workers, and everyone who has ever brushed up against us in life. I owe much to the doctors who have cared for me when I was sick or needed surgery, to the coaches who trained me in various sports, and to the Boy Scout leaders who invested their time in me. I am even indebted to the animals I cared for on the farm, and the pets I have had. We are benefactors of all the people and all of life that has surrounded us.

If this is true concerning all who have crossed our path, how much more it is true when it comes to matters of the Spirit. I am a pastor, but other pastors have pastored me, and they were pastored by others. Our experiences have piled one upon the other, and I am so much better off today because of those whom I have followed.

We must always remember though, that it is the Lord who does the sending. His Spirit speaks to us and we are called into His service, but in His providence He has already put people into place to help us in our journey. It is so true that others have done the hard work, but we have reaped the benefits of their labors.

The crop is eternal life, and being a laborer in that field is of the utmost importance. Whether we are clergy or a layperson we need to work together to make sure that the harvest comes in. Not only will it make us glad, but angels in heaven will rejoice when we help bring one new person into the Kingdom of God. We will never be worthy of such a calling, but I am sure that the disciples of Jesus in that first generation felt much the same way. So let's not give up when there is so much to do and many souls depend on our labors. Others have paved the way for us, so we must do our part to build on their work so that the next generation can build upon ours, to the glory of God.

JUST TELL THE STORY

John 4:39–41 *Many of the Samaritans from that town believed in him because of the woman's testimony, "He told me everything I ever did." So when the Samaritans came to him, they urged him to stay with them, and he stayed two days. And because of his words many more became believers.*

A personal testimony can be a very powerful thing. Courts of the world rely upon firsthand accounts from people who have witnessed events surrounding legal cases. History has given us examples of how a person's words can change circumstances of nations and people groups.

The same is true when people testify about Jesus and what He has done in their lives. This Samaritan woman had never met anyone like Jesus, and when He told her all about her life, she knew that He was more than just an ordinary man. Naturally, she wanted to tell someone about her new friend, and when she did, others got the opportunity to sit at Jesus' feet and learn from Him. Her testimony spread to her neighbors and then throughout the rest of the village, and as a result, more people came to know Jesus as their Lord and Savior.

This same scenario has played out countless times over the centuries. One person meets Jesus, and then they tell someone else about the encounter. That person tells other people, and the Kingdom of God is enriched with new members. One person telling the story of Jesus to another has produced more fruit that we will ever know in this life.

This is why it is so important that we who are believers, continue to do just that. Once we truly meet Jesus, we have an urge and an obligation to tell our spouse, our children, our parents, our siblings, our neighbors, and those whom God brings into our path. When we truly meet Jesus, something wells up inside of us that wants others to know the love and connection we have found. Good news like this should never be kept to ourselves.

As a result, history records that a village was changed. First, they came to Jesus because the woman's story made them curious. Later they followed after Jesus because they too had listened to His words, believed on Him, and set their life's course to follow Him. Sychar, the Samaritan village, would never be the same. Our hope is that God would continue to inspire people to tell the story of His love today. The world needs to hear it.

"We Have Heard For Ourselves"

John 4:42 They said to the woman, "We no longer believe just because of what you said; now we have heard for ourselves, and we know that this man really is the Savior of the world."

The witness of the woman that Jesus met at the well had a big impact on her community. But once the community met Jesus for themselves, they realized that God had literally come into their midst. Jesus has, and had, that kind of impact on people.

I guess this is the reason that I believe so much in the church. The Church of Jesus Christ has been at the forefront of sharing Him with the world for nearly 2000 years. It continues to tell the story of how He has made a personal difference in heart and life, and people are drawn to the Savior as a result. It begins with a testimony from someone who has met Jesus, then when others check out the validity of that testimony, they find themselves convinced that God truly changes lives.

The church begins with children, then it continues the story with those in their teens. By the time one reaches young adulthood, the church has provided multiple opportunities for people to meet Jesus, and thankfully, many do and are never the same again.

There is nothing so precious and special as the new life that is found in a relationship with Jesus. The people of the Samaritan village are just one case of how this is played out on continents around the world. People meet Jesus and then all doubts vanish as to His identity. They too proclaim that He is the Savior of the world. We don't hear any more about the woman that met Jesus at the well after this scene. We don't see Jesus interacting with other Samaritans either. We can only assume that since they were convinced about the Messiah, that other Samaritans would hear the story also. Only eternity will reveal how many lives were changed by that one meeting when Jesus was thirsty.

We today who have been touched by the Master's hand are to tell that Jesus will continue through the power of His Holy Spirit to change lives for time and eternity. It begins with our witness, but then others pick up on it and are changed too. The cycle continues and will continue until Jesus returns. Blessed are those who realize Jesus really is the Savior of the world.

THINGS ARE DIFFERENT AT HOME

John 4:43–44 *After the two days he left for Galilee. (Now Jesus himself had pointed out that a prophet has no honor in his own country.)*

Jesus had been on a journey that took Him from Jerusalem through Samaritan village of Sychar, but He was on His way north to Galilee. He was returning to His hometown, and the word about His demonstrations of God's power was beginning to spread over the area in a big way. News had to travel by word of mouth only, but what Jesus was doing was having a rippling effect from village to village.

His testimony had been wonderfully received by the Samaritans over the last couple of days, but Jesus knew that the scene would change when He got closer to home. Sceptics who knew Him from years gone by would be hard to convince that He was anything special, or that His message was life-changing. After all, He was a hometown boy, and it would have been hard to be accepted by neighbors and friends who had known Him for so long.

When I first acknowledged God's call on my life to preach the gospel, one of the greatest fears I had was to make the announcement in my home church and the people of my community. I was then, and am now, nothing special, but to think that God would single me out to do anything, was almost more than I could put into words. I thought constantly on these words from Jesus, that a prophet would not be honored in his own country. Thankfully, I was accepted much more readily that I ever expected, and I will always be grateful for the support I received.

It is vitally important that local church embrace and encourage those who are called from their number to do ministry. Friends and family may not always favor God's call on an individual, so the local church must realize that whether a called person succeeds or fails rests greatly in their hands. Certainly, ministry skills must be developed, and mistakes will be made, but every called person has enough headwinds to push against without having to go alone. The local church support of God's call on a ministerial candidate can make them or break them.

Jesus was stepping into dangerous waters, but He depended on the Father for His every move. Each called person must do the same, but if they have a team of prayer warriors behind them, it can make a huge difference.

THE HONEYMOON

John 4:45 *When he arrived in Galilee, the Galileans welcomed him. They had seen all that he had done in Jerusalem at the Passover Feast, for they also had been there.*

Expectations were running high when the Galileans came out to meet Jesus. We are not told by John of all that Jesus did in Jerusalem outside of the cleansing of the temple, but He apparently did enough that tongues were wagging and curiosity was running high. They wouldn't always show Him favor in the days to come, but this initial meeting appears to be a good one.

Every pastor who begins a ministry in a new church setting experiences what many call, a "honeymoon" period. It's that time when the pastor's possessions are unloaded from the moving van, and the lay people bring in food, drinks, and wishes for success as this minister is poised to do something new with this flock. These are special times because they may not last long.

Like the honeymoon after a couple is married, the hope is that everything will be wonderful through the duration of the times the bride and groom get to know each other intimately. Hopefully the days are filled with joy and memories are made that will hold them fast for many days to come. The reality is, however, that honeymoons end, and then life in the real world begins. What can start so tremendously can change quickly as circumstances begin to be altered from what was expected.

I love it, that the Galileans welcomed Jesus. He had a good start with them, and His ministry would always be remembered in light of the fact that He was a Galilean. This verse doesn't reveal any conflict between Jesus and anyone else, for it is an announcement of his past activities and actions that primed the people for some wonderful things to come.

Speaking as a pastor, for the sake of pastors everywhere, I hope that all churches will give their new ministers the benefit of the doubt concerning his or her ministry and allow a time of "honeymoon" before things get too busy and pressures start building. There will be time enough for challenges and we see next that Jesus was thrust right into the midst of the fray, but pastors need an opportunity to be accepted before they are judged. Like Jesus, they need to catch their breath before the needs come calling.

THE NEWS GETS OUT

John 4:46–47 *Once more he visited Cana in Galilee, where he had turned the water into wine. And there was a certain royal official whose son lay sick at Capernaum. When this man heard that Jesus had arrived in Galilee from Judea, he went to him and begged him to come and heal his son, who was close to death.*

When Jesus had attended the wedding feast back in chapter two, we weren't told how many people had been in attendance with Him. We aren't even told that when Jesus turned the water into wine, it was news that was widespread, or if John was simply referencing the event as he was inspired by the Holy Spirit to write. Jesus must have garnered some notoriety among the locals by this point though, because this local official was convinced that Jesus was capable of doing miracles, and his son's life hanged in the balance of that fact.

Cana of Galilee was about twenty miles from the city of Capernaum. We aren't told what position this royal official who came to Jesus held, but we can surmise that he was a man of significant importance. We might wonder what would make a man of his position travel such a distance on the basis of a rumor about a carpenter turned rabbi that all the people were talking about. There must have been something that he had heard that stirred up faith within him and caused him to hope that Jesus could bring about change. Going to Jesus was one thing but begging Him to travel the distance back to his home shows the desperation of the man. He was hoping against hope for the impossible, for a miracle, and his hope led him to Jesus. If Jesus didn't intervene, then the life of his son would be over.

Do you know what it's like to realize that unless Jesus acts, all is lost? Have you experienced the depth of seriousness that a crisis brings, causing a willingness to try anything for relief? If you have, then you know that coming to Jesus is the best thing you can do. Things may not always turn out as we anticipate, but we can be assured that Jesus will do whatever is needed to fulfill the Father's desire in the situation. Answers to our cries may sometime seem to be unheard but be assured that they are not. Our Father knows and cares about each one of us. What He will do is up to Him, but our part is faith that He will do the right thing. Our faith in Jesus makes all the difference, not only for us, but for those He puts in our path as well.

BLIND FAITH

John 4:48–50 *"Unless you people see miraculous signs and wonders," Jesus told him, "you will never believe." The royal official said, "Sir, come down before my child dies." Jesus replied, "You may go. Your son will live." The man took Jesus at his word and departed.*

We are told these words back in John 2:24-25, "But Jesus would not entrust himself to them, for he knew all men. He did not need man's testimony about man, for he knew what was in a man."

By this time in the ministry of Jesus, it is most likely that people were coming to Him on a regular basis because they wanted something from Him. There would no doubt be sincere believers, but also plenty of opportunists who wanted to witness the spectacular so that they would have their curiosity satisfied and have news they could exploit. It almost sounds here like Jesus was chastising the royal official for making his request, but actually Jesus was testing this man's faith. He wanted Jesus to come with him so that his son could be healed, but Jesus wanted the man to believe, whether He made the journey or not. Divine power and human discipleship are going hand in hand here.

It must have come as bittersweet news to hear Jesus say that the official's son would live. He would have been thrilled to hear the words, but there must have been a degree of disappointment because of the refusal of Jesus to make the journey. His faith was being tested to a great degree.

It's hard to take Jesus at His word without any physical corroboration. We want to see with our eyes, hear with our ears, and touch with our hands the workings of God. Faith is hard work and discipleship is a hard road, so Jesus knows that we need to be toughened up for the task. Not seeing yet believing is the true way of the believer with the Messiah. Jesus would later say, after the resurrection, "Because you have seen me, you have believed; blessed are those who have not seen and yet have believed" (John 20:29).

Today we once again are being asked to walk by faith and not by sight. The world clamors for a miracle, but the witness we are to give them is one of a transformed heart and life. Such a witness may or may not satisfy them, but we who experience that change, find it more important than a physical happening. As we walk blindly, our faith grows, and the Father is glorified.

"YOUR SON WILL LIVE"

John 4:51–53 *While he was still on the way, his servants met him with the news that his boy was living. When he inquired as to the time when his son got better, they said to him, "The fever left him yesterday at the seventh hour." Then the father realize that this was the exact time at which Jesus had said to him, "Your son will live." So he and all his household believed.*

It is true that some people only believe in the word and power of Jesus when they see a miracle with their own eyes, but when that miracle does happen, it would take a pretty skeptical person to remain in their unbelief. This royal official had his faith confirmed when he realized that his son was healed at the exact moment when Jesus had spoken the word and promised health upon the boy. No longer could there be any room for doubt. Jesus had made believers out of this family forever.

Every day there are opportunities for people to put their faith in Jesus, but often they pass because they don't really believe in the power of God, or they don't ask Him to get involved. Our Lord is a gentleman and doesn't intrude where He is not wanted, but when He is asked, there is never a request that He doesn't hear. That doesn't mean that we will always get what we ask for, because sometimes we ask with selfish motives and insincerely, but it does mean that when our request lines up with what is good for us, and will bring glory to the Father, we can rest assured that God will provide what we need when we need it.

It's important to notice that God's timing was involved in this story. The boy was healed at the seventh hour, which would be 1:00 p.m. by the way we tell time. It was easy for the royal official to recognize it to be the same time he had been with Jesus that day before. The miracle was too great to be considered a coincidence. His mustard seed of faith bloomed into a full flower of confirmed belief.

Today the Lord still wants us to trust Him. We may not have a need like the one in this story, but for Jesus to work in our lives we have to put our faith in Him. His grace is always sufficient to meet whatever is before us as long as we keep our trust in Him. This is the day of salvation and the day of renewal for our faith-walk. Talk to Jesus. Ask of Him. Put your faith in Him and know that He has the power to meet your needs to the Father's glory.

MIRACLE # TWO

John 4:54 *This was the second miraculous sign that Jesus performed, having come from Judea to Galilee.*

The first recorded miracle by John was when Jesus turned the water into wine in Cana of Galilee. The second was when He healed the royal official's son. However, there were other things that happened along the way that caused people to put their faith in Jesus to be more than just an ordinary guy. Down in Jerusalem He had stirred the pot by cleansing the temple, but He was having more of an impact than that. His conversations with Nicodemus, with the woman at the well, and with the people of her Samaritan village were producing changes in the lives of people that are not specifically recorded, but they were miracles of grace, nonetheless.

It's a common thing for us to put miracles into the category of being something spectacular, a special moving of God that couldn't happen any other way, but that God caused it to happen. While I believe that normal, but unusual events of time shouldn't be called miracles just because they can't be explained, I do believe that every time a person's life is made new by the power of God, a huge and significant miracle has occurred.

A new birth is something only God can bring about. The regeneration of our spirit by a divine encounter with the Holy Spirit, can't be duplicated by any power of man. The outward signs of turning water into wine and the healing of a sick boy were certainly things of which Jesus was responsible, but let's not downplay the lives that are changed miraculously through a person's faith in Christ.

We must remember that these events recorded by John are before the cross and before the resurrection. Jesus was still developing His ministry throughout the boundaries of Israel, and even though people were seeing wondrous things, the power of the new Kingdom of God was yet to be unleashed. The cross would change everything, and the resurrection would confirm that the new age of the Spirit had begun. The power within Jesus was being revealed on a small scale, but the resurrection from the dead would show the world something it had never seen before.

We don't want to belittle the physical miracles, but the miracle of a redeemed soul is the greatest thing God has ever done for any of us.

AT HOME WHERE THE NEED IS

John 5:1–3 *Some time later, Jesus went up to Jerusalem for a feast of the Jews. Now there is in Jerusalem near the Sheep Gate a pool, which in Aramaic is called Bethesda and which is surround by five covered colonnades. Here a great number of disabled people used to lie—the blind, the lame, the paralyzed.*

There are several things for us to notice in these verses. First, Jesus was a social person. He traveled widely, and though He spent much of His time in Galilee, He was also found in the city of Jerusalem in Judea. He observed the religious festivals, and though this passage does not make the connection, Jesus always seemed to go where people were, and this feast put Him squarely in the midst of a large gathering.

It can also be noticed that Jesus didn't just go where there were parties, though I would like to think that He always felt right at home there. He also went where people were hurting, and this scene is about as tragic as we can imagine. Disabled people, including the blind, lame, and paralyzed coming together, no doubt with the help of family members and friends, all with the faint hope of the pool's waters being stirred by an angel. If this strange event did happen, it was only the first one in the water that was expected to be healed. We are not told how this strange belief began, but from the setting we can see that a large number of people believed in the possibility.

The final thing for us to notice about these verses is how the stage is set for the image of hopelessness. We get the picture that this scene of misery was not just an occasional thing, but that it was the daily practice of people who had no hope for a better life outside of something miraculous to happen. Their best efforts hadn't helped them, so either God would intervene or there would be no better days for them.

It's at this point that I see in this crowd of desperate people, a microcosm of all mankind. The difference is that this crowd knew that they were helpless and hopeless without God's intervention. So many people in our world today haven't realized just how needy they are, and how only the Savior can produce a change in their life's condition. The spiritually blind are just as needy as the physically blind, but it is to both groups that Jesus came to minister.

"DO YOU WANT TO GET WELL?"

> **John 5:5–6** *One who was there had been an invalid for thirty-eight years. When Jesus saw him lying there and learned that he had been in this condition for a long time, he asked him, "Do you want to get well?"*

It seems like such a strange question. A man who has been unable to walk for thirty-eight years could certainly have only one response to the question about his healing, couldn't he? Wouldn't anyone jump at the opportunity to be well after they had been sick so long? Why would Jesus ask such a thing?

The truth of the matter is, that there are some people who even though their need is evident to many, just don't want to get well. These are the people who have not yet reached their lowest point or have not been convinced that they need help. There are also those who have hit rock bottom but have long since given up on any hope of restoration, so they reject the offer of healing as one more empty promise. Despair can take a person so far away from hope that even the option of change seems totally impossible.

It is pretty obvious from what we have previously seen in the actions of Jesus, that He knew that man's condition, and He knew what the response to His authoritative command would be. However, it was important for Him to ask the question. He needed the invalid man to understand that He was more than just someone who might give him alms, or offer sympathy. Jesus wasn't going to try and console this man with platitudes or speeches about positive thinking. He was there to do the work of God, and for Him to do that, He needed to get the man's attention.

We could turn His question on ourselves. Do we really want to get well? Do we really have the desire to do anything that God would tell us to do? Do we want to be singled out for God's special purpose regardless of what obedience to the divine command may bring about in our life? We see the compassion of Jesus and we see the need of the invalid man. We get the sense that something wonderful is about to happen even before we read the following verses. We also know that what Jesus did at this distant point in time is something that He is still capable of doing today.

Do you want to get well? Jesus knows your need and He knows how to take care of it.

MIRACLE # THREE

John 5:7–9a *"Sir,"* the invalid replied, *"I have no one to help me into the pool when the water is stirred. While I am trying to get in, someone else goes down ahead of me."* Then Jesus said to him, *"Get up! Pick up your mat and walk."* At once the man was cured; he picked up his mat and walked.

The Jewish legend at the time of this occurrence, was that on occasion an angel would come down from heaven and stir the water. Then the first people in after the water was stirred by this unseen presence, would be healed. Whether there is any evidence to back up this legend is not recorded here, but evidently a good number of needy people believed the story enough to gather by the water's edge each day.

We can picture in our minds the sad and grieving masses that cast their hope on something that *might be*, however improbable. The invalid man made his excuse in his answer to Jesus, that he was just too immobile and frail to get into the water ahead of quicker miracle seekers. However, Jesus just brushed aside the legend, and gave him a command of healing that met his need instantly. What a shock it must have been to the lame man, as well as everyone else who witnessed what was happening.

Some people say that miracles happen every day, because they equate any unusual, good thing that takes place, with divine intervention. However, a true miracle is something special. Having a parking spot open in front of you at a busy shopping center just when you pull up is not what we are talking about. When God moves, His action is clear and definitive.

We are not told why Jesus chose this one particular man to heal and not others who were also waiting, but He must have had His reasons. It's not likely that this man was more worthy that someone else, but again, we just don't have any more information on what happened, or why Jesus did what He did with the person He chose. What we can be sure of is that He always knows what He is doing. Jesus healed a man, which brought about good to him, but He also glorified the Father, which was His main focus in life. The order for the man to pick up his mat was to demonstrate that the healing was real, and that the presence of God was among the masses.

When God moves, we will have questions, but we can be assured that His moving will always be at the right time and be the right thing to do.

BREAKING THE SABBATH—AGAIN!

John 5:9b-10 *The day on which this took place was a Sabbath, and so the Jews said to the man who had been healed, "It is the Sabbath; the law forbids you to carry your mat."*

One of the things of which Jesus was regularly accused was the charge of breaking the Sabbath. The Pharisees were keen on Sabbath keeping to the point of the extreme. The restrictions concerning what a law-keeper couldn't do were more than what most average folks could remember.

There were also special Sabbaths, days much like what we in America would consider as national holidays. They might, or might not, fall on the seventh day of the week. We are not told which kind of Sabbath it was, but apparently it was significant, because immediately the healed man faced opposition for doing something that violated the cultural understanding of what was permitted. Naturally, this man who had been an invalid for thirty-eight years, was overjoyed at the prospect of being able to walk and having the strength to carry his mat while doing so.

His critics didn't seem to care about him, what he had been, or what he was now. They were only concerned with dotting the "i's" and crossing the "t's" of the Jewish law. Too many times in the present-day church we still have critics who can't handle a moving of God that overflows their preconceived box of what is allowed and proper. Certainly, chaos cannot be allowed to reign, but God isn't a God of chaos. He is always in keeping with His plan to bless His creation and bring glory to His actions. Most of all, He loves His creation and desires it to be filled with joy for all He is doing in it. The critics who can't see this miss what God wants to do to bless.

Jesus knew and knows the needs of mankind. He also knew and knows the plan of the Father. Since the Sabbath was created to be a blessing and a day of celebration for all of creation, putting restrictions and making it a day of drudgery was and is completely out of character with His purpose.

Today, we as Christians celebrate Sunday as our Sabbath because it was the day Jesus was raised from the dead. But in our observance, let us be mindful that it is the Lord's Day, and it is a gift from God to us, not a day to bind or restrict people into a mold. Remember, the Sabbath was made for man, not man for the Sabbath.

LAW OR GRACE?

John 5:11–13 *But he replied, "The man who made me well said to me, 'Pick up your mat and walk.'" So they asked him, "Who is this fellow who told you to pick it up and walk?" The man who was healed had no idea who it was, for Jesus had slipped away into the crowd that was there.*

It would have been quite a sight to see. Here was a man who had been an invalid for thirty-eight years, trying to explain to the Jewish critics as to why he was moving about and carrying his mat on a Sabbath. It's hard to imagine that he wasn't recognized because he had been crippled for all those years and lay at the pool's edge each day. It was only natural that when the one who had healed him gave him a command, that he should do it. Jesus spoke with authority and power, so who was he to disobey?

To many people, law and tradition are the same. Jesus was already crossways with the Jewish hierarchy because of His previous actions at the temple, but now the issue was the Sabbath, the sacred cow for many in the Jewish community. When the established norms were violated, someone had to answer for the disturbance. Jesus obviously knew that the man He had healed would catch flak for doing what He told him to do. Jesus knew it was the Sabbath, but He also knew that the Sabbath was about celebration and freedom, not bondage and rule-keeping. However, it was too early for Him to play His hand, so to speak, so He chose to slip away unnoticed, leaving the healed man with no idea who had delivered him from his long years of misery.

We must remember that this healing was not based on the faith of the one who had been healed. We don't even know anything about his spiritual condition. We only know that Jesus found a man in pain and brought healing to him. His pedigree or credentials didn't matter. It was through the faith of Jesus and His connection to the Father that brought about this miracle.

Perhaps we too shouldn't be so quick to qualify whether a person is deserving of mercy. In fact, we should recognize that God wants the best for everyone, and if we can be a part of the solution to their ills, then we should welcome the chance to do something about them. At least, that's what Jesus did, and out of all the role models we could choose, He's a pretty good example to follow.

STOP SINNING!

John 5:14–15 *Later Jesus found him at the temple and said to him, "See, you are well again. Stop sinning or something worse may happen to you." The man went away and told the Jews that it was Jesus who had made him well.*

I find it interesting that Jesus didn't leave the man that He had healed with no information, and no explanations. He chose to find him and let him know who was responsible for the healing that had taken place. He also wanted to warn the man against doing anything that would put him back into jeopardy. It wasn't a threat, or even the idea that God would get him if he didn't straighten up. It was an analysis of the toll that sin takes on a life. The words, "Stop sinning or something worse my happen to you," is prophetic, not an accusation. I mean, the guy had been an invalid for thirty-eight years. What could possibly happen that could be worse than that? However, the man needed to stop sinning or face the consequences.

There are a couple of ideas that I pull from this. First, it is possible to stop sinning. If it was not, then Jesus wouldn't have told the man to do it. Sin is a choice, not something we accidentally get ourselves into. Sin is deliberately disobeying God's instructions and plans for our life.

It's also important to note that when Jesus warned the man, He was warning him against sin in general. This is because sin always is destructive— always. Because God cares so much for us, He makes a way for us to live in obedience and enjoy fellowship with Him. When we choose to live in disobedience, we will find eventually that God's ways and God's rules are for our benefit. We violate His direction at our own peril. It's like telling a child not to touch a hot stove. We don't do it because we are just trying to flaunt our authority. We do it because we want to keep the child from being burned. That's the way God is with us. He wants us not to sin because sin always leads to pain, heartache, suffering, death. There are no exceptions.

When the man found out who Jesus was, he had to tell others. He went to the Jews who had confronted him first, but giving him the benefit of the doubt, I would say that he just couldn't keep quiet when his life had been so completely changed. As a matter of fact, we shouldn't either.

Working On The Sabbath

John 5:16–17 *So, because Jesus was doing these things on the Sabbath, the Jews persecuted him. Jesus said to them, "My Father is always at his work to this very day, and I too, am working.*

One's view of the Sabbath has a big impact on a person's religious practices. When people ignore the Sabbath as something irrelevant to their life, it speaks loudly of their personal arrogance and general disregard for the majesty and authority of God. However, when a person builds their faith on their ritualistic practice of Sabbath observances, then the day itself can become an idol and that's something God never intended for it to become.

Is there a middle ground between neglect and legalism? I think there is. As Jesus said in Mark 2:27, "The Sabbath was made for man, not man for the Sabbath." The Sabbath is for our benefit. The whole idea of a Sabbath observance is so that we might be renewed, refreshed, and restored as we focus on the Creator, who has made wholeness possible. If we could understand the Sabbath Day rest as a time for reflection and contemplation on eternal matters, along with devotion and worship of our Lord, then we could enjoy the freedom of doing what renews us personally and corporately.

Of course, after the resurrection of Jesus, the seventh day Sabbath eventually morphed into the Lord's Day, which we celebrate on the first day of the week, because it was on that day that Jesus was raised from the dead. The first-century Christian Jews no doubt observed both Saturday and Sunday, but as the Jewish church became more and more a Gentile church, the focus of the Jewish Law on the Sabbath Day became less of a focus.

The point Jesus was making in this passage was that He was doing the Father's work, and the Father never takes a break. The Sabbath is a day of celebration and giving glory to the Father so whatever causes that to happen is a good thing. Certainly, the deliverance of a man who had been captive to a debilitating illness would fall into that category. God was being praised for the man's healing, so it was more than appropriate on the Sabbath.

It's sad that Jesus was persecuted for doing what came naturally to Him. We too may face obstacles because of what we do, but if we set about doing all we can do to bring glory to the Father, then we can be assured we are doing right, just like Jesus. And again, that's pretty good company.

DEADLY SERIOUS

John 5:18 For this reason the Jews tried all the harder to kill him; not only was he breaking the Sabbath, but he was even calling God his own Father, making himself equal with God.

Boy! This escalated quickly! In the previous verses the Jews were persecuting Jesus because of His violation of what they understood the Sabbath to be about, but now they have moved from persecution to murder. It doesn't take long for sin to rear its ugly head when challenged.

Of course, such sinners are cowards also. They could have attacked Jesus on the spot with overwhelming numbers, but because what Jesus was doing was pleasing to the masses, they were afraid of the pushback that would come if they accosted Him publicly. The devious plots of the enemy's agents rarely show any level of boldness.

The ironic thing about this whole Sabbath issue is that Jesus is the one who instituted the Sabbath, and it was given for the purpose of mankind's benefit, not to be a battering ram to beat people into submission. The Sabbath is a gift and is about joy and rest, though people who manipulate it into a political tool and a power focus could never understand that.

When Jesus put Himself in the category of being God's Son, there is no doubt but that He was speaking to a clueless audience. The incarnation was not something they expected, nor understood. It would take many more events and a period of time before even His own disciples would grasp the context of His words. In the meantime, they were learning, even as the world got uglier around their Master.

We can all learn from this. We see that when we are doing the work and will of the Father, we shouldn't be surprised when people attack us for doing so. Such challenges may come because of ignorance, because of misunderstandings, or they may just come from the raised hackles of people whose evil ways are being called into question. In any case, as Jesus didn't practice ministry to people without making enemies, we should expect the same from those who are in our age.

The good news is that love always wins out. There may be a cross to face in the path of our labors, but righteousness ultimately wins—always!

THE HIGHEST FORM OF FLATTERY—IMMITATION!

John 5:19 *Jesus gave them this answer: "I tell you the truth, the Son can do nothing by himself; he can do only what he sees his Father doing, because whatever the Father does the Son also does."*

When we were young, we learned everything from watching others. Because others walked on two legs, the time would eventually come when we would pull ourselves up and become mobile. When we heard other speaking, our own vocal cords began to make efforts to imitate the sounds and before too long we were uttering simple phrases. This pattern would be repeated countless times over the early days of our lives and even beyond as we made our encounters with the world around us.

It shouldn't seem strange to us then that Jesus also did what He saw His Father doing. We shouldn't be surprised that the love of the Father for His creation would also flow from the Son, who was totally dependent on His Father for His every action and reaction. Jesus was an obedient Son that reflected His Father's wishes on every occasion.

This should be a challenge for each of us as we evaluate our own understanding of the Father and His plans for our lives. We see the Father in action through His Word, through nature around us, and through the situations of mankind, and like Jesus it should be our responsibility to do the Father's work of bringing about healing and restoration. We can choose to ignore the pain in people's lives around us, and let them go on in their blind and ignorant ways, just like Jesus could have walked on by the woman at the well, or that lame man by the pool, but that's not what would please the Father. The Father is always about love and redemption, and letting people blinding wander through life without hope and without purpose is not in His agenda for them.

Jesus took His cues from on high, and that is where we should get ours. Ministry flows out of realizing the pain and situations of our neighbors, and then our reaching out to help them, pointing them in the way of living water and healing grace. It may take a brief encounter or a lifetime, but people are worth investing our lives in because they were worth Jesus investing His life in them. Wherever we go we are to look to the Father for guidance and blessing for other's sake. Remember, we are His children too.

"GREATER THINGS THAN THESE..."

These words are interesting to me. It's not news that the Father loves His Son, or even that He shows His Son everything there is to see. What catches my attention is that Jesus was going to be seeing things greater than He currently saw at that time. The one who is Lord and Master of all, was about to be shown more than He had seen before. It seems interesting to contemplate.

When I think of all that Jesus did as a man here on earth in His mere three years of ministry, I am starting to consider that there may be more behind what He was doing that just the actions themselves. I mean, turning water into wine, restoring justice in the temple, offering living water to the woman, and bringing healing to an invalid man are all pretty amazing things, but what if the meaning of what He did went deeper? Could it be that the things Jesus did were just demonstrations of what He expects from those come after Him? Could the "greater things," referred to in this verse, be pointed to the many different ministries to mankind that Christ's church would bring about? When Jesus saw what the Father did, and His disciples saw what He did, there seems to be a correlation as to the impact that such things would have on all creation.

You see, the Father is all about redemption and restoration, not only of mankind, but of all He has created. When Jesus demonstrated healing, in days to come hospitals that brought about healing in His name would be built. Because Jesus brought about justice in the temple, Christians would impact the world with laws and practices for the lands of the world. When Jesus offered living water that would transform a wayward woman's life, He was pointing a way for His church to also provide redemption and restoration for the lives of the sin-sick everywhere.

Perhaps no one ever did anything in greater *quality* than Jesus did, for after all, He is the Lord. But those who follow after Him can do things in greater *quantity* than Jesus ever did. He set the standard and demonstrated His purpose, the purpose that He saw from the Father, and His disciples—then and now—followed suit. These are greater things indeed!

THE POWER OF RESTORATION

John 5:21 *"For just as the Father raises the dead and gives them life, even so the Son gives life to whom he is pleased to give it."*

It is at this point in this ongoing message from Jesus that we first hear anything about people being raised from the dead and the Son's part in bringing it to pass. We will later, in chapter eleven, see Jesus do this literally in the case of Lazarus, but at this point in time, Jesus is just talking about it.

Is this another example of what He expects from those who follow after Him? No, in this case we realize that it is only God who can raise the dead. Because the Father has given all authority over to the Son, that ability falls to Him as well. If we are talking about a literal corpse being raised to full life once again, that falls into the camp of something only God can do. However, I think that the woman at the well would have correctly said that Jesus brought her to life, as would the village to whom she had introduced Jesus. As for the man who had been infirm for thirty-eight years, but found strength in his legs, and strength to carry his mat, I believe that he would have said that Jesus brought him from death to live. His whole world had been turned upside down.

In this regard, the people of God can have a role in restoration and resurrection. We can't raise those who are literally dead, but we can provide access to the King of kings who can mend marriages, bring prodigal children home, restore broken relationship, and forgive the sins that has plagued people down through the ages. Because Jesus has the words of life, and we are followers and disciples of Jesus, we too have a role in God's plan of renewal.

Whether it be in our families, our neighborhood, our job setting, our school interactions, or something else, we can pass along the words of life because the Father has given Jesus the power of restoration to life, and we can work as His ambassadors. We also can work and do the will of the Father, in the name of His Son, through the power of His Spirit. That is the role of the church.

Someday there is going to be a great reunion when eternity unfolds, and we are going to hear stories and testimonies of the millions to whom Jesus has restored life. In fact, we just may be among that number.

JUDGMENT BELONGS TO JESUS

John 5:22–23 *"Moreover, the Father judges no one, but has entrusted all judgment to the Son, that all may honor the Son just as they honor the Father. He who does not honor the Son does not honor the Father, who sent him."*

Most people don't like to think about it, but the Bible is pretty clear about the fact that there is going to be a judgment day. And according to this scripture, all judgment matters are going to be placed in the hands of the divine, crucified Lamb, who was raised from the dead. I have no idea what that will look like, but if the Bible is true—and I am convinced that it is—then we will all stand before the judgment seat of Christ.

The claim is also made here that Jesus is due all the rights and recognition given to the Father. The two are one and in the special connection they share there is unity in all things. Again, understanding and explaining the Trinity in detail is far above my pay grade, but I accept the matter as given, by faith.

What we can gain from this teaching is found in the fact that Jesus is not one of many options to eternal life, but He is the only way. That's a bitter pill for the majority of people in the world who run after many different religions or no religion at all. They want to think that Jesus or Christianity is just another player on the world's religious stage, and that all roads lead to the same place eventually, but that's not what the Bible teaches. All authority has been given to Jesus, and He is to be honored just as God the Father is honored. There is no room for a middle road of compromise here. There is no room for Christians to say that cults and other religions are ideas with whom we can negotiate and agree to disagree concerning eternal matters. This scripture is talking about divine judgment, and understanding that Jesus is the only way, the only truth, and the only path to life is paramount.

The Church of Jesus has been given the responsibility of sharing the Good News of the Gospel with the world, and that means that we cannot make concessions with false religions. We are always to act in love and respect for all people, but if we allow people to think that any way but the Christian way leads to God and eternal life, then we are doing them a grave misjustice for we leave them in their lostness and sin. Judgment is coming and Jesus is going to be the Judge. It's time for folks to get ready.

MOVING FROM DEATH TO LIFE

John 5:24 *"I tell you the truth, whoever hears my word and believes him who sent me has eternal life and will not be condemned; he has crossed over from death to life."*

The transition from death to life seems like a tremendous span, but it's not as big a leap as some imagines it to be. Just as we will one day close our eyes in this world and open them in another world, even so, the change from death to life right now is possible for anyone who will take the leap of faith.

Believing in Jesus and believing His Word is the means by which we make the humanly impossible leap. Oh, we can believe, but it is Jesus who helps us have the faith to make the jump, and He is the one who provides the regeneration from our life where we are dead in our trespasses and sins to one where we have been adopted into the family of God.

Eternal life begins the moment we put our faith in Jesus as the Savior of the world and Lord of all things. It's not saying the right words, joining a church, or even being baptized, but instead it is a renewing of our way of thinking as we leave the idols of our old life behind, and pursue a way in the newness of the Spirit.

There are great advantages in making this leap of faith. First of all, we will not be condemned for the sins we have committed against God and man. Forgiveness is a great perk of Kingdom living. Second, we move from living for ourselves, which is a deadly spiral of idolatry, to new life in the Spirit of God, who comes to live within us and make us one with Him. Just as the new age began with the resurrection of Jesus from the dead, our new age begins when we transition from our sinful life to eternal life in Jesus. It's a wonderful gift and a wonderful experience.

Again, this is only possible by faith in the work of Jesus on our behalf. We put our trust in Him, pledge our life to Him, believe what He taught, and put into practice our life in the Spirit which He imparts to us when we turned from our old way and to His new way. This is the gift of God, that we should pass from death to life. With so many people struggling to find their purpose and their place in life, this avenue of faith is a real game changer for all who will believe. We can be raised to new life now and know that it has happened. Jesus makes all the difference for now and for eternity.

"THE DEAD WILL HEAR..."

John 5:25–27 *"I tell you the truth, a time is coming and has now come when the dead will hear the voice of the Son of God and those who hear will live. For as the Father has life in himself, so he has granted the Son to have life in himself. And he has given him authority to judge because he is the Son of Man."*

One of the questions that spurs the divide between the pro-choice and the pro-life movements in the abortion battle is the question of when life begins. According to these verses, it actually begins when one hears the words of Jesus. So, just what does it mean to hear the words of Jesus? It's more than just getting information to the ears, for it means that one must believe that God is who Jesus says He is, and realizing that the God of the Old Testament must be viewed through the lens of the New Testament.

Hearing the words of Jesus will change us and require something of us. It means that we are to accept the way of life that Jesus offers, however hard that may be and whatever sacrifices that may involve. It means to accept the help the risen Christ gives to us and the guidance the Holy Spirit has to offer us.

Life also begins when one believes God. We only have three accounts in the Gospels of God's voice. He said, "This is my Son whom I love, with him I am well pleased" (Matthew 3:17; Mark 1:11; Luke 3:22), as recorded at Jesus' baptism. At the Transfiguration, God said, "This is my Son whom I have chosen. Listen to him" (Matthew 17:5; Luke 9:35). And He spoke one third time after Jesus asked the Father to glorify His name. God said, "I have glorified it and will glorify it again" (John 12:28). Anyone who could not accept the fact that Jesus is the one and only begotten Son of God cannot enter into life. Whoever believes will not be condemned, so it is only reasonable to assume that whoever does not believe will be condemned.

We may ask, "Well, how is this life going to be possible?" The answer is found in God, the giver of life. It is possible now because to possess Jesus is to possess life. The dead will hear the voice of God for the Father has given the Son authority to also be the giver of life. We have life when we have Jesus and without Him we may have the activity and appearance of life, but it is only when we know the Source that real life begins.

THERE WILL BE A RESURRECTION!

John 5:28–29 *"Do not be amazed at this, for a time is coming when all who are in their graves will hear his voice and come out—those who have done good will rise to live, and those who have evil will rise to be condemned."*

The one great hope we as Christians have, is in the fact that there will be a bodily resurrection in the day when God will have the final trumpet of time sound. Just as Jesus was raised bodily from the grave, all who have put their trust in Him for their salvation will also be raised, and their old body will be made new. It will be a body that will never get sick, never deteriorate, and never grow old. We will be more alive than we have ever been, and we will live in the joy and service of the Lord.

The full details are unknown at this time and can be debated. However, the reality is undeniable if we believe the words of Jesus. These words are an echo of Daniel 12:1–2, and with them we set our hope on the collective writings of scripture as a whole.

In my own opinion, this is how I think it will play out. After we leave this world through the normal process of death, the essence of who we are will be in a time of rest in the presence of the Lord in a place that is often referred to as heaven, or paradise. This is where the saints will reside as Jesus promised in John 14:1–4, until the last day when the trumpet call will sound and time as we know it will be no more. At that point the great resurrection will take place as the graves will be opened, and then our bodies will be resurrected and united with the essence of our being, and heaven and earth will become one (Revelation 21:1–4).

Of course, there is much more to discuss than what we can do here, but when we take the words of Jesus seriously, along with Paul's words in I Corinthians 15:35–56, and II Corinthians 5:1–10, we have a good place to begin our study of the subject.

Regardless of how the debates about the next life play out in this life, of this one thing we can be sure. God is in control and He has promised to raise His followers up to live eternally, just like He raised Jesus. Therefore, we are to be encouraged, built up in our faith, and be determined more than ever to make His Kingdom come and His will to be done on earth until that wonderful day arrives.

PLEASING THE ONE
WHO CALLED US

John 5:30 *"By myself I can do nothing; I judge
only as I hear, and my judgment is just, for I seek
not to please myself but him who sent me."*

It will probably take us until we get to heaven before we can fully understand the relationship between the Father and the Son. We know that they are one, but we also know that the Son is totally dependent on the Father. It's a symbiotic relationship that is unlike anything of which we are familiar. But I'm sure that once we fully know the details, we will see it like everything else about the Godhead, namely, the epitome of perfection.

One thing that we do see about that relationship is that the Son is totally committed to pleasing the Father in all things. The incarnation was not about Jesus making Himself comfortable until His time here was concluded. It was about Him doing the work the Father sent Him to do, and doing it to the smallest detail.

Since we who are in Christ are brothers and sisters with Him, that should be our goal in life as well. Everything we do should be to the glory of the Father as we seek to please Him with our service in this life. By doing so we are not only helping our fellow humans around us, but we are laying up treasures for the world to come. As we work to bring God's Kingdom to pass on earth, so that the two will become one, then the Father will be pleased, and we will be doing good that will last for all eternity.

One of the greatest dangers the people of God face today is in the area of distraction. We too often seek to please ourselves more than we desire to please the Father. As we seek material things like cars, houses, clothes, appliances, retirement plans, vacations, and all the other stuff that Western society has prioritized, we could find ourselves stretching to make it all fit into God's plan, and working extra jobs to pay for it. We need to remember that they way of the Kingdom is not in the collecting of toys.

It's nice to have things, but it's not nice when those things have us. Whatever pulls us away from the focus we need to have on pleasing the Father, listening to the Father, and working for the Father needs to be put aside. Our time of service is limited and we need to remember that Jesus set the example for us to follow in this regard. God comes first in all that we have, for that is how we serve Him to the best of our ability.

EYEWITNESS EVIDENCE

John 5:31–32 *"If I testify about myself, my testimony is not valid. There is another who testifies in my favor, and I know that his testimony about me is valid."*

Don't you just hate it when people make outrageous claims about themselves? If I claimed to be able to hit a hole in one on any par three golf hole, people would just roll their eyes, unless they have seen me do it. It's a pain when airs are put on, but usually acceptable if they are proven true.

If I were to make the claims that Jesus does here, it would blasphemous, but when Jesus says these things, we look at Him differently. That wasn't the case when He was walking the earth during this time, however, so to make His case He points us to witnesses of the truth.

Any trial lawyer would recognize the value of having eyewitnesses. Having someone speak from personal experience, or demonstrate that they have first-hand knowledge of an event gives credence to claims that one has made or proves them wrong. Being a truthful witness has a powerful impact on settling matters of dispute. This is why it is so important that people who testify to being a follower of Jesus, have the fruit of that claim to back up their words. Going to church regularly, praying at the altar, being baptized, and taking communion are all good things that Christians regularly take part in, but there must be more than these things to prove our claim concerning whether or not we are a true disciple of Christ.

As Jesus said in these verses, a personal answer cannot be the final testimony as to whether or not we are a Christian. Anyone can say anything about oneself, but personal statements alone don't hold water as evidence. What does make a difference, however, is what others say about you. When people watch our lives closely and they consistently see the fruit of the Spirit flowing out from our words, our mannerisms, our temperament, and even through our presence of social media, they begin to form opinions about us, and they will decide if what we say about ourselves matches up with the truth image of Jesus.

We need to understand this clearly. What others say about us is more important than our personal testimony. What are people seeing and saying about us? It's something we ought to consider.

PUBLIC ENDORSEMENT

John 5:33–35 *"You have sent to John and he has testified to the truth. Not that I accept human testimony; but I mention it that you may be saved. John was a lamp that burned and gave light, and you chose for a time to enjoy his light."*

John, known as "the baptist," or "the baptizer," was sent by the Father to prepare the way for the coming of Jesus. As it was recorded in the first chapter of this book, "I am the voice of one calling in the desert, 'Make straight the way for the Lord'" (1:23).

John had several parts to his testimony about Jesus. First, John was the one who said that Jesus would take away sin. "The next day John saw Jesus coming toward him and said, 'Look, the Lamb of God who takes away the sin of the world'" (1:29). Second, John revealed that Jesus was the one who baptizes with the Holy Spirit. "I would not have known him, except that the one who sent me to baptize with water told me, 'The man on whom you see the Spirit come down and remain is he who will baptize with the Holy Spirit'" (1:33). Finally, John said that Jesus was the Son of God. "I have seen and I testify that this is the Son of God" (1:34).

These are pretty good endorsements as to the credentials of Jesus. It would have especially been true for those who lived in the first part of the first century in Israel. John had been building up quite a reputation, and people from all across the land and even to the Jewish palaces, were noticing him and being affected by his preaching. If John had not endorsed Jesus, it wouldn't have changed the fact of who Jesus was, but since he did—emphatically these three times—it was about as good a recommendation as a religious Jew could get at that point in time.

Again, this brings us back to the question, "What do people say about you?" How has your reputation affected the lives of people with whom you associate on a regular basis? How do your co-workers, schoolmates, social connections—in person and online—and family see you as related to your connection to Jesus and His message of salvation. Everybody influences somebody, and whether that influence or reputation is negative or positive, it reflects greatly on your impact for the Kingdom of God.

So again, what do people say about you concerning your faith in Jesus?

MISSING THE OBVIOUS

John 5:36 *I have testimony weightier than that of John.*
For the very work that the Father has given me to finish, and
which I am doing, testifies that the Father has sent me.

I read a story that caught my attention. A man and his dog were walking on the beach and met another man. The owner of the dog wanted to brag about a special trick his dog had learned, so he said, "Watch this!" and threw a stick out into the surf. The dog immediately ran over the top of the water, jumping over a wave, fetched the stick and ran back. The man shook his head as he stood watching in disbelief. The dog owner had the dog do it a few more times and then turned to the other man and asked, "So what do you think?" The other man replied, "Your dog can't swim, can he?"

It's amazing how many people miss the obvious. It was that way concerning Jesus and His time in Galilee and Judea as well. He turned water into wine (2:7–10), He cleansed the temple (2:15–16), He did miraculous signs (2:23), He taught truth to spiritual leaders (3:1–21), He brought new life to a Samaritan woman and her village (4:1–26), He healed a royal official's son (4:43–53), and He healed a man who had been lame for thirty-eight years (5:8). Yet with all these things bearing witness to His identity, there were still so many people who would not believe in Him. They might be curious, or even awed by His actions, but belief in Jesus as the Savior of the world had not yet been grasped by them.

We often find that the case is the same for our time. Jesus is continually at work in this world through His body, the church, and often people are unimpressed or apathetic about the whole thing. It's almost like we hear the words of the man in the dog story, "Your dog can't swim, can he?" Many assume that the church isn't real, or that its divine connection must surely be limited.

The point that Jesus was making here is that He should be evaluated in light of the works that He did. Not only was John's testimony valid, but anyone with eyes and a willingness to see the truth, could see that Jesus was doing things that were not only unusual and impossible, but were filled with the divine presence of the Father. This is evidence that Jesus said bore witness to who He was, and who He is. "O Lord, give us eyes to see!"

SENT BY THE FATHER

John 5:37-38 *And the Father who sent me has himself testified concerning me. You have never heard his voice nor seen his form, not does his word dwell in you, for you do not believe the one he sent.*

Jesus was continuing with His presentation concerning witnesses of His authority to do what He was doing. He had spoken of the witness of John, and then the very works of grace that He was doing, which bore witness to His validity. Finally, He went to the highest source of testimony of all, the Father Himself.

In difference places and in different ways, Jesus had made references to the fact that God was His Father. In verse forty-three He echoed these verses when He said, "I have come in my Father's name, and you do not accept me." He was, and is the only begotten of the Father, and as it says in the Nicene Creed, "I believe in one Lord, Jesus Christ, the only begotten Son of God, born of the Father before all ages. God from God, Light from Light, true God from true God, begotten, not made, consubstantial with the Father, through Him all things were made."

The Father sent Jesus to do a job. It was in His plan that Jesus should enter the world as a man and be the firstborn from the dead, pointing to the fact that those who follow in His path would also someday be raised from the dead. The Father's plan is about redemption for all mankind and all of His creation, and the Son was the person who would make all this possible.

Just as Jesus was given a task to do during His time here as one of us, we also are given a role to play in the plan of redemption. Each time we pray the Lord's Prayer, and say those words, "Thy will be done on earth as it is in heaven," we are declaring our faith and volunteering our help to do all we can to make that prayer come to pass. We are called to work where we are as His representatives to make our little piece of earth more like heaven.

As the Father had sent Jesus, He has also commissioned us and given us all the tools we need to do the work set before us. Paul makes reference to them when he wrote about "love, joy, peace, patience, kindness, goodness, faithfulness, gentleness, and self-control" (Galatians 5:22-23). These fruits are the evidence of Jesus in our lives, given to fulfill the plan the Father has given us to fulfill.

THE NEED FOR ANOINTING

John 5:39–40 *You diligently study the Scriptures because you think that by them you possess eternal life. These are the Scriptures that testify about me, yet you refuse to come to me to have life.*

Another witness to which Jesus made reference concerning His authority was the Holy Scriptures. He confronted the Jews at their own game as they appealed to Scripture to prove that He was a lawbreaker by His healing of the man on the Sabbath. Jesus turned the tables on them.

He showed here an example of diligent study, but in essence, useless study. When the Jews looked to the Law of Moses as their prosecuting witness, Jesus let them know that when Moses wrote he was writing about the role the Messiah would fill, which in fact Jesus was filling. Somehow though, the Jews couldn't put the actions of Jesus together with the writings of Scripture, so they missed the point altogether.

The problem was one of filling. Jesus was full of the Holy Spirit, and as they were one, He had complete and direct access to the heart of God and could see the purpose behind the commandments that had been given. The Jews were speaking from their study of the Law, but without the Spirit opening their eyes to the meaning of the words, they were just reading without understanding.

This is why we all need to have the anointing of the Spirit in our lives as we attempt to discern the will of God in our daily walk and continual ministry. In Hebrews 4:12 we find, "For the word of God is living and active, sharper than any double-edged sword. It penetrates even to the dividing of soul and spirit, joints and marrow. It judges the thoughts and attitudes of the heart." Not only does the Bible bear witness to Jesus, but it judges us, the reader, as we pour over its words, and through it the Father knows whether or not we are sincere.

The Scriptures point to Jesus. The Old Testament looks forward to Him, the Gospels tell what we need to know about Him, and the rest of the New Testament reflects upon Him. He had the words of life and He is the Judge who rules over all. By understanding this we avoid the trap of the Jews who saw the Law as a weapon, but not as a blessing. The Word testifies to the validity of Jesus however, and that's all we need to know.

JESUS KNOWS

John 5:41–44 *"I do not accept praise from men, but I know you. I know that you do not have the love of God in your hearts. I have come in my Father's name, and you do not accept me; but if someone else comes in his own name, you will accept him. How can you believe if you accept praise from one another, yet make no effort to obtain the praise that comes from the only God?"*

The difference in the amount of information that Jesus knows compared to the amount of information that we know is staggering. Being fully God and also fully man gave Him insights that go far beyond what we are able to discern, but there are some strong lessons that come from His encounter here with the Jews that challenged His authority.

Jesus knows whether or not we have the love of God in our hearts. People can be so deceptive at times and if we are not careful, we can fall into the traps they set for us. Too many times I have been met in a new church assignment by people who seemed so eager to help me adjust to my new surroundings, only to find out later that they had a personal agenda that was not always Christian. Someone once told me that I should beware of those who help unload the truck because they would be the ones who would rush to help me load it up again. That's a little harsh, but there is some truth in it.

We also see that Jesus always comes in His Father's name. His mission is always fully in line with that of the Father and ours should be as well. Whenever we go off on our own crusade, we are in danger of doing real damage to the church and our witness. Being an ambassador of the Father in Christ's name in all we do should be our top priority.

Jesus knows that we are fickle bunch. We have a tendency to run after the latest self-help guru, the latest church growth specialist, or the person who has all the attractive glitter. There is danger here and we should be very careful in our listening to the latest success story.

Finally, Jesus knows that our believe needs to center in on what comes from God and not on what comes from man. Staying God-focused and God-centered will help us to overcome many obstacles in our ministry to others. May we live lives where God is proud of us and draws us every closer to His heart each and every day.

THE FINAL WITNESS

> **John 5:45–47** *But do not think I will accuse you before the Father. Your accuser is Moses, on whom your hopes are set. If you believed Moses, you would believe me, for he wrote about me. But since you do not believe what he wrote, how are you going to believe what I say?"*

One final witness that Jesus called on to confirm His ministry before the crowd of Jews that were challenging Him, was the prophet Moses. Moses had lived some 1200 plus years before this time in the story listed, but more than anyone else, except perhaps Abraham, He cast a huge shadow on the lives of the Jewish people. He was the one God chose to lead the Israelite slaves in Egypt to the freedom of the Promised Land of Canaan. And though he didn't get to go in with them, he was the one responsible for getting them there.

The people of the first century attributed the writings of the book of the Law to Moses to the point it was and is often called the Law of Moses. Regardless of what modern scholarship has discovered over the centuries, at the time when Jesus was having this conversation with this group of Jews, Moses was *THE MAN* in Israel. However, the point Jesus made to these people was that though they put their hopes and faith in Moses, Moses had written about the Messiah, and Jesus was the person he was indirectly referencing. When Moses wrote, "The Lord your God will raise up for you a prophet like me from among your own brothers. You must listen to him." (Deuteronomy 18:15), he was writing about Jesus. The Jews of the Lord's time didn't recognize that fact though.

It would be easy to be Monday-morning quarterbacks here and second-guess the crowds in Galilee. We probably wouldn't have made the connection any better than they did. However, we have this account as a warning to recognize that God often does things in ways we didn't expect, and with people we didn't expect Him to use. Jesus was the answer to the Jewish community's prayers, but they failed to see how God was moving in their midst.

Today our prayer should be, "Oh God, give me eyes to see what You are doing in and around my life. Help me to trust You and glorify You in all I do, that Jesus may be seen in me, so that the world may know You."

CALLED TO SERVE

John 6:1–4 *Some time after this, Jesus crossed to the far shore of the Sea of Galilee (that is, the Sea of Tiberias), and a great crowd of people followed him because they saw the miraculous signs he had performed on the sick. Then Jesus went up on a mountainside and sat down with his disciples. The Jewish Passover was near.*

In a parallel account of this story told by Matthew, we find that when Jesus made this trip He was doing so because He needed to rest. He also needed time to reflect on the murder of His cousin, John, by King Herod. But what happened has happened so many times when one is in the business of ministry, is that the pressing matters on one's personal life don't always get the priority we would like to give them. Jesus needed rest. Jesus needed to pray. Jesus needed time alone to recharge His energy. However, the needs of others didn't stop just because He had needs.

Isn't it interesting? Jesus needed rest, but the people needed His care. His disciples needed some time for learning, but the crowds kept coming. The people following would eventually show that they weren't nearly as concerned about spiritual things as they were to get another free meal, but it didn't stop Jesus from looking to their needs first. Also, the days of Passover were upon them and that would mean that Jesus would need to make another trip to Jerusalem, which would be another long journey and take more energy from Him.

The scene in these four verses have been played out in churches and parsonage living situations on countless occasions. I think of how many times ministers have given up holidays, vacations, birthday celebrations, wedding anniversary dates, school events with their kids, and so many more things because the needs of the congregation and church obligations had to come first. I mention this not to create pity for these servants of God, but to remind them and others that this is what Jesus did.

We who are called to walk as Jesus walked must remember that our ministry is all about people. We are not at our jobs to be served, but to serve. Hopefully congregations will not take advantage of these servants, but even when they do, we are to do as Jesus did. As I learned long ago in Boy Scouts, "God first, others second, and myself last" is a pretty good example.

HE ALREADY KNOWS

John 6:5–6 *When Jesus looked up and saw a great crowd coming toward him, he said to Philip, "Where shall we buy bread for these people to eat?" He asked this only to test him, for he already had in mind what he was going to do.*

I often wish that the Bible came with pictures. I would love to have seen the look on the faces of the disciples when Jesus asked them about providing lunch for the masses. I would also love to have seen the face of Jesus as He must have smiled at the frustration of Philip and the others, when He already knew what He was going to do, and had the answer to His own question. Such is the testing of Jesus.

It seems to me that it brings Jesus pleasure to test those who would follow after Him. It certainly must be a good thing because we do seem to get tested a lot. However, when it happens, we are in good company because He has always prepared His disciples in this manner, for He knows what we are going to be facing in the future and what we need to get ready for it.

Sometime we are tested with a physical lacking like in this story. It could be in the form of food, shelter, transportation, clothing, or a myriad of other things that we worry over. The testing could come in the form of an illness, a financial challenge, a rebellious child, an obnoxious neighbor, or even in the form of challenging people in our church. The point here is that tough places, difficult decisions, and impossible circumstances are not there to defeat us, but to train us to trust in the only person who can resolve situations to the glory of God. We still walk by faith and not by sight (II Corinthians 5:7), and that is not going to change so long as we are in the world.

The lesson to be learned here is that Jesus already knows what He able to do and what He going to do concerning the test He places before us. What He needs from us is our willingness to do as He commands, and then believe that He has it under control. The disciples didn't have to find the food after all. Jesus had that covered. They just had to learn that when they couldn't, He could.

When tests come out way, we now like the disciples then, need to turn to the Lord and believe that all will be well. Remember, it's not about us. It's about Him, and He can do anything.

HOW BIG IS YOUR FAITH?

John 6:7–9 *Philip answered him, "Eight months wages would not buy enough bread for each one to have a bite!" Another of his disciples, Andrew, Simon Peter's brother, spoke up, "Here is a boy with five small barley loaves and two small fish, but how far will they go among so many?"*

Philip was taken aback by the question of Jesus. "Buy bread for all these people? Are you kidding?" In other Gospel accounts of this story, we find that there were approximately 5,000 men, plus all the women and children, so we are easily talking about 20,000 to 25,000 people, and maybe more.

Philip realized the unrealistic expectation that Jesus had put before him just wasn't possible by any stretch of the imagination. The group's treasury certainly didn't have that kind of money, or a place nearby to buy such food even if they did have the money. It wasn't like there was a McDonald's on every corner.

Enter Andrew. Yes, this is the same man who brought his brother, Simon, to Jesus in chapter one. He is the same Andrew, along with the same Philip, who would bring Greeks who were looking for Jesus, to the Master in chapter twelve. Whenever we see Andrew in the Bible, he is usually bringing someone to Jesus, and that's not a bad reputation to have.

When Andrew brought the boy who possessed the barley loaves and two small fish to Jesus, it not likely he did so because he had faith that Jesus would do a miracle and supply food for the hungry crowd. It seems more likely that he was presenting an object lesson to Jesus explaining that they didn't have enough food in hand, as an answer to the question that Jesus posed, but he was in for a big surprise.

We are so often in the same camp as Philip and Andrew. We may believe that Jesus has all power in heaven and earth, but many times we see situations with our eyes of flesh rather than with eyes of faith. We think of all the reasons why something won't work, why some need is too big, or how impossible society's sin is to conquer. Jesus was about to show that nothing was too big or difficult for Him. Because He is the Lord over everything, everywhere, He is the answer to our situation no matter what the details depict. Our task is to put our complete faith in Him, for when we do that, every need will be supplied—just in time.

LET JESUS HANDLE IT

John 6:10–11 *Jesus said, "Have the people sit down." There was plenty of grass in that place, and the men sat down, about five thousand of them. Jesus then took the loaves, gave thanks, and distributed to those who were seated as much as they wanted. He did the same with the fish.*

One piece of information left out of this story is how Jesus was able to communicate His wishes with so many people. Even the 5,000 men that are specifically mentioned, would today require some kind of public address system for everyone to hear adequately. Add to this number the women and children and one has a major audio challenge. Perhaps the vocal communication was another part of the miracle that was taking place, but even if it wasn't, there was certainly something very special happening among the people. We aren't told just how many people witnessed Jesus breaking and multiplying the food, but the masses had to be astounded that lunch was coming from somewhere.

It is a familiar process that Jesus showed by the story's example. First, He took what is given to Him. He thanked the Father for the gifts made available, and then He proceeded to take care of the problem at hand. He made it looks so easy, so natural that He should be able to do such a thing.

The truth of the matter is that this is still the way we are to address the problems that come into our lives. First, we willingly take the problem to Jesus, thank God that He has provided such a resource, and then allow our Savior to remedy whatever is needed to be remedied. It doesn't matter whether He decides to meet the need immediately, or if He chooses to test our faith by stretching out His response. The important thing is that He is actively on the scene, and we can put our trust in Him to supply an answer to the issue we have brought to Him.

Imagine what would happen if we handled our money problems this way. Just think of the results of bringing our marriage difficulties to Jesus and trusting Him to bless and change things, rather than just our throwing in the towel. What if we placed our health, our job, our children, and even our enemies in His hands and ask Him to take care of things. I believe we would be amazed as to how He is able to pick up the broken pieces and provide for the need presented. That's the kind of God He is.

The Lesson Of Twelve

John 6:12–13 *When they all had enough to eat, he said to his disciples, "Gather the pieces that are left over. Let nothing be wasted." So they gathered them and filled twelve baskets with the pieces of the five barley loaves left over by those who had eaten.*

There are some important lessons to be learned here. The first is simply this: Only Jesus can make what you have meet what you need. I love the fact that the people seated along the ground not only had some food to eat, but also that had enough to eat. They didn't have to scrimp on the servings, for what was provided to them filled the emptiness of their stomachs.

Another lesson to learn is that what we have will always be small unless Jesus touches it. That's true when it comes to our daily bread, our money, our faith, our expectations, and a host of other things. We see only with what our five senses can discern, but Jesus can take our little bit and magnify it through His divine power and turn it into something big. We can't make it happen, but there is no end to the possibilities of greatness to the glory of God when Jesus is given full control over our situations in life.

Finally, what we have will always be enough when Jesus gets through with it. We are told that there were twelve basketfuls left over from the five barley loaves that Jesus had to work with. I don't think that number is a mere coincidence. The number twelve is used one hundred and eighty-seven times in the Bible, and twenty-two in the book of Revelation alone. Jacob had twelve sons, who became known as the twelve tribes of Israel. Abraham's son, Ishmael, had twelve sons who became princes. The Old Testament priests were ordered to place twelve loaves of unleavened bread in the temple each week (Leviticus 24). Jesus is recorded as being in the temple at twelve years of age. There were twelve disciples that Jesus hand-picked. There are twelve gates surrounding the New Jerusalem (Revelation 21). Twelve seems to have a special significance in the Bible.

To me it seems that Jesus was using the number twelve because it would significant to those looking on, and thereby increase their faith. He could have made it eleven or thirteen, but twelve was recognized as something from God, and that's just what Jesus wanted them to see. This much I know for sure: Getting table scraps from Jesus is better than any banquet ever.

"LET'S MAKE HIM KING!"

John 6:14–15 *After the people saw the miraculous sign that Jesus did, they began to say, "Surely this is the Prophet who is to come into the world." Jesus, knowing that they intended to come and make him king by force, withdrew again to a mountain by himself.*

It was at the conclusion of this tremendous miracle of the loaves and fish that Jesus faced another great temptation. In fact, it was the kind of temptation that causes many a strong person to succumb, for it attacked the human craving for popularity and fame.

The power of peer pressure is an amazing thing. Our egos often get inflated when we are lauded and crushed when people disapprove of us. Jesus was on a roll here. He was doing the impossible, convincing skeptics and transforming lives, and His reputation was rising very rapidly. The sheer number of people that followed Him out into that remote area bears testimony to His popularity.

It is so natural to want to be accepted. It makes us feel good when people like us, and many a person has been swept into political activity because the masses called for them to take their place in public service. Jesus was fully human, and I am sure that it must have been gratifying at some level to know that people were seeking Him out.

The fact that Jesus was special made Him the perfect candidate for leading these people. He obviously could have done it. He was, and is, the King of kings, and would have had the most effective rule of any person in history. In days to come that will actually come to pass, but we will have to wait a bit to see His Kingdom come into its fullness.

But Jesus knew that popularity was also a trap. It makes people do things they never thought they would do, and can cause one to go a wrong direction just because masses of humanity would support such a move. But Jesus does a wise thing here. He didn't give in to their demands. They wanted Jesus to be their king, but they didn't want Him to be their Lord. He could fill their stomachs, but He wanted to fill their hearts. It would not have been within the plan of the Father to listen to this crowd, and the Father knows best. So, when the crowds are the loudest, Jesus shows us that such is the time to listen instead to the voice of the Father.

WALKING ON THE WATER

John 6:16–21 *When evening came, his disciples went down to the lake, where they got into a boat and set off across the lake for Capernaum. By now it was dark, and Jesus had not yet joined them. A strong wind was blowing and the waters grew rough. When they had rowed three or three and a half miles, they saw Jesus approaching the boat, walking on the water; and they were terrified. But he said to them, "It is I; don't be afraid." Then they were willing to take him into the boat and immediately the boat reached the shore where they were heading.*

At this point in time, I have never been to the Sea of Galilee, the body of water that is mentioned here. However, I have pastored along the edge of Lake Erie in Ohio, and I was always amazed at how different the water conditions can be from day to day, and how quickly the winds can turn a tranquil lake into a raging sea. The disciples had good reason for being concerned with the changing weather conditions.

What is interesting about this story is that Jesus was the one who put the disciples in the boat and sent them away. Matthew 14:22 says, "Immediately Jesus made the disciples get into the boat and go on ahead of him to the other side while he dismissed the crowd." The Sea of Galilee is a little over eight miles wide, so Jesus caught up to them somewhere near the middle of the lake. It has a depth of approximately 140 feet, so this was a dangerous situation in which the disciples found themselves. Jesus came to them when they were afraid and in desperation. He took charge of the situation and the wild waves were calmed.

This story is almost legendary, but it certainly depicts how the Lord intervenes in our lives still. At so many points in our lives we find ourselves like the disciples. Things get scary and things look bad, even dangerous, but we need to remember that Jesus is not unaware of our situation and He has the resources and power to get us through the storms we face, and help us get safely to the other side.

In the storm, His disciples gain faith. In the storm His disciples see the impossible happen. In the storm all is well because Jesus is there and takes charge when we let Him do so. There is nothing we will face today that the Lord can't handle. As we look to Him, God is glorified and we are delivered.

WHERE DID HE GO?

John 6:22–24 The next day the crowd that had stayed on the opposite shore of the lake realized that only one boat had been there, and that Jesus had not entered it with his disciples, but that they had gone away alone. Then some boats from Tiberias landed near the place where the people had eaten bread after the Lord had given thanks. Once the crowd realized that neither Jesus nor his disciples were there, they got into the boats and went to Capernaum in search of Jesus.

We are told in the gospel of Matthew that Jesus made the disciples get into the boat and shove off while He dismissed the crowds. Matthew also tells us that after the disciples and the crowd left, Jesus went off by Himself to pray. As the story continued, Matthew related that it was the fourth watch of the night, which would be between 3:00 a.m. and 6:00 a.m., when He came to the disciples, who were having a rough time battling with the storm out on the lake. When they saw Jesus, they thought He was a ghost and were scared witless.

The disciples didn't know that Jesus was well aware of their situation. They had been rowing and bailing for hours, but were finding that their boat was in trouble. Now, these were not amateurs, for some in their number were professional fishermen. They knew how to handle rough waters, and they also knew the danger they were in.

But on the mountain, before the Father, Jesus knew all about their situation. The disciples didn't know they were fulfilling a plan and learning a lesson about faith, but Jesus did. After all, He had put them in the water on purpose, and He was showing them that things don't happen by accident. We are under the guidance and care of Almighty God Most High. Jesus was in the process of coming to their rescue, and though He could have calmed the storm from His place on the mountain, this was a time for their faith to be increased. They didn't yet know that He truly was the Son of God, but by the time this event was over, they were a lot more convinced than they were before they left the shore.

Could your storm be Jesus testing your faith? Maybe you should consider it. Maybe God is up to something new. Nothing is impossible with Him and what you are experiencing may just be the plan you need to see.

Training For Success

John 6:25–27 *When they found him on the other side of the lake, they asked him, "Rabbi, when did you get here?" Jesus answered, "I tell you the truth, you are looking for me, not because you saw miraculous signs but because you ate the loaves and had your fill. Do not work for food that spoils, but for food that endures to eternal life, which the Son of Man will give you. On him God the Father has placed his seal of approval.*

Jesus was always in the process of training His disciples. Here He is teaching them how to deal with people who follow Him for the wrong reasons, for the disciples of Jesus have to learn how to handle success as well as failure. The truth of the matter is that we are not as good at it as we would like to think.

Some people follow after Jesus because the crowd does. We have to understand that there is peer pressure in the church also, but Jesus doesn't need "groupies." He calls out His followers to be disciples, and being a disciple takes discipline.

Some follow after Jesus because they want a handout. There will never be an end to the poor or an end to people who think that the church is around just to do their bidding and take care of their needs. Many people want the church for the christening of their babies, a place to get married, and a place to have a funeral, but don't have time for it or interest in it otherwise. These rituals become meaningless when they become just perfunctory. However, there are many who follow after Jesus because they have truly found a new life through Him. Only those who have experienced such a change that Jesus brings can fully understand the importance of His presence. We can't survive, let alone understand scripture or minister without Him. Jesus is the Source and Foundation for all that Christians aspire to be and do.

This would be a good day to evaluate the reasons as to why we are following after Jesus. Is our faith as good as our testimony? Are we following because someone else has put pressure on us to do so, or are we genuinely following for the right reason? If we are claiming to follow Jesus for any other purpose other than to recognize His Lordship and authority over our lives, then we may find ourselves slipping into the ranks of this crowd that wanted a handout. The old saying is true. He is Lord of all, or not at all.

"Just Believe!"

John 6:28-29 *Then they asked him, "What must we do to do the works God requires?" Jesus answered, "The work of God is this: to believe in the one he has sent."*

I t would appear to be a legitimate question, at least on the surface. What is it that God requires of us? That's a question that deserves an answer because sincerely seeking people often truly want to know. Jesus made His answer direct and simple: We are to believe on the Son whom God sent into the world. That is how we please the Father.

That seems too simplistic for us. We want to do something, achieve some great thing, and make our mark so that we will be worthy of God's notice. However, that is not what Jesus said. Our coming to Him is always going to require faith, and that faith is not in what we can do to be worthy of recognition. We are to believe in Jesus as God's only begotten Son, who was sent into the world to die on our behalf so that the new age of the Kingdom could begin, and we could therefore enter into everlasting life. That's it. It's not about rituals, rules, laws, or demonstrations of piety. Life in Jesus is a life of faith, for that is the work of God for us to do.

The Apostle Paul would later echo this thought when he wrote, "For it is by grace you have been saved, through faith—and this not from yourselves, it is the gift of God—not by works, so that no one can boast. For we are God's workmanship, created in Christ Jesus to do good works, which God prepared in advance for us to do" (Ephesians 2:8–10).

Faith is where our walk in Christ begins and where our daily interactions are sustained, but once we walk in faith then the Spirit of God will lead us into doing good for the bodies and souls of those around us, to the glory of the Father. We are not saved by good works, but because we are saved, we will do good works. The two ideas are not incompatible; they are complementary. The Kingdom of God expands as people, born again by faith, put their faith into the action of doing good for others, and causing others to follow their example.

The people John was writing about may not have been ready for this truth, but the message hasn't changed down through the centuries. We walk by faith in Christ, and that is how the work and mission of God is accomplished.

"HOW ABOUT A SIGN?"

John 6:30–31 *So they asked him, "What miraculous sign then will you give that we may see it and believe you? What will you do? Our forefathers ate the manna in the desert, as it is written, 'He gave them bread to eat.'"*

It is an interesting trait of the human condition is that we like to hunt down the scriptures that we can use to fit our present situation. An example of that is given here where the Jews pulled the "Moses" card on Jesus, and reminded Him that God's *real* prophet caused manna to come upon the land to feed the people of Israel. By inference they were saying that if Jesus really was the one from God, He should be able to feed them like Moses did.

It is true that God provided the miracle of manna for the Israelites, and it is also true that the scripture records that it lasted for forty years, until the traveling troupe reached the Promised Land of Canaan. The "bread from heaven" account is recorded in Exodus 15 and Numbers 11. This was a gift from God to the people of Israel so that they wouldn't starve while on their wilderness journey. By the time Jesus walked in Galilee, manna had become legendary, and adopted into the folklore of the descendants of those who had received the gift.

The point behind this account here though is that the people were still not acting in good faith, or in any manner of faith at all. Jesus had fed them the day before, so why shouldn't He do it again? After all, the food from God that Moses announced to the people of Israel came every day for a generation. Surely this prophet, Jesus, could give them lunch two days in a row.

This is a matter of people wanting a handout, not a group of people who were expressing faith. Because we as humans are a fickle bunch, there are always those who want to see a miracle or unusual event before they will believe. But like the people of this story who had just experienced a miracle the day before, most need more than one demonstration. People want God to keep repeating the spectacular before they will believe, or in other words, "God, what have you done for me lately?" Never satisfied, they live by sight and not by faith.

Jesus always requires us to believe in Him, not in the circus of religion. He is the way, and all other paths are just sideshows, for He alone is Lord. If we can grasp that fact and live like we do, nothing else is needed.

TRUE BREAD

John 6:32–33 *Jesus said to them, "I tell you the truth, it is not Moses who has given you the bread from heaven, but it is my Father who gives you the true bread from heaven. For the bread of God is he who comes down from heaven and gives life to the world."*

People often confuse the giver with the gift, and when it comes to spiritual matters, the messenger is often confused with the message, and the source of the message. I have been called by many titles throughout the years of my ministry, but often I am just called "Preacher," by folks in and out of the church. Who I am has been frequently tied to what it is that I do.

The people in this story confused Moses as the giver of manna with the Father who actually provides all things. It's like the building of a church facility. People often say, "Pastor So-and-So built this church," but what they mean is that he held the office of pastor while the church's physical structure was being erected. The pastor may not have driven a nail or painted a wall, but because it was under his administration, he often gets the credit for it.

Jesus set the record straight. Moses didn't provide manna; God did. Moses didn't deliver the Jews from Egypt; God did. Moses didn't dictate the Law; God did. Moses was just a tool used by God to accomplish His purposes. Moses served as a speaker for the voice of God to the people.

God also provided the Messiah. The prophets of old may have talked about Him in general terms, but the Father was the one who put the Son in place and gave Him direction for His mission. His mission was to be spiritual sustenance for the world. His mission was the incarnation—God becoming man so that man could better know God through the work of redemption that Christ provided on the cross.

The result of what God did is found in the offer of life. Though the physical signs that Jesus performed were astounding, they were a side issue to be an example of what His followers would do. The main purpose of the Son was to give life to those who would believe on Him, and trust Him for their salvation. Life abundant here, and life everlasting to come, have been made possible because Jesus willed it to be so. Moses pointed Israel in the right direction, but the focus of the direction was really from the Father, as found in His Son, Jesus the Christ.

THE BREAD OF LIFE

John 6:34-36 *"Sir," they said, "from now on give us this bread." Then Jesus declared, "I am the bread of life. He who comes to me will never be hungry, and he who believes in me will never be thirsty. But as I told you, you have seen me and still you do not believe."*

There is a bit of a play on words here that doesn't show us in the English translation. Jesus was born in Bethlehem, which when translated from the Greek language is literally, "House of Bread." Jesus, the Bread of Life, factually comes from the House of Bread. Even the name of the community our Lord came from gives authority to His testimony.

When Satan tempted Jesus to turn stones into bread in the Synoptic Gospels, he was attempting to get Jesus to do a miracle to meet His own needs. Jesus, however, was never about pleasing Himself, but always was about doing what would glorify the Father, and blessing the creation He had made. When Christ offered His body to this listening crowd, He was appealing for them to be focused on the eternal and not for what would satisfy them for only a meal, for taking in the life of Jesus puts one in company with the divine, and thereby produces everlasting life. The bread—the life of Jesus—sustains us like nothing else can.

Of course, the people listening to Jesus didn't understand this. Because they were so focused on the immediate circumstances, they couldn't project into the future to see what Jesus was talking about. They wanted satisfaction to their fleshly needs right then, and couldn't believe that Jesus was speaking about something beyond their human desires.

When the church takes communion, we are reenacting what Jesus was talking about here. We take the bread and the cup, and we eat and drink into the life of the Lord. We accept by faith the work that Jesus did on our behalf, and we accept by faith the reunion we are going to have with Him someday when we dine with Him in the eternal Kingdom of God. Such a day may seem very far away, but someday we will look back and see that it wasn't so long after all. But by remembering to share and partake of the Lord's body and blood, we draw a bit closer to that day being a reality.

We who have not seen but believe, are the worshipers Jesus wants. May we be faithful to the Master and feed on Him all the days of our lives.

GOD WANTS YOU TO HAVE LIFE!

John 6:37–40 *All that the Father gives me will come to me, and whoever comes to me I will never drive away. For I have come down from heaven not to do my will but to do the will of him who sent me. And this is the will of him who sent me, that I shall lose none of all that he has given me, but raise them up at the last day. For my Father's will is that everyone who looks to the Son and believes in him shall have eternal life, and I will raise him up at the last day."*

I believe in eternal security. I don't believe in it in the sense that it is impossible for a person to lose his or her salvation once they have begun a walk with Christ, because walking in faith involves a relationship and relationships depend on both of the parties involved. We can choose to walk away from Jesus at any time, and therefore the relationship with Him can be broken. However, what Jesus is saying here is that it is His desire to lose no one. He longs for a relationship with us, and He will not turn down anyone who asks to connect with Him. The Father has made such a thing possible, and Jesus continually longs for us to be one with Him.

He speaks here of those who belong to Him being raised up at the last day. This is about the bodily resurrection that awaits everyone who puts their trust in Him. We will go the way of the grave eventually, but after death, just as Christ was raised from the dead bodily, we will be raised bodily also. Between the grave and the resurrection of our body, our spirit, the part of us that makes us who we are, will abide in the place we call heaven. That is not our last stop though. When the last trumpet shall sound, the bodies that were buried will be raised to new life, and we will be wholly alive once more; in fact, more alive than we ever have been.

All this is possible by looking to the Son for eternal life. We put our trust in Jesus as the author and finisher of our faith and know that His sacrifice on the cross defeated the powers of darkness and death once and for all. His resurrection is the proof we need to know so that when the time for our resurrection comes, we shall be like Him with a glorified body that will never age, hurt, or die again. It may sound too good to be true, but these are the words of the Lord Himself, and He never lies. All who will come to Him, He will receive into His family and we will abide with Him forever. It doesn't get any better than that!

STEPPING OUT ON FAITH

John 6:41–42 *At this the Jews began to grumble about him because he said, "I am the bread that came down from heaven." They said, "Is this not Jesus, the son of Joseph, whose father and mother we know? How can he now say, 'I came down from heaven'?"*

When things don't turn out the way we have hoped for, grumbling is often the result. The crowds that came to Jesus really thought He was going to be their meal-ticket once again. After all, He had fed them the day before, so why couldn't He just do it again. If He was the promised Messiah, then certainly God would allow Him to take care of their basic needs.

But this is also a story of how familiarity breeds contempt. Since Jesus had a history of time in Galilee, people knew Him. They knew His parents, His siblings, and His story. How could He be saying now that He came down from heaven? Where did He get such an idea?

The incarnation is never an easy thing to understand, or an easy concept to explain. If we put ourselves in the sandals of those people from Galilee, we probably would find ourselves asking the same questions. How would we react if someone we grew up with started claiming that he was originally from heaven, and that God and he were one? I dare say that we also would be a bit skeptical.

We today have the privilege of hindsight, and as we look back over time, read the Gospel accounts concerning Jesus, see how the church came into existence, and witness the dramatic ways it has impacted our world, we can more readily agree that Jesus truly is the Son of God. We also have the witness of the Spirit in our lives, telling us that it is so. We, who are far removed from the scene, have a great advantage over those who lived in the first half of the first century and were seeing Jesus with their eyes and hearing Him with their ears.

Living by faith is not something that comes naturally. It comes as a result of the supernatural. The Jews who were around Jesus at this point were seeing with their eyes, but didn't yet have the experience of a changed heart, so their faith was small. As time would go on, and as Jesus would continue to amaze many with His teachings and miracles, more would believe. May God give us hearts of faith to believe as He reveals Jesus to us today.

IT IS THE FATHER THAT DRAWS

John 6:43–45 *"Stop grumbling among yourselves," Jesus answered. "No one can come to me unless the Father who sent me draws him, and I will raise him up at the last day. It is written in the Prophets: 'They will all be taught by God.' Everyone who listens to the Father and learns from him comes to me."*

It's awfully easy to take this passage out of context and use it in a variety of situations. Church people have a great tendency to grumble, even though they should have less to grumble about than anyone else. Oftentimes, however, when we begin to focus inwardly instead of outwardly, the people of God, well, we start to grumble.

Looking to minister to the needs of others instead of focusing on ourselves is a great way to put grumbling to rest. However, this particular scripture has to do with people who have not yet put their faith in Jesus as Savior and Lord, and as a result are grumbling about things they don't understand. These people only saw Jesus with eyes of flesh and not of the Spirit, so they weren't able to separate His human upbringing from His divine connection.

There's still a problem for a lot of people who regard Jesus just as a historical figure that lived and died. Some denied that He ever even existed, but many more recognize that someone provided the foundation for the three and a half billion people who see Jesus as more than just another faith healer of antiquity. Someone has to be behind the movement that transformed and continues to transform lives all over the world. It's important to remember the words that Jesus spoke, "No one can come to me unless the Father who sent me draws him." It is the power of God's Spirit that causes people to be attracted to Jesus, and it is His gift of faith that enables folks to put their trust in Him.

The new birth and life in God, is not something we can generate on the human level. We can prepare the atmosphere, provide information, and declare a testimony of what God has done in our life, but it is ultimately the Father who seeks out and saves the one who is lost. The Father will always lead people to Jesus, for He is the way to salvation. There is no other way to life everlasting, and we who have met Him need to keep telling His story, so that the Father will receive the glory.

EVERLASTING LIFE

John 6:46–47 *"No one has seen the Father except the one who is from God; only he has seen the Father. I tell you the truth, he who believes has everlasting life."*

The incarnation, the act of God becoming man, is one of the great mysteries of the universe, and one that we will never figure out completely while we reside in this life. It's no wonder that the people to whom Jesus was talking were perplexed at His sayings, and were baffled by His connection to His heavenly Father. They had watched Jesus, the man, grow up, and now He was saying that God was His Father. It was a big stretch for them to be sure.

Though we may have the benefit of centuries of time for such a truth to sink in, faith in the person of Jesus as the Son of God and Savior of the world, is still a big leap. After all, Jesus said it best, "No one has seen the Father except the one who is from God," and we are not from God, so we walk by faith alone.

However, the promise Jesus gives here, "he who believes has everlasting life," is our ace in the hole. We may not see, but we who believe are being rewarded in ways beyond our imagination. We need to be reminded from time to time that faith is not of our doing. Faith is a gift that comes from God alone. It is His gift to us. Paul reminds us of this fact in Ephesians 2:8–9 where he says, "For it is by grace you are saved, through faith—and this not from yourselves, it is the gift of God—not by works, so that no one can boast."

We don't save ourselves, and we don't even generate the faith that can save us. It's all God's doing as He makes our salvation possible from beginning to end. The salvation promised us is everlasting life. Because we measure time in years and we celebrate our birthdays every time they roll around, it's hard for us to grasp the concept of everlasting. We don't know of anything that lasts forever because everything and everyone around us eventually wears out. Here again is information that is beyond our grasp, but something we take by faith. Those who are in Christ and have gone before us are now experiencing everlasting life. What that is like is something we can only guess about, but we know that we want to join them there—and we will if we keep faith in Jesus. He is our pathway to get there.

LIVING BREAD

John 6:48–51 "I am the bread of life. Your forefathers ate the manna in the desert, yet they died. But here is the bread that comes down from heaven, which a man may eat and not die. I am the living bread that came down from heaven. If anyone eats of this bread, he will live forever. This bread is my flesh, which I will give for the life of the world."

No doubt the metaphor Jesus was using here was confusing to His listeners. They knew about the manna that came down from heaven. They had heard the stories of what happened in the days of Moses all their lives. They also knew that Jesus had just accomplished the impossible, a miracle, when He took the five loaves and two small fish and fed thousands of people with them. They knew that Jesus was like no one they had ever met, but they were having a tough time taking in all that He was saying.

Since we have the benefit of time in our favor, we can see the shadow of the cross that is looming just ahead of Jesus, and we can look into the upper room as He tells His disciples that they were eating His flesh and drinking His blood as part of the Passover meal. Of course, even the disciples didn't quite grasp what Jesus was saying at that point, so it's not surprising that people at this place in His journey were perplexed, but Jesus was speaking truth to them.

Whenever we eat food, even food that God provides, we are eating to satisfy our bodily needs only temporarily. We all know what it's like to have the hunger pangs that eventually return after we have gone without nourishment for a while. However, we who are in Christ also realize that once we have partaken of His life our hunger is satisfied, and as long as we remain in Him, we never long to be sustained again. We may long for a closer relationship with Him, and we will long to be renewed in Him daily, but we have lost that empty feeling deep inside once we find Jesus. He fills us in ways that people without faith cannot understand. His body is flesh indeed, and His blood is drink indeed. We are sustained by the fellowship and communion He shares with us continually.

As the manna came down from heaven, so did Jesus. As the manna provided life temporarily, Jesus provides life eternally. But as the manna eventually went away, Jesus never will. He is truly our gift of life.

"Eat My Flesh"

John 6:52-55 *Then the Jews began to argue sharply among themselves, "How can this man give us his flesh to eat?" Jesus said to them, "I tell you the truth, unless you eat the flesh of the Son of Man and drink his blood, you have no life in you. Whoever eats my flesh and drinks my blood has eternal life, and I will raise him up at the last day. For my flesh is real food and my blood is real drink."*

Most Christians of our day will recognize the similarity of what Jesus is saying, to the communion services in which we participate in our local churches. Though our Roman Catholic brothers and sisters insist that the bread and the wine offered to the congregation actually becomes the flesh and blood of Jesus in the offering of the mass, most Protestants adhere to the idea of the elements of communion as being symbolic, or a reminder of Christ's spiritual presence that is with us always via the Holy Spirit.

It's hard to blame the Jews for being confused by Jesus' words because they sound confusing to us still. If we take what He is saying literally then it sounds a whole lot like cannibalism, an accusation that would come back to haunt the first century Christians in the days to come.

We, who have devoted ourselves to Jesus, want to be as wrapped up in the life and person of our Master, regardless as to how strange it sounds, even if it is misunderstood. We desire eternal life with Jesus and we live in the faith of being raised up at the last day, the day of resurrection.

Many Jews believe in the resurrection at the end of the age, and the reference Jesus makes to it here would not have been a shock to them. They knew that God was going to raise up the righteous in the age to come, but they didn't expect that He was going to begin that new age in the person of Jesus. They expected all people to be raised at the same time. But when Jesus was raised from the dead, He showed that God was breaking into history and doing something different from their expectations. Jesus would become the firstborn from the dead, and though the rest of us won't receive our resurrected bodies until the last day arrives, we can plan on being with the Lord after this life is over as we wait in the heavenly realms for that day to come. Eternal life has been promised to God's faithful, and eternal life we shall have, for through the Holy Spirit we can be filled with Jesus right now.

FEEDING ON JESUS

John 6:56–59 *"Whoever eats my flesh and drinks my blood remains in me, and I in him. Just as the living Father sent me and I live because of the Father, so the one who feeds on me will live because of me. This is the bread that came down from heaven. Your forefathers ate manna and died, but he who feeds on this bread will live forever." He said this while teaching in the synagogue in Capernaum.*

The lesson that comes out of this story is actually pretty simple. If we rely on the bread of this world to eat, we will die, for it only provides a temporary sustenance. But if we partake in what Jesus has to offer, we will live forever, for in Him we have access to the source of all life, the presence of God.

Back in the Garden of Eden there were various trees. The two that are mentioned are the *Tree of Knowledge of Good and Evil*, and *The Tree of Life*. Adam and Eve were warned not to eat of the former, but they ate daily of the latter. It was the *Tree of Life* that gave them the ability to live without aging and experiencing death. After they ate from the *Tree of Knowledge of Good and Evil*, against the command of the Lord, they were barred from the Garden, and therefore deprived of the fruit from the *Tree of Life*. As a result, they could no longer sustain their lives, and death eventually came to them.

Some may consider this a fable, or a bit of historical melodrama, but when one reads through the story of Genesis, it makes perfect sense. What Jesus was offering to the people listening to Him was a path back to the source of life that would keep on giving. If they just kept toiling for their daily bread, they could be assured for their possibility of life for as long as they could eat of it. But if they would feed on the teachings of Jesus, they would have the words of life that would cause them to be able to live forever. It wouldn't be an eternal life in this world, but His words would feed them and prepare them for a heavenly home, and a resurrected life on God's new earth.

Across the miles and across the years, the words of Jesus would no doubt be misunderstood and misconstrued. Still, the truth remains, if we set our hearts on dwelling in the life and mission of Jesus, we will live forever. Rebellion and rejection of the Son will be understood as a rejection of the Father as well. We can't have one without the other, for they are one. Therefore, let us feed on Jesus, breathe in Jesus, and live for Jesus today.

HARD STUFF

John 6:60 *On hearing it, many of his disciples said,
"This is a hard teaching. Who can accept it?"*

Being a Christian is not hard, for the grace that overwhelms us is full of joy and peace. However, understanding everything that Jesus communicates to us takes a bit more effort. It's not that He is trying to confuse us, but it is because that in our humanness we doubt and question everything, we find His words problematic.

When Jesus spoke of the necessity of His being indwelt by those who would come after Him, on the surface it seemed very strange. In fact, it was so strange that His listeners found His unacceptable, because this was a concept they couldn't grasp. Hard teachings are that way. They are accepted by those who are really serious about discipleship.

There have been many times in my life when I have heard Jesus telling me something that was too big for me to grasp at the first hearing. When He called me to preach His Word was a big one. So was leaving my first college setting to move to the second so that I could better prepare for what He had me to do. Moving from assignment to assignment in ministry always took some serious prayer and careful consideration. Leaving the nation that was home to all of my friends and family for the unfamiliar sights and sounds of East Africa was another. The idea of retirement itself is a hard saying; one that I have to confess that I am still wrestling with.

Who can accept the words of Jesus? Not just every person. Those who accept the words of Jesus are those who first give up their own rights and pledge themselves to be willing servants, regardless of what that commitment may mean. So long as we continue to have to have control of our lives, and set the direction in accordance with our own personal desires and wishes, we will find what Jesus has to say to us to be very hard.

The good news is that Jesus never speaks to us with words that are too difficult for us to receive. All He asks is that we allow Him to be indwelt within our lives so that we can know fully that He is with us every step of the way. When we do this, we find an awareness of the goodness of God that we never knew was possible. Some tasks may be hard to us, but the way of the Master never is. His presence makes every journey a joyful one.

LIFE IN THE SPIRIT

John 6:61–65 *Aware that his disciples were grumbling about this, Jesus said to them, "Does this offend you? What if you see the Son of Man ascend to where he was before! The Spirit gives life; the flesh counts for nothing. The words I have spoken to you are spirit and they are life. Yet there are some of you who do not believe." For Jesus had known from the beginning which of them did not believe and who would betray him. He went on to say, "This is why I told you that no one can come to me unless the Father has enabled him."*

It's really hard to teach lessons to people who are not ready to receive them. Jesus found difficulty in getting people to accept Him for who He was. During this conversation He had more in mind than being a daily source of food for the people who were following after Him. Instead, He provided a classroom of instruction that gave the crowds what they needed to hear.

In the church we like it when the crowds come in and we can report numerical growth for our congregations. However, real character comes to the surface when we have to give out a message that people don't want to hear, and then suffer loss when people walk away from that message, and perhaps our ministry. Jesus was about to experience just that.

The uncertainly that comes when our faith is weak leads to grumbling. We want to see results. We want to see them in a tangible way that we can see with our eyes and touch with our hands. But spiritually created words often cause offense to earth-based ears, and that is what was happening in this passage. Without the Spirit of God, we can't interpret the divine word, gain insights in prayer, or be effective in ministry but people without the Spirit don't usually understand that.

It boils down to the realization of divine knowledge and power. It's a matter of what He knows and what we know. We may ask, "What does God know about our future? Of what can we be sure?" There are some answers for which we have to wait to understand, but we can know that salvation never begins with us. It is the gift of God. Spiritual growth doesn't happen because we try harder. It happens because we listen and follow His plan. We know that the Spirit gives us life, and God draws whomsoever He wills. Our part is to believe and know that He is always right.

TURNING AWAY

John 6:66–69 *From this time many of his disciples turned back and no longer followed him. "You do not want to leave too, do you?" Jesus asked the Twelve. Simon Peter answered him, "Lord, to whom shall we go? You have the words of eternal life. We believe and know that you are the Holy One of God."*

I believe that this is one of the saddest scenes in the Bible. To read the words, "From this time many of his disciples turned back and no longer followed him," brings pain to my heart, and I'm sure it did to Jesus also. When people refuse to walk in the path that Jesus has for them, and accept the teachings He gives them, there is inevitably a split in the company. Jesus' words were hard, but always based in truth. Sadly, many people just don't want to hear the truth or yield to its claims on their lives.

Jesus asked a good question here. He needed to hear that His chosen twelve would not be leaving with the rest of the miracle seekers. After all, Jesus never stops anyone from leaving Him. He is the King of all the universe and has unlimited power, but He always choses to limit Himself on our behalf, based on our own free will concerning our relationship with Him. He could make us follow Him, but He always leaves that choice with us.

Simon Peter seems to be the man on the spot, though he will be more so in the coming days. His answer is classic and spot-on for all thinking people. Where else can we go? Who else has the ultimate truth about eternal life? Who else can change water into wine, heal the lame, feed the multitude, walk on the water, and change people's lives? Of course, the answer here is obvious: No one! Jesus alone can do all those things—and more.

We see how Jesus qualified those who would stay with Him. He wants us to say that we will remain true and hear our testimony that we will obey Him in all areas of our lives. This is important because He will either be God to us or He will be nothing at all. We can't just add Him on at the points of our lives where we need help. He won't just settle to be a healer, a forgiver, a counselor, a teacher, and a comforter in bad times, though He is all of those things. We either make Him Lord of our life or we break fellowship with Him. He isn't interested in just putting on a show or drawing a crowd, for He is in the redeeming business and it is redemption that we need.

REACHING OUT TO THE LOST

John 6:70–71 *Then Jesus replied, "Have I not chosen you, the Twelve? Yet one of you is a devil!" (He meant Judas, the son of Simon Iscariot, who, though one of the Twelve, was later to betray him.)*

I've often wondered why Jesus chose Judas Iscariot to be one of His disciples. It seems very obvious that Jesus knew before He even met Judas, that he was full of wickedness and was literally hell-bent on causing the eventual betrayal. Later, as John would write from hindsight, he would declare that Judas was a thief (John 12:6), and that he actually couldn't be trusted with money even he seemed to serve as the group's treasurer.

If Jesus knew all this, why in the world would He call Judas to follow Him? Why not just pick someone more worthy? I could also ask the questions, "Why did Jesus ever pick me to follow Him as be His disciple? Why did He pick you to follow Him and be His disciples?" We could protest and say, "Well, I would never do what Judas did. I would never betray Jesus in the way that would lead to His death!" Maybe not, but Hebrews 6:6 speaks of those who would crucify Jesus all over again by their unfaithfulness to continue in the journey. If we walk away from Him, like the crowd in this story, we too are guilty of betrayal.

The bare facts of the matter are that God always wants everyone to be saved, even Judas. Even Judas deserved a shot at redemption, and no one ever had a better opportunity than those who were hand-picked by Jesus to be His disciples. There was a hope for turning Judas around, but then there is always that "free-will" thing. We always have the God-given privilege of following Jesus faithfully, or putting on the show when people are watching, but choosing a different path when in secret. God gives us all a chance for change, but when we decide whether or not we will make the most of the opportunity, it's on us.

It's so easy to throw stones at Judas. He was a pitiful and despised creature in the story of Jesus and ever since. People don't name their children, "Judas." They shy away from any connection to him because we don't want anyone to be like him. Still, Judas had a soul, and Jesus reached out to redeem that soul. He would do the same for anyone. In fact, He did the same for us.

IT'S ABOUT TIME

John 7:1–5 *After this, Jesus went around in Galilee, purposely staying away from Judea because the Jews there were waiting to take his life. But when the Jewish Feast of Tabernacles was near, Jesus' brothers said to him, "You ought to leave here and go to Judea, so that your disciples may see the miracles you do. No one who wants to become a public figure acts in secret. Since you are doing these things, show yourself to the world." For even his own brothers did not believe in him.*

Timing is such an important factor when we try to understand the Gospel of John. Six months had passed between the close of chapter six and the opening of chapter seven. We know this because John 6:4 tells us that the Jewish Passover was near. Chapter seven lets us know that it was now the time for the Feast of Tabernacles.

There were three main feasts in the Jewish culture of that day: Passover, Pentecost, and Tabernacles. All male Jews who lived within twenty miles of Jerusalem were obliged by Jewish Law to appear at these feasts in person. Passover was in the spring, Pentecost was at the beginning of summer, and the Feast of Tabernacles was in late fall. This was a harvest festival.

During the time Jesus spent in Galilee, He had been ministering among the people and had done many miraculous signs. The other Gospel writers include more of what happened during this time than John does. Although we are only in chapter seven of John's twenty-one-chapter book, we are already to the start of the last six months of Jesus' earthly ministry. John had been led by the Spirit to focus His Gospel on these last six months.

It is in this particular passage that we begin to see the beginning of the end. We closed chapter six by looking at how Jesus had already reached the peak of His popularity during His three-year ministry. John 6:66 (an appropriate reference for the occasion) told us, "From this time, many of his disciples turned back and no longer followed him." We begin to notice at this point that the attitudes of the people changed toward Him. It's also where we start to look within ourselves and ask, "Will we still follow Him?" We find that outward attitudes often tell the story of what is happening on the inside of us, and it is certainly true in this setting. May we all be honest at this point and be determined to follow Jesus, no matter what.

WHEN THEY ARE OUT TO GET YOU

John 7:1 *After this, Jesus went around in Galilee, purposely staying away from Judea because the Jews there were waiting to take his life.*

By this time the attitude of the Jewish authorities and leadership of the Jewish community toward Jesus was very simple: Kill the blasphemer! Jesus had already gone over into Galilee four or five times as recorded here by John, and He continued there because He found that the hatred of the Jewish and political leaders was such that they wanted to murder Him if they could catch Him alone in Judea.

However, Jesus knew that His time to suffer had not yet arrived, so He did what He had to do to stay out of their reach. In this one chapter we find there are no fewer than seven references to the Jews desire and attempts to kill Jesus. They are found in verses 1, 13, 19, 23, 25, 30, and 35. There is no doubt that by this time in the life of Jesus, the plan of the Jewish leadership was to get rid of Him.

How sad it is that our Lord had to suffer the worst that mankind had to offer. When we are entertaining special guests, we normally want to put our best efforts forward so that they will feel welcome and honored to be with us. When the heavenly Father sent His divine Son into our world, He received just the opposite. From the cradle to the grave Jesus saw what sin has done to our world, and how it has affected every person in it.

Whether or not we will ever have people plotting to take our lives, we have all found the necessity of working around situations that would hamper and hinder our ministerial efforts. Jesus warned us that we are to as wise as serpents and harmless as doves, so we can't always rush headlong into the battles. Like the example of our Master, we must be patient as we plan our strategies that will bring glory to God in the midst of our situations.

Today we will experience opportunities that can lead us into wonderful areas of ministry, but we will need to be aware that in the midst of these encounters, the enemy of our souls will do all that he can to bring defeat to our best efforts. Where we find our strength is in our reliance on the Father to provide the timing and connection that will produce success. As Jesus had the ear of the Father, so do we, and we ought to always rely on His guidance. Tests will be many, but the final victory is assured in Christ.

HURT BY THOSE WHO ARE CLOSE

John 7:2–5 *But when the Jewish Feast of Tabernacles was near, Jesus' brothers said to him, "You ought to leave here and go to Judea, so that your disciples may see the miracles you do. No one who wants to become a public figure acts in secret. Since you are doing these things, show yourself to the world." For even his own brothers did not believe in him.*

It has been said that blood is thicker than water, so it would seem to be a very natural thing that the family of Jesus would be among His biggest supporters. We would like to think that, but unfortunately that is not what the Bible teaches us. When Jesus really needed people to have His back, in the midst of dwindling numbers of disciples, His own brothers had not only not caught the vision of the message He was sharing, they didn't even believe His words.

It does appear that they wished to capitalize on His fame. However, they were totally unaware at this time as to the true identity of Jesus. In spite of their having lived in the presence of His perfect life, the Lord's brothers failed to see Him as the promised Messiah. They credited Jesus with power to work miracles, as we see in verses three and four, but they totally misunderstood His mission.

They suggested that He was too modest, and that He should promote Himself. It was one thing to dazzle the simple-minded hillbillies of Galilee, but they thought He should make a name for Himself by convincing the more sophisticated people of Jerusalem. They thought He would never establish the prestige He needed by hiding His gifts in a corner.

Jesus had chosen not to go to the feast with His brothers, or to show up at the feast publicly. His brothers could go anytime they wanted, for they weren't in any danger. It wasn't that Jesus didn't want to go to the festival; He just didn't want to go with them.

Family can be hurtful. On many occasions the called of God have had to leave their families behind because that is what their task required. We can never allow blood relatives to thwart the mission of the Master, however. When God calls us into service, we follow, whether our family is in agreement or not. If the Lord is not first in this area of our lives, He will not be first in any area. We belong to the Father more than we belong to our families.

SIDESTEPPING THE TRAPS

John 7:6–9 *Therefore Jesus told them, "The right time for me has not yet come; for you any time is right. The world cannot hate you, but it hates me because I testify that what it does is evil. You go up to the Feast. I am not yet going up to this Feast, because the right time has not yet come. Having said this, he stayed in Galilee.*

The Jewish leadership didn't have anything against the family of Jesus. It was Him they were after. They didn't have any reason to stand against the brothers of Jesus because at this point in time they were just like the rest of the Jews. They didn't really believe in Jesus either. The brothers weren't making any waves, so they would be safe among the masses in Jerusalem.

Sin hates to be called out, and call it out is exactly what Jesus did. Because He was not willing to let injustice and ungodliness become the practice of the day, Jesus made enemies. He made enemies of the Jewish leaders because they had become the enemies of God, though they supposedly represented Him among the people.

It almost seems like Jesus was talking out of both sides of His mouth when it came to whether or not He was going to the feast though. His motives reveal a matter of timing, however. It wasn't the truth that He wasn't going, but just that He wasn't going—yet. He had to wait for the right time, for His life was ordered by the Father, and He would not be cornered into a box when He had more important things to be about.

Perhaps there are times in our zeal to do the work of the Lord that we rush headlong into various types of ministry without ever counting the cost, or evaluating what the most effective way to serve would be. There are times, when in the sincerity of trying to meet a need, we jump into something that we are not prepared to do. If we don't wait on the Lord's direction and timing, we may find ourselves causing more harm than good, and not being very happy with the outcome.

Jesus was wise because He depended on the leadership of His heavenly Father. He avoided the traps of men and accomplished more in a shorter amount of time than most because He prayerfully and thoughtfully approached all of life in accordance with God's direction. We can learn from that and serve more effectively if we follow His example.

WHERE IS HE?

John 7:10–11 *However, after his brothers had left for the Feast, he went also, not publicly, but in secret. Now at the Feast the Jews were watching for him and asking, "Where is that man?"*

There are some who would say that Jesus went back on His word, or that He had lied to His brothers. However, if we will look closely at what Jesus said we would find Him saying in verse eight, "The right time for me has not *yet* come." He didn't say that He wouldn't go, but that He wouldn't go with his brothers because timing was always a big part of His strategy in ministry. He would go, but He would do so on His own schedule so that He wouldn't fall into the traps of evil men.

We cannot say enough about using strategic plans in our ministry. Jesus didn't just blunder along through life, taking whatever came His way. He was methodical and measured because He knew His time was limited in this world, and everything had to go according to the plan of the Father for His life.

So, He went up to the feast a little later than His brothers, and He went in secret. He was going to be like a fly on the wall for a little while so that He could hear what people were saying about Him, and what was being plotted against Him. He wouldn't have to wait long because the city was buzzing with conversations and discussions about this prophet from Galilee, and everyone—for one reason or another—wanted to see Him up close and personal.

We may never have people clamoring after us, or wait in line wanting to get our autograph, but folks will take notice of us if we just live a consistent holy life like Jesus did. We can't control what people will say about us, or even what motive they may have in making a connection with us, but we can live our lives in such a way that people will ask "Why?" when they see how we live. In fact, one of the greatest things we can do with our life is to present ourself in such a fashion that others will wonder about us, and wonder what the basis is for our behavior. When that happens, and we are asked about why we do or don't do certain things, we can say that it's because of Jesus and the change He has made in us. That's the kind of strategy that will change the world for Christ.

MIXED REVIEWS

It's too bad that the modern news media didn't have their polling reporters in place on that day in Jerusalem. They could have had quite a story on the evening news concerning what the people were saying about Jesus. They seemed to be divided right down the middle about Him.

At this time in the story, Israel was divided into three regions. The southern region was Judea, where Jerusalem was located, and where the political and national religious powers were concentrated. These rulers had much to lose if the Messiah came and excluded them from His anticipated new Kingdom. The middle region was Samaria, which was populated largely by partially Jewish mixed-blood people, who were despised by the full-blooded Jews. The northern region was Galilee on the western shores of the Sea of Galilee. The population there was regarded by Judean Jews as simple, and kind of "back-woodsy."

It appears from the verses read that many of the people looked favorably on Jesus, but they dared not admit it publicly for fear of the Jewish rulers. Jesus didn't travel in disguise, but He did go without a prior announcement for public display, for He was the main topic of the festival conversation. The religious leaders wanted to kill Him, while another faction rallied to His support and pronounced that He was a good man. A third group denounced Him as an imposter and a deceiver of the people.

Isn't it interesting that the one who is King and Lord of all seems to always be the great divider among men? There is a good reason for this. It's because Jesus never claimed to be just a good man; He claimed to be the Son of God. Either we accept that as His identity with all that the title means, or we reject Him completely. He did not come to the earth to just be a prophet, a philosopher, a dictator, or even just a good role model. He is the Messiah! He is the Master! He is the Lion of the tribe of Judah! He is the Lamb slain from the foundation of the world! He is the one and only Savior of the world! So, we must never water-down or forget these facts.

LEARNING FROM THE FATHER

John 7:14–15 *Not until halfway through the Feast did Jesus go up to the temple courts and begin to teach. The Jews were amazed and asked, "How did this man get such learning without having studied?"*

The people around Jerusalem hadn't been able to decide what to think about Jesus. Some wanted to kill Him, some wanted to use Him, and others were unsure as to whether He was good or bad. Jesus watched for four days in silence, and then He decided to take action. He had been walking the tightrope of going from private to public, and He was truly controversial, for He had the people talking. They couldn't understand how He could do so much and know so much when He didn't have any formal training.

What they didn't take into account though, was that He had had the best of teachers. He listened constantly to His Father and acted in perfect harmony with the lessons that were handed down to Him. There was nothing man could teach Him, for He already knew what was in the hearts of men, and He knew how sin would twist every good word He spoke and every good intention He had.

My grandmother, who never finished high school, had very little use for people who got, "book learning." I remember her saying, "If preachers have to go to school to learn to preach, then God didn't call them." She meant well, but being uneducated she didn't realize the value of learning outside of what she needed to make it in life where she lived. Grandma was right about one thing though. Though I disagree strongly about her opinion concerning education in general, I do believe that until the people of God get their spiritual information from the heart of God, they really have got anything to say. We can learn much from scholars who have gone before us, but it is in the quiet and private place of prayer that the greatest matters of life are settled. We should never forget that.

Jesus amazed the crowds, but what He was saying really wasn't new. He was speaking from the heart of God and God has not changed since before the beginning of time. As Jesus said, "For out of the overflow of his heart, the mouth speaks," (Luke 6:45b). Jesus was filled with the Holy Spirit and the Holy Spirit filled Him with the words of the Father, so when He spoke, He was saying what God told Him to say. Maybe we should try that too.

STAGES OF EDUCATION

John 7:16–18 Jesus answered, "My teaching is not my own. It comes from him who sent me. If anyone chooses to do God's will, he will find our whether my teaching comes from God or whether I speak on my own. He who speaks on his own does so to gain honor for himself, but he who works for the honor of the one who sent him is a man of truth; there is nothing false about him."

The simple truth about what Jesus was saying was that His teachings were found in His Source, God, His heavenly Father. We depend a lot on the Bible, especially the New Testament. But though Jesus inspired the writing of it, He focused on what was written in the Hebrew Bible, as did those who heard Him. He did, however, have access to the Author, and having that access set Him apart from the masses who came to hear and judge Him.

The stages of education can actually be distilled into four steps. First, there is the requirement of finding a teacher. No one can go beyond what they know without some source of instruction to help them along. Second, there is the step of listening to the teacher. Whether it is the school of hard knocks, an article in a magazine, a podcast, or with an in-person instructor, learning depends on really listening to the lessons that are taught so that understanding can begin. Then there is the step of asking questions of the teacher. Feedback, give and take, and challenges are all part of the learning process. Finally, there is the giant step of imitating the teacher. We learn by doing what others have shown us, told us, and displayed for us. As we copy those instructions and instructors, we find ourselves learning.

Learning things of spiritual value is no different. The crowds around Jesus may not have understood what He was saying, but Jesus was demonstrating the Father's work through His actions. He showed that doing God's will is found through knowing God Himself. To know what the Father's will for our life is, is not found in seeking information; it is found in seeking the person. We find Him as our teacher, we listen to His voice, we ask questions of Him in prayer, and we act in accordance with what He teaches us.

In short, we do what Jesus did, and get to know the divine path through seeking interaction with the divine One Himself. Our time in prayer is essential, not for getting what we want, but for getting to know the Teacher. He is our Source for all that we need to know.

NO ONE KEEPS THE LAW

John 7:19–20 *"Has not Moses given you the law? Yet not one of you keeps the law. Why are you trying to kill me?" "You are demon-possessed," the crowd answered. "Who is trying to kill you?"*

Sometimes it's hard to tell just who in this story is doing the speaking. We have seen that the leaders of the Jews have already been plotting to kill Jesus because He threatened their authority. This part of the crowd seems to be oblivious to the idea of such a plot, or it may be that they are just denying what Jesus knew to be true. After all, He knew the hearts and motives of all men (John 2:24).

Jesus was so right when He said that no one in this crowd kept the Law faithfully. The Law was a spiritual matter, but the masses had turned it into a checklist of material things that had to be acted out, or avoided. What was designed to bring people closer to the heart of the Father turned out to be a stumbling block because no one was doing what the Law said.

All of this was part of the Father's plan from the beginning. When He gave the standards that He expected from His people in the form of the Ten Commandments, He knew that they would not be able to keep them. But over the years afterwards the expectation of God for His people didn't change, for He held them accountable to walk in the way He prescribed. But it would take time for mankind to reach the understanding of what God expected, and they would eventually find that they could only keep the Law through the Son He sent into the world. Without Jesus, the Law is just a list of rules that men run up against, and then they crash. In Christ, we have a guide for our lives found in His Spirit that aids us in obedience.

Jesus would be labeled as demon-possessed, not because they found attributes of evil in Him, but because He couldn't be jammed into their mold for a Messiah. He knew they were plotting to kill Him, but untruthfully they denied His accusation. They were breaking the Law through the plotting of His murder and then bearing false witness about it. Jesus knew them and their intentions so well.

Jesus knows us well too. He knows that we can't keep the rules on our own. He knows that we need to be fully invested in the Father, if we even desire to do so. We keep the Law through our relationship with the Christ.

JUDGING FAIRLY

John 7:21–24 *Jesus said to them, "I did one miracle, and you are all astonished. Yet, because Moses gave you circumcision (though actually it didn't come from Moses, but from the patriarchs), you circumcise a child on the Sabbath. Now if a child can be circumcised on the Sabbath so that the law of Moses may not be broken, why are you angry with me for healing the whole man on the Sabbath? Stop judging by mere appearances, and make a right judgment."*

It seems amazing that the crowd was still focused on something that happened back in chapter five, when Jesus was walking among the sick and lame by the pool called Bethesda near the Sheep Gate in Jerusalem. Since that time, He had traveled back to Galilee, fed the 5000, walked on the sea, and taught the masses of followers who trailed after Him. It has been a season that has last almost from the Passover until the Feast of Tabernacles, basically from spring until the fall, yet folks are still talking about Jesus healing the invalid man on the Sabbath Day. This shows the intensity of interest in what Jesus was doing, as well as the huge amount of animosity His actions were arousing.

Jesus made a very good argument here. A male child was to be circumcised eight days after his birth, and this ritual wasn't put off just because the eighth day would happen to fall on a Sabbath. If the action of the priests were not considered work, how could merely speaking a word of healing to a lame man be put into the category of laboring. These people were not thinking and speaking logically, but only out of the ritual and tradition that so completely blinded them.

We would like to think that we have come a long way, but we still have our biases. Democrats and Republicans refuse to bend from their political ideologies, Calvinists and Wesleyans huddle with their own groups, and Protestants and Catholics hardly speak to each other. Instead of looking for common ground, rationally examining the Scriptures, and questioning the "whys" of our particular bent, we often band with our own clique and refuse to budge on any issue. When Jesus said that we should make a right judgment, I believe He was saying something that applies to us all. We aren't the final word, and none of us have the whole truth. So, let's be gracious and allow love to be our binding chain.

IS HE THE MESSIAH?

John 7:25–27 *At that point some of the people of Jerusalem
began to ask, "Isn't this the man they are trying to kill?
Here he is, speaking publicly, and they are not saying a
word to him. Have the authorities really concluded that he
is the Christ? But we know where this man is from; when
the Christ comes, no one will know where he is from."*

M y education has taught me a lot of things over the years, but most of all it has taught me how much I don't yet know. My walk with Jesus has done the same thing, as does prayer, divine healing, the call to ministry, and the church in general. The more I know the more I find I have yet to discover.

Just imagine how confused the Jews of the first century were. Previously the crowds had been discussing the Sabbath Law and whether or not Jesus had broken it by healing a lame man on the Sabbath. Now the Jews at the Feast of Tabernacles were turning to a more direct question. Just who was this Jesus really? He had been accused of being a lawbreaker, praised for being a prophet, and admired as a miracle worker and healer. Just who was He?

Though He had come on the scene secretly and had remained hidden for four days, now He was teaching boldly and declaring the Kingdom of God. How could He get away with such public exposure when it was common knowledge that the religious authorities wanted Him dead? This had to baffle the crowds, because either Jesus was a criminal or He was not. By allowing Him to speak in the temple courts, the common people were starting to question what the authorities were saying about Him. Could this man really be the long-awaited Messiah? There were some of the common people who probably thought this to be the case.

No doubt the disciples of Jesus were starting to get some clues. Not only were they amazed at His teachings, but that saw Him turn water into wine, drive merchants from the temple, bring faith to the Samaritans, heal a public official's son, restore a lame man to health, feed the 5000, and walk on the water. If they weren't getting a few insights then they were pretty dense indeed.

What about you? Have you concluded that Jesus is the Christ, the Savior of the world? How you answer that question will change your life forever.

KNOWING THE FATHER
THROUGH THE SON

John 7:28–29 *Then Jesus, still teaching in the temple courts, cried out, "Yes, you know me, and you know where I am from. I am not here on my own, but he who sent me is true. You do not know him, but I know him because I am from him and he sent me."*

"Could this man be the Messiah?" That idea wasn't even considered by some. One of the commonly held beliefs about the Messiah was that He would come out of obscurity, make some grand entrance, and the establish His kingdom then and there on earth. Many people believed that no one would know where the Messiah came from.

This is not to say that they didn't believe the prophecies about Him being born in Bethlehem, but sometime after that He was supposed to disappear and remain hidden until He came to deliver them, by force if necessary. The Jews had several presuppositions about their expected Messiah and Jesus didn't fit these ideas. That's why so many rejected Him and were so terribly disappointed in Him. Though the crowds knew about Him, they did not really know Him because they didn't know the One who sent Him, for in the Bible, knowing is on a very intimate level.

People still do the same thing today. The biblical Jesus doesn't fit their world view because He is too confrontational, too exclusive, too intolerant, and too politically incorrect. So, they try to replace Him with their own version of Jesus. Like them, we too can know all about Him without ever reaching a level of intimacy with the Father and truly knowing Him.

This means that it is vitally important that we get to know the Father if we want to enjoy fellowship with the Son. It also means that we need to know the Son if we ever hope to get in close with the Father. They are one and they are the source of our hope and salvation. Through the work and power and intimacy of the Spirit, who lives within our lives, we work for the Son to the glory of God the Father. We too can say that we are not here on our own, but that the One who sent the Son also sends us, and we know all about Him and His mission for us is true.

Jesus is our elder brother, the firstborn from the dead. We can call Him "Lord" because we are working alongside Him to build His Kingdom, and in the process, we get the blessing of getting to know the Father also.

PUTTING FAITH IN THE CHRIST

John 7:30–31 *At this point the tried to seize him, but no one laid a hand on him, because his time had not yet come. Still, many in the crowd put their faith in him. The said, "When the Christ comes, will he do more miraculous signs than this man?"*

It was natural for the people to wonder as to why Jesus had not been arrested by the religious leaders in the temple. The reason behind His freedom was that everything Jesus did was on God's timetable, and the hour for His death had not yet arrived. Because the temple leaders could rage about Him, but not stop Him, it must have been incredibly frustrating to them, but they would get their time to vent their anger all too soon. There were many who did believe on Jesus. As the prophets of old had performed great miracles to validate their messages, the same was expected from Jesus. He certainly didn't let them down in this regard because talks of His acts of grace were spreading all throughout the city and countryside.

Jesus gave signs that led to personal faith. Still today, seeing is believing for many and though people can be duped by technology, slight of hand, and slick talkers, the power of Christ still leads many to faith. He also gave them signs that witnessed to His relationship to the Father. This got Him in trouble with the temple leaders, but they couldn't ignore His claims.

Today people are watching what we do, what we say, and how our lives have been changed since meeting Jesus. They will want to know if the change that they see in us will last, or if it is just a phase that we are going through. We need to remember though, that when Jesus really transforms us, something real happens, not just a relative appearance of change. There is no greater sign or testimony of our faith than a changed life because people who watch us notice, and many opportunities to share Christ open up as a result.

The crowd asked lots of questions, but today, we on this side of the cross, have the answers. Jesus came from the Father and He was God in the flesh as He lived among us. He not only lived, but died, and was raised from the dead for our sakes, showing that He would be the first one to experience victory over the grave, pointing out the way for us. He lives today and is preparing a place for His followers. This is the good news of the gospel.

SURROUNDED BY ENEMIES

John 7:32 *The Pharisees heard the crowd whispering such things about him. Then the chief priests and the Pharisees sent temple guards to arrest him.*

This is the first time that we see a specific listing as to who the enemies of Jesus really were. Strangely enough, His Kingship was not being challenged by the ruling Roman authorities because that this point, they really couldn't care less about Jesus. The attack on Him came from those in His own religious circle.

His enemies were unlikely bedfellows. The chief priests were Sadducees. During the time of the New Testament era, the Sadducees were aristocrats. They tended to be wealthy and held powerful positions, including that of the chief priest and high priest, and they held the majority of the seventy seats of the Jewish ruling council, called the Sanhedrin. The common man related better to the party known as the Pharisees.

Though the Sadducees held the majority of the seats in the Sanhedrin, history indicates that much of the time they had to go along with the ideas of the Pharisaic minority because the Pharisees were popular with the masses. Religiously, the Sadducees were more conservative in one main area of doctrine. The Pharisees gave oral tradition equal authority to the written Word of God, while the Sadducees considered only the written Word to be from God.

Because the Sadducees were more focused on politics than religion, they were unconcerned with Jesus until they became afraid that He might bring unwanted Roman attention. It was at this point that the Sadducees and Pharisees united and conspired to put Jesus to death.

It would be a terrible thing to be an enemy of Jesus. One might succeed in the short term, but in the long run, His Lordship will be seen by all. This is why it is true for us today that we must always seek the heart of God in all things. Politics and power grabs are not God's way. The way of the love that requires a cross is the way God chose for His Son, and for us. It's better to suffer now and be a friend of God than to be an enemy even for a season.

The crowds would continue to whisper, the ruling Jews would continue to plot, and the guards would be unknowing dupes in the drama of the ages.

WHERE IS HE GOING?

John 7:33–34 *Jesus said, "I am with you for only a short time, and then I go to the one who sent me. You will look for me, but you will not find me; and where I am, you cannot come."*

He was truly with us for such a short time. According to church tradition, Jesus lived among us as a Palestinian Jew for only about thirty-two or thirty-three years. In that time, He grew from infancy to childhood, through His teen years, and into manhood. He learned what other Jewish boys learned, but His education was extended. His Father was not of this world and He picked up much more information from Him.

We are never told when it was that Jesus realized His truth identity and purpose for life. It's unlikely that a baby in a manger would have any idea about anything, other than what other babies experience. We see a clue when He went to the temple at age twelve, but that's the only record we have of His early life until He met His cousin, John, down at the edge of the Jordan River as a young man.

If I had to guess, I would say that the baptism of Jesus was a monumental event that changed His life forever. It was at that point that the Holy Spirit settled upon Him and directly led Him into the wilderness for forty days of fasting and enduring the temptations of the enemy. It was also at that point that the Father and Son got reacquainted with each other in a very intimate way. When He came out of the wilderness experience, Jesus seemed to be sure of His mission, and how that mission was going to work out. Those forty days changed the world for time and eternity.

We can almost hear the homesickness in Jesus' voice as He spoke of returning to the One who sent Him. The world was His creation and He loved it with all the energy He was able to produce, but His connection to the Father trumped everything, and soon He would be going home.

I believe that this is a foreshadowing of the relationship the Father wants to have with us. The more we spend time with Him the more we want to be with Him, and we too long to see Him face to face. We are so blessed to have the example of Jesus, for as He finished His task and went home, we too have a job to do, and then we also can go home. This life is a gift and a blessing, but I wouldn't miss what is ahead of us for the world.

GOD'S PLAN AND GOD'S TIMING

John 7:35–36 *The Jews said one to another, "Where does this man intend to go that we cannot find him? Will he go where our people live scattered among the Greeks? What did he mean when he said, 'You will look for me, but you will not find me,' and 'Where I am, you cannot come'?"*

The crowd that surrounded Jesus thought that they knew His origin. After all, they knew that Jesus came from Nazareth. He had been there since He was a boy. They had heard of His carpenter connections and knew that His educational opportunities and experience were limited. However, they didn't have a clue as to where He would go next. Jesus had just announced that He was going to return to the Father, but those who heard those words couldn't begin to imagine what He was talking about.

All this group of festival-goers could imagine was the diaspora, the scattered ones, or Jews who lived outside Palestine. Perhaps Jesus was going to take His band of disciples and go teach them. Maybe going beyond the confines of the borders of Israel was where He was referring.

The words here were really a "put-down." It was if they were saying, "Take your show on the road to the Greeks; this is the kind of thing they would swallow." At least if He went away, He wouldn't be causing any more trouble in Israel.

There is little doubt but that Jesus raised more questions for those who heard Him than He gave answers. He was not about to tip His hand as to what was coming next, yet every step He made and every comment that He spoke led Him closer to the climax of His mission, which would come at the next Passover season.

What can we take way from this entire conversation? Well, we can realize that nothing trumps God's plan and God's timing, and we can also learn that just because we don't understand what our Lord is saying, it doesn't mean that He is not speaking. In the same way that we may not know we are being used for God's purpose, it doesn't mean that He is not working through us. Our every action is leading us closer to the conclusion of our mission as well, and if our hearts are as they should be, we will be used by God to further His Kingdom in our world. Being like Jesus is our goal and our mission, so let's live like it before the world who is watching us.

"Streams Of Living Water..."

John 7:37-39 *On the last and greatest day of the Feast, Jesus stood and said in a loud voice, "If anyone is thirsty, let him come to me and drink. Whoever believes in me, as the Scripture has said, streams of living water will flow from within him." By this he meant the Spirit, whom those who believed in him were later to receive. Up to that time the Spirit had not been given since Jesus had not yet been glorified.*

All throughout this chapter of John's Gospel, we have been reading about what happened at the Feast of Tabernacles. It's important for us to review it because during the feast Jesus finally took center stage and showed us what His mission was all about.

The Feast of Tabernacles was the third of the great Jewish festivals, which also included Passover and Pentecost. Attendance was compulsory for all adult male Jews who lived within twenty miles of Jerusalem. The feast was held for seven days, followed by an eight day of spiritual observance which included an offering to God.

This offering was a water celebration. The crowd assembled for the ceremony of water libation, which was the climax of the feast. Each day the people came to the temple with their palms and marched around the altar. Then a priest would go to the pool of Siloam, six hundred yards to the south of the temple, dip his golden pitcher in the pool and lift it out as the people would chant, "With joy you will draw water from the wells of salvation" (Isaiah 12:3). The crowds then went back to the temple, and the priest would empty his pitcher at the base of the altar. While this was done, the Levite choir would sing the Hallel (Psalm 113-118). When they came to Psalm 118:1, "O, give thanks to the Lord," and 118:25 "O Lord, save us," and 118:29 "Give thanks to the Lord," the worshippers would shout and wave their palm branches toward the altar. It was a celebration of praise to God for the water supply that met the needs of the people over the centuries.

On the last day of the feast the people would march around the altar seven times, in memory of Jericho, as they praised the Lord. It was at this point that Jesus cried out and gave His invitation to the people. It's good to know that in the midst of all the activity of life and worship, Jesus still calls to us today. We have in Him, the true water of life.

DIVISION

John 7:40–44 *On hearing his words, some of the people said, "Surely this man is the Prophet." Others said, "He is the Christ." Still others asked, "How can the Christ come from Galilee? Does not the Scripture say that the Christ will come from David's family and from Bethlehem, the town where David lived?" This the people were divided because of Jesus. Some wanted to seize him, but no one laid a hand on him.*

It's so hard to put ourselves back into the sandals of the people who were speaking about Jesus in these verses. We are used to going to our computers to research information on any topic or person of our choice, that we can hardly imagine a time when most people didn't even read, let alone have access to the personal information of anyone.

If the crowds would have done their research, they would have found that Jesus was indeed born in Bethlehem, and that it was only after a stent in Egypt that Joseph settled his little family in Nazareth. As to the character of the man they knew as the carpenter turned prophet, Jesus had already made His defense by the means of able witnesses back in chapter five. The words of John the Baptist, the works Jesus did, the testimony of the Father, and the Holy Scriptures bore witness of His identity and proved that He was on a mission from God. But the people of Israel had a long history of not being able to make up their minds about spiritual leaders, and over the centuries it had cost them dearly.

Today people are still divided about Jesus. We are divided by political party affiliations, religious dogmas, denominational focuses, and even to the point as to whether Jesus was a good man, a charlatan, or even if He ever actually existed. Where all of us stand concerning our beliefs about Jesus is going to be affected by some of these factors.

It's easy to throw stones at the unbelief of these people because we are so far removed from their situation. What is harder for us to determine is where we stand on the person of Jesus, and what impact we will allow Him to have on our lives, and whether or not we will stand up for Him regardless of the impact such a stand will have on our lives.

They didn't arrest Jesus because His time hadn't yet come. However, the indecision of the masses pulled the necessity of the cross ever closer.

THERE IS NO ONE LIKE HIM

John 7:45–46 *Finally the temple guards went back to the chief priests and Pharisees, who asked them, "Why didn't you bring him back?" "No one ever spoke the way this man does," the guards declared.*

The temple guards had been sent by the chief priests and Pharisees back in verse thirty-two of this chapter, to arrest Jesus. When they found Him, they found more than they expected to find, however. This may have been the first time for these guards to hear the words of Jesus. After all, on the previous occasion when Jesus cleansed the temple, His actions were very brief and then He left. There most likely wasn't time then for the temple guards to be alerted.

Now, though John doesn't record the full messages of Jesus, we get the impression that the crowd was hanging on His every word, and the temple soldiers were part of the listening audience. So, the assignment given by the chief priests and Pharisees was not carried out.

No doubt this unusual turn of events made the authorities even more nervous and fearful about Jesus. We are reminded again of the fact that this arrest didn't happen was not a matter of chance or fate, but a fulfillment of the plan of the Father. Jesus was right on schedule with the Father's timetable, and there was no power in the universe that could change that arrangement.

It's a good lesson here for us when we are tempted to worry about events in our lives. The Father has a plan for us too. We are not to throw caution to the wind and do foolish things to tempt God, but we can rest assured that if we are attempting to walk in the center of the Father's will for our lives, that He will honor that, and we will not have anything happen to us that will take us out of His plan.

Is God responsible then for the terrible things that have happened to the saints down through the centuries? No, but God is able to take the horrible events, like the cross, and turn it into something that will be for our ultimate good, and for His glory. We who are in Christ have been stamped with the seal of redemption (Revelation 7:3, 9 and 14:1), and our days are numbered by the Lord. Just as Jesus could teach and walk among the guards without fear, we can live boldly for Him, knowing that our times are in His hands.

A FIST OR A KISS?

John 7:47–49 *"You mean he has deceived you also?"*
the Pharisees retorted. "Has any of the rulers or of
the Pharisees believed in him? No! But this mob knows
nothing of the law—there is a curse on them.

Eight days of celebrating and partying was about to come to an end. The Feast of Tabernacles was winding down, but the impact Jesus had had on the people there was profound. He arrived under fire for the healing of a lame man on the Sabbath some six months earlier, but He was popular for feeding the multitudes, and for other miracles that He did. He arrived late to the feast and didn't make Himself known until four days after His arrival, but once He did, He was the focus of everyone. He had just declared Himself to be the source of living water at the water festival, and His name was on the lips of visiting pilgrim. Some wanted to praise Him and others wanted to kill Him. Yes, He certainly had had an impact and was a polarizing influence at the feast.

The Pharisees hated Him! They were the religious rule-keepers of Israel, and for the most part was the most favored group of the common people, compared to the rest of the political Jewish hierarchy. The temple guards were generally tough and fiercely loyal, but they had been so taken with Jesus' words that they couldn't act. This only angered the Pharisees, and they spat out their venomous attitudes about the people who even gave Jesus a second look.

Religious people have such a huge role to play in the overall plan of God. The Jewish leaders had initially been instituted by Moses, under the direction of the Almighty, but over the years had digressed into a power-hungry group that couldn't' see beyond their pre-conceived notions. Jesus also represented a religious faction, but His focus on the Father, His love for all people, and His refusal to be cowed by the attacks again Him, set Him apart from the Jewish leaders.

The church can learn something here. It can speak out with poisonous anger against what it judges to be evil, or it can take the role of love, while holding the line of holiness of heart and life for all people, instead of cursing them. Jesus only wanted to bless the crowds. Likewise, we are to reflect Him, so we can stand up with a clinched fist, or a warm embrace.

NICODEMUS—ACT 2

John 7:50–53 *Nicodemus, who had gone to Jesus earlier and who was one of their own number, asked, "Does our law condemn anyone without first hearing him to find out what he is doing?" They replied, "Are you from Galilee too? Look into it, and you will find that a prophet does not come out of Galilee." Then each went to his own home.*

Nicodemus came to Jesus at night for a conversation back in chapter three. Later, in chapter nineteen of this book, we find that he will be instrumental in the burial of Jesus also. He was a member of the Jewish ruling council, the Sanhedrin, and was a Pharisee. In fact, he is one of the few Pharisees in the Gospels that seems to be presented in a favorably light.

He brings up a good point concerning the attitude of the ruling Jews. He realizes that they are breaking their own laws with their talk of condemnation without even the semblance of a trial. Jesus had not been sufficiently questioned, and He had not had an opportunity to explain His views, yet as we have seen from earlier statements, the ruling class had already been plotting His murder.

Is it fair to pass judgment on someone who has not been thoroughly heard out? Nicodemus didn't think so, but it seems that his voice would be lost in the setting of angry shouts that came from his peers. Their limited connection with Jesus, and their fear of how He might cause them financial and political loss, drove them to irrational and sinful conclusions. They could only see that He was a threat that had to be eliminated.

Here's an important lesson for all generations. Everyone deserves a fair hearing before informed opinions can be developed and choices are made. It is so easy to listen to the sound bites of current news sources, and then make up our minds about people, their positions and topics, before we have all of the information we need to make right decisions. If Jesus had been subjected to our mass and social media sources, He most likely wouldn't have gotten a fair hearing by anyone, because too often our ideologies are so biased by the continual pounding of misinformation.

Nicodemus was a brave man who took a stand for Jesus when others within his social circle wouldn't listen to anything good about Him. Let's follow the example of fairness and extend it to all people in all situations we face.

GRACE ON DISPLAY

John 8:1–2 *But Jesus went to the Mount of Olives. At dawn he appeared again in the temple courts, where all the people gathered around him, and he sat down to teach them.*

As we move into chapter eight, we find that the Feast of Tabernacles had come to its conclusion and the people of Israel had started moving back into their regular routines and homelife. Jesus, however, continued with what He previously had been doing. After spending the night resting on the Mount of Olives, He returned to the temple in Jerusalem and taught the people.

It has to be acknowledged at this point though, that the verses from chapter seven, verse fifty-three through chapter eight, verse eleven, are missing from the oldest copies of the Greek manuscripts of which we have access. Most Bibles will point this textual issue out in a footnote that accompanies the passage. That being said, there are scholars on both sides of the issue who have problems with the legitimacy of the story.

What we can know for sure about this story, is that whether it is a part of the original text or not, this is certainly something like what Jesus would do. From reading the rest of the accounts of His life and ministry, there is nothing about this passage that would us to think of it as being unusual, or outside the character of Jesus.

When I first attempted to preach my very first sermon, this was the passage that I chose to preach from. In those days I only had access to the King James Version of the Bible, and there was no disclaimer questioning the validity of the words from John. I assumed that it would genuinely an approved part of Scripture, and that was good enough for me. When I preached that first sermon, it was in the middle of a twenty-three-inch snow storm in the thumb of Michigan on a Sunday evening. In my fear of this new endeavor, I stammered, stumbled, and sputtered out about seven minutes or oration before a congregation of about fifteen people, who were graciously patient with that eighteen-year-old preacher.

The one thing that remains of my futile attempt to do justice to this text, are the words of Jesus. "Neither do I condemn you." I had done my best, and I have always been grateful that He gave me another chance to preach. He is like that for all of us. His grace is sufficient, and His mercy never ends.

"Caught In The Act"

John 8:3–6 *The teachers of the law and the Pharisees brought in a woman caught in adultery. They made her stand before the group and said to Jesus, "Teacher, this woman was caught in the act of adultery. In the Law Moses commanded us to stone such women. Now what do you say?" They were using this question as a trap, in order to have a basis for accusing him. But Jesus bent down and started to write on the ground with his finger.*

It must have been such an embarrassing moment. It's one thing to be accused of adultery, but to caught in the very act and exposed in front of everyone would be the extreme in mortification. It does speak to the timeframe of this story thought that there is no mention of the man involved. It was definitely a patriarchal society and the woman was left with much less protection that any man would have had.

But this story was not about the woman. This whole situation was a trap designed to catch Jesus and get Him to say or do something that would get Him in trouble with all the people. The woman was just a pawn in this sick game that the teachers of the law and the Pharisees were playing.

Obviously, Jesus did not approve of adultery. Since they had caught this nameless woman in the act, she was guilty. It was also true that the Law of Moses required that this woman should be executed by stoning. It looked like any reaction that Jesus would make would be costly to Him.

I love the picture we see of Jesus here. He didn't speak and He didn't act. He didn't do anything that would cause His adversaries to have an advantage over Him. He simply stooped down and wrote in the dust. We don't know what He wrote although people down through the ages have speculated on what it might have been, but there is no record to satisfy our curiosity. He simply took time and patiently waited for the right moment to say what He had to say.

We can learn so much from Jesus here. All too often in our zeal to set the record straight, to express and opinion on social media, and in our attempt to balance the scales of justice, we rush into a situation without proper forethought. Jesus shows us the value of waiting, thinking things through, evaluating, and being deliberate in our actions before making a move. It's always best to follow the example that Jesus gives in all things.

SINLESS?

John 8:7–8 *When they kept on questioning him, he straightened up and said to them, "If any one of you is without sin, let him be the first to throw a stone at her." Again he stooped down and wrote on the ground.*

Jesus was under attack. This ploy with the woman was just a diversion. The Jewish leaders wanted to trick and trap Jesus, and they would use anyone and anything to get Him. But Jesus just wrote silently in the dirt. This is the only record we have of Jesus ever writing anything and we are clueless as to the message He was conveying. Was it just scribbling, doodling, or was He actually saying something to the group that was gathering around Him? If we only knew what Jesus was writing that day, it might explain a lot about the men's actions that followed.

It is more than obvious that the scribes and Pharisees were not in the least interested in seeing true justice executed here. Had they been in pursuit of justice they would have taken the woman to the appropriate authorities to settle the case. Instead, they brought her to Jesus, which proved to be to the woman's great benefit.

When Jesus finally stood up and spoke to the rabble, He reinterpreted the Law through the lens of love. Everything that Jesus did was based on God's love for people, and dealing with sin was no exception. Without accusing anyone of anything, He let the men who had dragged the woman before Him, face their own sin as they realized that they too fell short of perfection's standard. They had forgotten their own shortcomings in their zeal to condemn the woman and catch Jesus in their trap.

No doubt there are some of us today who have been tempted at times to go after someone who's sin seemed egregious and we would love to see them get what they had coming to them. What we have to remember is that we too have been guilty before the Lord, and He has always had patience with us when we were less than perfect. We want to be careful about wanting someone else to experience wrath when we ourselves crave mercy.

Jesus returned to His writing in the dirt after catching the accusers in their own trap. His mercy, wisdom, and love won the day. Perhaps what He wrote in the dirt that day we just the word, "Grace." May we apply it to all we encounter also.

MAKE A CHANGE

John 8:9–11 *At this, those who heard began to go away one at a time, the older ones first, until only Jesus was left with the woman still standing there. Jesus straightened up and asked her, "Woman, where are they? Has no one condemned you?" "No one, sir," she said. "Then neither do I condemn you," Jesus declared. "Go now and leave your life of sin."*

The Jewish leaders, who had only a few minutes before been willing to take this woman to task and pin her judgment on Jesus, began to melt away as the silence of guilt mounted upon their own heads. Though they had dragged the shamed and embarrassed woman out into the street and threw her down before Jesus, demanding that He give a verdict upon her, now they were not to be found when Jesus rose from His writing in the dirt.

Seeing that the woman was alone and that there were no accusers about, Jesus spoke directly to her with words of forgiveness. He was not going to condemn her, but released her to consider her lifestyle and ways. The big message of the story was that not only she was not to be condemned, but also that she should leave the life of sin that had brought her to this moment of crisis.

It is so vital for the church today as the representatives of Jesus, that we learn to do just as Jesus did here. It is not our job to condemn or acquit, but to offer forgiveness, but with that forgiveness to admonish people as to the consequences of sin. This woman was not forgiven so she could go back to the way she had been living, but that she would change her ways and put the life of adultery behind her.

That's what real repentance is all about. It's not repentance when we say we are sorry, when we apologize, or when we promise to do better. Repentance takes place when we change from the direction we had been traveling to a new direction. It's doing what Jesus said for this woman to do. We go and leave our life of sin.

It's wrong for us to pronounce forgiveness on people without calling them out on their sin. Sin destroys—always! We don't want people to return to that so we admonish them to leave their wicked ways behind. Without change there is no repentance. Without repentance there is no salvation. Without salvation there is no hope. But with Jesus, sin can be vanquished.

LIGHT VERSUS DARKNESS

John 8:12–13 *When Jesus spoke again to the people, he said, "I am the light of the world. Whoever follows me will never walk in darkness, but will have the light of life." The Pharisees challenged him, "Here you are, appearing as your own witness; your testimony is not valid."*

It sounds like a courtroom drama. Proclamations, witnesses, challenges, and testimonies all to bring the words of the printed page to reveal real life situations: *Jesus the Messiah vs. the Pharisees*. It's quite a battle of wits in a duel of perspectives. We get to be the spectators as if we were attending a debating competition on the highest level. The message is gripping because the outcome sets the stage for who truly has the authority to govern our world and our souls.

Jesus spoke those powerful words: "I am." These words ring clear back to the Old Testament account of Moses when the Father revealed Himself in that manner at the burning bush (Exodus 3). The Gospel of John records at least seven remarkable claims by Jesus. He said, "I am the bread of life" (6:48), "I am the light of the world" (8:14), "I am the door" (10:9), "I am the good shepherd" (10:11), "I am the resurrection and the life" (11:25), "I am the way, the truth, and the life" (14:6), "I am the vine" (15:5).

Specifically, Jesus says here that He was "the light of the world." When light is interrupted, we have a shadow. When light is not there, darkness reigns. Darkness is the absence of light in the same way cold is the absence of heat, and evil is the absence of God.

He is the light of the world that dispels darkness, and certainly in this story the Pharisees are taking the role as the purveyors of darkness. They insisted that Jesus had no witnesses, and that His own testimony was not valid. They saw Jesus as alone, but previously He had pointed out in chapter five that John the Baptist, the miracles He Himself did, the Father, the Scriptures, and even Moses had testified on His behalf. His claim was on solid ground.

There are varying degrees of darkness in which people find themselves. The Pharisees were darkened in their thinking and blind, but Jesus came to open the eyes of the blind. He could have done so much to help them as well, but blindness is hard to be dispelled when one's heart is hard. It's always possible, but we have to will let Him in before healing can take place.

OVERCOMING DARKNESS

John 8:14–18 *Jesus answered, "Even if I testify on my own behalf, my testimony is valid, for I know where I came from and where I am going. But you have no idea where I come from or where I am going. You judge by human standards; I pass judgment on no one. But if I do judge, my decisions are right, because I am not alone. I stand with the Father, who sent me. In your own Law it is written that the testimony of two men is valid. I am one who testifies for myself; my other witness is the Father, who sent me.*

When Jesus answered the Pharisees, He proved that divine knowledge trumps human ignorance every time. His righteousness triumphed over their rage and He showed that judgment is not a human privilege because God alone will have the last words.

When we see here that the Father cannot be separated from the Son, we see that they are eternally one, so that's never going to change. And with the Father and the Son in their intimate connection, our oneness in Christ—and therefore with the Father—is also meant to last forever. Our faith is not a private thing that we can keep hidden, for we are what we are every day of the week. Just as Jesus couldn't deny His relationship with the Father, neither can we. Ethics that change depending on the situation are not Christian, because as the Son could not be separated from the Father's plan, we are meant to be crafted into the divine mission as well.

There are some basic theology lessons that come from this account. The world's darkness is only overcome by divine light; therefore, the presence of the Lord is more important than the presence of any law. We also see that judgment without divine input is faulty, but when we are connected to the King, we too can give a testimony that is without stain or reproach.

As we look back over the pages of time to this conversation, we almost have a tendency to feel sorry for the Pharisees. They came at Jesus to present a battle of wits, but left the scene appearing to be totally disarmed and defeated. Jesus stood alone, but victorious, except for the presence of the Father, who saturated His life always.

In this we find our example. Though the world may hate us and persecute us, when we have the Father in our corner we really don't need anyone else. His grace is sufficient, both now and forever.

DEALING WITH NAY-SAYERS

John 8:19–20 *Then they asked him, "Where is your father?" "You do not know me or my Father," Jesus replied. "If you knew me, you would know my Father also." He spoke these words while teaching in the temple area near the place where the offerings were put. Yet no one seized him, because his time had not yet come.*

Jesus spoke a lot about His Father, so it really isn't curious that the Pharisees would want Him to clarify just who it was He was talking about. That they didn't know Him was a pretty clear fact, based on what Jesus said here. They may have heard about Mary's husband, Joseph, but probably didn't know much about the background of Jesus. After all, He was just a country bumpkin to them, so He hadn't merited their consideration until recently.

Before we get too hard on the adversaries of Jesus, maybe we should ask ourselves just how we would react if we heard someone say that God was his father. I don't mean in the generic sense, but if we met someone who claimed to have a relationship with God unlike anyone else, I would imagine that we too would have a hard time believing them, just like the Pharisees. But the relationship given here was real and intimate.

The divine Godhead may be hard to understand or explain, but that doesn't mean it doesn't exist. It just requires us to see with eyes of faith rather than our physical focus. What we have to remember is that knowing Jesus is the prerequisite for knowing God. If we want to know what God is like, we look at Jesus, for His is the human personification of God, who is Spirit.

Because the Pharisees couldn't catch Jesus in their traps, and because they had no basis at this point for arresting Him, Jesus kept right on teaching in the temple courts. It's hard to teach when people are plotting against you, but Jesus set the standard for the rest of us.

As we live for the Lord, there are always going to be nay-sayers. Sooner or later someone will scoff at our faith, and we will not be believed by certain people no matter what we say. The important for us is to be faithful to our Lord and to the task He has put before us. As Jesus continued on in the work of the Father, we are to soldier on also, regardless as to who believes us or not. The Father is the judge, and He is the only one we have to please.

DYING IN SIN

John 8:21–22 *Once more Jesus said to them, "I am going away, and you will look for me, and you will die in your sin. Where I go, you cannot come." This made the Jews ask, "Will he kill himself? Is that why he says, 'Where I go, you cannot come'?"*

There are a number of similarities between these two verses and what was recorded in John 7:33–36. In both places Jesus revealed that He was going away, that the Jews would look for Him, but that they could not come where He was going. In both places the Jews misunderstood what Jesus was saying, even when they repeated the words He had just spoken.

In both misunderstandings that are listed the Jews ironically reveal a truth. In chapter seven, they foretell the Gentile mission. In chapter eight, they stumble upon the sacrificial death of Jesus.

It was a pretty shocking thing for the Jews to hear that they would die in their sin. No one wants to hear that. In fact, the idea is so troubling that it is very rare in a funeral service that one even hears a mention of the wrong-doing of the deceased. It seems like all one has to do to go to heaven is die. The truth of the matter is that more people die in their sin than not, for Jesus Himself said, "For wide is the gate and broad is the road that leads to destruction, and many enter through it. But small is the gate and narrow is the road that leads to life and only a few find it" (Matthew 7:13–14).

It is also true that though the number be few that find their way to eternal life, it is possible for everyone who desires to be saved to achieve that goal. We cannot reach the next world to be in the presence of God on our own, but by putting our faith in Jesus as our Savior, we can accomplish through His grace the hope that we have for heaven and eternity.

The Jerusalem Jews in these verses were only confused by it all. The time for Jesus to be glorified had not yet arrived, so actually they were trying to make their judgments based on only half the information they needed. The resurrection would change that for them, just like it has for us. Though it was once impossible for anyone to escape dying in their sin and facing judgment, through Jesus that escape is not only possible for us, but promised. We can't make it alone, but hand in hand with Jesus, the Savior, we too can be redeemed.

TO WHAT ARE YOU ANCHORED?

John 8:23–24 *But he continued, "You are from below; I am from above. You are of this world; I am not of this world. I told you that you would die in your sins; if you do not believe that I am the one I claim to be, you will indeed die in your sins."*

It's an interesting thought process upon which to focus. Jesus was not of this world. The Pharisees were of this world. Jesus would go on from the grave to live forever. The Jews would die in their sins.

What does all this mean to me and to you? When Jesus said that those around Him were of this world, I think He would have to include all of us. Though He had His start somewhere else, we have our start right here. Earth, this time, and this dimension is all we know. Because we are of this world, we are anchored to it. In fact, different people are anchored to it by different things so a good question to ask is, "What has hooked your heart?" Whatever our anchor is hooked onto is where we remain. Jesus was hooked on doing the will of the Father and that connection was unbroken throughout His earthly ministry and beyond. For us, well, we have a tendency to get anchored to other things.

One of the strongest anchors I see is the family. That can be a very good thing because those family ties bind loved ones together and make them a force to be reckoned with, should someone try to hurt one of their number. But it can also be a very bad thing. Some people are so tied to their family that it becomes a god to them. Family sometimes comes before their faith and the real God, and that's when it becomes a problem.

Some are of this world because they are anchored to their job, their pleasures, their money, or a myriad of other things. In the midst of grabbing for all the toys they can, they neglect their relationship with Jesus, and as He said, they will die in their sin. That is a tragic loss indeed!

Our task as Christians is to love people into a relationship with us so that we can point them to a relationship with Jesus. He is our anchor to the next world and our Rock for this one. He is the one who can free us from the fear of dying in our sin, for He produced life in us that even the bonds of death and the grave can't contain. In Him we have life, and without Him there is no life. It's best to tie our anchor to things in the world to come.

HERE COMES THE JUDGE

John 8:25-26 *"Who are you?" they asked. "Just what I have been claiming all along," Jesus replied. I have much to say in judgment of you. But he who sent me is reliable, and what I have heard from him I tell the world."*

When I read the question asked by the Jews, "Who are you?" I wonder if what they really were saying was, "Who do you think you are? Who are you to talk about being God's Son, judgment, and having a divine mission? Who are you to say you are from somewhere else and not here?"

One thing we have to say about Jesus is that He never changed His story. His message was simple and it was consistent. He came from the Father and the Father had left all things concerning judgment into His hands. He was announcing the coming Kingdom and recruiting all He could find to be a part of it. He was and is the King of that Kingdom. That's His real identity.

It is in the communication conduit between Jesus and His father that we need to focus our full attention. Because Jesus was sent, He had a mission to fulfill. Because the one who sent Him is always reliable, His mission had to be completed as given. Because the Father and the Son were one in purpose, in essence, and in communication, Jesus could speak the words of the Father and show us just how God feels about things.

People sometimes wonder why the God of the Old Testament and the God of the New Testament seem so different. As I understand the Old Testament, it was given to the writers by the Holy Spirit for the benefit of all mankind. However, though I believe God's transmitter is always perfect, I do at times wonder about man's receiver. That doesn't mean they got it wrong, but it does mean that what was written possibly needed some clarity because future readers didn't always seem to fully understand what sometime was passed along.

Jesus came not only to die and be raised from the dead to show us the way to eternal life, but also to help us understand what God had previously said in the Old Testament. At different points in His ministry Jesus would say, "You have heard that it was said, but I say unto you..." and thus clarify what men had misunderstood. Because the Father is reliable and the communication between He and His Son is reliable, we receive first-hand information from God for our lives through Jesus. We look to Him for clarity.

THE CROSS CHANGED EVERYTHING!

John 8:27–30 *They did not understand that he was telling them about his Father. So Jesus said, "When you have lifted up the Son of Man, then you will know that I am the one I claim to be, and that I do nothing on my own but speak just what the Father has taught me. The one who sent me is with me; he has not left me alone, for I always do what pleases him." Even as he spoke, many put their faith in him.*

What does it take for people to put their faith in Jesus? Is it about going to church, reading their bibles, praying, and doing good deeds for people who are around us? No, those are all things that we hope will come about because we do put our faith in Jesus, but they are not what directly cause us to believe. There is something much simpler involved for those who would be followers of Christ.

We believe in Jesus as the Son of the Father only through the lens of the cross. Once we view the cross and its importance in the plan of God, then we see everything else start to fall into place. Jesus had to be lifted up on the cross so that men would see Him suffer death, because death is what we all have to face. The cross was the graphic instrument of torture that depicted mankind at its worst, but through that tool God was able to do something wonderful. If Jesus had just died and stayed dead, then there wouldn't have been anything accomplished. If He could have escaped the Jewish and Roman injustice, or if the crowd would have chosen Him instead of Barabbas to be set free, then we would still be lost in our sins. He had to die and people had to see Him die so that there was no doubt concerning His fate.

But the resurrection changed everything. Many of the people who saw Him die were also witnesses to His resurrection. It was then that they really began to understand the relationship between Jesus and His Father, and that understanding caused them to believe.

After all these years, there are still many people today who do not understand Jesus any more than they did then, but if they are ever going to believe they will believe through the venue of the cross. The crucifixion was not a plan from Jesus that went bad, but the plan of the Father being fulfilled to perfection. And that, my friend, is what makes faith possible.

REAL DISCIPLES

John 8:31-32 *To the Jews who had believed him, Jesus said, "If you hold to my teaching, you are really my disciples. Then you will know the truth, and the truth will set you free."*

There are few passages in the New Testament that contain such a complete picture of being disciples as this passage provides. John gives us a map and a goal as a way of discipleship.

Discipleship begins with belief. It begins when a person accepts what Jesus says is true. This includes what He said about the love of God. It also includes what He said about the destructive nature of sin and what He said about the real meaning of life.

Discipleship also means continually remaining in the word of Jesus. It involves listening for His voice as we pray, as we read the Bible, and in all aspects of our worldview. Being a disciples mean making our decisions to take or not take action until we have been directed by Jesus as to what we should do or not do. This also includes our constantly learning more and more about Jesus, for the shut mind is the end of discipleship.

Discipleship grows with the knowledge of the truth, for it causes us to ask some questions, like: "To what am I giving my life? Is it to a career? To making money? To getting pleasure? To providing a comfortable retirement? What reasons do I have for gathering material possessions?" Jesus helps us get our values right.

Discipleship ultimately results in freedom. It brings us freedom from fear, for the person who is a disciple of Jesus never has to walk alone. He is always with us. It also brings us freedom from our selfish nature. Many a person has realized that he or she is his or her own worst enemy, but the power and presence of Jesus can re-create a person until he or she is totally a new creation in Christ. Discipleship frees us from what other people think, and it provide us freedom from the chains that binds us to sin, enabling us to be the person we ought to be, and the person Jesus wants us to be.

The answer to getting free from the sin that binds us is by understanding that the way out is up. Being a disciple of Jesus puts us on the road to eternal life, but it also opens our eyes to our role in God's plan in this world.

SLAVES, REALLY?

John 8:33 *They answered him, "We are Abraham's descendants and never been slaves of anyone. How can you say that we shall be set free?"*

This has to be one of the most ironic and misinformed statements in the New Testament. It is true that the Jewish people were bloodline descendants of Abraham, although Jesus would expose just how far this group of people had drifted from the focus and purpose Abraham had. What is crazy though, is for them to say that they had never been slaves of anyone. A brief look at Jewish history tells a completely different story.

The book of Exodus settles the matter when it reveals that the Jews were slaves in Egypt for over 400 years, a story which any Israelite would know by heart. At various times in the book of Judges they were oppressed and enslaved by different groups before the nation of Israel set of a kingdom and began their progression of kings. At the end of the age of the kings, the Assyrians conquered the northern kingdom of Israel and sent the remnants of those tribes into exile and bondage. When Judah fell, they became slaves of the Babylonians, and even after they returned to their homeland, they would eventually serve the Greeks and then the Romans. It's a wonder that Jesus didn't laugh out loud when He heard the claims of this crowd.

This is good example of how sin so often blinds the sinner to the point that he doesn't even know that anything is wrong. The alcoholic often claims that he can stop drinking anytime. The drug user just needs one more fix and then everything will be okay. The spouse or child abuser really didn't mean to do what they did, so it will be different the next time. The list could go on and on, for sin is a great deceiver and people who are under its spell don't even realize that they are really slaves to the sin they are committing.

Jesus came to bring freedom to the captive, but before freedom can be found, the captives have to know that they are slaves to the desires that rules their lives. Jesus has the ability to change anyone, anywhere, and at any time, but the realization and confession of wrong doing must precede the healing. No one gets up until they realize that they are down. No one chooses freedom until they realize that they are a slave. The Holy Spirit's role is to convict, but freedom only comes when our denial of sin is confessed. Then the personification of Truth will truly set us free.

HEARING WHAT WE
NEED TO HEAR

John 8:34–38 *Jesus replied, "I tell you the truth, everyone who sins is a slave to sin. Now a slave has no permanent place in the family, but a son becomes to it forever. So if the Son sets you free, you will be free indeed. I know you are Abraham's descendants. Yet you are ready to kill me because you have no room for my word. I am telling you what I have seen in my Father's presence, and you do what you have heard from your father."*

Family is a wonderful thing. It's great to have friends with whom we can spend time and enjoy their company, but there is nothing like belonging to a family. Ours may not be perfect, and we certainly don't get to choose which one we were born into, but there is something about having a heritage that we can claim that helps us to know who we really are.

The Jews in this passage were in the same bloodline as Jesus and Abraham, but they weren't acting like family. In fact, they were betraying their family roots because they weren't living like Abraham and they certainly weren't filled with the love of God. Because they were living in their sin and were blind to their addiction to it, they couldn't find a way for Jesus to fit into their ideology. He was only a problem that they needed to get fixed.

Jesus was doing a wonderful thing here. He was telling His listeners what they needed to hear, even if it was not what they wanted to hear. He was pointing them to the way of freedom and eternal life, but they were so set in their ways and bound by their hatred that His words were having no effect on them.

Jesus always does that though. He doesn't condemn us in our sin without showing us where it is that we have sinned. He cares for us all enough to show us where change is needed, but then we are left with the decision of what to do with the information He has provided to us. These Jews couldn't hear the words of Jesus because they were too focused on hearing the words of their father, the devil. Murder was in their hearts and on their minds, so the words of freedom that Jesus offered just couldn't find a place to take root.

May we never be so hard of heart, deaf in our hearing, and blind to our situation that Jesus can't speak to us with words of healing. May our lives be ever tuned to the Master's voice so that we can be free indeed.

WE ACT LIKE OUR FATHER

John 8:39–41 *"Abraham is our father," they answered. "If you were Abraham's children," said Jesus, they you would do the things Abraham did. As it is, you are determined to kill me, a man who has told you the truth that I heard from God. Abraham did not do such things. You are doing the things your own father does." "We are not illegitimate children," they protested. "The only Father we have is God himself."*

The claim of the Jews was that Abraham is their father, but Jesus reminded them that they didn't act like him. How would He know that? Well, it's because He knew Abraham face to face. As He would say later in this chapter, "Before Abraham was, I am." Since Jesus is from everlasting to everlasting, all the history of the world was within His view.

This was not the case with the Jews who were plotting to kill Jesus. They were following their basest desires, and they couldn't see Him as anything but a problem that they needed to get rid of. There is a not-so-subtle dig at the background of Jesus here. The rumor was that He was the illegitimate son that came from some affair of His mother, Mary, before she married His father, Joseph. Of course, there wasn't a shred of evidence to back up their smear campaign, but gossip often has no basis in fact. When Jesus spoke of His heavenly Father, He was speaking truth, but this was a truth that the masses were not ready to accept.

It was quite a claim for the crowd to say that the only father they had was God, since they hadn't been acting very godly at all. After all, if Jesus could make such a claim, then they could too. This backwoods son of a carpenter wasn't going to get a leg up on them.

But I think Jesus makes a good point here though. We have a tendency to act like our fathers even if we are of a totally different personality from the one who sired us. We connect with him through various points of how we look, our blood type, and the words and actions that we observed from him.

If this is true physically, how much truer is it in the spirit? If God is our Father and His Spirit has come to reside within us, then we are going to act like Him, for the fruit of His Spirit flows forth from our being. If we are not of God, then we are going to act like whatever spirit has possessed us. We either belong to Him or not, and the truth of the matter is going to show up.

CALLED TO LOVE

John 8:42 *Jesus said to them, "If God were your Father, you would love me, for I came from God and now am here. I have not come on my own, but he sent me."*

T he pure essence of our heavenly Father is love. There is no getting around that fact. When we are filled with Him, we too show forth His love to the world. When we are filled with self or something else, then that will be on display for the world to see as well.

Jesus, being God in the flesh, was overflowing with love toward all of his creation, and that even included the people who were making life tough on Him. He was challenged by them, tempted by them, accosted by them, and even scorned by them, but it didn't stop Him from loving them. He could not do otherwise, for as we said, the essence of God is love—and Jesus was God in a human form.

Because He was full of love and because His mission was directed by the Father, His actions came out of that source of love to all mankind. It would have been so much better if man would have loved Him back as He loved them, but what filled their lives was so much different from what filled His life. He lived to fulfill the purpose and plan of the Father while they lived to fulfill their own selfish desires. The contrast is staggering!

I believe it is the hope of His Father that all of His children would love Him, serve Him, and love and serve each other. That's the way things were supposed to go from creation right up to the present time. However, because He gave us a free will and the ability to choose who or what would be the top priority in our lives, we have the results of what happens when we think we know better than what God does. Sin runs rampant among the nations because sin takes priority among the nations.

We are called to adopt the mission of Jesus and do what He did. What did He do? He came to fulfill His Father's plan for the span of time that He was given as a man in this world. We too are given a certain number of years on this planet and then our time will be up. If we are going to do anything for the Lord and for our fellow human beings, it has to be done within the time frame with which we have been allotted. We too have not come to be served, but to serve, that the glory of the Father may be fulfilled through us.

ON ONE SIDE OR THE OTHER

John 8:43–44 *"Why is my language not clear to you? Because you are unable to hear what I say. You belong to your father, the devil, and you want to carry out your father's desire. He was a murderer from the beginning, not holding to the truth, for there is no truth in him. When he lies, he speaks his native language, for his is a liar and the father of lies."*

We know from personal experience as well as from the Bible that sin is the enemy of the good God wants us to have. In this passage we come to understand that even the words of Jesus are muffled by sin, and those who are under its influence can't grasp what the Master is trying to get across. The devil's impact on unbelievers is huge, and they don't even know that it is happening.

What we learn here also is that everyone is in one of two camps. Either God is our Father and we are on His side, or the devil is our father and we are on his side. As much as people would like to straddle the issue, there is just no middle ground. To believe that there is, is to believe a lie, and the devil is the master and father of lies according to Jesus.

Sin is a great deceiver on our world. People think they can play with it, indulge in it, and live in it without consequences, but that is a lie from the father of liars. Sin always leads to pain, loneliness, destruction, and death, but the lie that entices us to try is wrong and many succumb to its wishes. We always think that we will be the exception. We think we will be the one who will play with fire and not get burned. However, the case against sin is 100%. No one ever sins without paying the price for doing so.

For this reason, the people who were surrounding Jesus were blinded by their sin, and were convinced that they were right by the father of lies, who happened to be their father. Though the people in this story are limited in number, there are legions just like them down through the ages. We who belong to Jesus need to make sure that we hear what He is saying. Since He is our Good Shepherd, we will know His voice if we will listen for it. If we don't want to be hurt and suffer the pains of sin, then we need to listen carefully to what Jesus has to say to us. If we do otherwise, then we will be in the same camp as those who tried to kill Him. He who has ears to hear, let him, or her, listen to what the Spirit is saying.

WHEN YOU DON'T
BELONG TO GOD

John 8:45–47 *"Yet because I tell you the truth, you do not believe me! Can any of you prove me guilty of sin? If I am telling you the truth, why don't you believe me? He who belongs to God hears what God says. The reason you do not hear is that you do not belong to God."*

Later Jesus will tell His disciples that He is truth personified (John 14:6), just as we have seen in this chapter that He is the Living Water and the Bread of Life personified. Because He is the essence of truth, there is no way that any sin could be in Him. Whatever He said, or says, is true, because His source for truth is found in the Father, who knows everything.

It must have been so frustrating for Jesus to have the antidote for sin that was binding His hearers, and yet was restrained from sharing it with the masses because they couldn't hear what He had to say. Because their god was the devil, there was definitely a conflict of interest in play. The enemy of our souls had stopped their ears from hearing the words of truth that could redeem them and free them from bondage.

We need to remember this when people of our day refuse to hear what we want to tell them about Jesus. Many times, people just turn us off if we speak concerning the Master who can change their lives and free them from their sins. We must remember that even Jesus didn't change the minds of those who had been taken over by the tricks of the devil, and refused to see the truth that was presented to them.

That doesn't mean that we should give up on people, but realize that God may have to other means, other people, or perhaps another time before they will have their eyes opened. At one point, the Apostle Paul was just like this crowd—and worse—but eventually God opened his eyes to see Jesus like he had never seen Him before.

We don't stop praying for people, loving people, or hoping the best for people, just because the enemy has them at this time. As long as there is life, there is hope, and we have the greatest power in the universe on our side. These people wanted to kill Jesus, and eventually they would get their wish fulfilled. That didn't stop Jesus from loving them though, for from the cross He forgave them and us. Sin is a blinder and a problem for all, but victory for all can be won through Jesus. Faith wins the day in the end.

"Us And Them"

John 8:48–51 *The Jews answered him, "Aren't we right in saying that you are a Samaritan and demon possessed?" "I am not possessed by a demon," said Jesus, "but I honor my Father and you dishonor me. I am not seeking glory for myself; but there is one who seeks it, and he is the judge. I tell you the truth, if anyone keeps my word, he will never see death."*

John had been building a case for the deity of Jesus. Since the healing of the lame man in chapter five, Jesus had been continually hounded by the Pharisees who were trying to trip Him up, discredit Him, and even kill Him if possible.

He was accused of being a Sabbath breaker and a blasphemer (5:18), but He continued to amaze the crowds by feeding the five thousand to the point that people wanted to make Him their king (6:15). There was even talk of Him walking on the water (6:19), but the crowd began to turn against Him (6:66), when He wouldn't feed them anymore. At the Feast of Tabernacles He was continually confronted. He was tested by a mob with an adulterous woman (8:1-11), and wherever He spoke He sparked controversy.

The Pharisees were not going to let Him alone because He had called them children of the devil in the previous verses. One basic rumor that the Pharisees tried to attach to Jesus was that He wasn't really one of their crowed. His identity was questioned and His legitimacy was questioned. Instead, they claimed, "You are one of them!" They wanted the crowd to be divided so that the influence of Jesus would be diminished.

How often today do people put us into the camps of "us" and "them?" If you are not one of "us," then you must be one of "them." If you are not one of us, or with us, then you must be our enemy. Difference is bad and likeness is good; it sounds like this could be taken from the news of the 21st century.

Socialism, Communism, Fascism, and so many other "isms" use the same tactics. Divide and conquer. It doesn't matter whether people are called saints or sinners, angels or demons, the other side is "bad," and we are not.

However, Jesus came with a message of love that says we all are included in God's grace. In Him we are one, and without Him we are just another angry voice.

GREATER THAN ABRAHAM

John 8:52–53 *At this the Jews exclaimed, "Now we know that you are demon-possessed! Abraham died and so did the prophets, yet you say that if anyone keeps your word, he will never taste death. Are you greater than our father Abraham? He died and so did the prophets. Who do you think you are?"*

The chants continued, "You are not who you say you are!" The Pharisees got pretty wound up over Jesus saying that He and Abraham were contemporaries. After all, Jesus was in His early thirties and Abraham had been gone for a couple thousand years. How dare Him also say that He was God's Son? Wasn't it blasphemous for Him to declare Himself the "I AM?" Why, the only way that Jesus could have been with Abraham and also for Him to be the "I AM," was for Him to be God. That was a concept that could have stopped them in their tracks if they had thought His words through.

No, none of that could be true, so He must be demon possessed. There was no way that Jesus could be what or who He said He was. Abraham was dead and there was no denying that. The prophets also died; how dare Jesus to make such claims!

We are finding here that in the minds of radical terrorists, which is what the Pharisees were proving to be, disagreements can be fatal. Fear, ignorance, and jealousy are powerful motivators. In fact, they are like an unholy trinity, and there is only one cure for such maladies, namely Jesus the Messiah. Love conquers fear, enlightenment conquers ignorance, and the Holy Spirit conquers jealousy.

Without Jesus as the antidote to the hate these men were festering, there was no real hope for them to change their ways or point of view. Yes, Abraham died and so did the prophets, but what the Pharisees didn't understand was that even though they left this world, they did not leave the presence of God. They are as much alive today as they ever were, but they are with the Father, out of view from those of us who remain.

Of course, we know that Jesus really is greater than Abraham and all the prophets combined. He is the only begotten Son of God. As John builds his case in this book, that truth is going to become more and more clear, but for those who won't believe, darkness and lostness is all that's left to them.

"NO BRAG, JUST FACT!"

John 8:54–56 *Jesus replied, "If I glorify myself, my glory means nothing. My Father, whom you claim as your God, is the one who glorifies me. Though you do not know him, I know him. If I said I did not, I would be a liar like you, but I do know him and keep his word. Your father Abraham rejoiced at the thought of seeing my day; he saw it and was glad."*

It was the humorist, David Runyon, who said, "He that tooteth not his own horn, the same shall not be tooteth." That seems to be the motto of many people throughout the ages, for we all like to make ourselves appear in a good light, and some try to do that by bragging on their own accomplishments.

Jesus wasn't that way though. He knew that if He only had His own words as testimony about Himself, it would never be convincing to His hearers. Therefore, He allowed the Father who sent Him into the world to glorify Him. It was the Father's plan, and His Son filled the role He was given perfectly, so the Father was pleased with all that He said and did.

The big difference between Jesus and those confronting Him in this story is that Jesus knew the source of all truth intimately. He could not deny who He was, or the relationship that He had with the Father, or He would be a liar. The Father was glorified through Him, and in turn the Father glorified Him. Those listening were clueless because they didn't have any kind of relationship with the Father. Their religion was based on rituals and rules, not on a oneness of mind and mission.

Jesus really got their attention when He told them of His relationship with Abraham. He was the epitome of all that Abraham hoped for when He believed the word of God. As Abraham glorified the Father, so did Jesus, only more completely.

What would it be like if we lived in such a way that we not only glorified the Father with our words and deeds, but also in return had the Father glorify us? Every time I start to count my blessings, I realize anew that the Father is the source of all good things that have happened in my life. Every victory I win, every achievement I accomplish, every life that I touch for Jesus is the result of God working in me and through me. Whether I am glorified as result really doesn't matter, but that God is glorified is worth everything.

THE "I AM!"

John 8:57–59 *You are not yet fifty years old, the Jews said to him, "and you have seen Abraham!" "I tell you the truth," Jesus answered, "before Abraham was born, I am!" At this, they picked up stones to stone him, but Jesus hid himself, slipping away from the temple grounds.*

I feel kind of sorry for the Jews who surrounded Jesus here. They were in water so far over their heads that they didn't have a hope of coming up for air. They were trying to match wits with their Creator and appeared to be coming to the contest totally unarmed. When Jesus told them that He knew Abraham and that Abraham was glad to see His day, that was too much for them. They just lost it. No one could know a man who lived two thousand years in the past and they just couldn't let that kind of talk go unchallenged.

What really hammered them was when Jesus said, "before Abraham was born, I am." "I am who I am" was the name that God gave for Himself to Moses back in Exodus 3:14. This was Jesus actually revealing His own true identity, and it was more than they could handle because of their hard hearts.

So, when every argument has been exhausted, the usual next step is violence. When a man can't get his way or get his point across, it historically has been the carnal order of man for him to strike out and hit the person who has contradicted him. This is the root cause of wars, nation conquering, and even family squabbles.

Here's a pretty good rule of thumb for us to consider: If circumstances in life cause us to attack someone else, we can be pretty such that such a reaction is not of God. Jesus could have crushed His opposition with a whisper, but instead chose to defuse the situation by leaving.

When we are pushed to violence for the sake of getting our own way, we can be assured that it is not God who is doing the pushing. The enemy of our soul always wants people to fight; he wants us to destroy each other.

That doesn't mean that fighting is never justified. It just means that it is not justified when it is done it is done for personal gain. Christians respond for the benefit of others and to the glory of God. The way of sin is the way of aggression and is not God's way, for it doesn't benefit man or bring glory to His name.

"THE WORK OF GOD"

John 9:1–3 *As he went along, he saw a man blind from birth. His disciples asked him, "Rabbi, who sinned, this man or his parents that he was born blind?" "Neither this man nor his parents sinned," said Jesus, "but this happened so that the work of God might be displayed in his life."*

The Bible is made up of many things, but for most people the most endearing parts of it are the stories. They are more than just stories though; they are lessons of life that feed our souls. The Bible is full of drama, and drama gives us insights into who God is and what He is about.

Consider the following examples: One-hundred-year-old Abraham and ninety-year-old Sarah had a baby, for nothing is impossible with God. Joseph was sold into slavery, and from this act God had a plan to save all Israel. God allowed the kingdoms of Israel to be destroyed, for God will not be mocked, but God restored His people, because His mercy endures forever. God sent His Son into the world because He will not give up on us.

In this story we have the sixth miracle that John would record. The others were Jesus turning water into wine, healing an official's son, healing a lame man at a pool, feeding the multitudes, and walking on the water. John records Jesus' ministry in a very dramatic fashion, almost like it was a play.

Here the disciples questioned Jesus. They wanted to know who it was that sinned against God and caused this man to be blind from birth. It's natural for people to see bad things and think that God's wrath must be in play. However, God gives us life and then says, "Look up!" The Apostle Paul would put it like this, "And we know that in all things God works for the good of those who love him, who have been called according to his purpose" (Romans 8:28).

Jesus set the record straight. God can be glorified through our misfortunes even if we can't see the reason for them. He works on His timetable and for His purposes, not ours. We don't always understand any more than the disciples or this blind man understood his handicap, but God was setting up the scene in such a way that would produce great joy as well as bring glory to His name. Bad things do happen to good people, but never without God knowing about it and working in it to bring good out of the bad. We may have to wait to see it, but that's the way He always works.

TIME IS ON THE LINE

John 9:4–5 *"As long as it is day, we must do the work of him who sent me. Night is coming when no one can work. While I am in the world, I am the light of the world."*

It was Henry Ford, the founder of the Ford Motor Company, that first popularized the eight-hour work day in 1914. Up until that time there were no definite restrictions by employers on how many hours a day a person could work. Other companies followed suit eventually because it proved to be a good business practice and helped them to make money. An employee can, and often does, work more hours than that to this day, but the standard for American society for that time and in this time is still the eight-hour day.

Different countries have different policies concerning the age of retirement. Again, the standard for workers in the United States at this time is somewhere between the ages of sixty-two and sixty-seven. Some will take an earlier retirement and some will work longer, but most people will officially retire somewhere in their sixties.

Jesus brings about a different focus on the time one has to work. He knew that His time before the cross was limited and He had much to do before the eternal Kingdom would be launched through His resurrection. He also knew, and knows, that our days in this world are numbered. We may live to be 100-years-old, but eventually our life will come to an end. When that time comes, our time for working for the Lord—or for any job for that matter—will be over for good.

This is why it was so important for Jesus and so important for us, to be at our best for the Father all the days of our lives. We are not given a time or day for retirement from Kingdom work until the Lord calls us home. Our skills and abilities will diminish eventually as our years advance, and some will be able to work longer than others, but we are called to work in Christ's harvest field for as long as He gives us strength, opportunity, and ability. Every day is filled with new occasions for us to find ways to minister in our Lord's name. It may be to our neighbors, to our family, to our co-workers, to our schoolmates, or even to other church folks, but we are called to serve, not to be served, just as Jesus was. Soon we will enter into the night and our work here will be done. Let's be what we can be for Jesus while we are able.

OBEDIENCE IS KEY

There is a very simple principle of life at work here. If you are in need, do what Jesus tells you to do and your situation has a better ending. I can see the surprise in the blind man as Jesus makes a poultice of mud and spital, and begins to smear it on eyes that had never seen anything. He was no doubt a bit curious as to what this stranger was doing to him, but when he was told to wash it off, he did it without delay. The rest is history. One touch from Jesus and the man was never the same again.

I wish every story in the Bible, and in life, turned out that well. Without a doubt there were many blind people in Israel at the time of this event, but Jesus made a difference for this man so that God would be glorified. I'm sure that if He had wanted to do so at this point, He could just have just spoken the word and every blind person in the world would have been able to see, but He doesn't seem to work like that. This was done to bring glory to God in the midst of a crowd that could not understand. His reasons for choosing this man and this time remain His own, but His power was demonstrated completely.

I also wish that everyone who is blind to the truth of new life in Christ could see that He is the answer that they need. I wish that every family situation where relationships are strained or non-existent, could be mended so that God could be glorified, and lives separated would be united. There are a lot of problems in the world that Jesus could fix if only people would let Him, but willingness to obey lies at the root of the cure. Jesus applied a remedy, gave a command, and watched the man walk away. He didn't have to follow him to see if he would do what he was told, for Jesus saw something in him that showed a spark of faith, brought about by a divine touch.

There would be great joy and great surprise when the water from the pool of Salome ran down his face. Jesus had done it again. The good news is that He is still able and willing to provide what we need for our lives too. The key is obedience to do what He tells us.

IS THE CHANGE REAL?

John 9:8–9 *His neighbors and those who had formerly seen him begging asked, "Isn't this the same man who used to sit and beg?" Some claimed that he was. Others said, "No, he only looks like him." But he insisted, "I am the man."*

Not everyone believes when the impossible happens. Some people will look for every excuse in the world to explain the unexplainable rather than just admit God was involved. Change in a person's life is hard to realize, but when the evidence of that change is standing right in front of you, it's a pretty hard thing to deny.

Down through the corridors of time, since Jesus first walked the earth as a man, there have been billions of stories of real change. Drunkards are sobered up, killers are made into lovers, and abusers are transformed into people who become protectors, as sinners are made into saints of God. The way that change takes place is as different as the people themselves, but when Jesus moves into a person's life, the change is real.

This is why our personal testimony before those who know us is so vital. It's necessary for people to hear about the change Jesus has made in us, and then it's mandatory that we live out the new life we have been given so that our testimony will be proven true. Christian transformation is not an act, but a reality as stark as a man who has always been blind being made able to see. There will be the naysayers who will deny that such change is possible, or real, just as there were in this story, but when the Son of God forgives, cleanses, and empowers us for His service, and we act as He instructs us, the doubters will eventually have to face facts.

This man once couldn't see, but then suddenly he could. Only Jesus could have done that. We once were lost in our trespasses and sins, but we were set free. Only Jesus could do that too. Let them talk about us all they want. Isn't this the person who used to swear, and lie, and couldn't be trusted? Aren't those people down at the church just a bunch of phonies and hypocrites who talk about things out of both sides of their mouth? Isn't religion just a crutch for the weak and the old?

Doubters will come and doubters will go, but when the change is real, it will be noticed because Jesus is the change agent for all time.

TRUST AND OBEY

John 9:10–12 *"How then were your eyes opened?" they demanded. He replied, "The man they call Jesus made some mud and put it on my eyes. He told me to go to Siloam and wash. So I went and washed, and then I could see." "Where is this man?" they asked him. "I don't know," he said.*

Sometimes even when evidence to truth is standing right in front of some people, they don't see it. Miracles like curing lifelong blindness doesn't happen very often, so when it happened to this man, there was plenty of reason for the crowd and the religious authorities to be skeptical of it.

Jesus apparently never gave His name to the man He healed, so there was no way that He could be identified when the man who had received His sight was asked about the healing. This only confused the authorities even more and caused them no small amount of consternation.

However, the main focus of these couple of verses is found in the fact that Jesus had touched the man, and then given him a command. If he wanted the healing to take place then he had to do as he had been told. The healing didn't happen until the instructions that Jesus gave him were completed.

How like that is our relationship with Jesus still. Our faith may seem so weak and uncertain, but when we sense the leading of the Lord in our life to do something, we will never get relief until we follow up on what we have been instructed to do.

I have heard many stories from people over the years who have sensed instruction from on high that caused them to change their activity, only to see the hand of God at work when they obeyed. It could happen when we are reading through a section of the Bible and we get an impression that the Lord is speaking to us directly about some that requires our action. Whether or not we follow up on what we have been told often makes a huge difference in someone's life.

Obedience to do what Jesus tells us to do is one of the most vital habits we can ever develop. It may or may not lead to a miracle like the one that happened to the man in this story, but it will always lead to a better result than if we ignore what the Lord is telling us. May God make us willing and obedient servants always.

RULES? WHAT RULES?

John 9:13–15 *They brought to the Pharisees the man who had been blind. Now the day on which Jesus had made the mud and opened the man's eyes was a Sabbath. Therefore the Pharisees also asked him how he had received his sight. "He put mud on my eyes," the man replied, "and I washed, and now I see."*

When the local neighbors and friends couldn't make physical and rational sense out of what had happened to the man who had been born blind but now could see, they naturally gravitated toward a more spiritual answer. Who would know about spiritual things better than the Pharisees, the religious "rule-keepers" of the people of Israel? They were more popular with the common people than the Sadducees who operated the temple and government, so the healed man was pushed their way. Just as the man's acquaintances had required an answer concerning the source of his healing, the Pharisees wanted to know also. Blind people didn't just suddenly start seeing in those days any more than they do now, so there had to be a reasonable explanation behind what had happened.

It's almost a sidenote in this passage, but John does slip it in. "Now the day on which Jesus had made the mud and opened the man's eyes was a Sabbath." This is at the crux of the story, for the Pharisees were very strict on matters concerning the Sabbath Day, and they felt that any activity that took place between sundown on Friday and sundown on Saturday had to be carefully considered and regulated. If Jesus had healed the man on a Tuesday, this healing would have no doubt draw attention from the man's friends, but it wouldn't have gotten attention from the religious crowd. But healing on the Sabbath? Well, that sounds a lot like work and as such could never be allowed. How blind the Pharisees were in such matters! Though skilled in the written Law, they had long since lost the meaning of what they were reading. Jesus would bring that to light in the coming verses.

Being overly zealous for rules and keeping order has plagued the church down through the centuries. Have a balance between theological chaos and liberality over against legalism has challenged many a saint and finding a middle ground isn't always easy. However, a good rule of thumb is to always land on the side of love and grace. That's where Jesus stood and where He is remains a pretty good place to be.

HE DOESN'T DO IT LIKE I DO!

John 9:16–17 *Some of the Pharisees said, "This man is not from God, for he does not keep the Sabbath." But others asked, "How can a sinner do such miraculous signs?" So they were divided. Finally they turned again to the blind man, "What have you to say about him? It was your eyes that he opened." The man replied, he is a prophet."*

We may hear it said a bit differently these days. "He can't be a Christian; he smokes." "He can't be a Christian; he drinks." "She can't be a Christian; she doesn't believe like I do." Lots of people like to categorize others when how they act and think doesn't match up with what we think is correct.

The Pharisees were like that. "Jesus couldn't really be from God because He doesn't live like we do." They were all about keeping the rules while Jesus was all about helping people. The Pharisees were rigid in their focus on what it meant to keep the Sabbath Day holy. Jesus was more concerned with what would help to make men whole.

Of course, there were some on the other side of the discussion. After all, how could someone do all the good things that Jesus was doing if God wasn't involved with him somewhere? They may or may not have heard the stories about Jesus turning the water into wine, healing a city official's son, restoring health to a man who had been lame for thirty-eight years, feeding thousands with just a pittance of food, or heard tales of Jesus walking on the water, but there was one thing they couldn't deny. This man before them had been blind since birth and after Jesus got through with him, he could see. It's pretty hard to deny evidence like that.

The man who was healed could only confess that Jesus was a prophet. He had no doubt heard about what the prophets of old could do, but of course he hadn't seen them himself. In fact, he had never seen anything for himself. He hadn't even seen Jesus because Jesus sent him away to wash the mud off his eyes and was gone by the time the healed man returned from the well. He had to be a prophet though. What else could He be?

It would be great to have access to a video recording of that day's events. God was working through His Son in a big way and some would acknowledge it and some would not. It kind of sounds like our world today. As for me, I'll choose to believe. Jesus is just too good to do otherwise.

PASSING THE BUCK

John 9:18–21 *The Jews still did not believe that he had been blind and had received his sight until they sent for the man's parents. "Is this your son?" they asked. "Is this the one you say was born blind?" How is it that now he can see?" "We know he is our son," the parents answered, "and we know he was born blind. But how he can see now, or who opened his eyes, we don't know. Ask him. He is of age; he will speak for himself."*

One has to feel sorry for the parents of blind man that Jesus healed. On one hand there must have been such joy at seeing their son moving about with two fully functioning eyes after years of having to take care of him because of his physical affliction. Now he could not only take care of himself, but also provide care for his parents as they aged, which was and is the rightful role of any able-bodied son.

However, on the other hand they were gripped with a new fear. They couldn't explain what happened to their son any more than anyone else could, but the consequences of saying the wrong things to the Jewish leader could cost them dearly. They seemed to caught between the proverbial rock and a hard place emotionally and practically.

Because they testified that their son was of legal age to speak for himself, we can assume that he was at least in his late teens or older. Therefore, he could take responsibility for his own actions and words—especially now that he was able to see. Since the tone of the Pharisees appears to be an accusatory one, rather than one purely interested in investigating the details, speaking directly to them would have been a challenge for either the healed man or his parents. He had already testified that he thought Jesus to be a prophet, so the parents were willing to let him stand alone in his evaluation of his healer.

Fear can be a powerful force when we are questioned about our faith. There is so much skepticism and unbelief around us from people who are not Christians, and sometimes even those within our church circle may not believe our testimony when we speak of the way God moves within us. In this regard we have a wonderful example of faith from the healed man, even if not the same level of faith from his parents. Sometimes we have to stand alone, but when we stand with Jesus we are always in good company.

UNHOLY DICTATORS

> **John 9:22-25** *His parents said this because they were afraid of the Jews, for already the Jews had decided that anyone who acknowledged that Jesus was the Christ would be put out of the synagogue. That was why his parents said, "He is of age; ask him." A second time they summoned the man who had been blind. "Give glory to God," they said. "We know this man is a sinner." He replied, "Whether he is a sinner or not, I don't know. One thing I do know. I was blind but now I see."*

Maybe we need to read that first sentence once again a little more slowly and carefully. "His parents said this because *they were afraid of the Jews...*" What does it say about a religion when people are afraid of the leaders of that religion? Where is the focus on God? Where is the fairness and value of individual rights and opinions? How do these people have such power over the masses of believers?

The only answer to these questions is that the Jewish leaders at this time, the Pharisees, had moved from the arena of being God's ambassadors to being dictators who were ruled only by their own opinions and warped views of what there so-called distorted understanding of their illustrious history really was. It is true that in time to come that there would be other leaders who would also abuse their power, but here we are seeing the Jewish religion gone bad in a big way, showing very unjust actions.

The penalty that brought fear to the healed man's parents was that they would be deprived of their place of worship and praise to their God. They would be banished from the group that gathered each week to hear words from God's book and sing psalms as a family. This is what would happen to anyone who dared to think and express the idea that this person who healed the lame, restored sick children, fed the multitudes, and opened the eyes of the blind, just might be the one God had promised His people He would send. Without a trial, without a hearing, and without any formal declaration concerning guilt or innocence, Jesus was considered to be off-limits for people to consider as even a prophet. It was truly a sad state of affairs.

Heresy cannot be allowed to stand in any legitimate religion, but every voice needs to be heard and every challenged considered fairly. Only bullies rule without mercy and justice—and that's what the Pharisees were.

A QUESTION AS AN OPEN DOOR

John 9:26–29 *Then they asked him, "What did he do to you? How did he open your eyes?" He answered, "I have told you already and you did not listen. Why do you want to hear it again? Do you want to become his disciples too?" Then they hurled insults at him and said, "You are this fellow's disciple! We are disciples of Moses! We know that God spoke to Moses, but as for this fellow, we don't even know where he comes from."*

If there ever was a story of good news and bad news then these verses tell that story. To begin with, we see the kind of questioning from the Pharisees that true lovers of Jesus would be excited to get. After all, how long has it been since someone has confronted you with a question concerning your interaction with Jesus and ask, "What did he do to you?" Talk about a door for sharing our faith! I always love to have people ask me that question!

Of course, though this man had met Jesus, he really didn't know Him. He didn't even know His name or how to point others to Him. That would change in the days to come, but at this point in time he probably felt overcome by his newly discovered sight, the huge amount of attention he was getting, as well as from the badgering from the Pharisees—which perhaps brought a bit of the fear that plagued his parents. It must have been an overwhelming time in his life.

This is where the bad news comes in. Once he didn't give his questioners the answers they were looking for, they began to insult him. They didn't care that this was the first day he had ever seen anything in his entire life. They didn't care that he was stunned with emotion on all kinds of levels and was probably having a hard time processing it all. They didn't care whether they had embarrassed the man's parents with their questioning. They wanted Jesus and they wanted Him out of the way as soon as possible, and they would stop at nothing to achieve their devious goal.

The Jews said that they were disciples of Moses. Though Moses wasn't on the scene to confirm or deny their claims, a brief look at the life of Moses, or even the Ten Commandments that he presented to people of Israel would reveal that their discipleship was lacking in some key points.

Sin is always like that. It destroys what it can't control. Thank God Jesus frees us from its clutches.

SPEAKING TRUTH TO POWER

John 9:30–34 *The man answered, "Now that is remarkable!
You don't know where he comes from, yet he opened my eyes.
We know that God does not listen to sinners. He listens to the
godly man who does his will. Nobody has ever heard of opening
the eyes of a man born blind. If this man were not from God, he
could do nothing." To this they replied, "You were steeped in sin
at birth, how dare you lecture us!" And they threw him out.*

Speaking truth to power is rarely a fun or easy thing to do. This man who had been healed from his blindness spoke boldly here, as he chastised the blindness of those who were out to get Jesus. He would pay a social and religious price for his daring, but he spoke words that needed to be said. He had a wonderful argument. The Jewish leaders first said that they knew where Jesus came from (7:27), that He was a Galilean (7:52), and that knew His father, mother, and siblings (6:42). Then they accused Him of being an illegitimate son (8:41), as they tried to smear His name and dampen His influence. Now they say that they don't know where He came from (9:29). They were digging themselves into a hole, and this recently healed man was spot-on to call them on it.

He was also right in his assessment of the situation. God had healed him through the work of Jesus, but he said that God doesn't listen to sinners, so if Jesus was a sinner, then God wouldn't have worked through Him. The Jews had no answer for such a rational argument, so they just threw him out of the synagogue to shut him up.

That's the way of the irrational. When their arguments get weak and are bested, then the next step is to silence the person who makes a sane argument. We see this in the realm of social and public media all the time. When one makes a statement that goes against the current popular thought, no matter how factual or rational it is, then that person making the statement is banned, censured, or expelled from public communication.

It would be easy to get political here and name specific examples, but with every generation the case is made. The names and situations change over the years, but when correct thinking and righteousness confront sinful powers, there is going to be a social and political pushback. Speaking truth to power is never easy, but it's the way Jesus wants us to go.

THE JOY OF BEING REJECTED

John 9:35–38 *Jesus heard that they had thrown him out, and when he found him, he said, "Do you believe in the Son of Man?" "Who is he, sir?" the man asked. "Tell me so that I may believe in him." Jesus said, "You have now seen him, in fact, he is the one speaking with you." Then the man said, "Lord, I believe," and he worshiped him.*

The blind man that Jesus healed had answered the questions of the Pharisees honestly. He had given them a very intelligent argument concerning the righteousness of one who could give sight to the blind. The reward that he got for his boldness however, was to excommunicated from the local synagogue. In today's terms, he was kicked out of the church. It doesn't seem right, and it wasn't. It doesn't seem fair, and it wasn't. But sin doesn't pursue rightness or fairness. Sin always seeks its own benefit and power, regardless of how it affects others.

When Jesus found the rejected man, He qualified his faith. "Do you believe?" was the question. The sad reality was that he didn't even know who it was that he was supposed to believe in. But when Jesus revealed His identity to him, everything changed. Ignorance changed to faith and faith led to worship. It's a path that we have seen many people follow down through the years.

This progression from ignorance to faith to worship is the pattern we are called to share with others because that's the way we found the truth in Jesus. No one knows the truth about Jesus until He reveals Himself to the heart that has been made hungry by the wooing of the Holy Spirit. Once faith has been achieved, worship is the by-product of such a revelation.

As we continue in our walk with Christ, we find joy in being rejected for the sake of being able to find the Master who has delivered us. There is no price that is too high to pay, no loss too great to sustain that would equal the value of knowing Jesus, the Son of Man and Son of God. Like the man of this story, we would sacrifice all relationships and connections to be a follower of Jesus. Others continue to pay heavy prices for this privilege around the globe where freedom of worship is not available in certain societies. But it is in the sacrifice that we offer that our faith is solidified. Only when much has been required will the reward achieved be appreciated.

JUDGING THE BLIND

John 9:39 *Jesus said, "For judgment I have come into this world, so that the blind will see and those who see will become blind."*

It was in Jeremiah 5:21 where the prophet wrote, "Hear this, you foolish and senseless people who have eyes but do not see, who have ears but do not hear." Later in 1546, John Haywood would expand upon these words and write, "There are no so blind as those who will not see. The most deluded people are those who ignore what they already know."

Jesus was dealing with much the same thing when He was dealing with people who couldn't see what was right in front of them. Jesus comes as the ultimate Judge in this situation for He always knows the truth and always puts things in the proper perspective. There was no way that the man who had been blind could have been healed unless someone or something healed him. Because he had been blind since birth, the miracle was even more dramatic. But these leaders of the Jews, who may have had 20-20 vision physically, couldn't perceive the presence of God right in their midst. They were truly the "seeing" blind.

We live in a world like this. In more recent years as radical ideologies take center stage, and the post-modern world calls for the abolition of absolutes, except for their opinions, of course, that we see this kind of blindness on a massive scale. Babies are murdered in the womb right up to the point of birth and the blind call it, women's healthcare. People are paid to stay home from their jobs rather than go into the workforce and be productive, and the blind call it, compassionate welfare. A nation's borders are breached to the point of anarchy and violence, but the blind call it, fairness and equity.

In America we have had our share of blindness over the centuries. Manifest Destiny saw the spiritually blind ravage the land as they pushed out and murdered native Americans, imprisoned slaves to work their fields, and persecuted anyone who stood in their way. Sin always leads to spiritual blindness. We can put other labels on it, but when we are so full of ourselves that we can't see the hand of God working in others, we have truly lost our sight. It was for this reason that Jesus came, so that we could be freed from our darkness and be brought into the light. In Him, and in Him alone, can we truly see as the Father wants us to see.

REFUSING TO SEE

John 9:40–41 *Some Pharisee who were with him heard him say this and asked, "What? Are we blind too?" Jesus said, "If you were blind, you would not be guilty of sin; but now that you claim you can see, your guilt remains.*

Talk about putting your own foot in your mouth! These Pharisees always showed up with the intent of putting Jesus in His place, but then continually found themselves on the short end in the battle of wits when they challenged Him. No matter how angry it made them, or how hard they tried, they just couldn't catch Jesus off guard and trap Him with their words.

The very sad reality of this story is that it began with Jesus doing a tremendously generous and needful thing, namely healing a man who was born blind and giving him sight for the first time. The man went from a world of darkness and dependency on others for everything, to a world of light and colors and shapes that he couldn't have even imagined before. The healing was all because of Jesus, and there was no one who could argue the miracle away. Once he was blind, but after meeting Jesus he could see.

The Pharisees wanted to deny it, but there was no way that they could. The proof was standing right in front of them, and in front of all the people who had witnessed the change in the man. The issue was that Jesus did the healing on the Sabbath. Jesus instructed the man to wash his eyes on the Sabbath. He was the one responsible for the change, but He was also the one who saw a different purpose for that Sabbath Day than did the Pharisees.

At this point, Jesus made His message clear. The physically blind had been made whole and the spiritually blind were guilty because they wouldn't accept what was plainly seen by everyone else. They weren't physically blind, or even ignorant of their actions, but they were inwardly dead and therefore incapable of allowing Jesus to do what came naturally to Him.

We meet people all the time who know better, but don't do better. They know they should give God their lives and give Him the glory He deserves, but their hard hearts and selfish motives won't allow themselves to be humbled and be healed from what blinds them. Jesus came to bring spiritual sight to all men. The Pharisees are just examples of people who won't yield. The light of Jesus is around all of us, but we must open our eyes to see it.

The Role Of The Shepherd

> **John 10:1–2** *"I tell you the truth, the man who does not enter the sheep pen by the gate, but climbs in by some other way, is a thief and a robber. The man who enters by the gate is the shepherd of the sheep.*

It's a jungle out there. That seems to be the case for living in the twenty-first century, no matter where we may be located. Whether we live in a high-rise inner-city dwelling, a small town, in the suburbs, or out in the open country, there are sheep, and there are robbers who try to take advantage of the sheep.

Jesus knew this all too well, for He knew what was in the heart of a man (John 2:25). Because there are so many thieves and robbers trying to accost the sheep, He stands out as the Shepherd guarding the flock for the sake of His Father, and for our sakes as well. I have witnessed too many pastors who have betrayed their charge, and either took advantage of their flock, or left them defenseless against society's wolves because they were not adequately fed on God's Word or watched over by a caring leader. Some people who hold the job of shepherd are more in the position because of what they can take from the sheep than what they can provide for them. When pastoral candidates apply for a church position and lay out a list of requirements that must be filled concerning salary, benefits, and expense accounts, it's a pretty good sign that they are merely hirelings.

The shepherd puts the needs of the sheep before his or her own personal comforts. If God directs a shepherd to a flock, then all other considerations are peripheral. If the call of God is not the primary focus, then it's best for the flock to consider other candidates.

Jesus never sneaks in a window or climbs over a fence to get to a flock. Being the Good Shepherd He enters into the gate into our sheep pen, and when He gets there, He is interested in binding up the wounded, inspiring the lambs, feeding the whole flock, and leading them to safe pasture. In this simply analogy, Jesus gives guidance for every person who would ever entertain a call to be a shepherd. A shepherd is real, not a phony. Regardless of his or her personal needs, the needs of the sheep come first. When that doesn't happen, the church just degenerates into a club or business, and the wolves take over.

FOLLOWING THE
SHEPHERD'S VOICE

John 10:3–5 *"The watchman opens the gate for him, and the sheep listen to his voice. He calls his own sheep by name and leads them out. When he has brought out all his own, he goes on ahead of them, and his sheep follow him because they know his voice. But they will never follow at stranger; in fact, they will run away from him because they do not recognize a stranger's voice."*

I have to confess that my memory is not as sharp as it used to be. I tell my wife that I don't remember ever forgetting anything, but then, that could be part of my problem. What I do remember, however, is the sound of the Master Shepherd's voice. It's not a definitive tone, or even an audible sound, but I know it when I hear it, and I know when He is speaking directly to me.

The role of a pastor is to be a watchman as much as it is to be a shepherd. Both hats need to be worn if the job is to be done effectively. The watchman has the responsibility of providing an avenue to the Great Shepherd, who is the Savior of our souls. Anything that a pastor can do to open the way for the members of his or her flock to get to the Good Shepherd is vital ministry. On the other hand, the role of shepherd, or perhaps more accurately put, the role of under-shepherd, is also desperately needed. Members of the flock have a tendency to drift apart, and the audible voice of the under-shepherd is needed to call them back into the group. Hours spent in the pulpit are necessary, but so is time in the counseling room, or praying by a sick lamb in a hospital bed, or spending and being spent in daily activities with members of the flock in social and crisis situations.

Home visits by the pastor were once considered essential for the job, but now they are almost unheard of. It makes one wonder if many shepherds are more interested in virtual connections than actually getting the smell and feel of real flock-life.

It takes time and direct involvement with the sheep for a shepherd to get to the point where his or her sheep know the voice that is calling out to them. There are so many voices calling for the sheep's attention that without a strong presence and the voice of a shepherd, the sheep may get lost. But where the shepherd is faithful and the sheep know that the shepherd is around, there can be peace in the flock and safety in the sheep pen.

THE GATEKEEPER

John 10:6-9 *Jesus used this figure of speech, but they did not understand what he was telling them. Therefore Jesus said again, "I tell you the truth, I am the gate for the sheep. All who ever came before me were thieves and robbers, but the sheep did not listen to them. I am the gate; whoever enters through me will be saved. He will come in and go out and find pasture."*

The idea of Jesus saying that "I am the gate" is a unique concept. He identifies Himself with the Father by using the "I Am" language, for He does it seven times in John's Gospel. He said, "I am the bread of life (6:35, 41, 48, 51), "I am the light of the world (8:12), and here in this passage, "I am the gate for the sheep." He would also say, I am the good shepherd" (10:11, 14), "I am the resurrection and the life (11:25), I am the way the truth and the life (14:6), and "I am the true vine (15:1, 5). It was this "I am" talk that raised the anger of the Jewish leaders because they immediately identified it with how God labeled Himself when He spoke to Moses all those centuries ago (Exodus 3:14).

One thing that I notice about gates is that they are not for offense, but for defense. When a soldier is suiting up for battle and collecting weapons, he never takes a gate. Gates are for protection, for being a barrier, and for defending a place or people that are behind it. When Jesus said in Matthew 16, that the gates of Hades would not overcome the Kingdom He was building, He was not telling the disciples to hide behind a gate. Instead, He was instructing His followers to break down the gate that leads to death so that the kingdom of darkness would be conquered by the Kingdom of light.

Jesus here is providing protection for His sheep. Those who will come to Him will find safety from the thieves and robbers who would do them harm. We enter the Kingdom of God only through Him, and once we are a part of that Kingdom, we are secure in the protection of His powerful arms.

Of course, we are speaking of spiritual matters here. Being in Christ doesn't guarantee that no bad thing will ever happen to us physically, in fact, just the opposite may be true. But in spiritual warfare and for eternity, Jesus, the Gate, provides us safe passage and secure dwelling in the presence of the Father. He cares, He points the way, He leads us, and He protects us as we put our lives in His hands. Praise be to the Gate!

LIFE ABUNDANT

John 10:10 *"The thief comes only to steal and kill and destroy;
I have come that they may have life, and have it to the full."*

Our society has gotten very brazen in its ability to flaunt its own importance in God's face. Sin is a concept that is either totally disregarded as some medieval holdover, or is caricatured as something to be laughed at, sneered at, or considered out of touch with reality. There was a point in time when most everyone had some concept of right and wrong, but in our post-modern world there are no absolutes, so what is permissible changes from person to person, and is in the eye of the beholder.

Jesus took, and takes, a different view of things. He knows that sin is a destroyer, and the thief mentioned in this verse is representative of sin personified at work. The destructive nature of sin is presented clearly as something that is not good for the flock of God, nor for mankind in general. Sin always leads people to a bad place, and Jesus wants more than anything to save us from that.

This is why He told the multitude that He had a better option. While living for the moment is the way many people live, Jesus offers life that builds people up instead of tearing them down. He wants us to not only have life, but to have the best life we could ever possibly experience.

The only way to this kind of fullness of life is found in the person of Jesus. He is the Good Shepherd who knows what is best for His sheep and knows how to put us in touch with circumstances and people that will shape us into something that we could never be on our own. Because we have in Him such a powerful ally, we can avoid the pain that sin brings, and claim the promises God offers to those who will by faith enter on to the way of holiness.

I have found that life is not always easy. There are struggles financially, physically, emotionally, and yes, even spiritually. However, along with those struggles we find the Good Shepherd there to encourage us, protect us, empower us, provide for us, and lead us. He never leaves those who trust in Him as their Lord. We may not see Him, or even have the sensation of His presence, but we do have His promise for His people, "I have come that they may have life, and have it to the full." Because of Jesus we don't just exist, we live!

THE GOOD SHEPHERD

John 10:11-13 *"I am the good shepherd. The good shepherd lays down his life for the sheep. The hired hand is not the shepherd who owns the sheep. So when he sees the wolf coming, he abandons the sheep and runs away. Then the wolf attacks the flock and scatters it. The man runs away because he is a hired hand and cares nothing for the sheep."*

Have you ever stopped to consider what the world would be like if God were not good? It's hard for me to even imagine such a thing, but I know there are some people who have developed bitterness toward God over things that have happened in their lives, and feel like He is anything but good. Nothing could be farther from the truth though.

When Jesus said that He is the Good Shepherd, He is relating to His disciples a fact that goes back to the core of His very nature. He is kind and compassionate in all His doings. In fact, when the Apostle Paul wrote about the fruit of the Spirit in Galatians 5:22-23, he was not just making up these attributes out of his own imagination. He was describing Jesus, who is the Divine Shepherd that has only the best of intentions for all His flock.

It is because there is so much danger in the world that the Good Shepherd stands between the harm that can come to His sheep and the adversary that is always ready to attack the flock. The very fact that Jesus came to the earth as a man shows the extent of love that the eternal God has for His creation, and the lengths to which He will go to protect it.

The hired hand is not presented in a very good light here, but it's because he cares for the sheep only up to the point that it would cost him something. If he becomes endangered, he runs and sacrifices the sheep because they don't mean as much to him as does his personal safety. This is just the opposite of the shepherd and the distinction is clear.

Again, we have to consider the goodness of God. The divine mission of Jesus was precisely to lay down His life for His sheep. He didn't come to avoid conflict, but to walk into the face of it for our sake. Though He didn't have to die, He chose to die in order that He might break the power of death and sin through His resurrection from the dead. He showed His flock not only His love, but the path we are to follow after Him. Because He was raised, we also shall be raised at the time of God's choosing.

KNOWING AND BEING KNOWN

> **John 10:14–15** *"I am the good shepherd, I know my sheep and my sheep know me—just as my Father knows me and I know the Father—and I lay down my life for the sheep."*

It's a wonderful thing to know, but an even more wonderful thing to be known. We may know who the leader of our country is, but if we are known by him then our self-worth and self-esteem is boosted greatly. It feels great to know how to do a trade or a hobby, but even more gratifying to realize that we have become known as someone who is proficient and celebrated for the that talent or ability.

Hear clearly the announcement that Jesus makes here. As we follow after Him, we are known by Him. He knows our name, where we live, what we do, and what we like and don't like. He knows us right down to how many hairs we have on our head and how many cells we have in our bodies. We are known in ways we can't even imagine and we are invited to know Him as well. What a wonderful realization! We matter to the King of kings!

Being the Good Shepherd, we can rest assured that He will always do what is in our best interest. He went so far as to go to the cross on our behalf, so why would we ever think that He wouldn't give us exactly what we need when we ask Him for it. He doesn't provide everything we want because that wouldn't be in our best interest, but He does specialize in giving us what we need. In fact, there are things Jesus gives us that we didn't even know we needed, or deserved. Like He knows us in ways that we can't imagine, He also looks out for us in ways that are beyond our ability to comprehend.

Only eternity will reveal the full love of the Savior for those who belong to Him. We will then see how what we considered to be missed opportunities, unscheduled interruptions, along with pleasant and unpleasant surprises often turned out to be the Master stepping in on our behalf to provide opportunity and protection for us.

Today I am so thankful that I know Jesus. He is the most wonderful friend I could ever have, for His mercies to me never end. But I am even more thankful today to realize that He knows me. He is fully aware of my limitations and knows how to lead me in the way that will be for my good. Being in the flock of the Good Shepherd is the greatest gift I will ever know.

YOUR PEN OR MINE?

John 10:16 *"I have other sheep that are not of this sheep pen. I must bring them also. They too will listen to my voice, and there shall be one flock and one shepherd."*

These words from Jesus have caused a bit of speculation over the centuries. Just who was it, or is it, that He was talking about? I have heard people say that this is proof of life in outer space because they felt like Jesus was referencing extra-terrestrial life on other planets. Some have suggested that this was simply Jesus' way of saying that the Jews scattered throughout the world at His time were in His scheme of priorities, while others have purposed that He was referring to those who were Gentiles and not of the Jewish family.

All of these ideas may be right in some regard because we don't have a lot of commentary from Jesus Himself about what He actually meant, but it appears to me that what He was speaking about concerned the masses of our world who had never yet heard His words of life. That includes those who were alive in the first century and all of us who have been born since then. We too are part of His flock today and are very concerned about hearing His voice and following the one true Shepherd.

This is a good verse for being more ecumenical in our faith practices. The members of Christ's flock often like to segregate and be with those of our similar ideologies and practices. There is nothing wrong with that if done in moderation, for we all have our own likes and dislikes when it comes to styles and formats for how we do worship. Too many times, however, we forget that we are all a part of the same flock and that the Master Shepherd doesn't favor one group over another. Whether we be Nazarenes, Methodists, Wesleyans, Lutherans, Presbyterians, Anglican, Pentecostal, Independent, Protestant, or Catholic, we have one Shepherd and His name is Jesus.

Because we are all a part of His royal bloodline, we are to consider the other members of the family truly as brothers and sisters. The size of our congregation doesn't matter and the focus of our emphasis for ministry is not on trial, as long as it glorifies the Father through His Son and brings peace and benefit to the body of Christ and our world. We may not be a part of Christ's original sheep pen, but we can give thanks that we are included now.

TRUE AUTHORITY

John 10:17–18 *"The reason my Father loves me is that I lay down my life—only to take it up again. No one takes it from me, but I lay it down of my own accord. I have authority to lay it down and authority to take it up again. This command I received from my Father."*

I love my two children, but because I love them so much, there is no way that I could ask them to lay down their life for me. That seems to be what Jesus is saying the Father is asking Him to do in these verses, but if we stop at the fact that the Father loves the Son, we have missed a big part of what is being said here.

When Jesus says that the Father is pleased that He lays down His life, it is closely connected to the fact that He has the power to take it up again. As awful as the cross was for Jesus, He knew that He was doing it because the Father wanted Him to, but also because He knew that death would be temporary. The resurrection to come was as sure as the nails that were driven through His hands and feet.

Each night I lay my head down on my pillow and go to sleep. When I do this there is no fear in losing consciousness, in fact, it is a welcome thing because my body and my mind is tired. To not sleep would be unnatural because we are designed to be renewed by rest after a time of activity.

The same is true when we think about death and the resurrection. Jesus didn't want to experience the torturous pain and suffering that was heaped upon Him. No sane person would want that. But He didn't fear death. The reality of waking up from death was as sure as our waking up from a night of sleep. He would rise to never die again, and this is what pleased the Father and led Him to do it.

We are promised a resurrection that is just as sure as the one that Jesus experienced. If we put our trust in Him for our salvation, when our time to face the last enemy called death comes, we can approach it with the same confidence that Jesus did. We too will awaken never to die again. It was the Father's plan for Jesus and it is the Father's plan for us. We will not sleep forever, but we will be changed into a new existence and will be more alive than we ever have been. This is done because the Father loves us, just as He loved the Son. It's a family thing and our "Dad" is the best there is.

AVOIDING DOUBLE-MINDEDNESS

John 10:19–21 At these words the Jews were again divided. Many of them said, "He is demon possessed and raving mad. Why listen to him?" But others said, "These are not the sayings of a man possessed by a demon. Can a demon open the eyes of the blind?"

There is no doubt that Jesus caused division wherever He went. He said that such a thing would happen in Matthew 10:34, "Do not suppose that I have come to bring peace to the earth. I did not come to bring peace, but a sword." Then He went on to quote from Micah 7:6, "For I have come to turn 'a man against his father, a daughter against her mother, a daughter-in-law against her mother-in-law—a man's enemies will be the members of his own household.'" Micah had been speaking against the waywardness of the nation of Israel, but Jesus spoke in the context of people becoming divided because of faith, or lack of faith, toward Him.

To this very day people are divided over the very concept of Jesus. Some see Him as the eternal Lord of all, the Son of God who has no equal in any other religion anywhere. Others see Him as a historical man only, or equal to all other religious figures, or an idea of a person that really never even existed. A public survey of people on any street corner would find folks all over the map in their opinions about Jesus.

It was the biblical author James that wrote about those who refuse to give Jesus the priority that He deserves when he said that the doubter "should not think he will receive anything from the Lord; he is a double-minded man, unstable in all he does" (James 1:7–8).

Christians today need to learn to take a stand and publicly defend their belief in Jesus as the Savior of the world. We don't need to obnoxious about it, but there should be no doubt in our minds about who He is or what He has done on our behalf. Either He is our Savior and Redeemer, or He is not. We can't find a middle ground here, for there is no room for compromise on this subject. We serve a King who requires complete loyalty from His subjects if we are going to have a place in His Kingdom.

The Jews of His day were confused concerning what to believe about Jesus, but on this side of the cross and this side of Pentecost, there should be no doubt in the mind of any believer. Jesus is Lord over all, forever!

WHY DO YOU DO WHAT YOU DO?

John 10:22–24 *Then came the Feast of Dedication at Jerusalem. It was winter, and Jesus was in the temple area walking in Solomon's Colonnade. The Jews gathered around him, saying, "How long will you keep us in suspense? If you are the Christ, tell us plainly."*

Inquiring minds want to know. At least the people surrounding Jesus at the Feast in Jerusalem certainly wanted to know about Him. This event was the Feast we would call Hanukkah, the celebration of the Jewish victory over the Greeks, and the rededication of the temple in Jerusalem. The belief of Hanukkah is that a miracle had taken place during the rededication of the temple that caused the eternal flame to burn for eight days on one day's worth of oil, hence the reason for the eight days of the Feast.

Because Jesus was a Jew and knew the Jewish customs and Feast schedules, He was there to celebrate along with His fellow countrymen, and because He was always comfortable being about His Father's house, He was a common figure at such events. But He had become a point of controversy because of His miracles and His words, so He had the crowds talking about Him continually, and the Jewish leaders were feeling threatened by this man they couldn't silence or control.

They demanded that He identify Himself, but He had not been keeping who He was a secret. He had spoken openly about His relationship to His Father, but what He was saying was not something that the religious leaders could accept, so they just kept pressing Him for more information. What they were actually after, was some way to trick Him, or trip Him up with His own words so that they would have grounds to negate His influence.

People today may ask such a thing about us. They might put it like this, "If you are a follower of Jesus, a Christian, then tell us plainly why you believe like you do?" It probably doesn't come out exactly like that in most situations, but once people have an awareness of our Christian testimony, they will not look at us the same way afterwards. They may scoff or make fun of what we say, or they may look for chinks in our armor of public witness in order to prove that there is nothing different about us, but they will see us differently once we go on record for Jesus. That's good, because then we can shine for Jesus, as He gives us grace to be a reflection of His light to the world.

HIS SHEEP LISTEN

John 10:25–27 *Jesus answered, "I did tell you, but you do not believe. The miracles I do in my Father's name speak for me, but you do not believe because you are not my sheep. My sheep listen to my voice; I know them and they follow me."*

If you could see Jesus do a miracle, I mean doing it now right in front of you, would it make any difference in what you believe about Him? As strange as it sounds, I believe there would be some who would say yes and some who would say no. Some would say yes because they say they have doubts right now, and seeing something impossible to happen, really happen, would push them in the direction of believing that Jesus truly is divine. Those who would say that seeing a miracle wouldn't change what they believe about Jesus, would most likely take that stance because they already have faith in Him as the eternal Son of God.

However, in this setting of scripture the people around Jesus have already seen what He had been doing: healing the lame, feeding the multitudes, and opening the eyes of the blind. But though these things convinced some that He was the promised Messiah, other witnesses remained blind to the possibility that God was involved in His actions in any way.

Human nature being what it is, the skepticism of this crowd has to be expected. Moses called down plagues on Egypt and at God's direction caused the Red Sea to be parted, but only days after the miracles occurred, there were those who grumbled, complained, and wanted to go back to Egypt. When Jesus spoke words of life and performed mighty acts of God, the mood of the crowd hadn't changed much from the days of Moses. Even the Apostle Thomas wanted to see the nail prints in the hands and feet of Jesus—after the resurrection—but Jesus put His blessing on those who had not seen, but still believed.

Today we are in the camp of those who have not seen. The question is whether or not we will join the number who will believe in Jesus as the Christ of God anyway. We may not have had a Damascus Road experience like the Apostle Paul, but we do have the Holy Spirit who is always ready to draw us to the Savior. Jesus longs for us to be His sheep, the members of His flock. If we hear His voice and follow, His desire for us is fulfilled.

A RELATIONSHIP WITH CHRIST

John 10:28–30 *I give them eternal life, and they shall never perish; no one can snatch them out of my hand. My Father, who has given them to me, is greater than all; no one can snatch them out of my Father's hand. I and the Father are one.*

These verses are some of the favorite proof-texts for those who chose to believe in the doctrine of eternal security. At first glance it may appear that they have a case, because it sounds like once we are in Christ, no one can change that state of grace, regardless of one's beliefs or actions after that time. In this view, no one who has been saved can fall from grace.

However, when we take this view, we are missing a very important piece of what Jesus is saying. Once we are in Christ it is true that "no one can snatch us out of the Father's hand," but it nowhere declares that we can't change our minds and go a different direction.

Certainly, anyone who comes honestly to Jesus in repentance and a desire to follow Him will truly have a life-changing experience. When we are changed from darkness into the light, we would be hard-pressed to call it something else. But the truth of the matter is that we don't live continually on the introduction level with Jesus. We are to go deeper in His grace and develop a relationship with Him that will cause us to be intimate friends.

I met the woman who would become my wife back in 1973. That introduction was an experience that can't be repeated because you only have one opportunity to make a first impression. But after we started dating and eventually married, and then lived together for the decades that have followed, a relationship has developed that is far deeper than what we experienced at our first meeting, or even in the first days of our marriage. We have grown in this relationship over the years because we chose to do so. Either of us could have ended it if we had so desired, but are together because we choose to be.

Walking with Jesus is like that. We are in a relationship with Him and we can get out of it if we want. It would be poorest choice we could ever make, but Jesus does not hold us hostage. We are His because He chose us, and also because we choose to remain in that relationship with Him. Love grows as our walk with Him continues, and that love keeps us securely together.

STONES AGAIN?

John 10:31–33 *Again the Jews picked up stones to stone him, but Jesus said to them, "I have shown you many great miracles from the Father. For which of these do you stone me?" "We are not stoning you for any of these," replied the Jews, "but for blasphemy, because you, a mere man, claim to be God."*

If I claimed to be God, it would be incorrect and blasphemous. If you claimed to be God, we would have to draw the same conclusion. However, when Jesus claimed to be God, it was as true as any statement could ever be. The problem with the claim to the Jews who were threatening to stone was in the fact that they didn't believe He was who He said He was.

There is it. Reality is one thing, but perception of reality usually determines the outcome of what we claim to be real. In the realm of scientific dogma, I can claim that gravity doesn't exist, but the facts and data that have been proven over and over again state that gravity on our planet is very, very real. A theory is not reality, no matter how desperately we want to believe it.

Jesus had proved His claim to be the Son of God repeatedly throughout John's Gospel. John carefully recorded the miracles of Jesus turning the water into wine, healing a lame man, feeding the multitudes, walking on the water, and opening the eyes of the blind. His teaching in the temple courts and throughout His travels had borne truth like no one had ever heard before. He could make the claim of His connection to the heavenly Father because He had the proven track record to back it up.

What we have to realize is that when people make up their minds as to their version of the truth, stubborn pride and ignorance take priority over any level of facts that can be presented. We see that played out continually on social media and in the current political atmosphere. We want our side, our views to be true, we believe them to be true, and no one is going to change our minds and convince us to think differently. This is why social media arguments as such a waste of time.

These Jews were like that, so they picked up stones and threatened to use them on Jesus to shut Him up. Somehow, the message of love that Jesus was teaching was lost on them. Sadly, it's lost on a lot of people still, but Jesus will keep right on loving just the same.

DOING WHAT THE FATHER DOES

John 10:34–39 Jesus answered them, "Is it not written in your Law, 'I have said you are gods?' If he called them 'gods' to whom the word of God came—and the Scripture cannot be broken—what about the one whom the Father set apart as his very own and sent into the world? Why then do you accuse me of blasphemy because I said, 'I am God's Son'? Do not believe me unless I do what my Father does. But if I do it, even though you do not believe me, believe the miracles, that you may know and understand that the Father is in me, and I in the Father." Again they tried to seize him, but he escaped their grasp.

Jesus had a wonderful way of using scripture to confound those who would attack Him. Because He is the Creator of all things, there is no doubt that He would have a better grasp of what the writer's original intent was than His enemies would, for He had inspired the prophet to write what he did. We are not told of any limitation He may have had concerning His understanding, but even if He had to have relearned everything as a man, by this time in His earthly walk He was the Master of all that was written.

The main point of these verses though is that Jesus was defending His actions because He was only doing what His Father does. The Father is always in the business of restoring, redeeming, and healing, so it is a natural thing for the Son to be in the same line of work. Jesus had just brought sight to a man who was born blind. In doing so He not only showed His power and ability to bring about the healing, but also the love and compassion that compelled Him to do so.

The Jews who were constantly trying to trap Him and trip Him up couldn't understand Him. He spoke to them as the Good Shepherd, but they had no interest in being a part of His flock. Their propensity for violence toward Him only condemned their actions, because Jesus never did anything that would be worthy of stoning or any other kind of punishment. He did what His Father does, just as His enemies did what their father does.

We each have to choose which side to which we are going to belong. We can side with the one who cares about people and the challenges they face, or we can side with the group that cares about themselves and keeping score. Jesus' way calls for love, and that is the way we are called to also.

BE IT EVER SO HUMBLE...

John 10:40–42 *Then Jesus went back across the Jordan to the place where John had been baptizing in the early days. Here he stayed and many people came to him. They said, "Though John never performed a miraculous sign, all that John said about this man was true." And in that place many believed in Jesus.*

Going home can be a wonderful thing. When I am away for an extended period of time, it's always a special feeling when I arrive safely and get to enjoy the things that are familiar to me, and I have the privilege of just relaxing. As has been said many times, "There's no place like home!"

Though this setting by the Jordan wasn't exactly home for Jesus, it was where His ministry began at the time when He was baptized by John. It was here that the heavenly Spirit settled on Him, the same Spirit that would lead Him out to the desert for a period of prayer and fasting before He would launch out into His preaching, teaching, and healing ministry.

This homecoming was no vacation for Jesus. Though He had left the limelight of Jerusalem, the water's edge offered Him no rest. The people still came, the needs were still there, and He continued to meet those needs in accordance with the power and will of the Father. The end result of all this activity at the Jordan River was that many more people believed in Him—and that made His journey and the sacrifices involved in it, worth the trip.

It's hard not to feel a bit sorry for Jesus here. He has been under attack by the Jewish leaders because of His mighty works and His relationship to the Father. He had come away from the city to rest, to regroup, and to find a place to continue teaching His disciples. In the coming days He would be facing many trials, pressures, and even more sacrifices as He made His way toward the cross. The Jordan River was a place of refuge that had special memories for Him, but a place of rest it was not.

Could we take a lesson from this? Could we possibly take from this passage that the followers of Jesus, like their Master, are never off duty. We don't take vacations from representing Him, loving our neighbors, doing good works, and glorifying God. As long as people are coming to faith, can we not be about the Father's business as a lifetime commitment? Our time too is short, but so is the time of those who need Jesus, so let's not quit too soon!

SICK, BUT FOR A REASON

John 11:1–3 *Now a man named Lazarus was sick. He was from Bethany, the village of Mary and her sister Martha. This Mary, whose brother Lazarus now lay sick, was the same one who poured perfume on the Lord and wiped his feet with her hair. So the sisters sent word to Jesus, "Lord, the one you love is sick."*

John was getting a little ahead of himself here. The story of Mary anointing Jesus with perfume will not happen until we reach chapter twelve of this book, but John used a little bit of writer's license as he foreshadowed what will take place later.

We are not told much about Lazarus. We only know from the Bible that he was a friend that Jesus loved, along with his two sisters, Martha and Mary. Martha was the busy bee, working to supply the needs of Jesus and His disciples (Luke 10:38-42), while Mary seemed more content to just be near Jesus and listen to His words. Luke also tells us that the home belonged to Martha, so how Lazarus fits into the story isn't exactly clear.

What is clear though, is that Lazarus was in a bad way. From these verses we learn that he was ill, but we are not told the cause of the illness. It was serious enough, however, that Martha and Mary saw the need of calling upon Jesus to come to their aid. Like a good example for the rest of us, when we face needs in our lives, these ladies realized just how vital Jesus was to their situation.

We know a little more about Mary. The fact that she would pour her very expensive perfume on Jesus's feet and dry them with her hair in chapter twelve, tells of the appreciation she felt toward Jesus as a result of what He would do for her brother, and for her humble devotion to one she considered to be not only her friend, but also her Master.

The sickness of Lazarus was not something that was sent from God, but it was something God would use to bring glory to His Son and cause many people to put their faith in Him. Bad things sometime end up being good things when they result in people finding faith in Jesus in the midst of their crisis. Therefore, we shouldn't always pray for healing, but for a heart to bring God praise out of whatever situation we may find ourselves. Giving God an opportunity to work will be the best thing that could happen to us.

GLORIFYING THE FATHER
AT ALL COSTS

John 11:4–6 *When he heard this, Jesus said, "This sickness will not end in death. No, it is for God's glory so that God's Son may be glorified. Jesus loved Martha and her sister and Lazarus. Yet when he heard that Lazarus was sick, he stayed where he was two more days.*

In the most recent statistics to which I have access, in the year 2015, fifty-five million people on our planet died. Every day in almost every newspaper around the world there is an obituary page which lists the deaths of people who have recently died in that particular area. Death for mankind has been around since Adam and Eve were barred from the Garden of Eden, so by now one would think that people would be getting used to the idea. However, we all know that is not so.

Like most of us, the people in this story were accustomed to death and also most of us consider death a foe to be conquered for as long as possible. In fact, even the Apostle Paul stated that "The last enemy to be destroyed is death" (I Corinthians 15:26). Though death is inevitable for all people, we usually go down fighting it to the very end.

Therefore, it should have been a happy bit of news when Jesus assured His disciples that the sickness Lazarus was experiencing would not end in death. They knew by this time that Jesus had the power to do what He wanted to do, and if He said that Lazarus was going to get well, then he was going to get well.

Of course, we who know the rest of the story know that Lazarus does indeed die, but we also know that death was not the end of his story. Actually, death is what gave Lazarus his story. Without death there is no resurrection, for when Jesus comes on the scene, even the forces of physical death cannot win.

All of this was coming to a head so that the Father and the Son would be glorified. Jesus lived to bring His Father glory and because of that, He too would be exalted. This opportunity sprang out of the love Jesus had for Lazarus, Martha, and Mary, but most of all for His heavenly Father. Some waiting would be required, but when the situation was eventually turned over to Jesus, an amazing miracle would happen. Come to think of it, that's just what happens when we turn things over to Him today.

WALKING IN THE LIGHT
OR THE DARKNESS

John 11:7–10 *Then he said to his disciples, "Let us go back to Judea." "But Rabbi," they said, "a short while ago the Jews tried to stone you, and yet you are going back there?" Jesus answered, "Are there not twelve hours of daylight? A man who walks by day will not stumble, for he sees by this world's light. It is when he walks by night that he stumbles for he has no light."*

We are not told exactly how long Jesus had been residing along the Jordan River after He left Jerusalem, but we know it was some period of time between the winter Feast of Dedication, or Hanukah (10:22), and Passover (11:55), which took place in the spring. He was there following extreme confrontation with the Jewish leaders in Jerusalem, and it would seem likely that His disciples were relieved to be out from under the pressure that such powerful leaders in their capital city could produce. It had become common knowledge that these leaders despised Jesus to the point that violence against Him was a real possibility.

However, when Jesus announced His return and received the obvious questions concerning such a decision, there was no hesitation. Jesus knew what the disciples did not know. He knew that His next action would bring glory to the Father and glory to His own person and ministry, and such a miracle would never happen if He stayed safely by the water's edge at the Jordan.

To His disciples it seemed that Jesus was walking blindly, possibly into a trap. But Jesus knew that this trip would end up in a good way for those who were hurting, for Lazarus, and for the plan that the Father had worked out for Him. He wasn't walking in the darkness of indecision, but in the daylight that communion with the Father brings. He was in no danger of stumbling because the Father ordered His every step.

This is where Jesus shines brightly for us. Fear can be such a paralyzing factor when we are trying to make decisions. That fear is only multiplied when we have to make a decision and it has the possibility of going badly. But if we will learn from Jesus' example, we will see that when we walk in fellowship with the Father, we never have to be afraid of the outcome. God is in charge. We must never forget that fact. We can rest in His Lordship and know that He never fails or makes a mistake.

HE KNOWS WHAT WE DON'T

John 11:11–13 *After he had said this, he went on to tell them, "Our friend Lazarus has fallen asleep, but I am going there to wake him up. His disciples replied, "Lord, if he sleeps, he will get better." Jesus had been speaking of his death, but his disciples thought he meant natural sleep.*

I love it when the plan that Jesus had already decided on started coming together. The very idea that He knew exactly what steps to take to get the glory to the Father, showed the level of confidence and faith that flowed through Him.

The fact that He had waited for two days after the message of Lazarus's sickness had come to Him from Martha and Mary, only sharpened the impact of what He was doing. He wanted to make sure that Lazarus was dead and that everyone knew it. This miracle wasn't going to be about opening the eyes of the blind or healing a lame man. This mighty act was going to demonstrate that He was Lord over the very powers of life and death. He wanted Lazarus to be pronounced dead, buried, and beyond the time of any possibility of recovery before He would intervene. There would be no doubt about His abilities when people would later witness this upcoming miracle.

As confident as Jesus was, the disciples played a role that was just the opposite. They were in the dark concerning the real condition of Lazarus, just as they were in the dark concerning why Jesus would want to take a chance on His life and go anywhere near Jerusalem. People hated Him there. People wanted to kill Him there. Lazarus was just too close to where the enemies of Jesus resided, so since they didn't know at this point that Lazarus was dead, it would seem foolish to venture back into Judea. We really can't blame them. It's just that Jesus knew what they didn't.

Jesus still knows far more than we do, and there are times when we wish He would just speak plainly to us so that we could be on the same page with His plans for our life. However, just as He gradually broke the news about Lazarus to His disciples then, He will slowly give us what we need to know also if we will trust in Him and listen for His voice. He doesn't want us to live in ignorance, but He does want us to live in faith. He will bring us in on His plan for our life just when we need to hear it, and when He does, then like the disciples are soon to discover, we will be glad He did what He did.

DEATH IS NOT THE END

John 11:14–16 *So then he told them plainly, "Lazarus is dead, and for your sake I am glad I was not there, so that you may believe. But let us go to him." Then Thomas (called Didymus) said to the rest of the disciples, "Let us also go, that we may die with him."*

At this point the cat comes out of the bag. Jesus no longer shields His followers from the grim reality that is facing His friends back in Judea. Lazarus is dead. He is not just sick, not just sleeping a natural sleep, or even experiencing some kind of induced coma, he is dead, buried, and his family is in a deep state of grief.

It may sound surprising then to hear that Jesus is glad. He is not saying that He is glad that Lazarus is dead, per say, but He is glad that his death is going to provide an opportunity for faith to be initiated in the unbelievers, strengthened for those who already believe, and solidified completely for His disciples. All of a sudden, the prospect of going back to Judea to die with Jesus, as Thomas suggests, changes in its meaning as they would start to realize that their Lord dominates even the dark world of bereavement.

Certainly, it is commendable for Thomas to want to stay with Jesus right to the bitter end, but it doesn't say much for his understanding of the situation or of his knowledge of the King of kings' capability. At this point in time his reasoning is clouded by his personal devotion to Jesus as a man, but His divinity is still being questioned on some level. In fact, even after the resurrection of Jesus, it was Thomas who wouldn't believe his Lord was truly alive until he would be allowed to put his fingers in the nail prints on Jesus' hands and feet. There was a lot of growing to do and a lot of revelation to come for these disciples over the ensuing days.

We have to ask ourselves the question at this point, "What would we have done?" Knowing what we know about the plots against Jesus in Jerusalem, knowing that there was possibly death waiting for Jesus just down the road, would we have acted any differently from these disciples if we had been in their shoes? It's highly unlikely.

This is why the resurrection makes a difference. Because Jesus came back from the cross, our faith can be solidified. Like Lazarus and millions of others, we can know that Jesus is Lord over all, including life and death.

TOO LATE?

John 11:17–20 *On his arrival, Jesus found that Lazarus had already been in the tomb for four days. Bethany was less than two miles from Jerusalem, and many Jews had come to Martha and Mary to comfort them in the loss of their brother. When Martha heard that Jesus was coming, she went out to meet him, but Mary stayed at home.*

When a person has been pronounced dead and has been in the tomb for four days, it's usually a pretty good sign that said person is not coming back. It's no wonder that Martha, Mary, and their friends had given up all hope of seeing their brother and friend again, but when Jesus arrived on the scene, something must have started a flicker of faith within the heart of Martha. She determined to go and meet Jesus even if her sister was too deep in her grief to be moved to action at this time.

We can only wonder what was going through Martha's mind as she made her way to meet Jesus. Perhaps she was rehearsing what she would say to Him, or maybe form the question that she had to have been thinking, "Jesus, where have you been?" She had sent word to Jesus that Lazarus was sick days ago. Even from the banks of the Jordan River, which was less that twenty miles to the east, Jesus could have been walked that distance in much less time than He actually took to get there. There had to have been some angst within her because she had no doubt been waiting day after day for some sign that Jesus had gotten her message, and was on His way to save the day. "Jesus, where have you been?"

We can identify with Martha. When we go to the Lord in prayer, we often have the same kind of impatience that we can imagine that Martha had here. "Lord, don't You know I have a need?" "Lord, don't You care that I'm hurting?" "Are you going to come to my aid, or aren't You?" In our microwave religious fervor, we want results and we want them now.

It was the biblical writer, James, who said, "that the testing of your faith develops perseverance" (James 1:3). Who are we to rush the Lord and tell Him what He should do anyway? If we stand firm in our faith, we will find that Jesus always provides what we need, so if we need deliverance from this world, He can provide that. If we need an answer in this world, He can provide that. We stand in our faith because He's always worth waiting for.

"WHY, LORD, WHY?"

John 11:21–22 *"Lord," Martha said to Jesus, "If you had been here, my brother would not have died. But I know that even now God will give you whatever you ask."*

If Martha demonstrates anything here, she shows her faith. She believed in Jesus to such a degree that she is convinced His presence would have kept her brother from dying, and that even in this late hour there was still a glimmer of hope He could do something. She believed Jesus had the ear of His Father and that all He would need to do was ask of Him and it would be done. That, without a doubt, is faith.

Martha is an example for the rest of us. She knows Jesus as her Lord, she has faith that He can change the circumstances of life—even the impossible ones—and she believes that the Son and the Father are one in power and purpose. I would gladly serve the Lord alongside a person like Martha.

Perhaps then, this is a good place for us to do a little self-examination. Do we have this kind of faith? Do we commit our daily walk to Jesus, knowing that His presence in our life and activities can actually have an impact on all we do? Does our relationship with Jesus reflect the belief that He has the ear of His Father in all things?

These questions and the answers that we would be put with them tell a lot about our level of faith in Jesus. We may have some hesitation because we don't have the face-to-face encounters with Him that Martha had, but we have something that Martha didn't have, namely the Holy Spirit of Christ that has come to live within us. Martha had access to Jesus when He was in the neighborhood, but we who have received His Spirit into our lives have access to Him twenty-four hours a day, seven days a week, three-hundred and sixty-five days a year. We are never out of His sight or out of His care.

For me, it all goes back to the first word that Martha uttered in this verse, "Lord." Though it could have been merely a term of respect that she offered to Him, for me it goes much deeper. Allowing Jesus to be the Lord of our lives is key to the level of faith we are going to put in Him. Knowing that He is the King of kings, Savior of all mankind, and Redeemer of all His creation, gives me a new level of hope and faith that I could never muster on my own. Because Jesus is Lord, all things are possible.

THE BEST IS YET TO COME

John 11:23–26 *Jesus said to her, "Your brother will rise again." Martha answered, "I know he will rise again in the resurrection at the last day." Jesus said to her, "I am the resurrection and the life. He who believes in me will live, even though he dies; and whoever lives and believes in me will never die. Do you believe this?"*

Christians seem to be really confused about the resurrection these days. Often the discussion about it leads to a mixing of going to heaven after we die, and a belief in a rapture of the church out of this world, which though popular since the inception of the idea in the 1820's, is found nowhere in the Bible. Because so many ideas float around church circles, it pays for us to hear what Jesus says on the matter.

In Jewish thought, there will be a resurrection of both the good and the bad at the end of the age. A good start in checking this out can be found in Daniel 12:1–2. That idea is reinforced in the New Testament by the Apostle Paul in I Corinthians 15. Someday, when God declares that it is time for the world as we know it to come to an end, it will happen, and all the bodies of the faithful dead will be resurrected and be made into new eternal bodies just like the one Jesus had when He was resurrected. The essence of our existence that goes to be with the Lord after we die will be reunited with our resurrection body, and we will then serve the Lord for eternity as heaven and earth become one. This subject is too complex to deal with in this short space, but that's the gist of what the Bible teaches.

What Jesus is saying here, however, is that He is in charge of the resurrection. Lazarus didn't have to wait until the last day to be raised, for Jesus has the ultimate say over life and death, which is why the grave could not hold Him. We who believe in Him will live in His presence in this life, but after this life we will continue to enjoy Him, but on a much more intimate scale.

There really is no reason for any Christian to ever fear death. It may be natural to fear the process of dying, for no one wants to go through the pain of that experience any more than Jesus wanted to go to the cross. However, with our faith in Christ for our salvation we can face the last enemy and know that the Lord we served here will be waiting for us over there.

DO YOU BELIEVE?

John 11:27 *"Yes, Lord," she told him. "I believe that you are the Christ, the Son of God, who was to come into the world."*

Finally, someone gets it and spells it out! We only have the written word to relay this message to us, but I have to think that if we had a video recording of this conversation, at this point Jesus would break into a huge grin and give Martha a big bear hug. After all the lies being told about Him, after all the enemies trying to smear Him and threaten Him, even after the bumbling disciples not grasping what He was putting right in front of them, Martha, a Jewish first-century small-town woman, finally gets it. Jesus is the Christ, the long-awaited Messiah, the Son of God who has come into the world. What an astounding revelation from the lips of His humble servant!

Martha's words came in response to the question that Jesus asked in the previous verse, namely, "Do you believe this?" He was asking if she believed that He was in charge of resurrection matters. Her answer here, declares that she does indeed, believe.

When a person gets to the core of Jesus' message, this is the conclusion that comes to light. We get so much fluff spread through our world concerning Jesus that it's hard to wade through it sometimes. We are told that He was a good man, a great teacher, a radial revolutionary, and some even claim that He didn't actually exist. There is no end of speculation about Him, for no one ever has impacted, or ever will impact our world to the degree that He has. Certainly, He is bigger than life and the most influential person of all time.

What matters though is whether or not we can declare with Martha, "I believe you are the Christ, the Son of God." Only faith like this can save us from our sins and connect us with His Holy Spirit that will transform our lives. This is not about church attendance, donations in the offering, being baptized, being busy, or taking communion. This is about faith, raw faith that elevates the position of Jesus in our life to the place of Lord.

Today is a good day to make sure that our faith in Him is sincere and complete. Others are entitled to their opinion about Him, but we who have met Jesus know that Martha was absolutely on the right track, and someday in eternity I want to thank her for her testimony.

THE GOOD SISTER

John 11:28–29 *And after she had said this, she went back and called her sister Mary aside. "The teacher is here," she said, "and is asking for you." When Mary heard this, she got up quickly and went to him.*

We are not told why Mary didn't come with Martha to meet Jesus while He was still outside the village. We don't know if it was because her grief was so great that she was unable to function, or whether she didn't know that Jesus had arrived, or if there might have been some other reason. We do know that when Martha relayed to her that Jesus was asking for her, she didn't waste any time responding to His summons.

Mary is often thought of as the "good sister." She is the one who sat at the feet of Jesus rather than busying herself with household duties like her sister Martha in Luke 10:38–42. However, on this occasion, it was Martha who took the initiative to go to Jesus while Mary had to be called to His side.

What we can take from this is that Jesus is faithful to call for us even when we don't ask for Him. Though He initiates the divine call upon all our lives, when we don't respond to His presence, He seeks us out, just like He did Mary. As He asked to see her, He continually is asking us to draw near to Him as well. I don't think it is stretching this story too much to realize that John's recording of this event has a lesson for all of us who read it.

When did Jesus first ask for you, and how did you respond? Did you go running to be with Him like Mary in this story, or did it take some coaxing for you to yield to His invitation? Some run from His presence, or run from His call on their lives, but that doesn't stop Jesus from calling those He loves. Whether we answer immediately, or stray away from His request for years, He never stops caring about us and never stops wanting to heal the hurt that we feel.

Both Martha and Mary are in a bit of shock because of all that has happened in recent days. Jesus was informed about their brother, but He didn't get there in time to save Him from dying. He does come on the scene days later, but no one knows what He is going to do. The important thing is that when His call goes out, we are to respond as quickly as possible. If we will, then we will find that He is able to meet our need in ways we couldn't imagine. If we don't, then we will be left to wonder what He could have done.

"WHY, LORD, WHY?" (ROUND TWO)

John 11:30–32 *Now Jesus had not yet entered the village, but was still at the place where Martha had met him. When the Jews who had been with Mary in the house, comforting her, noticed how quickly she got up and went out, they followed her, supposing she was going to the tomb to mourn there. When Mary reached the place where Jesus was and saw him, she fell at his feet and said, "Lord, if you had been here, my brother would not have died."*

Though they came to Jesus at different times, the reaction to His presence was the same for both Martha and Mary. Each of them said to Him, "Lord, if you had been here, my brother would not have died." Their confidence in the ability of Jesus to fix broken situations was firm, for Jesus had never met a foe He hadn't conquered.

However, death was a new enemy for them. They hadn't dealt with it before in this manner, and now from all that their previous experiences had taught them, there was no turning this around. People just don't come back from the dead. Jesus was too late, and though He might have been able to do something if He had gotten there sooner, now Lazarus was dead and buried, and they didn't see any way to fix that.

Mary came with an entourage. They weren't requested by Jesus, but because they were a support system for Mary, they followed her when she suddenly went out. Perhaps they hadn't heard Martha speak to Mary and tell her that Jesus wanted to see her. Most likely they just wanted to be near Mary in her hour of grief to help supply whatever needs she might have. Friends like that are dear and precious, and for their care here they are going to experience something that they would never forget.

If this story were an opera, the music would be building in its intensity as it approached the climax of Jesus at the tomb. Jesus is aware of all that is going on, but within Himself He is also being stirred by the pain experienced first by Martha, then Mary, and now also the friends that have come along with Mary. We get the feeling that something is about to happen. The King is about to make His move.

This is a story about how the Master feels when we bring our needs to Him. He is not unaware or unconcerned, but ready and able always to meet us at the point of our pain. He is able to do more than we can imagine.

"COME AND SEE"

John 11:33–35 *When Jesus saw her weeping, and the Jews who had come along with her also weeping, he was deeply moved in spirit and troubled. "Where have you laid him?" he asked. "Come and see, Lord," they replied. Jesus wept.*

The stage is set. Martha is in tears. Mary is in tears. The crowd of friends and mourners that have followed Mary are also grieving. It's getting to be too much for Jesus and He is troubled in His Spirit.

This is where the story really gets interesting. You see, Jesus already knew what He intended to do about the death of Lazarus. He made clear to His disciples back at the start of this chapter that this death wouldn't end in death, but would result in the Father being glorified. He knew that He had the power to do what He intended to do, and that there is nothing that could hinder His divine will. He would raise Lazarus from the dead, all would be well with everyone, God would be exalted, and it certainly wouldn't hurt His own reputation any either. So, the question is, "Why did Jesus cry?" With everything going exactly according to His plan, why did He weep?

Verse 35 is the shortest verse in the Bible, but perhaps it has the biggest message of any two words in the Holy Scriptures. Jesus wept because He cared. He cared about the pain His friends were feeling, and He couldn't bear to see them in such agony. We are told earlier that He loved Lazarus, and Martha, and Mary. It was this love that caused Him to feel what they felt, and He cried because He cared for them.

I hope we can realize from this that Jesus still cares. He notices when we hurt. His compassion extends to us to the point that He can feel our pain. When we have been moved by sadness, He grieves along with us. When we feel hopeless, He cares enough to provide hope for us.

Certainly, there are enough bad things at work in our world to keep Jesus crying all the time. Wars, poverty, sickness, abuse, and sadness are all from the impact of sin on our world. As a result, Jesus is building His Kingdom that will eventually deliver all those who come to Him from its effects. Lives are being changed one at a time, and though we may have to go through a time of grief like the folks in this story, the resurrection is coming and sadness will be turned to joy. Because He cares, the Kingdom of God is ours.

DOES HE CARE?

John 11:36–37 *Then the Jews said, "See how he loved him!" But some of them said, "Could not he who opened the eyes of the blind man have kept this man from dying?"*

The people who stood outside the tomb of Lazarus were in many ways in awe of Jesus. They had heard of His exploits, and perhaps some of them had even seen the mighty works He had brought to pass. But watching Him as He stood weeping next to the burial place of Lazarus, they saw something they hadn't witnessed before. They saw the heart of God. Though they may not have been convinced yet that He was truly the Son of God, when they saw His tears, the fact that He was the Son of Man was very evident to them.

The old saying goes, "People don't care how much you know until they know how much you care." Jesus was putting His humanity on full display and was vulnerable enough to reveal His broken heart. He wept because there was such a sense of grief among the people that surrounded Him, and the fact that He cared didn't escape those who looked on.

In an age when church altars are non-existent, or barren too much of the time, there is a danger for the people of God to appear calloused to the needs of our world. When the saints of God are under a burden for the lostness of mankind, for our societies that ignore their Creator, and for families that have lost their way, it shows up in our tears. When the tears dry up, the watching world assumes that we don't have any more answers than they do, and that we have just given up hope along with our concern for their well-being.

These verses should be a wake-up call for the representatives of Christ to fall on their faces before God until the pain of a world in need brings us to tears. Such tears on behalf of others are the seeds of revival that will move us personally, and the church around us, to our God-called place of ministry and evangelism. Nothing can ever replace the need for burden-bearing saints of God. No church can honestly claim to be alive without them.

"O Lord, break our hearts for the sake of others, like the heart of Jesus broke because of the pain people felt around Him at the tomb of Lazarus. Give us tears as our food, and sleepless nights in sorrow as we cry out to You for the souls of our family and friends. In the name of Jesus we pray, amen."

WE REALLY WANT TO BELIEVE!

John 11:38–40 *Jesus, once more deeply moved, came to the tomb. It was a cave with a stone laid across the entrance. Take away the stone," he said. "But, Lord," said Martha, the sister of the dead man, "by this time there is a bad odor, for he has been there four days. Then Jesus said, "Did I not tell you that if you believed, you would see the glory of God?"*

It looked as if Jesus was about to expose a distressing sight to the world. After four days being buried with no embalming or preservative of any kind, the body of Lazarus would not be a pleasant sight to look upon. The smell from the decomposing corpse would be strong and difficult to stomach, as Martha was quick to point out. After all, she loved her brother and she wanted to remember him as he was, not see the rotting flesh that would no doubt greet them when the tomb was opened.

Martha had said earlier that she believed that Jesus was the Messiah, but when push came to shove, and Jesus was calling for the grave to opened, her faith wavered. Jesus had to gently remind her, "Did I not tell you that if you believed, you would see the glory of God?" It's easy to forget faith when facts seem to be to the contrary.

Martha is like so many of us. We want to believe in Jesus, no, we do believe in Jesus. We believe that He is the Son of God and that all power is within His grasp. But like Martha, we have a tendency to see the physical evidence of life before us and forget that Jesus operates on a different plane. He is not limited to the natural, for He is supernatural. The grave may be a difficult place for us, but Jesus has power over both death and the grave.

When we are faced with the difficult moments of life, that is when we need Jesus the most, and that is when He shines the brightest. Whether it is in the hospital room, the prayer room, the morgue, or the mountaintop, we can know that He is able to meet our need and display His Lordship before our eyes. Those times of doubt may sweep over us, but the gentle whisper of His Spirit will remind us, "Did I not tell you that if you believed, you would see the glory of God?"

Today there may be challenges to our faith, but the challenge is all on our part, not the Lord's. He can do the impossible and provide us faith to hold fast to Him. In these times, God is able, just like always.

THE STONE MUST GO

John 11:41–42 *So they took away the stone. Then Jesus looked up and said, "Father, I thank you that you have heard me. I know that you always hear me, but I said this for the benefit of the people standing here, that they may believe that you sent me.*

Moving the stone was an intricate part of what happened at this grave. Jesus was ready to do a miracle, but there was this big rock that was in His way. Inside the tomb it was dark, and the tomb was sealed to keep the odor in and keep people out. Inside there was death, but Jesus was ready to change that reality into a new one.

If the stone had not been moved, then even if Lazarus came back to life, no one would know it. He had been wrapped in grave clothes. His hands and feet were tied. His face was bound up with a cloth. Even if he heard the voice of the Master calling him to life, he would be unable to respond, and no one on the outside of the cave would know that life had returned to the inside of the cave. The stone had to go or there would be no miracle witnessed that would bring glory to the Father.

How often our churches are like this cave. Inside the sanctuaries of churches, wonderful things happen. God is praised, people are restored from sin's bondage, and joyful experiences take place. The problem is that like the cave in this story, if the good things that happen on the inside of the church don't get witnessed by people on the outside of the church, then no one is aware that miracles are still taking place.

The task for the church of the 21st century is to remove whatever stones are impeding the Good News from getting out into the neighborhoods of our land. The Father needs to be glorified, and sometimes all that it takes to make that happen is for people to move the stone when Jesus tells them to. Jesus never specified who should move the rock. It wasn't an angelic rock or a demonic rock. It was just a rock, and anyone could move it. But obedience to do what Jesus said to do made the difference between Lazarus coming out of the tomb, or remaining in it until he died again.

It's so true that only Jesus Christ can raise the dead and bring life where there was none. But it's also true that anyone of us can take away the stone so that the miracles of God can be seen by others.

"Let Him Go!"

John 11:43–44 *When he had said this, Jesus called in a loud voice, "Lazarus, come out!" The dead man came out, his hands and feet wrapped with strips of linen, and a cloth around his face. Jesus said to them, "Take off the grave clothes and let him go."*

If it weren't in the Word of God, no one would ever believe that such a thing had happened. Jesus merely spoke the word and Lazarus, that lifeless corpse in the tomb, immediately had his heart start beating again, his brain began functioning, blood started flowing through his previously deteriorating veins and arteries, as new life was restored to a body that was dead to the dead, dead, dead. The miracle could not be denied.

I would love to have been there to see the faces and hear the shrieks of delight from the people that stood around the grave of Lazarus. I would also love to have seen the expression on the face of Lazarus as he slowly hopped into the light so that his friends could unwrap him from his mummy-like state, and free him from his death bonds garb. He would be telling this story for years to come, and probably gained celebrity status that he would never be able to evade until time would take its toll, and he would die a natural death once again. We have plenty of testimonies on record as to how people have been born again because of their encounter with Jesus, but Lazarus is one of the few people who would ever experience death more than one time. We aren't told what happened to him after the Gospel of John record, but we can imagine that he saw life in a completely different perspective.

This is the climax that John was working toward in his Gospel account. The miracles of changing the water into wine, the healing of the lame man, the feeding of the 5000, the walking on the water, and the event of opening the eyes of the man born blind were all just precursors to this event. Through this miracle John proclaims, "Jesus is Lord!" He is fully convinced of that fact, for no one could do what Jesus did if he were not divine.

Even though we weren't there to see the literal return to life in Lazarus, and can't comprehend all that people experienced that day, with eyes of faith we can joy in on the celebration. This event did just what it was supposed to do, and that was to bring glory to the Father. Jesus is the way, the truth, and the life. The raising of Lazarus settled that question once and for all.

SEE...AND BELIEVE!

John 11:45–46 *Therefore many of the Jews who had come to visit Mary, and had seen what Jesus did, put their faith in him. But some of them went to the Pharisees and told them what Jesus had done.*

When we perceive something with our own senses, it's hard to deny anything to the contrary. Everyone knows that people don't come back from the dead, but when these people saw for themselves that Lazarus came out of the tomb and took up his place among the living, they could do nothing but believe the facts that were before their eyes. No doubt we would act the same way if we saw such a thing, but these people didn't just realize that Lazarus had been changed from a dead man to a living man, they recognized that Jesus was the one who made it happen. They may have had doubts about Him before, but if a person can raise the dead, well, that sealed the deal for many of them concerning the divinity of Jesus.

Each of us who have experienced a new spiritual birth because of Jesus can testify to a similar thing. We may not see a dramatic miracle like in this story, but we know when the old life died and the new life within us began. We also know that Jesus was the person responsible for this change, and we too have put our faith in Him as the Son of God and Savior of the world.

When we have been genuinely changed, there is no way that this change will remain secret anymore. We don't have to preach, or even talk about it—though most will want to—but our character and countenance changes, and people around us will notice the difference even if they don't know what caused it.

There are places in our world where a public acknowledgement of Jesus would result in an instant death sentence, and for that reason many are naturally hesitant to share of their transformation. Others may be introverts who have a real struggle speaking publicly about any subject, but when we have been raised to new life from the deadness of our sins, the word will get out somehow. The presence of Christ in us will testify as His fruit bears evidence of the transformation. The fruit of Christ's Spirit will eventually be seen even if we don't know how, or aren't able to express it with our words.

Critics may look at this change as something negative, but people will find out, for Jesus has a way of being seen in His followers, even us.

THINGS CHANGE WHEN JESUS COMES

John 11:47–48 *Then the chief priests and the Pharisees called a meeting of the Sanhedrin. "What are we accomplishing?" they asked. "Here is this man performing many miraculous signs. If we let him go on like this, everyone will believe in him, and then the Romans will come and take away both our place and our nation."*

The Sanhedrin was the highest governing authority for the Jewish society at that time. It was under the overall rule of the Roman government, but it was given liberty to make decisions on local matters so long as they were peaceful, and didn't go against Roman authority. It was similar to what Americans would consider their Supreme Court, for it had the final say on all legal matters and even routine matters of the land. The fact that the chief priests and Pharisees were discussing the case of Jesus before them gives an indication as to just what kind of ripples He was making throughout the country, and especially in Jerusalem.

This council was right on this occasion about three things. First, they were accomplishing basically nothing in regard to Jesus. His foes had tried to trick Him, trap Him, and threaten Him without any effect whatsoever, except that with each of His victories over them He was gaining supporters among the common people. Second, they confirmed that He had been doing miraculous signs. There were too many examples of Jesus ministering to the needy of the nation for them to be denied or ignored. One would think that such power being demonstrated before them would have softened their attitude to at least consider that He might be sent on a mission from God, but their sin blinded them from seeing what many others saw.

Finally, it was true that if they let things go on as they were currently going, He was going to have a huge impact on the faith of the Israelites, and eventually on the Romans, for these matters could not be kept from them forever. They could only speculate as to what the Romans might do, but they knew that if the Romans got involved that the Sanhedrin stood to lose authority, power, and wealth, along with the possibility of their personal freedom.

Nothing stays the same when Jesus gets involved. People choose sides about Him when He is presented before them. It was true then and true still.

PROPHECY ON DISPLAY

John 11:49–50 *Then one of them, named Caiaphas, who was high priest that year, spoke up, "You know nothing at all! You do not realize that it is better for you that one man die for the people than that the whole nation perish."*

The series of events and comments that are included in these verses prove the fact that not everyone who sees what Jesus does believes in Him. The high Jewish council would not believe because they were afraid of what believing in Jesus as the Son of God, the long-awaited Messiah, would cost them. These Jews were afraid of the Romans, since the Romans held the ultimate authority over life, death, and power in the land, and it was the loss of power especially that produced a madness that would cost these greedy men to pay any price to keep control.

At this point we could ask ourselves, "What are we afraid of?" What would keep us from declaring before everyone that Jesus is Lord of all? Some cannot make such a claim because darkness hates that light, and too many people play in the realm of darkness just enough to keep Jesus at bay in their loyalties. Surrendering all of life to Him would take the control out of our hands, and like the Pharisees in this biblical account, control is a power some are not willing to relinquish.

Caiaphas was more than willing to give Jesus up for the sake of his own power-grab over the Jewish nation. The high priest was the highest level of authority that any Israelite could hold at that time, and because he had gotten a taste of power, he wasn't going to let some carpenter-prophet from the hills of Galilee take it from him. Because he and others had come to hate Jesus so completely, they saw Him as the ideal scapegoat to get the nation off the Roman hook, and get this nuisance out of their own hair at the same time.

Since we have the advantage of time, and a perspective from the biblical account, we can see just how foolish this devilish plan was. Though he held the top religious post of the land, it didn't stop Caiaphas from being the enemy of God, and more than willing to play into the hands of darkness.

This is a picture of religion at its worst. When a religious body loses its divine purpose and mission, it will always degenerate into a selfish mob. We must let a lesson from the past remind us of this danger even in our time.

JESUS DIED FOR US ALL

John 11:51–53 He did not say this on his own, but as high priest that year he prophesied that Jesus would die for the Jewish nation, and not only for that nation but also for the scattered people of God, to bring them together and make them one. So from that day on they plotted to take his life.

Regardless of one's belief, whether Christian, some other religion, or no religion at all, Jesus died for all people. He was railroaded by the Jews and crucified by the Romans, but He died for them as well. From the cross they were all forgiven because from the cross He held no grudges. His love was poured out for mankind in a measure that we will never deserve nor understand, but it is a fact that history and the Bible records.

Even to this day He is often betrayed by the nations of the world, but He still died for every person of every country. Personally, I am saddened by the godlessness exhibited by the leaders of my own country, but I know that He died for them too. His sacrifice on behalf of everyone reminds us that we will never vote ourselves out of our sin and problems, but that His love for us will win the day eventually.

Faithlessness, like the example demonstrated by the Sanhedrin, always leads to a downward spiral. In this case, it restricted Jesus' ministry to a certain degree because He knew that these men wanted to kill Him. Though nothing would have brought Him more joy than to bring the kind of renewal and life-changing experiences to the lives of the Jewish nation that they needed, there was literally a price on His head calling for His death.

The good news of the story is that though He would die for the nation of Israel, and for all the people of all centuries, He would do it because of the Father's love for His creation. He would be raised from the dead to demonstrate that the Father's plan will ultimately win the day and that everything then and now is going along right according to His divine will. God is establishing His Kingdom here on earth in this present age, and it is coming to pass because of what Jesus did on our behalf.

That's the gospel message. The scattered people of the nations can now be forgiven, cleansed, and set free from the sin that has always bound them because of Jesus. He died once so that all people can live. It was a blessing then and is a blessing now, because in the end, because of Jesus, we win.

SANCTIFIED HIDING

John 11:54 *Therefore Jesus no longer moved about publicly among the Jews. Instead he withdrew to a region near the desert, to a village named, Ephraim, where he stayed with his disciples.*

J esus was at this point a wanted man. The Sanhedrin might as well have put out posters with a "Wanted, Dead or Alive," focus on them, because their goal was to capture Him, and get rid of Him once and for all. Because they had all the might of the Jewish hierarchy, and the authority under Roman law to handle local disputes, they had the final word on whether Jesus remained free or not. The problem was that they couldn't find Him.

Jesus was also on a mission, which was to complete the Father's plan, the Father's way, and on the Father's schedule. He was going to be the Passover Lamb that would take away the sins of the world, but until the Passover Feast time arrived, He had to stay one step ahead of the Jewish ruling authorities in order to postpone what He knew would happen if He were to be caught. His decision to go the region near the desert could be very easily described as a "hideout," as He bided His time until Passover.

We don't see this image very often as we consider the storyline of Jesus' life. Television programs and movies portray the miracles, the teachings, and even the conflict with authorities, but it almost seems out of character for Jesus to be relegated to the isolated regions as He ran from the grasp of the Sanhedrin until the appointed time.

Throughout the coming years and centuries, right up to the present day, there would be many disciples of His who would have to remain hidden at times because their faith had made them criminals in the eyes of the ruling authorities. This was true in the years of persecution leading up to the days of Constantine early in the fourth century A.D., where Christians were often hunted down, tortured, and martyred for their faith, and reality for our present brothers and sisters in Muslim or Communist countries where a public profession of their Christianity could cost them their freedom or their lives.

As I read these words over and over, I am reminded of how once again Jesus was setting a precedent for His followers. The Father has a plan for each of us, and there is no disgrace in doing whatever it takes to allow His plan to be fulfilled, even if that means hiding at some point.

JUST WHERE IS HE?

John 11:55–57 *When it was almost time for the Jewish Passover, many went up from the country to Jerusalem for their ceremonial cleansing before the Passover. The kept looking for Jesus, and as they stood in the temple area they asked one another, "What do you think? Isn't he coming to the Feast at all?" But the chief priests and Pharisees had given orders that if anyone found out where Jesus was, he should report it so that they might arrest him.*

The days until the Passover Feast celebration were counting down and the city was buzzing with talk about Jesus. It seemed like every time He showed up in person that strange and wonderful things happened, and usually controversy followed. More than likely, the Jewish religious leaders would end up on the short end of the public debates, for Jesus really knew how to hold His own ground when He was challenged.

Even though it was the annual ceremonies and rituals that drew people to Jerusalem, while they were there it was possible that anything could happen. The people didn't know what was about to transpire, for this would be a Passover like no other, one that would change the course of history forever.

Isn't it interesting that Jesus stirred the curiosity of people to the point that all over the city and countryside people talked about little else? It's especially enlightening because when we compare the drive to discover Jesus that both His friends and foes alike had, with the apathy that people have concerning Him today, it is staggering.

In far too many communities the presence of Jesus evidenced through His church in the twenty-first century hardly creates a ripple in society. The only times that people talk about the church and its place in our world is when people admire the architecture of its buildings, the controversy that goes with a scandal, or because of some kind of "giveaway" the church is conducting. Scarcely do people outside the church have much of a desire to come into the church because the Jesus that is witnessed by them seems very far removed from the scene.

Maybe it's time that the church returns to its power source, as found through His Holy Spirit, so that people who seek Him can still find Him. After all, why else are we even here?

ALL BECAUSE OF LOVE

John 12:1–3 *Six days before the Passover, Jesus arrived at Bethany, where Lazarus lived, whom Jesus had raised from the dead. Here a dinner was given in Jesus' honor. Martha served, while Lazarus was among those reclining at the table with him. Then Mary took about a pint of pure nard, an expensive perfume; she poured it on Jesus' feet and wiped his feet with her hair. And the house was filled with the fragrance of the perfume.*

Matthew 26:6 and Mark 14:3 records this event taking place at the home of a person called Simon the Leper, who also lived in Bethany. Luke 7:36 reveals to us that Simon was a Pharisee and that Mary is just listed as a sinful woman. In these accounts Martha is serving while Mary breaks open her alabaster jar that holds a precious perfume, and anoints Jesus with it.

Nard is a spice that is said to originate in the Himalayan Mountains of China. It has had various uses over the years as a perfume, an incense, a sedative, and an herbal medicine. Since China is a far distance from Bethany, where Mary, Martha, and Lazarus lived, it would no doubt be a rare commodity and therefore be valued at a high price. In fact, according to people who know much more about these things than me, the amount of nard listed would have been equivalent to 300 denarii, or about $54,509 in current U.S. monetary standards. That's a lot of money to be spent on Jesus, or anyone. The fact that Mary possessed such a prize tells us that she most likely had some financial means herself.

What a group had gathered for this meal! Simon the Leper, a Pharisee, who probably had been healed of his disease by Jesus, Lazarus, the man Jesus had raised from the dead, Martha, the faithful and dutiful servant-minded worker, the disciples, who followed after Jesus nearly everywhere, and Mary, the woman of means who was previously just referred to as a wicked woman. A more unlikely group picture would be hard to imagine.

The common denominator in all of these lives is that Jesus loved them. He loved the lepers, the Pharisees, the disciples, and John specifically mentioned that He loved Lazarus, Martha, and Mary (John 11:5). The gift Mary offered was an outpouring of the love she wanted to return to Him for all He had done for them.

We too are loved. Therefore, we too are to love. It's the Jesus thing to do.

GIVING OUR BEST FOR JESUS

John 12:4–6 *But one of his disciples, Judas Iscariot, who was later to betray him, objected, "Why wasn't this perfume sold and the money given to the poor? It was worth a year's wages." He did not say this because he cared about the poor but because he was a thief; as keeper of the money bag, he used to help himself to what was put into it.*

Though the attitude Mary showed in this chapter was one of love and giving, the same could not be said for Judas, one of the Lord chosen disciples. His idea was that he wanted to get his hands on the money that the nard could bring on the market, so that his own situation would improve. He really didn't care about the poor, but though he thought no one else realized that fact, he wasn't fooling Jesus at all. In fact, his actions and attitude here show that he didn't even care about Jesus, let along the poor. He only cared for what he might get out of the situation, for he had either forgotten the teachings from Jesus on Kingdom values of gaining and losing, or he wasn't listening when that lesson was given out.

The attitude of Jesus here shows a complete contrast to Judas. No motive of the heart will ever go unnoticed by Him, and that included Mary as well as Judas. Jesus knew about the poor, and He knew that it was the responsibility of those who would follow after Him to be merciful to the poor continually, but He also knew that as long as sin ruled in this world, the fact of poverty would never go away.

Our Lord knows when we give our best for Him. He knows when we think of ourselves first and when we don't. Too often we think too small and focus on our little kingdom rather than the big picture of the eternal Kingdom. He appreciated the gesture by Mary, for she gave from her heart. Her story has been told in all four Gospel accounts and has gone around the world over centuries as an example of selfless devotion and love for her Savior.

We too are never at a loss when we give our best for Jesus. There are many roads we could choose to trod, but we will never be sorry when we make the decision to go the way Christ leads. He will bless us for what we give Him, for He will be in no one's debt. He also will do more with our little gift than we could ever do with it, for what we keep for ourselves we will lose anyway, but what we give to Jesus will have eternal rewards.

We Will Always Have The Poor

John 12:7-8 *"Leave her alone," Jesus replied. "It was intended that she should save this perfume for the day of my burial. You will always have the poor among you, but you will not always have me."*

If anything is clear in this Gospel account, it is that Jesus is in charge. His words reprimanding Judas were no doubt heeded, and it probably caused Judas a little embarrassment along with his chagrin at not getting his hands on the money the perfume could bring. But when Jesus spoke, people listened, and Judas apparently fell in line with the command.

People probably looked around the room at each other when they heard the remarks that Jesus made. Perfume for the day of His burial? What was He talking about? He had proven that death was not a barrier for Him by the way He brought Lazarus out of the tomb. Surely a person who could bring life to others didn't have to worry about His own death.

Jesus wasn't worried, but He did know what was coming. In less than a week He would be hanging on a Roman cross, and the full weight of the world's sin would be weighing down upon Him. For a time, Satan would be gleeful, for he would seem to gain the victory he had wanted for eons. The hour of darkness was getting closer.

When Jesus made mention of the poor always being among us, He was not belittling the needs of the poor, nor was He telling the listeners that they should have no interest in meeting the needs of the poor. He had demonstrated His compassion for those living in poverty on more than one occasion, but in this one particular instance the needs of the poor had to be put aside so that glory would come to the Son, as well as the Father.

The reality of Jesus telling those around Him that He would not be with them much longer must have baffled them. Perhaps they sensed the tide of opposition rising up again Him and understood that the power of organized religion and the state were awesome foes for even the Messiah to take on. But it is just as likely that they were not yet ready to grasp the events at hand. Jesus was going to leave them, but they didn't know He would be back.

How thankful we should be that Jesus, though gone in the body, is ever present with us in the Spirit. It is that presence that makes life worth living.

A DOWNHILL SLIDE

John 12:9–11 *Meanwhile a large crowd of Jews found out that Jesus was there and came, not only because of him but also to see Lazarus, whom he had raised from the dead. So the chief priests made plans to kill Lazarus as well, for on account of him many of the Jews were going over to Jesus and putting their faith in him.*

I t was Saturday evening and the Sabbath had come to a close. People sought Jesus out as they always did, but on this particular night there was something afoot that was more than just requests for healings or blessings. There was something more sinister in the hearts of several people who just didn't know what to make of Jesus.

One has to wonder how the leaders of a religious movement intent on doing good, could become so murderous and treacherous. Judaism had a solid beginning, but by this point in history its leaders were more bent on self-serving atrocities than holiness.

Religion takes a downward path when its own self-interests become more important than the truth. We see it all the time when people don't think the rules were made for them, and self-interest dictates policies and actions. The chief priests were threatened by the very presence of Jesus, as well as what He was saying and doing. For them to survive, He had to be destroyed.

We also see this downward trend when people try to destroy evidence that threaten long-held belief systems, as in this case, the resurrected Lazarus. Nobody likes to be told that they are wrong, but if there is evidence that what we believe is wrong, then it needs to be seen. The priests were not concerned about right or wrong, however. They believed what they wanted to believe and nothing, not even one returning from the dead, was going to change that. The downward path of religion reached a climax as we see it become more form than faith. Our past experiences and traditions play a bigger role in our belief system that we often like to admit. However, when these things don't lead us to a personal connection with God, then they are no longer means of grace, but just rituals without purpose.

Killing Lazarus and eventually killing Jesus were just efforts in futility. These leaders didn't know it, but their actions were playing right into the plan of the Father. Jesus, the King, would not be stopped, no matter their actions.

THE TRUE SOLUTION

> **John 12:12–13** *The next day the great crowd that had come for the Feast heard that Jesus was on his way to Jerusalem. They took palm branches and went out to meet him, shouting, "Hosanna!" "Blessed is he who comes in the name of the Lord!" "Blessed is the King of Israel!"*

Have you ever dealt with a problem that seemed unsolvable? We are at a point in the Gospel of John where the text records what happened just one day after the chief priests had decided that both Jesus and Lazarus should die. They couldn't deny the miracles that Jesus was doing, they couldn't explain how they were doing them, they couldn't accept His criticisms of them, and they didn't have any answer for Him except to get Him out of the way and off the public stage. But here He was again, in a parade.

In this familiar story, the crowd was on its way to the Passover Feast. When they came upon Jesus, they recognized Him as the Savior and Deliverer that they had been hoping and waiting for. When they called out, "Hosanna!" they were in essence saying, "Please save," and "Save now!" The common people could see what the Jewish religious leaders could not.

A lot of people cry out to God when the want to be delivered from hard times. The Jews had been under bondage from the time of the Babylonian exile hundreds of years earlier, and they had experienced the same treatment from the Medes, the Persians, the Greeks, and now the Romans. The people wanted and needed deliverance, and they saw Jesus as just the person who would be able to give them what they called for.

In this passage they were acknowledging that Jesus was anointed by God, as they said, "Blessed is he who comes in the name of the Lord!" This very association proclaimed Him as royalty. They were blessing Him as the King of Israel, but the "kingdom plans" they had in mind for Him were nothing like what the Father had planned. They were seeing Him as a means to an end, while Jesus in actuality *was* the answer they were looking for, but in their short-sightedness, they didn't know it.

He is still the answer for us today. Jesus is not *a way* to a solution for us. He *is* the solution for us. In Him we have all that we need to operate in this world and prepare for the next. The crowds were on the right track though, for their King was before them, and He is always worthy to be praised.

SETTING THE STAGE

John 12:14–15 *Jesus found a young donkey and sat on it, as it is written, "Do not be afraid, O Daughter of Zion; see, your king is coming, seated on a donkey's colt."*

Jesus wasn't just sitting on a young donkey that day. He was sitting on the means of transportation that would take Him right into Jerusalem. This was a high-water mark in His ministry and it came at a very high point on the Jewish calendar. People could feel it! He was bigger than life, and just being near Him was something everyone was clamoring to do.

It was inevitable that He would be praised. The crowd felt free to display their emotions about this amazing man. This day on the calendar was like the Super Bowl for the Jewish nation and Jesus was the star quarterback who was coming to town to be the hero of the day. The people joyfully joined in on the praise because it just seemed right to do it.

However, it was also inevitable that He would be misunderstood. The imagery of the donkey certainly wasn't lost on this group that greeted Him. The words of the prophet Zechariah were well known by the population, and Jesus seemed to fit the prophesied role perfectly. Because He was so flawless in His fulfillment of the prophet's words, He was gaining the kind of notoriety that would make Him a threat to power. Even though He was just sitting there as the donkey moved slowly through the crowed throng of worshipers, the fact that He was receiving such praise had to have driven His enemies to their highest levels of frustration.

But by the end of the week, people would realize that this donkey was carrying Him to a crucifying death. A showdown was coming and every step that the animal took brought Him closer to the pain that He knew was waiting.

The only recorded account of a donkey talking in the Bible is found in the book of Numbers, in the Old Testament with the story of Balaam. However, if any donkey ever had a story to tell, it would be this donkey. It was young; it was a colt; but it was an animal of destiny.

We really can't downplay this story because this trip to town set the stage for all that was to come, for the crowd praising Him here would soon be calling for His head. The cross casts a huge shadow over this parade.

CONFUSED AND CLUELESS

John 12:16 *At first his disciples did not understand all this. Only after Jesus was glorified did they realize that these things had been written about him and that they had done these things to him.*

The disciples were clueless as to what was happening. We could write it off to the fact that we as part of the male species are often pretty much out in the field when it comes to being observant, but it seems very strange that the obvious was oblivious to them.

Of course, some understanding comes best from hindsight. We understand God more completely when we look backwards in time and see how He has been working in our lives. I have made many hard decisions over the years as I moved from place to place, and took on different types of ministries, but I would be the first to confess that I see things more clearly when I look backwards in time than when I try to look ahead.

The disciples were like that. Their understanding increased as time went along and they were able to look back and connect the words of Jesus with the events that took place. When they began to study the Old Testament Scriptures, the only Bible they had, they began to get a new appreciation for what Jesus said and what He experienced.

Of course, the most effective way for us to understand the workings of God is through the avenue of revelation. When God so chooses to reveal things to us, all questions are settled. We would think that the disciples would pick up on things more quickly since they were around Jesus continually, but somehow, they seemed to miss the messages over and over.

Almost two-thousand years have gone by since Jesus rode into Jerusalem on the donkey. We today have the luxury of time on our side as we look back on those events. We know about the cross, the resurrection, and the eventual coming of the Holy Spirit in power upon the church. We are blessed in a way that the disciples were not, but unfortunately far too often we too are slow to understand all the Jesus wants us to grasp.

This is why it is important for Christians today to seek the Lord in earnest and spread the news about Jesus to all we meet. We have received much, so let's pass it on.

"This Is Getting Us Nowhere!"

John 12:17–19 *Now the crowd that was with him when he called Lazarus from the tomb and raised him from the dead continued to spread the word. Many people, because they had heard that he had given this miraculous sign, went out to meet him. So the Pharisees said to one another, "See, this is getting us nowhere. Look how the whole world has gone after him!"*

It's hard for us to imagine how news traveled in the world two thousand years ago. Because we have so many avenues to get information through the various social media outlets, television, radio, and newspapers, we often hear conversations decrying the loss of personal communication. People in the twenty-first century spend more time interacting with their electronic devices than in face-to-face, one-on-one personal conversations.

It was not that way in the days following the raising of Lazarus from the dead. The people that were on the scene when Lazarus came out of the tomb, talked about it, talked about it, and then talked about it some more. Though there were a limited number of eyewitnesses to the fact, before long the news spread through second-hand, third-hand, and even more distant rumors about this incredible happening. Jesus had earlier said, when the news of Lazarus's sickness reached him, that this event would be for God's glory and the faith development of His disciples (John 11:4, 14). Certainly, the Father was being praised and the disciples' faith was being strengthened, but the glory coming to Jesus was piling on fast and furious as well.

The Pharisees had no answer to all of this. Nowhere do we see them denying that Lazarus had been dead, or that Jesus had raised Him to life. When a formerly dead man is seen walking around in public, it kind of puts the deniers to shame. But because they had no answer to the Jesus problem, and His influence was overshadowing them, the only solution was to get rid of Him, and they were scheming to do so.

People still don't have an answer for Jesus. Though some claim to be atheists and agnostics, they don't have a compelling reason for the behavior change of someone who has been raised from the deadness of sin to a new life abundant. When treachery, lying, stealing, and abusive behavior is changed to holiness in heart and life, the contrast is not only apparent, but baffling. The world is still seeking the one who can change their lives.

SEEKING AFTER JESUS

John 12:20–22 *Now there were some Greeks among those who went up to worship at the Feast. They came to Philip, who was from Bethsaida in Galilee, with a request. "Sir," they said, "we would like to see Jesus." Philip went to tell Andrew; Andrew and Philip in turn told Jesus.*

This is certainly an interesting passage of scripture. It just screams questions. Who are these Greeks? What are they doing at a Jewish Passover? Were they also worshippers, or did they just happen to be passing through? Why and how did they find Philip? More importantly, what was John trying to tell the readers of this story in the first century, and what can we take away from it for the 21st century?

I don't think it is an accident that the previous verse reads, "Look how the whole world has gone after him!" John was saying that through the connection with these foreigners, the statement by the Pharisees was true. The whole world would eventually be affected by the person of Jesus, the Christ, the Son of God.

In spite of all the questions that this story brings to the stage, we can deduce some pretty obvious things from it. First, the Greeks were looking for Jesus because people were talking about Jesus. Society was saturated with stories about this guy. Perhaps we could learn a lesson here. Maybe we need to be talking more about Jesus because the more people hear about Him the more possibility there is that they might want to meet Him.

Second, the Greeks came to Philip because they had a connection with him. We are not sure what the connection was, but something pulled them together and something told them that he had access to Jesus. O that the world would see and say that about us.

Third, the Greeks were asking of Philip the same thing the world is asking of us. "Where is Jesus?" "How do we get to Jesus?" How would we answer these questions if they were put to us? Can we help those who seek Him, find Him? Can we help people to see that Jesus is in the church He created? Can we really help people to get to know Him up close and personal? People may come to us this week. Hopefully we will be able to show them Jesus for He is still the Light of the world, the Savior of mankind, and the only hope we will ever need!

THE HOUR HAS COME

John 12:23–26 Jesus replied, "The hour has now come for the Son of Man to be glorified. I tell you the truth, unless a kernel of wheat falls to the ground and dies, it remains only a single seed. But if it dies, it produces many seeds. The man who loves his life will lose it, while the man who hates his life in this world will keep it for eternal life. Whoever serves me must follow me; and what I am, my servant also will be. My Father will honor the one who serves me.

Where did we get the idea that Christianity is a safe way to live? The more I read the words of Jesus the more I realize that being a Christian is the most radical, most dangerous, and most intensive way to live. The principles that Jesus puts before us in this text are not for the faint of heart.

He first lets us know that God's schedule is not our schedule. He is never late and He is never early, for His schedule is always what is best for His followers. Jesus was on the Father's schedule always, and in these verses He lets us know that on that schedule, His time had come.

He said we also need to remember that God is to be glorified. For that to happen our life here must come to an end. It means that transformation will take place and we will be equipped to live forever. Jesus demonstrated this truth with His own death and life and we who put our trust in Him will someday follow the path He walked before us.

He wants us to think about the need for multiplication. The disciple's goal is not to just get to heaven, but to take as many people with us as possible. We will not achieve that task without loss, but we do it to help others to enter the Kingdom as well, so that they too will live forever. Jesus made this clear when He spoke about being like a seed that dies in the ground.

He reminds us that what we gain here stays here, but what we lose for His sake goes into eternity with us. There is not an area of our life where this is not true. These words should cause us to re-evaluate what we hold on to.

Finally, He tells us that to be His follower we must be His servant. That means we must go where He goes and do what He did, but in doing so we will not lose our reward. All these lessons show us that the way is tough, but possible through Christ, and the trip is worth any price we could pay.

THE VOICE OF GOD

John 12:27–29 *"Now my heart is troubled and what shall I say? 'Father, save me from this hour'? No, it was for this very reason I came to this hour. Father, glorify your name!" Then a voice came from heaven, "I have glorified it, and will glorify it again." The crowd that was there and heard it said it had thundered; others said an angel had spoken to him.*

We see a very human side of Jesus here as He turns His eyes and thoughts to the cross. Since He is now within just a few days from going there, it is completely rational that He would be a bit preoccupied. These words show His concern. No sane person would ever want to endure what was facing Him, and even though He was fully aware of the glory that would fall on the following Sunday morning, there was no way He could ignore the pain that was coming.

There was a branch of people in the early days of the church called Gnostics, who didn't believe that Jesus was actually human and that He didn't really feel the pain of the torture and the cross. The words in these verses prove that idea completely false.

Because Jesus was troubled in His spirit, there were some options He could consider. He could go ahead with the Father's plan and go to the cross, or He could choose another route. It was within His power and ability to change His mind if He wanted to. If He was not able to choose, then He was not really tempted to avoid the pain, but because He could choose and still chose the way of death, we see just how much He loves us. He became what we are so that we could become what He is—holy.

When the voice of God sounded and reinforced His decision, it surprised everyone but Him. After all, it's not every day that God speaks audibly to His creation. We don't know if Jesus expected His Father to speak as He did, but He recognized the voice immediately because He had heard it often. The Father spoke to confirm Jesus to the hearers.

This voice brought about a mixed reaction. Some couldn't accept that it was God and others thought that at least it was the voice of an angel. Most probably didn't know what to think. What we do know is that it came right on time, for the Father is always on time. The Word made flesh was on the brink of completing His mission, and His Father was proud of Him.

HEARING GOD'S VOICE

If you want people to think you are crazy, just tell them that God talks to you. However, just because others don't believe it doesn't mean that it didn't happen. In these verses the Lord is being glorified.

Jesus revealed to His followers that the defeat of their spiritual enemy was at hand. Judgment was about to fall upon Satan and the penalty would settle his future once and for all. The day of reckoning was getting closer.

The world was about to do a terrible thing and these words make clear that the enemy of our souls was behind it. Because the enemy had such a stranglehold on mankind, it made the sacrifice of Jesus all the more important. Sin was deeply intrenched and only the blood of the spotless Lamb of God could break its power.

The cross would do just that. It was to be the example of the devil doing his worst to bring down the King, for I John 5:9 tells us that Satan was still ruling over the world until Jesus put an end to his reign. Because of what Jesus did, we who reside in Him are free from the bondage of sin and the power our enemy wants to use to rule over us.

The coming victory over the grave would settle matters forever. The cross is magnetic in the sense that Jesus draws us to Him through the sacrifice that He made there. But it is also majestic because the victory won there would never have to be repeated again, for the Lord conquered once and for all. But the days of victory were still in the future at this point, and Jesus was preparing Himself to face all that the devil could throw at Him.

Each of us will have times in our lives when we will be tempted to quit and take an easier route than the Christian walk. However, we find strength and grace to withstand those temptations because Jesus walked this path before us. He could have changed His mind. He could have returned to the Father, or called down angels to defeat the devil another way. But He didn't. He didn't quit because He needed to set an example for us to follow.

QUESTIONS, QUESTIONS, QUESTIONS...

John 12:34–36 *The crowd spoke up, "We have heard from the Law that the Christ will remain forever, so how can you say, 'The Son of Man must be lifted up'? Who is this Son of Man'?" Then Jesus told them, "You are going to have the light just a little while longer. Walk while you have the light, before darkness overtakes you. The man who walks in the dark does not know where he is going. Put your trust in the light while you have it, so that you may become sons of light." When he had finished speaking, Jesus left and hid himself from them.*

If anything is obvious from our reading of the Gospel according to John, we are learning that people did not agree in their opinions about Jesus. There are a lot of questions that people asked about Him—and a lot of questions that people still ask about Him. Our task is to keep pursuing, to keep searching to know all we can possibly know.

In the previous verses we have seen Jesus wrestling with the idea of the cross. He knew it was coming, but He also knew that it was the only way to accomplish His mission. In the meantime, He still had to deal with the crowds and their questions because they had lots of questions, and among them was the whether or not the Christ would be with them forever. Lots of scriptures implied that fact (i.e. Psalm 110:4; Isaiah 9:6-7; Daniel 2:44), but Jesus kept talking about leaving them, and that didn't seem to fit with the image of what they expected from their Messiah.

They were no doubt confused about His use of the term "Son of Man." They had read these words in the scriptures also, but hearing Jesus refer to Himself by this title was unusual to them. As the New Testament would unfold, the connection would be more evident, but these folks didn't have the New Testament, so questions lingered.

They were probably confused about His use of the term, "Light." From the ancient Persians the concepts of light verses darkness had evolved into a religious idea, but Jesus took it to a new level. He Himself was, and is, that light. Only those who put their trust in Him as the light of God could ever walk in the light as He did.

One thing is sure. We today see all of these titles as reality for Jesus. He is the eternal Son of Man, the Son of God, and the Divine Light for our world.

BEING WHO GOD WANTS US TO BE

John 12:37–41 *Even after Jesus had done all these miraculous signs in their presence, they still would not believe in him. This was to fulfill the word of Isaiah the prophet: "Lord, who has believed our message and to whom has the arm of the Lord been revealed?" For this reason they could not believe, because, as Isaiah says elsewhere: "He has blinded their eyes and deadened their hearts, so they can neither see with their eyes, nor understand with their hearts, nor turn—and I would heal them." Isaiah said this because he saw Jesus' glory and spoke about him.*

John quotes here from Isaiah 53 and Isaiah 6 as he emphasizes the irony of how Jesus fulfilled the words of the prophet. Just as Isaiah bemoaned the wayward state of Israel hundreds of years before Jesus walked as a man in Galilee and Judea, the same spiritual deadness remained these many generations later.

Jesus didn't hide the power of God from the masses. Though there were times when He healed someone and then instructed that person to not spread it around, though they usually did anyway, there were plenty of occasions when Jesus did mighty acts publicly. When people observed these miracles with their own eyes one would think that all doubt about the legitimacy of Jesus being the Messiah would be removed, but that was not the case. Some who were eyewitnesses to the power of God still wanted to kill this carpenter turned preacher.

Verses like these often make me wonder how blind we are today. We live in a time of gloom and doom as politics runs amok throughout the airwaves and bitter partisanship battles for dominance around our world. Jesus is still doing many mighty acts of healing, restoration, renewing, cleansing, and empowering, but these things are often overshadowed by people whose minds are locked into other matters.

Just as Jesus came to bring light and understanding to a blinded world, His body, the Church is called to do the same work. There will always be a faction that will not listen or heed the announcement of the Kingdom of God, but we see here that Jesus faced the same thing. However, this is not the time to quit, but to make sure that our church is doing its part to proclaim the Good News that transforms lives. This is why God put us where we are.

AFRAID TO BE FREE

> **John 12:42–43** *Yet at the same time many even among the leaders believed in him. But because of the Pharisees they would not confess their faith for fear that they would be put out of the synagogue, for they loved praise from men more than praise from God.*

When I read these verses, I am reminded of people who go out to eat in restaurants and feel the need to pray for God's blessing on their food before they eat their meal, but look around to see if anyone is watching before they bow their head. It's easy to be spiritual when we are in church or when no one in watching us in public, but fair-weather Christian don't rank very high in John's estimation that is contained in these verses.

Leaders become leaders because they get a consensus of people to follow them. They get them to follow the leader by doing and saying things that will win the approval of the people that the leader considers to be important. Politicians go where the votes are when they are campaigning, and while on the campaign they are usually careful not to do anything that would cause them to appear in an unfavorable light to their constituents.

The leaders here were more concerned about the influence of the Pharisees than they were with the applause of God. After all, they could see the Pharisees, and hear the threat they had made concerning anyone who decided to follow after Jesus. They believed in God, but, well, they couldn't see Him, so it was easier to just bow to the present pressure than to worry about judgment that would come later. How blind and short-sighted they were.

We should all take a lesson here and make sure that our stand for Jesus and our devotion to Him is not just something we can turn off or on like a water tap. He is the King of kings and deserves to be acknowledged as such. We cannot let our fears of being embarrassed by the comments of people around us when it comes to our loyalty to Christ. He certainly isn't ashamed of us, so we should never be of Him.

The Pharisees had already committed murder in their hearts, and their minds concerning Jesus was all made up. We who follow Jesus should be just as convinced as to our standing in Him, and be public as to where our loyalties lie. Someday, when standing before God, we will wish we had.

BEING PART OF THE FAMILY

John 12:44–46 *Then Jesus cried out, "When a man believes in me, he does not believe in me only, but in the one who sent me. When he looks at me, he sees the one who sent me. I have come into the world as a light, so that no one who believes in me should stay in darkness.*

A truth that is not always fully understood, is that when a man and a woman marry, they marry into a whole new family. Their personal identity is retained, but it is forever connected to a new group of people. When I got my wife, I got her family, and when she got me, she got my family too. That's the way family works.

The same thing is true when we consider the Holy Trinity. One cannot put his or her trust in God without putting his or her trust in Jesus. When we get the Son, we get the Father, and the Holy Spirit as well. For centuries people wondered what God looked like and what He really was like, but when Jesus came on the scene, He settled those questions. God looks like Jesus and Jesus looks like God. God acts like Jesus and Jesus acts like God. If we desire to see how those acts are displayed in our world, we only have to go to Galatians 5:22–23 and see that Paul listed the divine attributes as "love, joy, peace, patience, kindness, goodness, faithfulness, gentleness, and self-control." This is the way Jesus acted while He walked in our world, and it is the way the Father acts in all He does.

This is where the work of the Holy Spirit comes to bear in our lives. Since the fruit of the Spirit show the attributes of the Trinity, and we have received the Holy Spirit into our lives, we have a bit of God in us. The Apostle Paul called it a deposit, or down payment (Ephesians 1:14) on what we are to receive in full when we are finally perfected. Throughout our walk in this world, we are to be ever pursuing the things of God so that the fruit that has been deposited in us will continue to grow and transform us into the being that can enjoy fellowship with a holy God throughout eternity.

God makes this possible so that we will not walk in darkness and stumble. Since Jesus is the Light of the world, He allows His brilliance to guide our steps so that we will not fall, but reach our full potential as His servant now, and reach our reward when this life is over. Bad trees don't bear good fruit and good trees don't bear bad fruit. Our fruit should make us look like Jesus.

JUDGMENT AND CONDEMNATION

John 12:47–48 *As for the person who hears my words but does not keep them, I do not judge him. For I did not come to judge the world, but to save it. There is a judge for the one who rejects me and does not accept my words; that very word which I spoke will condemn him at the last day.*

These verses take some careful thought. Here is a truth that is not fully understood by a lot of people because it says that Jesus is not the judge over those who reject Him. How can this be? Isn't Jesus the King and Creator of all things, the one who will have the final word on everything?

In the previous verses we have acknowledged that Jesus and the Father are one. When we see Jesus, we see the Father and when we see the Father, we will see Jesus. They are of one essence and with the Holy Spirit make up the Divine Godhead we know as the Holy Trinity. So, if Jesus is not our judge, then neither the Father, nor the Holy Spirit judges us either, for they are one. This seems very confusing.

I believe what Jesus is telling us through John's Gospel account here is that our own actions produce natural reactions, which will in turn prove to judge us for our unbelief. It's like someone not believing in gravity and stepping off a high bridge. The result of their unbelieving action will result in its own judgment. Sin takes a terrible toll on everything and everyone it touches, and no one who goes that way will escape unscarred. Sin deceives, distorts, and destroys as it plunges its victims into a life of darkness that blinds them to the path that leads in the way of God's Spirit.

In book VIII of Plato's Republic, the ancient philosopher Socrates said, "A man who is accustomed to indulging any pleasure as it comes to him— absolute freedom from restraint—will soon find himself mastered by strong desire." This is the destiny of the one who refuses to believe in Jesus and refuses to walk in His light. He will create his own hell here on earth that will eventually lead to eternal separation from God. This judgment is of each person's own choosing, for God's desire is that no one perishes.

Separation from God is separation from everything that is good, beautiful, peaceful, and wonderful. It takes a person to an eternity that is full of selfishness, pain, disappointment, fear, and loss. It is an awful destiny that is chosen by those who go there. It sure sounds like hell to me.

THE REAL POSSIBILITY

John 12:49–50 *For I did not speak of my own accord, but the Father who sent me commanded me what to say and how to say it. I know that his command leads to eternal life. So whatever I say is just what the Father has told me to say.*

The mystery of the divine Father-Son connection will probably not be fully understood until we reach the next world. We know God is one, but we also know that the Son prays to the Father and is directed by the Father. We see this picture of two entities acting in lockstep as if two personalities are present, but with one body. I can hardly wait to be in the Great Praise Party of heaven to witness first-hand how it all really is.

Something that we do know from these verses is that all the Father's efforts and focus is on redeeming His creation. Eternal life is not just a pipe dream, or a religious fantasy, but a reality that is made possible by plans made in the eternities of time beyond our abilities to grasp. Because we are so conditioned by the boundaries of time and space, getting to see beyond those limitations is truly a matter of faith. But we know that faith is a gift from God (Romans 10:17), that He gives to us who need it so desperately.

The commands of God that lead to eternal life have been written for us in this book we called the Bible. Though it has a long history of being constructed, the guidance for us that it contains can't be rated high enough. It is food for our souls because the Holy Spirit inspired every thought that goes into it. The fact that this ancient text that began in Hebrew, Aramaic, and Greek has now been translated into languages that the vast majority of the world can read in their own native tongue is amazing in itself, but the additional fact that this book transforms lives is even more astounding. God, working through men, inspired by His Holy Spirit, telling the story of His divine Son, is a collaboration and masterpiece that will never be equaled.

Eternal life is the possibility for all of us. The commands that lead us to it are found in His book. His book is available for us to access, and God gives us faith and insights to understand it, so we have no excuse not to find that path into eternity that has been marked out for us.

The church continues its mission to spread that news. God is in the business of redeeming the world—and that includes every one of us.

PASSOVER PONDERINGS

John 13:1 *It was just before the Passover Feast. Jesus knew that the time had come for him to leave this world and go to the Father. Having loved his own who were in the world, he now showed them the full extent of his love.*

Passover had been a main focus of religious observance for the Jewish people since the time of Moses, which was approximately 1200-1500 years B.C., depending on which scholar one believes. This particular Passover would have more of an impact on the Jewish nation and the whole world than even the first event did, for the slaying of this Passover Lamb would provide the blood necessary to save people on a scale not previously imagined.

For the needed sacrifice to be made, however, Jesus had to die. It was the way that He would be able to return to the Father and fulfill the mission that brought Him into the midst of His creation some thirty-three years earlier. The time had no doubt passed rather quickly, but at this point all the necessary pieces of the puzzle for redemption were in place and awaiting the culmination of God's divine plan.

What has been written about since that time, and has been made into song, movies, and stories told, was the amount of love that was required of Jesus to be this sacrifice. There was no profit in it for Him, for He had all He could ever desire by just asking of the Father. No, He did what He did for selfless reasons that go beyond human understanding.

The closest we could ever get to grasping the concept of this kind of love is found in our own family. Any parent worthy of being called such, would gladly give up his or her own life for the sake of our children, the life that we created through natural childbirth. Our children and grandchildren are the most precious gifts we have ever received, and most of us would do anything within our power for them.

Jesus takes this example to the extreme, however, because He didn't just go to the cross for His own kin, but for all of His creation. He went to the cross to redeem humans, whether good or bad, but also to redeem all that He had made in the days of creation. His love didn't just reach to humans, but to bring about a Kingdom where utopia and paradise would be restored on our planet. That's what was at stake and that is how much He loved. It is also why He still loves us, and still draws us to His heart to this very day.

WE ALL HAVE A CHOICE

John 13:2 *The evening meal was being served, and the devil had already prompted Judas Iscariot, son of Simon, to betray him.*

This has to be one of the saddest verses in the Bible. Judas had all the same advantages that the rest of the disciples did, but what a different outcome. After hearing all the sermons and teachings of Jesus, seeing the healings, the dead being raised, the feeding of thousands with a small amount of food, and all the other miracles, one would think that he would have been convinced to take a different route, but infamously, he did not.

We don't know a lot about Judas. Many Bible teachers don't believe that Iscariot was actually his last name, but a clue as to where he was from. Iscariot is not a word in any known language, but Kerioth was a small village in southwestern Judea. That would make him Judas of Kerioth, rather than Judas Iscariot, which actually does make sense. It is possible that his last name, "Iscariot," is a corruption of the Hebrew word Ish Kerioth (man of Kerioth).

If Judas was from Judea, then he would have been the only one of the disciples that was. The other eleven were from Galilee, in the northern section of Israel. We know nothing about Judas' family except his father's name, "Simon" (John 6:71). Judas was called a traitor (Luke 6:16) and a thief (John 12:6), but the most damning of his titles was used by Jesus who called him, "the one doomed to destruction so that the Scripture would be fulfilled" (John 17:12).

It could have been so different. Judas had the best teacher, the kindest friend, and the most skillful leader that any person could ever hope for. Jesus knew that Judas would betray Him, but He still loved Him, and even washed his feet. No one had more opportunities to get it right, but he got it about as wrong as was humanly possible.

The key to understanding this verse is to realize that Satan already had his claws in Judas. He would not be fully possessed by the evil one until later in this chapter, but already Judas was listening to the chief of liars.

We, like Judas, have a choice. We get to decide who will be our Lord. Pray for wisdom and grace to avoid Judas' mistake, and choose correctly.

THE HUMBLE LORD

John 13:3–5 *Jesus knew that the Father had put all things under his power, and that he had come from God and was returning to God; so he got up from the meal, took off his outer clothing, and wrapped a towel around his waist. After that, he poured water into a basin and began to wash his disciples' feet, drying them with the towel that was wrapped around him.*

This had certainly been a time for miracles. In just the few days before this event Lazarus had been raised from the dead, the voice of God was heard from heaven, the crowds had adored Jesus as He made His way into Jerusalem on the donkey, and in Luke 11:13 we are told the story of how Jesus verbally cursed a fig tree, and it dried up from its roots. There seemed to be no end to what Jesus was able to do, for the power of God swept over Him and was being seen everywhere He traveled.

But now the scene had changed. No longer do we see Jesus as the exalted miracle worker and King, but instead as a lowly servant who would take on the job of washing feet. Jesus was not just making an object lesson here, though we can easily see what He was getting at. No, this was not a made-up job, for these disciples had been walking through dirty streets that were filled with animal droppings, and mankind's refuse. These dirty feet really did need a bath, and Jesus took it upon Himself to make it happen.

I have seen foot-washings in church services. Though it is a moving act of humility and submission, it is usually more ceremony than of necessity. When Jesus did it, He was doing what needed to be done because no one else had stepped up to perform this menial task.

Does this speak to you? It certainly does to me. It tells me that I need to look for where the need of mankind is and then do something about it. I need to get my hands dirty so that someone else can find cleansing. This is not about putting on a show for others to see. This is about making right what is wrong, even if no one else ever knows that we were responsible for doing the work.

Our world is crying out for genuine healing, cleansing, restoring, and nurturing. Perhaps it's time for the church to get down into the gutters where much of mankind is living, and find ways to help them back to wholeness. Jesus saw the need and filled it. I believe He calls us to do the same.

THE "BLESSEDNESS" OF RECEIVING

John 13:6–8 He came to Simon Peter, who said to him, "Lord, are you going to wash my feet?" Jesus replied, "You do not realize now what I am doing, but later you will understand." "No," said Peter, "you shall never wash my feet." Jesus answered, "Unless I wash you, you have no part with me."

We are told in the account presented by Dr. Luke, that the Apostle Paul had related that Jesus said, "It is more blessed to give than to receive" (Acts 20:35). Jesus may have actually said this, for we have no reason to doubt Luke's account, Paul's words, or the Bible in general, but there is no reference in any of the four Gospels where it records Jesus as actually saying this. Still, it does sound like something Jesus would say, so I am willing to accept the fact that this statement is indeed true.

However, there is something we need to consider here in light of this passage in John's Gospel. If it is true that one is *more blessed* to give, one must be *some blessed* to receive. If no one ever is willing to receive, then there can be no giver who is more blessed in his or her giving. It takes both givers and receivers to open the blessing pipeline.

Jesus was doing a wonderful and yet humble thing here as He moved from person to person in that upper room and washed stinking feet. Later He would share in what we call, "The Last Supper," with His disciples, but first He once again qualified Himself as the ultimate servant so that these slow-to-learn followers would get the delusions of grandeur out of their heads and start thinking like members of the divine Kingdom.

In Luke 22:24, it is recorded that in this very setting of the Upper Room, a disagreement broke out among the disciples as to which of them should be considered the greatest. Though John doesn't specifically mention it here, I have to think that this demonstration by Jesus quieted the room and caused a sense of shame to fall upon the disciples as they saw what their Master was doing.

Peter was slow, as he seemed so often to be about things, to grasp the insight of what this action of Jesus really meant. He was too proud, too full of himself, to allow Jesus to wash his feet. But he quickly learned that what Jesus does is always right, and that he needed to yield to His wisdom always. As a matter of fact, that's a good lesson for us to learn as well.

MORE THAN SKIN DEEP

John 13:9–11 *"Then, Lord," Simon Peter replied, "not just my feet but my hands and my head as well!" Jesus answered, "A person who has had a bath needs only to wash his feet; his whole body is clean. And you are clean, though not every one of you." For he knew who was going to betray him, and that was why he said not every one was clean.*

It seems interesting to me that Peter was the only one of the disciples who is recorded to have made an objection to having his feet washed by Jesus. One would think that Judas, who was about to betray Jesus on that same night, would have been hesitant to have Jesus anywhere near Him. He knew the power that His Master had demonstrated in knowing the thoughts and intents of the hearts of those who challenged Him, so we would think that Judas would have felt pretty weird about getting his feet washed by the one he was about to betray.

Still, all we have in the biblical record are Peter's words of protest. It is striking though, that after realizing the cost of refusing the offer of Jesus, Simon Peter was all for the idea, and even more so. He wanted more than just his feet washed. He wanted to show Jesus that he belonged to Him from his head to his toes and everywhere in between.

That is a pretty good guide for the rest of us. Once Jesus shows us that we must yield to His plans for our lives completely, we need to offer Him the complete package of our lives. He doesn't call us to be baptized in water to only dedicate a portion of ourselves to Him, but to surrender to His will completely.

It would be great to hear Jesus say to us, "You are clean!" To be His, to be filled with His Spirit, and committed totally to His Kingdom is to be clean. To hold back anything from Him moves us out of the state of purity and causes a return to a soiled life. It doesn't have to happen, for Jesus doesn't want it to ever happen, but being clean requires not only a cleansing from the hands of Jesus, but a desire and willingness to stay that way.

Judas didn't get it. What Jesus did was not a symbolic act, for the cleansing was real, but there was great symbolism in it. As He did, we should do also. As He gave up everything for us, we should give up everything for Him. Judas couldn't do that, and the stain of sin would be with Him forever.

LIVING THE LESSON

John 13:12–15 *When he finished washing their feet, he put on his clothes and returned to his place. "Do you understand what I have done for you?" he asked them. "You call me 'Teacher' and 'Lord,' and rightly so, for that is what I am. Now that I, your Lord and Teacher, have washed your feet, you also should wash one another's feet. I have set you an example that you should do as I have done for you."*

Like a lot of people, I learn best when I can learn with visual demonstrations. Computers drive me crazy as I try to read manuals and instructive information, but if someone would sit me down in front of the screen and walk me through a program I can usually catch on.

Object lessons are made for people like me. Jesus surely knew that His disciples needed such demonstrations also. He probably could have preached a sermon about foot-washing and they would have missed the point, but when He did it right in front of them, they got the idea.

In order to make sure that the lesson stuck, Jesus did what a master teacher does, He asked questions to see if there was any confusion, then He reinforced what He had demonstrated with instructive words to clear up any doubt that might somehow still have remained in His follower's minds. It's as though He said, "You saw what I did. You heard why I did it. Now, it's time for you to imitate me before the world." John surely got the message, for he records it for us very candidly.

Let's now fast-forward to the present. The need for physical foot-washing as a public service is not necessary in most situations, at least in Western society. However, the principle behind what Jesus taught is still very valid and needed. First, it was among the intimate group of followers that Jesus made His demonstration as He provided for them what they needed physically. Perhaps that is a good place for us to begin. Whether it would be with our family, our Sunday School class, our church staff, or some other group of close friends, we could apply the teaching of Jesus to help meet some physical need in their lives. It might be food, a hug, words of encouragement, an act of physical labor, or some other way to demonstrate our willingness to serve. From there it may flow to the world, but kindness begins with the family of God.

IN DEBT, BIG TIME

John 13:16–17 *"I tell you the truth, no servant is greater than his master, nor is a messenger greater than the one who sent him. Now that you know these things, you will be blessed if you do them."*

I have been blessed throughout my life to have had some wonderful people who have taught me many things. My dad taught me how to work, my mom taught me how to love, my siblings taught me how to share, my pastors have filled my mind with an appreciation for God's Word, and my professors have taught me how to think about what I read. The list could go on and on for I owe so much to so many, like my wife, my children, my grandson, the people in the churches I have served, and many more. In various ways the lessons I have learned from these people are countless.

But the person to whom I owe the most is the Lord Himself. He has not only been my greatest teacher, but the Master of my destiny as He has directed my path of service. I certainly owe Him everything I have, I am, or will ever have, or be.

Since I owe Him such a debt, I feel the truth of His words in these verses. Though I am His servant, I will never be able to serve on a level that is worthy of His plan for me. Though I am one of His messengers, I am under no illusions that the messages come from me. If He doesn't give me the words to say then I have nothing worthwhile to contribute to anyone.

Sometimes I am convinced that I am the favorite of all His servants and messengers because of the amount of blessing His has poured all over my life. His pay scale is off the charts and His retirement plan is out of this world. Being able to be considered His friend is the highest award I will ever receive.

Because of such blessings, I realize that His example of foot-washing calls for me to imitate Him. There are many others whose needs require my care and my attention to their situation. As much as He has blessed me, I have an obligation to be a blessing to others in a way that would reflect well on Him. Because He called me and hasn't uncalled me, it is not possible for me to quit until I am unable to serve any longer, regardless of what the calendar says, or how many years stack up. Being a servant and a messenger for the King is the best job in the world, and I wouldn't trade it for the balance of the national debt. His approval should be all the pay I will ever need.

A NIGHT THAT CHANGED
THE WORLD

John 13:18 *"I am not referring to all of you; I know those I have chosen. But this is to fulfill the scripture: 'He who shares my bread has lifted up his heel against me.'"*

One advantage we have this side of the cross is that we know how the story of Christ's passion ends. We don't have to wonder about the final outcome, but we have the advantage of being able to put everything into slow motion, reverse, and replay in order to get the big picture of what really happened. The disciples couldn't do that, so we need to cut them some slack for their ignorance.

There has never been a night in the history of the world that had more of an impact on humanity than this night. We don't hear of people naming their children, Judas. I am filled with wonder when I consider all that was going on surrounding that last supper of Jesus with His disciples, and it causes me to ask some questions.

I have to ask, "Why did Jesus choose Judas in the first place?" Haven't you ever wondered about this? Didn't Jesus know the outcome of His choice? Surely, He wasn't duped by Judas. In considering this question, I have come to a few conclusions.

Perhaps Jesus included Judas in the number of the twelve disciples so that he would have no excuse for his unbelief. There was no way that Judas could ever plead that he wasn't given a fair chance. Perhaps Jesus chose Judas just to fulfill prophecy. Psalm 41:9 says, "Even my close friend, whom I trusted, he who shared my bread, has lifted up his heel against me." Psalm 55:12–14 records, "If an enemy were insulting me, I could endure it; if a foe were rising himself against me, I could hide from him. But it is you, a man like myself, my companion, my close friend, with whom I once enjoyed sweet fellowship at the house of God, as we walked with the throne at the house of God." Perhaps this choice was the only way that the plan of redemption could be finished. Without a betrayal there would be no cross and you and I would be guilty and die in our sin.

To fully understand whatever reason Jesus had for choosing Judas, we may have to wait until we can ask Him face to face. By faith we know He had His reasons, and we know that Jesus never makes a mistake.

HE KNEW WHAT THEY DIDN'T KNOW

John 13:19–20 *"I am telling you now before it happens, so that when it does happen you will believe that I am He. I tell you the truth, whoever accepts anyone I send accepts me; and whoever accepts me accepts the one who sent me."*

There is no doubt about it. Jesus knew things. He not only knew things, but He knew about them before anyone else did. In fact, He knew about them before they happened. The kind of insight that Jesus possessed was not natural because no one else possessed that level of awareness.

But if Jesus came to set an example for how we are to live, and we are to be holy as He is holy, and we are to be His light to our world, then how is it that He was able to see into the days ahead when we can't. There certainly must be an answer or else there is a serious disconnection taking place as we read these words.

It is my understanding that all Jesus was able to know and do was based on His connection with the Father. Jesus would spend all night in prayer at times (Luke 6:14), He would commune with the Holy Spirit and the Father in the wilderness (Matthew 4:11), in the city (John 12:28), in the quiet places with angels (Luke 22:43), and in the midst of crowds (Mark 1:11). It seems clear that the intense focus that Jesus had with the Godhead allowed Him to hear the words that He needed to hear in order to operate on the supernatural level in the midst of a natural world.

If this is true, then it stands to reason that we too could operate on a different plain spiritually if we were also willing to take the mission of the Father as seriously as Jesus did. If we were willing to set aside all distractions, obligations, and priorities of life, to instead concentrate on achieving the mission God has for us, then perhaps we too could tap in more effectively to the Father's voice.

It's easy to just say, "Well, Jesus was God, so of course He did things I could never do." I wonder though if that is just a cop-out for our lack of the commitment that Jesus had, for He told His disciples, "He will do greater things than these because I am going to the Father" (John 14:12). Maybe our refocusing will cause us to see and know things that only the Father can tell us. Would it be worth a try to find out? I wonder if we dare.

"Troubled In Spirit"

John 13:21–22 *After he had said this, Jesus was troubled in spirit and testified, "I tell you the truth, one of you is going to betray me." His disciples stared at one another, at a loss to know which of them he meant.*

We have seen this look on Jesus before. He was troubled in His spirit. It is no doubt hard to even begin to put into words what Jesus was feeling. He was hurt, disappointed, and saddened not only by what He was about to face, but even more so by the betrayal He was about to experience. He ultimately knew what was going to happen to Himself, because He has been telling His disciples about the cross since the time they first realized that He truly was the Messiah they had been waiting for (Matthew 16:16). Certainly, the cross that awaited Him and the torture He would face on it would cause Him to be troubled, but I think there is more at play here.

I believe what really troubled Jesus in His spirit was that He knew what would happen to Judas. There are probably no words that could ever describe the fate that awaited this disciple turned traitor. In Matthew 26:24 Jesus said, "The Son of Man will go just as it is written about him. But woe to that man who betrays the Son of Man! It would be better for him if he had never been born." Perhaps Hebrews 10:31 says it best, "It is a dreadful thing to fall into the hands of the living God."

The thing that was behind the way Jesus felt was the fact that He still loved Judas. We might think that such a terrible act of betrayal would produce bitterness and anger, but that's not what we see here. Jesus was experiencing a broken heart. Even though Judas wasn't worth the love that Jesus was feeling, He was loved just the same.

This is the story of us all. Who of us have not disappointed Jesus greatly at some point? Who of us is innocent when it comes to breaking the commandments of loving God with our whole being, and our neighbor as ourselves? Maybe we didn't betray Jesus to the extent that Judas did, but we have all come short of the glory of God (Romans 3:23). For that reason alone, we don't deserve the love of Christ, but He loves us just the same because love personified is who He is.

Judas blew it. We have too. Thanks be to God that we are loved anyway and cared for by the Savior of our souls.

FAITH BEING TESTED

John 13:23–24 *One of them, the disciple whom Jesus loved, was reclining next to him. Simon Peter motioned to this disciple and said, "Ask him which one he means."*

When we read the words, "the disciple whom Jesus loved," most biblical students understand this person to be the Apostle John himself. Since meals were not eaten while sitting on chairs around a desk-high table, Jesus reclined on His left side next to a low table with feet protruding out away from the table. John was located next to Jesus and most likely Peter next to John. In this setting, curiosity was high and suspicion was rampant.

Don't you have to wonder why Jesus didn't expose Judas to the other disciples outright. He certainly had plenty of time and opportunity before this night, and could have been more explicit on this night, but for some reason He didn't spell what He meant out for them.

He did tell the disciples, but they didn't understand what He was saying. These verses seem plenty clear to us, but apparently His words went right over their heads. Of course, if they had known what Judas was going to do, they probably would have put a stop to his scheme, but that wouldn't fit with the plan of the Father. I mean, if Peter would later be willing to take a sword and cut of the ear of the high priest's servant, one can only imagine what he would have done to Judas if Jesus had directly pointed him out.

The disciples didn't realize this at the time, but their future ministries and the destiny of the world would have changed if the events of the betrayal were not played out. Their view was short-sighted on their best days and they surely couldn't have been expected to see the unfolding plan of God from their limited perspective at this time.

We learn here is that faith is not developed in a vacuum, but through the fires of testing and waiting. On this night the disciples were confused about a lot of things. They didn't understand Jesus washing their feet. They had questions about Jesus telling them that the bread and the wine were really His body and blood. They were shocked and baffled by the announcement that someone would betray their Master, and they were genuinely surprised that they didn't know who that person would be. Prophecy was being fulfilled however, and the world would change forever. Thanks be to God!

SETTING THE STAGE

John 13:25–28 *Leaning back against Jesus, he asked him, "Lord, who is it? Jesus answered, "It is the one to whom I will give this piece of bread when I have dipped it in the dish." Then, dipping the piece of bread, he gave it to Judas, son of Simon. As soon as Judas took the bread, Satan entered into him. "What you are about to do, do quickly," Jesus told him, but no one at the meal understood why Jesus said this to him.*

We have to ask at this point, "Why didn't the disciples catch the hint that Jesus gave to them?" It could be said, and probably has been said by many wives, that sometimes men are just clueless. That may be a little cynical, but we of the male species sometimes really do need to have things spelled out for us.

It could be that the other disciples thought Jesus was sending Judas out on some kind of an errand. Since he was more or less the treasurer of the group, if something needed to be purchased then Judas would be the likely candidate to do the buying. Jesus had done so much for so many in the few years that they had known Him, that if wouldn't be unreasonable for them to think that He was about to extend another mission of mercy to someone. It was also true that just like with the parables Jesus told, they didn't always understand what He was talking about until they asked Him to explain it to them. They may have thought that this was just another lesson in the process of their training, and would yet be explained.

Maybe they were distracted by their own agendas. James and John had already been put in their place because of their desire to have a place of authority when Jesus came into His Kingdom (see Luke 22:24–26). Jesus dashed their immediate hopes, and pointed them toward a time when they would rule, but in a different way in a different kind of Kingdom.

Perhaps the disciples were still preoccupied with the evening's events. The foot-washing, the Passover meal, and Jesus' odd references to the finality of it all, and yet the beginning of something more. It was a strange night for them.

We might have missed the clues too, but if so, we would be in good company. One thing that could not be missed however, was that something big was about to happen. Shortly, everything would be much clearer.

"And It Was Night."

John 13:29–30 *Since Judas had charge of the money, some thought Jesus was telling him to buy what was needed for the Feast, or to give something to the poor. As soon as Judas had taken the bread, he went out. And it was night.*

Why did Judas do what he did? I guess we can only speculate about the reasons for his actions. He may have been confused by the circumstances that surrounded his situation, or he could have thought that a different path should be taken than the one Jesus was walking. He would not be the first or the last person who thought that they knew better that the One who created and knows everything.

He may have thought that there would be a different outcome. It's possible that he thought he was forcing Jesus' hand to take action and finally put the corrupt societal power-brokers of Israel in their proper place. The Pharisees, the chief priests, and the teachers of the Law had dominated the people for generations, and perhaps Judas thought that by forcing Jesus to go on the offense again them, the people of the land could finally be truly free.

We can't overlook the fact that by this time Satan had already entered Judas. There may never be any understandable answer as to why he did what he did because when the evil one has control, the end is always tragic.

This passage finishes with some terrifying words, "And it was night." Those four words paint a picture that screams doom. They remind me of when Samson had his head shaved by Delila and didn't realize that the Holy Spirit of God, as well as his strength, had left him (Judges 16:20). It also makes me think of what King Hezekiah of Judah did know. It is recorded in Isaiah 37:3: "This is what Hezekiah says, 'This is a day of distress and rebuke and disgrace, as when children come to the point of birth and there is no strength to deliver them.'" Doom can come at us from different directions, as these verses indicate.

The night of sin is a terrible place. Judas didn't even realize that he was in the midst of it because he had become blinded by his love for money, his self-serving purposes, and the entrapment of the devil. Sin destroyed him and will destroy all who yield to its leadings. The cross was ahead for Jesus, but a much worse fate awaited the one who would betray Him.

BRINGING GLORY TO THE FATHER

John 13:31–32 *When he was gone, Jesus said, "Now is the Son of Man glorified and God is glorified in him. If God is glorified in him, God will glorify the Son in himself, and will glorify him at once.*

The Kingdom of God is a subject that has two dimensions. There is the "here and now" and the "hereafter," and though they are different, they ought to be connected. Jesus is the bridge that gives evidence to both.

The focus of Jesus was on bringing glory to the Father, but this concept of glory is sometimes misunderstood because though it's common in the Bible, it is often distorted in our present-day society. It was not a selfish thing, for Jesus was not vain and He was not trying to promote Himself. His concentration was on doing the Father's will, because that is how the Father would be glorified to the world.

The idea of glorification is a matter of honor. Jesus wanted to bring honor to the Father in all He did. His life was an exhibit of holiness. This meant that His actions, His thoughts, and all He was about was to make the Father look good. Honoring the Father meant being the perfect role model for us to follow. Since the Father is holy, Jesus lived a holy life also, and His plan for those who would be His disciples is that they would be holy, and live holy lives as a reflection of His own life, who is the reflection of the Father. This is why we are specifically called to be holy in the Old Testament in Exodus 19:6; Leviticus 19:2; 20:7; 20:26; and 21:8. The New Testament records the same instructions in I Thessalonians 4:7 and I Peter 1:16.

Jesus wanted to bring praise to God. He set before us the example that living a holy life causes others to also want to exhibit the holiness of God. Christians sometimes get careless and forget their mission, but Jesus always calls us back to the way that will bring God praise.

It would seem very much like how we are when we want our earthly father's to be admired. The goal of every father should be to want to live in such a way that causes their children to imitate the characteristics of our heavenly Father, because they see that attribute in their father's life. Another way to put it is to say that I want to be like my earthly father because he is like our heavenly Father. That's the way it was with Jesus, and because His focus was constant, we have an example of how we should live.

SEPARATED FROM THE CHILDREN

John 13:33 *"My children, I will be with you only a little longer. You will look for me, and just as I told the Jews, so I tell you now: Where I am going, you cannot come."*

I find it interesting that in this passage Jesus refers to his disciples as His children. They were all adult men, but He had told them that they must become as children to get into the Kingdom, and they were reacting just like children to the news He was giving. Jesus was leaving them and going where they couldn't go, and the disciples didn't like it or understand it at all.

They were about to find out that separation is a painful but necessary part of Kingdom living. Later they would receive the Great Commission, with the first word being, "Go!" and they would come to understand that it is inevitable that someone will be left behind when someone else has to go. It is impossible to obey the divine command and not have someone leave.

Christian families have felt the pain of parting for the sake of the Gospel many times since Jesus spoke these words—and it's almost always hard. When we love someone, we long to be near them, so it's natural to have bittersweet feelings when family ties have to be severed.

This is why we must put Christ first at all times. When He takes the top position in our life's priorities, even our connections must be placed on the altar of sacrifice. It was this life of surrendering everything that Jesus was talking about in Matthew 10:37 when He said, "Anyone who loves his father or mother more than me is not worthy of me; anyone who loves his son or daughter more than me is not worthy of me." Serving Jesus involves making tough choices.

However hard it is for family to be separated, Jesus was telling His followers that *He* would be leaving them. To even think about Christ leaving us is an experience I never want to face. To live without Jesus would be harder and more painful the closer a person is to Him. When I try to put myself in the sandals of these disciples, the concept is almost overwhelming. Just imagine trying to do the work of the church on any level without the presence of Jesus to lead us, comfort us, and empower us. It would be impossible. We need Jesus for everything we do! I guess He was right, as usual. We are like children in need of our Big Brother all the time.

"LOVE!"

John 13:34–35 *"A new command I give you: Love one another. As I have loved you, so you must love one another. By this all men will know that you are my disciples, if you love one another."*

These verses make the mandate for Christian living as clear as it could possibly be: Love is the distinguishing mark of the Kingdom. The emphasis that Jesus puts on this directive is unmistakable, and it is not negotiable. We either put love at the core of all we do or we miss the mark Jesus set for us completely.

We have to realize that love is commanded by Jesus for His followers. This is not optional if we intend to be disciples of our King. Love is not necessarily an emotional thing at all, but instead is a choice that we make. The Greek word here for love is transliterated "agapate," or "agape," which is a love that comes from God for those who choose to be like Him. We decided whether we will follow the command or not. Again, it is a choice, not a feeling.

We also have to realize that this love is relational. It doesn't start with those who are not within our reach, but instead it begins with those close to us. The love we have is for one another; those nearest in our social connection. From there it can grow, but it begins at the starting point of our being. In this way it becomes more about a personal mission than "foreign missions," for all of life becomes a journey of learning how to love as Jesus does.

It is this love that becomes the evidence that Jesus really has taken control of our lives. The only thing that we have to prove is that what we testify to is real. Nothing else matters but our love.

What a strange night this was for the first disciples of Jesus. The foot-washing, the sacrament meal, the betrayal by Judas, and now this teaching and focus on what puts it all together. They were living out the Gospel while in the upper room, for it was love the caused Jesus to wash feet, to feed them the Passover meal, and to endure the disappointment in His heart caused by Judas. As His followers here would reflect back on this night some years later, they would be able to remember that they were to love in all circumstances because they saw that He loved regardless of what was happening. That lesson still holds true for us as well, for if we would be His followers, we will learn to live out the life of love. There is no other way.

"Will You Really?"

John 13:36–38 *Simon Peter asked him, "Lord, where are you going?" Jesus replied, "Where I am going, you cannot follow now, but you will follow later." Peter asked, "Lord, why can't I follow you now? I will lay down my life for you." Then Jesus answered, "Will you really lay down your life for me? I tell you the truth, before the rooster crows, you will disown me three times."*

If there was ever an example of how commitments are more easily made than kept, it is in these verses. It is a classic depiction of how will power alone is not enough to keep a person serving Jesus. There has to be a transformation in our very being by the power of the Holy Spirit for verbal commitments to become reality.

I would imagine that few people ever come to a place of prayer seeking a relationship with the living God without some level of commitment to the choice they are making with their lives. However, as we will find out later with Simon Peter, unguarded emotions often betray us. Physical fatigue can take its toll on us, as it would on Peter. The events in the upper room were emotional and draining, but what would happen after they would leave the room would lead to even more stress and physical weariness. Jesus knew what was coming, but at this point His disciples didn't have a clue.

We see here that impetuous boasts can belittle us. The claims of Simon remind me of I Kings 20:11, where Ahab of Samaria was challenged by Ben-hadad of the Arameans. Though Ben-hadad was confident of his army's ability to conquer Israel, Ahab simply told him, "One who puts on his armor should not boast like one who takes it off." In other words, don't brag until your victory is finished and secure.

No doubt the reply of Jesus to Simon's boast had to cause some bruising to the big fisherman's ego. He was about to learn though that it is better not to tell Jesus you will do something if you are not ready to back it up. Simon boasted that he would lay down his life for Jesus, but though Jesus knew that such would someday be the case, this is not the night it would happen.

It's a good lesson for all of us. Our testimony for Jesus and His Kingdom is vital, but it can't be just talk. A genuine relationship with Christ and being filled with His Spirit is essential before our words can become reality. Peter found this out the hard way. I hope we will learn from his mistake.

TRUST ISSUES

John 14:1 *"Do not let your hearts be troubled. Trust in God; trust also in me."*

I will always be grateful for the John W. Peterson's Easter cantatas that we sang back in the 1970's because these verses of scripture from John 14 were repeated over and over, in the King James Version, and therefore I put these truths to memory, and they have stayed with me over the years. The Word of God is food for our souls as well as great teaching for our minds.

We often forget that though these words of comfort are used at many funerals around the world, they come on the heels of the revelation of Peter's coming denial of Jesus in the upper room. They follow the washing of the disciple's feet and the betrayal by Judas. Deep things have been discussed, so probably the disciples needed a lift.

This is a great example of what Jesus is like. He doesn't take us to the depths without providing words to comfort us and lift us up. However, there are some issues of life that Jesus relates to His disciples and to us in this verse and the verses that follow.

There first is the issue of trust. We all know what it is to trust someone and the importance of having people to trust us. In our humanness we have a tendency to worry about the economy, political elections, our families, and our churches, and many other things, but with these words Jesus gives us an antidote for this problem of worry. He simply says, "Stop it!"

What He does is to remind the disciples and us, that all we have to do is trust Him. We don't have to focus on all the stuff that normally occupies our minds as we deal with the changes of life that we can't seem to comprehend or handle. We can leave the details to Him. We know that we have a limited number of years here on this planet, and then the future gets a bit blurry for us. We know that we can't control what we can't be sure of, so we focus on trying to be lords over our own little spot of the world. Jesus reminds us that we can put everything in His hands. He is big enough to provide everything we need, everything that will involve our families, and everything else we care about. He says, "You have trusted God, so now trust me. I am here for you and I will there for you when you face the unknown." If we will really trust Him, we will never have to worry about anything ever again, for what is unknown to us is already known to Him.

A PLACE IS WAITING

John 14:2 *"In my Father's house are many rooms; if it were not so, I would have told you. I am going there to prepare a place for you."*

This verse has been a source of speculation concerning what life is like after this world. What is translated as "rooms" here in the New International Version of the Bible is translated, "mansions" in the King James Version, as "dwelling places" in the New Revised Standard Version, simply "dwellings" in the Wycliff Bible, and "many places," in the Complete Jewish Bible. Many other English translations phrase it is similar fashion, having only slight differences in the wording. The Greek literally list the word as "monai," which could also be translated "remains," or "abodes." Words can be confusing because sometimes we don't know, and sometimes we don't even know what we don't know.

The fact of the matter is that we don't know what happens after death. After we close our eyes for the last time it is all faith and speculation. We don't really know what life is like after death. All we have is the Bible and that's why this is a faith walk that we are taking.

Because it is a faith walk, we who have put our faith in Jesus to be the provider for our salvation, really don't care whether we will be rewarded in the heavenlies with a mansion, or just a dwelling place, or abode. The important features of what Jesus is telling us here is that there will be a place for us, and it is being prepared by Jesus.

Think about that for just a moment, based on what John has already told us about Jesus. "Through him all things were made; without him nothing was made that has been made" (John 1:3). Jesus is the Master Architect and Creator of all the universe, and it appears to me that He has done a pretty good job. Can we not trust the One who has made all that there is to do well by us in our heavenly place of residence?

Our home is waiting for us. He would have let us know if it were to be otherwise. We can count on the fact that all of our friends, loved ones, family, and saints of the ages who have put their trust in Jesus for their salvation, are waiting there for us. We may not know exactly what it will be like, but we are given enough clues to make it sound wonderful. As for me, I can hardly wait to get there because my Master never does anything halfway.

HE'S COMING BACK!

> **John 14:2–3** *"In my Father's house are many rooms; if it were not so, I would have told you. I am going there to prepare a place for you. And if I go and prepare a place for you, I will come back and take you to be with me that you also may be where I am."*

In these verses there is a promise issue that we need to consider. Either Jesus can be trusted to keep His word, or we have been fooled about a lot of things. After all, we believe in the hope of eternal life because of Him.

Here He gives a promise as to where we will be. I especially love reading in the book of Revelation, chapters four and five. Those chapters contain what I call the "Great Praise Party," as all creation gathers around the throne of God in chapter four and celebrates His majesty and power. In the fifth chapter Jesus, the Lamb that was destined to be slain from the foundation of the world, enters the picture and is proclaimed worthy to open the seals of the scroll/book that will explain the mysteries of the ages. Though sometimes hard to understand because of the apocalyptic style of writing, we are given a view that everything is under control and going right along the plan and schedule of the Master.

There is a promise concerning the return of Jesus. We must never forget that He truly is coming back. II Peter 3:3–9 reminds us that though some people may scoff at the idea, Jesus is not lax or forgetful in fulfilling His promise, but is patient, waiting for as many people as possible to enter the eternal Kingdom before the end of time comes.

There is also a promise concerning His plans for us. He is taking us to meet the Father. We are going to finally be able to stand in the presence of the Eternal One from whom everything comes into existence. I doubt if we will stand long, for no doubt we will join the others who are bowing at His feet and worshipping.

There are certainly a lot of questions that remain concerning the mysteries of eternity and the path that takes us there, but one thing we can count on is the fact that the promises of Jesus are sure. We can rest on His words and live out our days in the expectancy of life everlasting to come when our days here are over. How, when, and where really don't matter because they are all answered in the Who. The Who is Jesus, and that's all we need to know.

WE OUGHT TO KNOW BY NOW

John 14:4 *"You know the way to the place where I am going."*

Something we may not have considered as we have read through this chapter before is the expectation issue that Jesus has with us. He speaks to His disciples in no uncertain terms as He prepares for the questions that He knows are coming. We will see them start in the next verse. However, there are most likely many questions about the place to which He is going that caused concern over the centuries. Sometimes the scriptures slip some things in on us so that we have to focus more closely if we are going to grasp their significance.

Jesus expects us to know about these things. Even the first disciples had been told repeatedly about events concerning the cross and the resurrection, but we who have had the words in print all our lives should certainly have developed an understanding that leads to confidence. The Bible has been given to us so that we might have faith, and Jesus expects our faith to be secure and solid. What He has proclaimed on this occasion should lead us to "know the way" to the place that He was going.

It is not from a lack of information that we suffer. Any doubt that may come our way comes from the fact that we want to be told and retold about such things. Too many of us are like the disciples here and want someone to lead us by the hand to discover things that Jesus has spoken about, without having to live by faith to achieve such understanding.

Again, we discover that our following after Jesus is totally a faith-walk. But though we walk by faith, that doesn't mean that we can't walk in confidence and assurance. Jesus has led the way, pointed us in the right direction, and will be waiting on the other side to receive us. These are all the things we need to know as we make our journey to the eternal Kingdom.

Before the days of our global navigational systems (GPS), we had to learn to read maps and discern directions by the placement of the sun and stars. On occasion we might need to obtain verbal instructions to help us get to where we were going, but we usually found our way without the help of a satellite. We have gotten a bit soft and dependent on electronic devices. However, Jesus offers a more secure way. We know the way because He has told us the way. Our assurance rests on His credibility.

NOT KNOWING

John 14:5–7 *Thomas said to him, "Lord, we don't know where you are going, so how can we know the way?" Jesus answered, "I am the way and the truth and the life. No one comes to the Father except through me. If you really knew me, you would know my Father as well. From now on, you do know him and have seen him."*

Do you know what it's like to be lost? I have a pretty good sense of direction, but there have been a few times when I have gotten completely turned around, like in a snowstorm, or a fog. It's possible for the most seasoned travelers to lose their bearings once in a while. These disciples were confused about where Jesus was going and how they were going to be able to follow after Him. Jesus cleared the matter up a lot for them and us.

It is true that we don't really know much about where we are going. We are perplexed and amazed by the stories of people who have supposedly died and then come back to tell us of their experiences. Even the Old Testament is a bit unclear as to our final destination. We read words like, "dust," "Sheol," "the pit," "destruction," and "the grave." Equally vague are some of the images we receive from the New Testament. Passages in 1 Thessalonians 4:13–18; 2 Timothy 4:6–8; Philippians 4:20; and John 5:24–29 are road signs, but not clearly defined pictures.

However, we do know the path that gets us there. Christians are convinced by faith that Jesus is the only way to eternal life with the Father. There is not a way for each religion or belief group—just Jesus. He is the only way. Therefore, we do not compromise with other theories. It is always good to discuss and listen, but as we walk with faith in Christ, we do not bend on this issue. Jesus is the one and only way to God. That is non-negotiable.

We actually don't know a lot about God, but we are continually growing in our insights and awareness the longer we walk with Him. We only know what He chooses to reveal to us. In the Old Testament He is shown as Creator and Judge, and in the New Testament we see Him as our benevolent Father.

What we do know we know because of Jesus. He is God in the flesh. He is God with us. He is eternal. It is His Spirit that lives with us and within us today. Others may doubt, but we know the way because of Jesus, and someday we shall see Him face to face!

"SHOW ME"

John 14:8 Philip said, "Lord, show us the
Father and that will be enough for us."

There are lots of analogies that describe the church. We are called the body of Christ, the salt of the earth, the light of the world, the remnant of faith, and the sheep of the flock, but no term is truly more descriptive than, "the family of God."

We are family because we have in-laws and outlaws, spiritual parents and spiritual children, and we have brothers and sisters in the Lord. We are often closer to our spiritual family and spend more time with them than we do our own blood relatives. Families have strong points and weak moments, and it is one of these weak moments that is depicted in this verse.

It takes time for faith to grow, even when it is in a family setting. We readily believe in cars starting, keys opening locks, stores being open, and roads being clear for travel. We've automatically come to expect these things without thinking, but spiritual faith takes a little longer to become fact for us.

The first disciples had a problem with their faith development too, and in many ways, we often find ourselves just like Philip and Thomas. We find that Philip says, "Show us the Father," but what he is really saying is, "We still are not quite convinced about You."

Like these disciples, we too sometimes have short memories. They had seen the miracles and heard the teachings of Jesus. They had heard the voice of the Father speak back in 12:28, in response to Jesus' asking Him to glorify His name, saying, "I have glorified it, and will glorify it again." One would think that they would have had ample evidence of who Jesus was in relationship to the Father, but still their faith was weak.

For people to reach the level of spiritual maturity that carries them through the storms of life, they have to grow to the point that they believe even when they don't see empirical evidence before our eyes. We too will find ourselves with short memories if we don't abide "the Source," who continues to display His greatness before our world.

If this is going to be the time that we will go deeper in our faith, we must trust Jesus even when we don't see Him with our eyes. It's hard, but required.

"Don't You Know Me?"

John 14:9–10 *Jesus answered, "Don't you know me, Philip, even after I have been among you such a long time? Anyone who has seen me has seen the Father. How can you say, 'Show us the Father'? Don't you believe that I am in the Father, and that the Father is in me? The words I say to you are not just my own. Rather, it is the Father, living in me, who is doing his work."*

It really seems like Jesus was taken aback and surprised by the comment from Philip when he asked Jesus to show them the Father. There aren't many places in scripture where Jesus appears to be amazed, but this is one of them. When He responds it is as if He is saying, "Is it because you have seen me, but don't really know me that you are asking this?" He comes across as flabbergasted that His disciples are still in the dark.

Knowing Christ and knowing the Father is so different from knowing about Christ and knowing about the Father. I know about many important people in the world and throughout history, but it's not the same thing as knowing them personally. I have read many books on Abraham Lincoln, so I have gleaned much information about him, but there is no way that I really know him.

It takes time and opportunity to build a relationship. I have more time than I ever have had these days, but I don't have the opportunity to know the current president, let alone ones from the past. Knowing and knowing about people are two totally different things.

Jesus calls for His disciples to understand that we get to know the Father by connecting with the Son, and allowing Him to do His work in us. God can, and will become one with us if we allow Him to do so, and if we take the time and effort needed to connect intimately with Him.

We hear people all the time say, "I don't know what people do without the Lord!" It's a legitimate question because we who put our trust in Him and get to know Him see what a difference He makes in our lives. Once one has the relationship, we wonder why everyone doesn't want to go deeper and experience the person of Jesus.

We have not seen the Father, nor the Son with our eyes at this point, but someday that will change. Until then, we meet and see our Savior in prayer.

DOING GREATER THINGS
THAT JESUS DID

John 14:11–12 *"Believe me when I say that I am in the Father and the Father is in me; or at least believe on the evidence of the miracles themselves. I tell you the truth, anyone who has faith in me will do what I have been doing. He will do even greater things than these, because I am going to my Father."*

At this point Jesus was nearly pleading with His disciples. "Believe my words or believe on the evidence—but believe!" He knew that His time with them was drawing to a close and it was so very important that their doubts about Him would be erased.

A lot of families try to use Santa Claus as a system of belief with the young. Some go through great pains to pull off the hoax so that children have an imaginary character with which to identify. We however, have the Word of God, and we have it in written form so that there would be no doubt as to what God wants us to know. We don't have to have a fictional focus to set our minds at ease, for we can know Jesus today in a real and intimate way. We see the evidence of what He has done and what He can do.

It is the evidence of changed lives that stands out above all the others. Countless numbers of people down through the ages have given witness of a transformation in their lives because of Jesus. Though the disciples in this setting didn't have the advantage of a historical view concerning Jesus, we believe because of all that Christ has done in our world.

When Jesus said that His followers would do greater things because He was going to the Father, He was in essence telling them and us that we are to be doers as He was a doer. As a child my first verse of scripture to memorize was from James 1:22, "But be ye doers of the word and not hearers only, deceiving your own selves" (KJV). The importance of that verse—and the words of Jesus here—still ring true.

We can do what Jesus did. We can teach, heal, rebuke, love, disciple, and show the self-control and discipline of the Spirit as we work for the glory of God. We can also do greater things than Jesus did. This most likely will not be in quality, for Jesus set the standard for ministry in all areas. However, we can put more "boots on the ground" as we minister in greater numbers, reaching more people with the good news, and declaring the wonders of God. We can believe and live out our faith in the power of the Spirit.

IN HIS NAME

John 14:13–14 *And I will do whatever you ask in my name, so that the Son may bring glory to the Father. You may ask me for anything in my name, and I will do it."*

One of the most important things that Jesus relates to His disciples of all ages through these verses, is the fact that we are not alone. He is in this journey with us all the way. There is no greater promise for us in the Bible than the promise of the eternal "I AM" is walking with us continually.

We who walk with Him, have come to realize that He is our resource. We depend on Him to figure things out. He is our power source. We depend on Him for strength to run our ministries, and face the challenges that such ministries bring. He also is our advocate. We depend on Him to defend us and intercede for us to the Father. Because of our relationship to Jesus, we have access to the highest level of authority that exists.

Throughout these verses Jesus has been emphasizing to His disciples the lessons about seeing, believing, doing, and abiding. In the few remaining hours He had before the cross, He wanted them to realize that such things were what the life in Him was all about.

The lessons are passed down through the centuries to us. We are called to see Jesus for who He is. We are asked to believe that He is who He said He is. He helps us to realize that ministry is not just for ministers, but for all who would follow after Him. We learn to trust His abiding presence to walk with us and enlighten us all along our life's pilgrimage.

There have been some who have taken these words from Jesus out of context and have taught that since we can ask anything in Jesus' name and we will receive it, regardless of what we ask. It's as though people make their wish list and then tag on, "In Jesus' name," at the end of it. That's not what Jesus was talking about.

Jesus was all about ministry. Those who say that Christians should name and claim wealth, health, authority, and prestige have no concept of the context of this story, or the looming cross that would lie just ahead. Jesus could have asked anything of the Father, but He chose the way of the cross. Selfless service and sacrifice will always be the path of ministry.

OUR PROMISED COUNSELOR

John 14:15–17 *If you love me, you will obey what I command. And I will ask the Father, and he will give you another Counselor to be with you forever—the Spirit of truth. The world cannot accept him, because it neither sees him nor knows him. But you know him, for he lives with you and will be in you.*

When we think about Jesus and the things that are connected to Him, we usually think on one of two levels. We often focus on what it's going to be like when we get to see Him face to face. Every time we attend a funeral, we think about His promise that He left to prepare a place for us (John 14:2).

As wonderful as that promise is, there is another promise that is just as important, and it involves how we are going to survive and thrive until He takes us home. He promised us that His Holy Spirit would be with us forever, and what a difference that has made!

In these verses Jesus speaks about love. He lets His followers know that real love requires action to prove its legitimacy. Words are cheap and easily found, for words are like opinions. We usually have more than enough of them to go around. However, actions are costly and require discipline. Jesus was obedient to the plan of the Father, and it is required of us to be obedient to Jesus, if we are to be His followers and demonstrate that our love for Him is real.

When Jesus speaks of the Counselor who was to come, He spoke of Him as being the reward for our love. God will never be in our debt, so He always gives us more than we could ever give Him. In this case, He sent a part of Himself, the Holy Spirit to be indwelt in our lives.

What do we know about the Holy Spirit? Well, we know that He is a gift from God, for He was promised in Acts 1:8. We know that He is eternal. Some friends will leave us, but not this Friend, for He will be with us forever. We know that He is completely honest, therefore we never have to wonder if we are being led in the right direction when we listen to what the Counselor is saying to us. He is invisible, and that is the snag for people without faith, but He is perceivable. Though we can't see Him, His voice can be heard and His guiding presence can be felt.

He lives within the believer and He is the best gift we could ever receive!

NO ORPHANS IN THE KINGDOM

John 14:18–20 *I will not leave you as orphans; I will come to you. Before long, the world will not see me anymore, but you will see me. Because I live, you also will live. On that day you will realize that I am in my Father, and you are in me, and I am in you.*

People have different reactions to the idea of having a counselor. I married one and I am one, so my perspective may be a little different from others. For some, going to a counselor invokes a sense of fear and frustration. For others, it's an opportunity to talk out ideas and make progress in our relationships, our marriages, and even in our own self-worth.

This Counselor is the presence of Jesus Himself. Jesus knows our status in life, and He knows that if we were left on our own, we would be orphans, so He doesn't want to leave us that way. When He sends the Counselor to be with us, He is not sending a stand-in, or a proxy, for the Divine Counselor is the presence of Jesus Himself in spiritual form. We cannot separate the presence of Jesus from the person of the Holy Spirit. We don't get Jesus in our lives at one point and then the Holy Spirit later, for the presence of Jesus is the Holy Spirit. When we choose to follow Jesus, we get all of God there is to get, and that includes the Holy Trinity.

Our hope for life is wrapped up in the person of Jesus the Messiah. His resurrection provides the hope for our own resurrection, for if Jesus was not raised from the dead then all we do and all we believe is for nothing. There is a time coming when we will see the Christ with our own eyes. This is a direct promise that Jesus made to His followers. Now we see through eyes of faith, but someday we will see Him as He is, and we will know Him as we are known.

Because Jesus is one with the Father and one with the Holy Spirit, when we become one with Him then we too are interconnected with the divine. We can know the joys of fellowshipping with the Trinity because of what Jesus has done and provided on our behalf.

It may seem like a long time has passed since Jesus made these statements, but as we look back over our own lives, we realize that the years pass quickly. We are closer now to seeing Him than we have ever been, and before long our faith will be sight! Glory be to God!

REAL LOVE

John 14:21 *Whoever has my commands and obeys them, he is the one who loves me. He who loves me will be loved by my Father, and I too will love him and show myself to him.*

We find here that Jesus is basically saying, "What goes around, comes around." If we love, then we will get love. If we love the Son we get the Father, but we don't love the Son we will get neither. If we obey the Son, then we will find He and the Father. In fact, Matthew 5:6 spells this out, "Blessed are those who hunger and thirst for righteousness, for they will be filled." Jesus is righteousness personified.

We learn from this section of Scripture that the Holy Spirit of God is not an "it," but a person of direct connection in the Holy Trinity. He is the presence of Jesus, He is the power of the Father, He is the promise for all believers, and He is the partner we need until we get home. When we love Jesus we get the whole package of Father, Son, and Spirit. It's beyond our full comprehension, for it is a blessing too big to describe or fully explain.

All of this comes at the price of love. Earlier Jesus had told His disciples that the first and greatest commandment was to love God with all of our heart, soul, mind, and strength, and to love our neighbor as ourself (Mark 12:29–31). In fact, He said that there were no greater commandments than these. We will spend a lifetime learning how to do either of these things as well as we should, but when love is at the core of all of our intentions toward God and others, we are on the right track for receiving all the blessings that have been promised to us.

I love the idea of Jesus showing Himself to us. We have many different renditions of what Jesus looked like from the minds of artists across the centuries, but probably no one really did Him justice. We see Him with eyes of faith, though we are blind to the spiritual form, but someday that is going to be completely different. As surely as the disciples saw Him on the Road to Emmaus (Luke 24) and Thomas was able to touch the nail prints in His hands and feet (John 20), we too are going be able to witness the bodily resurrected form of Jesus, our Redeemer.

Again, the ticket to seeing Him is love. It is the answer to the world's problems and the key to life everlasting, for love never fails!

WHY, INDEED?

John 14:22–24 *Then Judas (not Iscariot) said, "But, Lord, why do you intend to show yourself to us and not to the world?" Jesus replied, "If anyone loves me, he will obey my teaching. My Father will love him, and we will come to him and make our home with him. He who does not love me will not obey my teaching. These words you hear are not my own; they belong to the Father who sent me."*

We spend a lot of our time and energy asking, "Why?" That's not necessarily a bad thing though. In fact, it may be a very good thing because we rarely make progress without asking questions.

Sometimes, however, we may not be in a position to understand "why" even when the answer is clearly given. That seemed to be the case when Jesus talked with His disciples about things that were yet to come.

Doubt leads to fear and fear is a topic that comes up over and over in the Bible. People are often afraid of anything outside of their ordinary experiences, and we haven't progressed much in that department. Maybe the words of Judas are words with which we can identify on some level.

It seems like a fair question. Why did Jesus intend to show Himself to the disciples, but not to the world? We could still ask that question. Why are we so blessed, and have been treated so well in the matter of spiritual revelation? Why did He choose to let us in on the membership information for the Kingdom of God? Why has the Word of God found such a valued place in our hearts? We could ask, "Why not others?" Why have we been privileged to hear the words of life while millions in the world have still never hear the name of Jesus?

Apparently, love is the qualifier here. Love leads to obedience and obedience leads to fruit that can be witnessed by others. When there is no love there is no obedience, and when there is no obedience then new teaching is not received—even when God sends it.

The Father is at work and is responsible for sharing the Good News of salvation with mankind. How and why He opens the door of life to some and not others initially is known to Him alone. However, now that we know, it is our duty to share the gospel so that all people can know what we know.

THE COUNSELOR IS COMING

John 14:25–27 *"All this I have spoken while still with you. But the Counselor, the Holy Spirit, whom the Father will send in my name, will teach you all things and will remind you of everything I have said to you. Peace I leave with you; my peace I give you. I do not give to you as the world gives. Do not let your hearts be troubled and do not be afraid.*

A wonderful proclamation comes out of this passage. Jesus promises to be with us forever in the form of His Holy Spirit, the Comforter. Those who have walked with Jesus for a time have come to realize that there is nothing more healing than being in His presence. The fact that He wants to share in our walk and has guidance for us as we journey through life provides a great sense of security and blessing.

The Counselor speaks to us about new things. He reminds us of things we have heard from Him before. He provides peace for us that is divine in origin, and we find that what Jesus has to offer we can't get from anyone else on earth. No matter how wise our human counselors and advisors may be, we need the presence of God that only the Holy Spirit can provide.

The peace that the Spirit provides calms our troubled hearts and takes away our fears. He reminds us that Jesus is the One who has overcome the world and that He will remain triumphant forever, in every situation.

It is so true that family membership has its privileges. Christians get to know what others don't know. Christians get to experience a love like no other love. Christians get the presence of Jesus to be with them always in the person of His Spirit, and Christians get the real and lasting benefit of life to the full in this world, and life everlasting in the world to come.

We continue to have much we need to learn from the Spirit of Jesus. Every day provides new opportunities for us to make choices and all of those choices need divine direction. While others may turn to surveys and polls to help them determine which way the political and social winds are blowing before they choose a path, we who are guided by the Spirit of God have inside information that will lead us in the best option possible.

We are people of the Spirit and that provides peace to our hearts. No one else can give or do what Jesus can, and that alone sets our hearts at rest.

HAVING FAITH IN THE OUTCOME

> **John 14:28–31** *"You heard me say, 'I am going away and I am coming back to you.' If you loved me, you would be glad that I am going to the Father, for the Father is greater than I. I have told you now before it happens, so that when it does happen you will believe. I will not speak with you much longer, for the prince of this world is coming. He has no hold on me, but the world must learn that I love the Father and that I do exactly what my Father has commanded me. Come now; let us leave."*

One thing that we really love is for someone to reassure us that everything is going to be okay. Children expect it from their parents, and in crisis moments we all need to hear it.

The disciples must have been hanging on every word Jesus was saying about peace, but He had more to say to them (and us) than just peace. This was still a teaching time. His time with the disciples before the cross was coming to a close, but there was more that He wanted them (and us) to know.

This lesson lists what seem to be spiritual platitudes. Normally we don't like them because usually they are dull, trite, and simplistic. However, when Jesus is involved even the simple becomes amazing. There are some wonderful truths here that the disciples needed to hear on that fateful night. Maybe we need to hear them too.

There was truly a historical Jesus. Our faith is based on His life, death, and resurrection, and although we can't prove these things with empirical evidence, they are the bedrocks of our faith. Take any one of them away and Christianity is a worthless religion and truly just an opiate for the masses.

Jesus was looking forward to His homegoing. He knew that there was something beyond the grave, for His own ministry had proved that. In the same way we should be happy for those who die in the faith, for even though we grieve for ourselves, we rejoice for those who finally crossed over.

Jesus was bold enough to make predictions. He told His disciples that later they would remember and understand. He predicted the defeat of Satan, and He predicted that love would win the day. Doing the Father's will means having faith in the outcome, for though there would be a cross, glory was sure to follow.

LESSON OF THE VINE

John 15:1–2 *"I am the true vine, and my Father is the gardener. He cuts off every branch in me that bears no fruit, while every branch that does bear fruit he prunes so that it will be even more fruitful."*

If there is anything that the people of all stages of belief in Christ can agree on, it is that He was a Master Teacher. One of the keys to His teaching success was that He knew how to relate on the level of His hearers, for He spoke in reference to things that they knew. Jesus and His disciples had just left the upper room, and as they walked along, Jesus looked around and began to give a lesson to His companions.

Most of the people I know are country folks or have been country folks at some point in their lives. We all know about gardens because we have raised gardens. In these verses Jesus is teaching His disciples—and us—about something we all know.

He says that in the Father's Garden, fruitlessness is not tolerated. There was nothing politically correct about Jesus. We may want to soft-soap the truth sometimes, but Jesus never does. He lets us know that excuses don't matter because bearing fruit is not something we learn. It's something that we do naturally for it flows out of our relationship with Jesus. Productivity is all that counts because it's important to grow to show we are alive, and it's important to grow to show we are healthy.

Jesus also stresses that in the Father's Garden, pruning is a regular event. I've not worked much with vines, but I've trimmed a lot of hedges and trees, and there are some lessons I have picked up about pruning. First, pruning always involves change. The reason that we trim such things is to make them different, and that is exactly the reason God prunes us. We need to be crafted into His image and that is ever a work in progress. Second, change often involves pain. This is the reason why major adjustments are so difficult, or why change on any level of our lives is often so strongly resisted. It's also why Christians often don't grow in their faith and bear more visible fruit. Jesus wasn't just throwing words into the air when He talked about taking up a cross. Pruning is painful. Finally, it makes us dependent. When I get really pruned, I'm not much good on my own. The Lord allows those testing times so that we will always remember just how much we need Him.

THE IMPORTANCE OF CONNECTION

A lesson that Christians tend to ignore or drift away from, is that in the Father's Garden, no branch survives alone. Plants depend on other plants for pollination, for a plant by itself will have a very short life. The church was designed by Jesus for the very same purpose. We really do need each other to survive, let alone thrive.

We can't successfully bear fruit if we are alone for long. The topic that Jesus is talking about here is not about survival, and it's not even about gaining eternal life, or being able to go to heaven. What Jesus was trying to get across to His disciples was that they were going to need each other if they were going to bear fruit, and fruit bearing is why they, and we, are here.

If we don't bear fruit we are separated from the branch, but we are not the ones doing the separating. God knows who we are and who is producing fruit that will bring Him glory. When we are separated from the branch, our destruction will soon follow, for spiritual isolation has deadly results.

This is not to say that there are not extenuating circumstances. Though it is very valuable for the body of Christ to come together for encouragement, worship of the Lord, and to learn how we can allow Jesus to bear fruit through us, we know that there are times when going alone is the hand we have been dealt. People who are isolated because of sickness, age, imprisonment, and even for the sake of the gospel many times do not have the support system they need or would receive if they were actively participating in the ministries of a local church.

However, those are exceptions to the rule and Christ will provide grace for such times. In fact, finding people in those situations should be the mission of the church as it looks for new ways to exhibit the fruit of Spirit that Christ provides them. But the reality of Christian living is that we were designed to be connected to each other in the faith, and connected to the Vine, Jesus the Christ, so that together we can cause God's will to be done on earth as it is in heaven. It may not require a village, but it does require a church.

FRUIT OR FIRE

> **John 15:5–6** *"I am the vine; you are the branches. If a man remains in me and I in him, he will bear much fruit; apart from me you can do nothing. If anyone does not remain in me, he is like a branch that is thrown away and withers; such branches are picked up, thrown into the fire and burned."*

These two verses are loaded with contrast. First, we see that the possibilities found in Jesus Christ are limitless, and they are offered to all who will follow after Him. Being the vine, or the source of all that matters, Jesus has the power to enable His followers to accomplish much in His name. If I think of the term "much fruit," even in my wildest dreams it has limitations, but when I put it in the context of the power of the "Vine," then even the impossible becomes possible. Truly, we serve an amazing Savior!

Of course, all of this is contingent on whether we remain plugged into the Source of all possibilities. Jesus is the one who has the vision, the power, the wisdom, the riches, and the blessing to make anything good happen. He can construct great things for His Kingdom, while we are not even able to make mudpies in comparison. He must remain the center of our focus and the hope for all we dream to accomplish for His glory.

The contrast of this is a very dark picture. Not only can we do nothing if we don't stay fully attached to the vine, but without Jesus we are less than nothing. Our efforts are only doomed for destruction and disappointment. The very picture of withering branches being discarded to the fire is very graphic, but I don't think they are meant to be a threat. It's just more a statement of reality. When we try to do anything of value without being connected, fed, and led by the "Vine," we find that our best efforts come to nothing.

This is why so many well-intended Christian ministries crash and burn. Enthusiastic followers of Christ find a bit of success, and then start to think that they were the ones who caused good things to happen. The servants never truly accomplish anything of value without the Master's blessing. All that is built on the sand of our own delusions inevitably produces failure.

No true follower of Jesus will ever think that they can succeed without Him. He is the embodiment of all good things and in Him we are strong. Without Him we can do nothing. This is the reality of Kingdom living.

"Bear Much Fruit"

John 15:7–8 *"If you remain in me and my words remain in you, ask whatever you wish, and it will be given you. This is to my Father's glory, that you bear much fruit, showing yourselves to be my disciples."*

In the Father's Garden, connectivity brings privilege. The joys of being in the Kingdom far outweigh the temporary pleasures of being out of it. Adam and Eve may have enjoyed the taste of the forbidden fruit, but the reality that came from their disobedience made the taste short-lived.

The Father takes pleasure in connecting with us. Just as we love to reconnect with family members after being away from them for a time, God feels that way about us. He enjoys time that we purposefully spend with Him.

The Father also takes pleasure in responding to us. In the same manner that we come to know what brings pleasure to those we love, when we ask for something that pleasures the Father, He is overjoyed to answer our request with His blessing.

We are repeatedly reminded throughout this section of scripture that in the Father's Garden His disciples produce fruit. After all, why would we plant a garden year after year if it never rewarded us with a harvest? That would not only be a waste of time, money, and effort, but would also make us look silly. The Father expects fruit from us in the same way.

It makes God look good when we bear fruit for His glory, therefore it is good to "show off" what God has done in us and through us. It is God's desire that we bear a whole lot of fruit, for the idea presented here is more than just breaking even with what has been invested. The "gates of Hades" (Matthew 16:18) are waiting for us to knock them down and help bring out those who are living in the valley of the shadow of death (Psalm 23:4).

Fruit is the evidence of our being one with the "Branch." It is not us, but Jesus who brings in the harvest, but we do get the joy of being used of the Master as we are vessels for His service.

So, two central issues are at play here. Being Christian requires connectivity with Jesus, and secondly, the natural result of connectivity with Jesus is reproduction. Fruit flows from the plan our Master has for us. When that happens, the angels rejoice, and we get to attend the party!

REMAIN IN THE VINE

John 15:9-10 *"As the Father has loved me, so have I loved you. Now remain in my love. If you keep my commands, you will remain in my love, just as I have obeyed my Father's commands and remain in his love."*

S ome may think that love makes the world go round, but the idea of love in our present society has often fallen on hard times. More than not, when we hear of love presented through movies or social media we get a picture of lust, not love.

Jesus has a different idea about love, however, and He wants His disciples of all ages to be able to tell the difference. This is not "eros" (sexual/emotional) love, or "phileo" (family/friend) love, but the word used here in the original Greek language, in which John used to write, is "agape" (non-emotional/willful) love.

This follows Jesus' admonition that the disciples (branches) must remain in the vine (Jesus). Because this is a part of the last message He will give them before the cross, it is most imperative. He knows that in the days ahead His disciples will have to do without a lot of things, but there is one thing they cannot do without—and that is to remain in Him to get what they need. One would think that just remaining would be easy, but there is more to it than meets the eye.

Remaining was a choice for Jesus. He was God, but He was also man. He could choose to remain in the Father or strike out on His own. But He knew the Father's way was always the best way, so that's the way He went.

It is a choice for us as well. The choice to obey or not obey has been presented to every person since Adam and Eve. Whether or not we will choose to obey today determines whether we will succeed or fail as we continue in the Christian walk.

Learning to remain in the love of the Father is part of the response to the constant love of God. The Father's arms are always wide open, but we have to be willing to come to Him on His terms, not ours. Whenever we find ourselves being too impatient to remain and start venturing forward in new branches of ministry without divine direction, we will soon find ourselves in trouble. Waiting and remaining are the first steps in Christian success.

COMPLETED JOY

John 15:11 *"I have told you this so that my joy may be in you and that your joy may be complete."*

Jesus has a purpose for His disciples in asking them to "remain," and it's more that *just because He said so*. Everything that Jesus does for His followers, and every instruction He has for us contains a purpose that directly impacts His mission, and our part in helping to fulfill that mission.

Here Jesus shares the purpose behind His instructions. He wants us to remain in Him, just as a branch remains in the vine, so that we may have joy. However, we need to understand that joy is not the same thing as happiness. Though it is true that a grumpy Christian is very unbecoming for our personal witness, happiness is an emotion that is very fickle and can ebb or flow in accordance with the circumstances that surround our lives, but joy is a completely different matter. Joy is only possible if we are one with Jesus. It is His continual presence within us that produces the awareness of the deposit of His Spirit. Such joy becomes a reality when Christ's mission and our mission find that happy place of connection, and both are being fulfilled to the glory of the Father.

It is in this place of joy that comes from abiding in the "Vine" that we develop the mind of Christ. As the joy of His presence rises within us, we begin to think and understand in the categories of the Kingdom that are so important to Jesus, and so needed in our world. When we work to build His Kingdom here on earth, we find His blessing, and that blessing produces joy.

Joy is complete when our love for Him is complete. It may happen in an instant, or it may take a period of time as we learn how to serve Him in a life of surrender. Certainly, Christian joy cannot be complete without being placed on the altar of sacrifice so that Jesus can use us for His glory, but when we find that "sweet spot" in His will we find that His joy not only settles upon us, but that it remains on a continuing basis. It is when entire sanctification takes place as Jesus becomes the Lord of all things to us personally, just as He is in actuality to the world.

This is why the sanctified life is so necessary. It's the only place where we can find lasting joy, and when we find that joy, we never want anything else. We are complete when we are completely His!

THE GREATEST LOVE

John 15:12–13 *"My command is this: Love each other as I have loved you. Greater love has no one than this: that he lay down his life for his friends."*

We don't live in this world for too long before we find that everything is relative. There must be a context for every situation to be understood and there must be some standard of measurement for recognizing the reasons and purposes for what we do and what we are asked to do.

A case in point comes in the form of this command from Jesus. Throughout this chapter He has been speaking about the importance of His followers remaining connected to Him just as a branch would connect to a vine. The result of that connection, that "remaining in Him," is an abundance of inner joy that such a relationship produces. But the standard of living that follows such a privileged connection is the outbreak of love, which Jesus fully demonstrated for us.

The standard for our degree of love is the level of love Jesus has. He was willing to literally put His life on the line for not only His followers, but even for His enemies. He died on that cross for our sins, but also for all the sins of all the people in the world throughout the centuries of time. He loved those who betrayed Him, falsely accused Him, spat upon Him, tortured Him, and crucified Him. That is the standard of love that Jesus expects from those of us who would follow after Him. Love for one another is required, but not just for those who love us. Our love must be for all people everywhere regardless of race, creed, color, nationality, or conduct. We love because He loves and because He has taken up residence within us.

What this means on the practical level is that either we are willing to lay down our life for others as Jesus did, or we fall short of the standard of love that He has commanded us to have. Selflessness for His sake is what Jesus asks of us, and that is the only standard we have with which to compare our walk with Him.

All this points back to the necessity of abiding in the vine. We need the sanctifying grace of God in us to cleanse us, empower us, and fill us with the love that is needed to live out the Christian life before a world who is unaccustomed to it. Because Jesus, as the true vine, has the resources that are needed, it is possible. But such love is doable only as we abide in Him.

FRIENDSHIP WITH JESUS

John 15:14 *"You are my friends if you do what I command."*

Not only is an ever-present joy a reward for our fully abiding in, and trusting in Christ, but there is an additional benefit. We can actually be friends with Almighty God, through the person of Jesus, in the power of His Spirit.

Friends are precious. If you have one or more people in your life that you really can count on to be your friend, then you are blessed beyond what many people ever realize. Hold on to such individuals with all your might, for they are worth more than their weight in gold.

Friendship with Jesus is even more precious than that. He is the Friend who will never leave us under any circumstances. Sometimes we may feel like we do what we do, without seeing a tangible reward for our labors materialize. That's why so many Christians are so focused on getting to heaven. They think that if they can just struggle through this life and make it to the other side then they will be filled with joy throughout eternity.

What such thinking misses is that the joy that Jesus was sharing with His disciples is not dependent on us arriving on heaven's shores. We are promised His joy within us right now, right here as we walk the concrete sidewalks instead of streets of gold. We are promised His friendship as we allow His love to be poured from Him into our lives, and from us on to the lives of people with which we have contact. As glorious as our heavenly dwelling and the world to come may be, Jesus was more concerned that His disciples realized His joy and His love while they were in this world.

We are in the presence of the King daily, and He is aware of all we take on or give up for Him. He is aware of the state of our hearts as we serve Him. Though we may think that our labors are largely unnoticed and unappreciated, that is never the case. Because the branch (us) is firmly connected to the Vine (Him), He knows all that is going on in us and knows just what we need to be fully empowered to do and face all that we are to experience. The result of such a relationship is friendship.

He is closer to us than any family member, for the "Vine's" blood supplies all the nourishment we branches will ever need. That's a benefit of friendship of the highest order.

BEING A FRIEND

John 15:15–17 *"I no longer call you servants, because a servant does not know his master's business. Instead, I have called you friends, for everything that I learned from my Father I have made known to you. You did not choose me, but I chose you to go and bear fruit—fruit that will last. Then the Father will give you whatever you ask in my name. This is my command: Love each other."*

How often do you consider the value of a friend? Proverbs 18:24 says, "One who has unreliable friends soon comes to ruin, but there is a friend who sticks closer than a brother." We in the church have found that person, that friend, to be Jesus.

Throughout this chapter Jesus was trying to get His friends to realize their weakness on their own and recognize that their true power source was in Him. He illustrated this fact with the analogy of the vine and the branches.

Being a friend puts a person on the inside track because such friends know their Master's business. Luke 19:10 tells us that the Master's business is to seek and save the lost. His friends also know that Jesus knows the Father. He was totally God, but also totally man, therefore He had the same access to the Father that we do. He learned about Him by spending time with Him, just like we are invited to do.

Being a friend comes about because of selection. This idea of walking with God didn't begin with us, for it started in the heart of God. Romans 8:29 reveals, "For those God foreknew he also predestined to be conformed to the likeness of his Son, that he might be the firstborn among many brothers." In other words, God desires that our friendship with Him causes us to be like Jesus. He chooses that path for us if we will accept it.

God does have a plan for our lives, but it involves our cooperation. Things don't just happen. That's fatalism, not Christianity. This is an issue that involves prevenient grace, the love that was extended to us before we ever looked for it, and because God loves us, He chooses us.

Because God loves us so much, He provides the choice of friendship with Him, but to please Him we must reproduce fruit for His glory. That fruit is displayed through love, and God gives it to those who ask Him for it.

HATERS GONNA HATE!

John 15:18–19 *"If the world hates you, keep in mind that it hated me first. If you belonged to the world, it would love you as its own. As it is, you do not belong to the world, but I have chosen you out of the world. That is why the world hates you."*

We don't like to think of Jesus using words like "hate," "persecute," and "guilt." We prefer words of love, compassion, grace, and forgiveness. However, Jesus did not live in a world of isolation. He faced what we face, and He wanted to warn us about what was to come.

The fact of the matter is that we are in a war. This becomes pretty obvious to see if we have any sense of current events that impact our world. Wars have opposing sides and that plays out in the spiritual world as well as the physical. There is the nation and the world, there is the world and the church, and there is the church and the Church. All these things have the potential of creating conflicts that can lead to all-out war.

Certainly, history has shown us that nations of our world have too many times become enemies that try to resolve their differences in war. In spiritual terms, the forces of the world are ever encroaching on the church, trying to break it down to its level. It has become common speech in church conversations to refer to evil in the world as "them" and the spiritually directed of the Father as "us." But then it is also true that our little corner of church is often at odds against the larger diverse body of Christ to the point that we sometimes include those who worship differently from us as a tool of the "world," more than as brothers and sisters in Christ.

Jesus made it clear that opposing sides don't get along well. In fact, there is no reason to think that the true Church should have a different relationship with the world than Jesus did. If His examples and His teachings are not followed, especially by those who profess His name, then the divide between real Christianity and heresy becomes pronounced and amplified.

Sometimes the church tries to compromise with the ways of the world in order to keep peace, or to show a higher level of love that will include everyone in the body of Christ regardless of their beliefs. This is when war between the saints and the false church breaks out. As Jesus faced a real enemy, we who follow Him won't get off without a battle either.

LIKE MASTER, LIKE SERVANT

John 15:20–21 *"Remember the words I spoke to you: 'No servant is greater than his master.' If they persecuted me, they will persecute you also. If they obeyed my teaching, they will obey yours also. They will treat you this way because of my name, for they do not know the One who sent me."*

It's not a pleasant thought to consider, but wars have casualties. Some may ignore that fact, but whenever there is a war of any kind, there will be collateral damage. Sometimes the losses are greater than expected and that should grieve us all.

The first casualty in spiritual battles is usually love, and the residue that remains when love is a casualty, is hate. There are times when the followers of Jesus are hated because they tell others that they are wrong, but our response to hate can't be retaliation or our love is lost. The church at Ephesus in Revelation 2:1–7 experienced this. Though they did a lot of things right, they had sacrificed their first love experience with Jesus and therefore became a casualty in the battle for holiness.

The second casualty in spiritual battles is the name of Jesus. Just speaking the name of our Lord is sometimes enough to put people into a rage, and at times even leads to persecution. We follow a name that is above all names and proclaiming such a thing sometimes makes people angry. However, Christians are to be like Christ, and are to live as examples of Christ to our world and catching flack for doing so is to be expected.

A third casualty in spiritual battles is Christian teaching. I have always felt that one my most important jobs as a local pastor was to be the resident theologian. This can be a precarious position because unlike other professions, the training, education, practical experience, and judgment of a pastor is often discarded because everyone has an opinion about spiritual matters that is many times considered just as valid as the pastor's. We wouldn't put the advice of a medical doctor, or even a plumber, or a mechanic in that category, but a pastor's doctrine is sometimes just taken as his or her opinion, and no more valid in spiritual matters than anyone else's.

Taking a stand for Jesus will always produce a battle, for sin hates to be confronted. But let us serve with a clean heart and minimize the casualties along the way as best we can, for the battle is ultimately the Lord's.

SIN WITHOUT EXCUSE

John 15:22–25 *"If I had not come and spoken to them, they would not be guilty of sin. Now, however, they have no excuse for their sin. He who hates me hates my Father as well. If I had not done among them what no one else did, they would not be guilty of sin. But now they have seen these miracles, and yet they have hated both me and my Father. But this is to fulfill what is written in their Law: 'They hated me without reason.'"*

For thousands of years mankind walked in darkness as decisions were made because of limited information, superstition, and ignorance of consequences. That was true not only for the human race in general, but also for people who were genuinely trying to know a God who seemed so far away. In their blindness they worshiped idols made by hand, along with the sun, the moon, the stars, and a host of other objects that proved to be useless over the course of time.

Jesus came to bring light to a darkened world and provide those who were truly seeking after the Father a way to get to Him. He Himself was the bridge that links a holy Creator with an unholy creation and made it possible for the two to become one. However, many people didn't take advantage of the offer of life, so they continued in their lostness and blindness brought on by their willful sin against God. In these verses Jesus relates that casualties have causes. All the animosity toward Jesus from the Jewish rulers didn't just come out of the air. There are reasons for the hate people hold and express.

First, we consider the ignorance of the Sender. People who don't know God can't possibly know what it is that God wants for their lives. Such ignorance produces fear and unbridled fear produces anger. Because Jesus was a threat to the status quo, He was hated. Second, we need to consider the fact of deliberate evil. There are those who are hell-bound and hell-bent on doing wrong. When light is shone on their evil, the gloves come off and attacks are made against the light. In the case of Jesus, He spoke the truth and His enemies couldn't handle the truth, so the divine Messenger was attacked. Finally, there is the matter of unrivaled hate. When people are confronted with their sin, they either turn from it or burn with hate toward the confronter. This is what they did to Jesus, and therefore did to the Father as well. As a result, sadly, unless they repent, the guilty die in their sin without redemption.

OUR JOB DESCRIPTION

John 15:26–27 *"When the Comforter comes, whom I will send to you from the Father, the Spirit of truth who goes out from the Father, he will testify about me. And you also must testify, for you have been with me since the beginning."*

Sometimes people quit learning when they graduate from school, but the word "commencement" should give us a clue that graduation only puts us at the beginning. It is just as true in the world of discipleship. Once a person comes to Christ and receives a new birth, then the walk of being a disciple starts, and it will continue for a lifetime.

Jesus let His disciples know that belief in Him was not enough to equip them for service. This probably surprised them a little, because by this time they perhaps thought there was nothing that Jesus couldn't do. However, we must remember that at the time of this event, Jesus was the God/man. His physical presence had not yet been glorified, so there were limits on Him.

For example, He couldn't be with them and be in them at the same time. He could not do for them and let them do for themselves at the same time. He was telling them that they should be expecting something more. They should expect Him to return to them in the power of the Spirit, for they would be nothing unless He empowered them for service.

Even though they had heard the teaching, seen the miracles, would later witness the resurrection and the ascension, they still weren't ready. They needed something that would narrow their focus beyond their abilities. They needed power from on high.

Jesus let His disciples know that the source of all power in ministry was in the Father. The Spirit would be sent by Jesus to them, and the Spirit emanated from the Father. The Spirit would have a particular purpose for their lives, for He always points to Jesus and would move in response to Jesus. The Spirit proclaims truth in relation to Jesus.

These disciples were to be teammates with the Spirit to accomplish the plan of the Father. The followers of Jesus must testify about Jesus because the Holy Spirit has been sent to them. That much hasn't changed. We are still only effective when we minister in the power of the Spirit.

DANGER!

John 16:1–3 *"All this I have told you so that you will not go astray. They will put you out of the synagogue; in fact, a time is coming when anyone who kills you will think he is offering a service to God. They will do such things because they have not known the Father or me."*

Jesus was speaking to His disciples the night before the cross. The foot washing was over, the Last Supper was over, He had told of the coming betrayal by Judas and the coming denial by Peter. He had told them about heaven and that He was the only path to get there, and then He told them about the coming of His Holy Spirit. He had promised them peace and instructed them to bear fruit that would last. Now He had a warning for them.

These disciples needed to understand that ignorance isn't bliss. There might be times when it is, but not here. There was too much at stake and Jesus wanted to prepare them for what was about to happen. There were three dangers of which they needed to be aware.

First, there was the danger of falling away. If eternal security was a reality, then Jesus would not have warned the disciples about the danger of losing faith and falling away. He knew that all people are susceptible to being lazy, getting careless, getting selfish, and falling.

There was the danger of being persecuted. This has happened to the followers of Jesus for 2000 years and is still happening in various parts of the world. The more the church confronts evil, the more they can expect to be persecuted.

There was also the danger of being the persecutor. Rarely have I faced any persecution to date from people outside the church, but from inside I have been lied to, slandered, called names, gossiped about, and faced things that have at times made me want to quit. Actually, the only thing that kept me going was the fact that I don't work for the church, but for the King.

The number of parsonage kids that have left the faith because of how their father/pastor was treated is legion. Folks may think they are doing God and the church a favor when spiritual leadership is challenged, but when the motivation of love is lost, the enemy wins. Our faith must remain in Jesus, not in the workings of men. The danger is real, and Jesus warned us.

WE HAVE BEEN WARNED!

John 16:4 *"I have told you this, so that when the time comes you will remember that I warned you. I did not tell you this at first because I was with you."*

To be forewarned is to be forearmed. Jesus once gave a parable about how the owner of the house needed to be prepared for a thief who might come in the night. He said, "If the owner of the house had known at what time of night the thief was coming, he would have kept watch and would not have let his house be broken into" (Matthew 24:43). Knowledge is a big key when preparation is needed for what is about to happen.

Jesus made clear to His followers that the things He was warning them about were not in the category of "if," but "when." They *would* face persecution. People *would* try to kill them. People *would* rise up against them and the message that they would share. The way of the cross was going to be laid upon each of them, and if they followed Him there would be no escape from that destiny.

This is a lesson that the church of the twenty-first century needs to hear. We are not followers of Jesus so that we can learn to be nicer people and get along with everybody. There is a price to pay for the Kingdom of God and when light clashes with evil there are going to be repercussions just as surely as a storm arrives when a cold front meets a warm front on a weather map.

Though the Apostle Paul would advise us to live at peace with all men as much as it depends on us (Romans 12:18), such words do not mean that peace will always be possible. Holiness can never mix with sin. Godliness can never accommodate unrighteousness, and the ways of the world and the way of the cross are always going to be at odds with each other. Sin is too deeply intrenched for us to be passive about our salvation. Jesus calls for His disciples to be willing to take a stand for the sake of the coming Kingdom to the glory of the Father.

So, He warned His disciples that night. In the same manner He warns us to be ever vigilant and on our guard against the enemy of our soul. Simon Peter would later warn us, "Your enemy the devil prowls around like a roaring lion looking for someone to devour" (I Peter 5:8). Let a word to the wise be sufficient. We have been warned!

HOME AT LAST

John 16:5 *"Now I am going to him who sent me, yet none of you asks me, 'Where are you going?'"*

Throughout most of my adult life, we have not owned a house, but we have always had a home. Most of our time in ministry has caused us to live in parsonages where we have had nice accommodations, but did not allow us to build up any equity. When I finally retired, we needed to obtain a mortgage and purchase our own home, but a little after one year there, it was destroyed by a fire, and we had to move again. At that point we had to come up with an answer to the question that is voiced in this verse as people would ask us, "Where are you going?" It took time for us to figure that out.

It is most likely that the disciples were very confused that night before the cross about a lot of things that Jesus had been telling them. They may have felt like the student who was afraid to ask the teacher a question because he didn't even know enough to know what to ask. Jesus had repeatedly told them that He would be leaving them, but for whatever reason, they didn't understand what He was saying.

In the course of this evening Jesus had made clear the fact that He and we have a home awaiting us in His Father's Kingdom. We who follow after Jesus have a destination after our life in this world is over. We can stand firm in our belief that we have an actual place to go because Jesus said that He was going somewhere, and that He would receive us unto Himself. That's good enough for me, for if Jesus is there then everything else will be just fine.

When we get where we are going, we will be ushered into a place we call heaven and be introduced to the Father by Jesus, who will receive us with open arms. To think of being able to live with the One who has given us our assignments in this life, and to hear the words, "Well done, good and faithful servant," will be music to our ears and more glorious that we can ever begin to imagine.

All this is going to be possible because Jesus left the disciples and went to be with the Father. Maybe the disciples didn't ask Him where He was going because they had already received enough information for them to understand. Maybe they were just overwhelmed. One thing I am thankful for though is the fact that where He is, I will one day be. Thanks be to God!

GOOD GRIEF

John 16:6–7 *"Because I have said these things, you are filled with grief. But I tell you the truth: It is for your good that I am going away. Unless I go away the Counselor will not come to you; but if I go, I will send him to you."*

"Good grief!" is more than just an expression from Charlie Brown. It's also an emotion of Kingdom living as we wait for the final consummation of the plan of God for our world. Back in the Sermon on the Mount in Matthew 5:4, Jesus had said that those who mourn would be blessed. At this point of the Gospel story His followers were starting to realize what He was talking about.

Fortunately, we today have the blessing of knowing the outcome of this series of events. The pages of history and the Bible give us insights as to how this night would play out, and having knowledge about the ending of the story puts us in a much better position than the disciples were in at that point.

We have also the blessing of Jesus watching out for us. Our Big Brother is ever on the job, looking out for our benefit. He knows that we are not strong enough to take on the enemy of our souls and face all the troubles that living in this world produces. He knows that we need a helper along the way, therefore He made plans to leave His followers for a brief time, but then to replace His physical presence with an eternal partner who would never leave us under any circumstances.

Not only do we have the blessing of the Spirit coming to us, but He resides in us as the Divine Counselor to guide us into all truth. He enters our lives when we are saved from our sins by faith in what Jesus has done on our behalf, and when we are willing to give over everything into His control, He sanctifies us completely. He changes our "want to" and makes it possible for us to be made perfect in love for the Father and for the sake of our fellow man. He cleanses us, and empowers us, and makes us ready to live in the presence of God for eternity.

The story of the cross certainly is a story of tragedy and grief, but thanks be to God, the cross isn't the end of the story. Jesus is alive! He has our backs and has sent His Holy Presence to abide in us forever. He is preparing a place for us to live with Him always and until we reach that point in our journey, we have continual contact with Him. It may start off as grief, but it's *good grief.* The best is yet to come!

THE SPIRIT'S ROLE

John 16:8–11 *"When he comes, he will convict the world of guilt in regard to sin and righteousness and judgment: in regard to sin, because men do not believe in me; in regard to righteousness, because I am going to the Father, where you can see me no longer; and in regard to judgment, because the prince of this world now stands condemned."*

There is a volume of information in the first thought presented here by Jesus. He shows us just what the Holy Spirit is all about, for He takes an active role in our world.

The Holy Spirit is not an "it." When we pray, we pray to the Father, in Jesus' name, through the power of the Holy Spirit. He is an intricate part of the Holy Trinity. He is not a guardian angel. Angels are created beings, but the Spirit is eternal. He empowers and directs the created beings. He is the presence of God that lives in each believer. When we sense the voice of God in prayer and in the Word, it is the voice of the Spirit who is interacting with us. He knows us intimately and loves us more than we can imagine.

The Holy Spirit convicts us of sin. He sets off an alarm when we don't believe in Him, for God is faithful to make Himself available to us through the presence of His Spirit. He sets off an alarm when we need to be forgiven. Conviction is a wonderful gift of God, for it is like the flashing lights we see on the highway to warn us of danger. He also sets off an alarm when we begin to drift. We count on the Holy Spirit to guide our attitudes, our words, and our responses to people and situations.

The Holy Spirit convinces us about what is right. When the world looks at the church, it ought to see what it saw in Jesus. We shoot ourselves in the foot when we allow carnality and self to reign and give such a testimony to the world. When the world looks at the church it ought to convince people of absolutes, for there are some things, like what the Bible calls sin and righteousness, that never change. And when the world looks at the church, it ought to see people walking by faith, for while we may not know what is in our path, we know what path to take. We may not always have the answers, but we can always point people to the One who does. The Holy Spirit is with us forever to convey Himself to the world, to convict the world of sin, and convince the world of His wonderful transforming power.

THE PERFECT GUIDE

John 16:12–15 *"I have much more to say to you, more than you can now bear. But when he, the Spirit of truth, comes, he will guide you into all truth. He will not speak on his own; he will speak only what he hears, and he will tell you what is yet to come. He will bring glory to me by taking from what is mine and making it known to you. All that belongs to the Father is mine. That is why I said the Spirit will take from what is mine and make it known to you."*

These verses continue in the last discourse of Jesus to His disciples. He knew that they wouldn't remember everything He told them. He knew they wouldn't last long without Him, and He knew that He was going to be taken from them, so He revealed to all the truth concerning the Holy Spirit.

The Holy Spirit has come to guide us. If we ever needed anything in our lives, it is guidance. We are constantly faced with new decisions and choices. The Holy Spirit picks up right where Jesus left off, and guides in things that are not specifically listed in the Bible. When we have need of wisdom and direction, we call upon the Lord and the Spirit will guide us. He shows us the difference between the true and the false.

The Holy Spirit confirms the Trinity. The word "Trinity" does not appear in the Bible, for it was first used by the ancient church leader Tertullian (A.D. 155-230). The doctrine was formally defined as one God, but three persons in the Nicene Creed of A.D. 325. The Spirit is always in agreement with the other members of the Godhead, and never contradicts the written Word of God. Holiness has always been God's plan for His creation, for Jesus taught it, and the Spirit confirms it still.

The Holy Spirit also gives us a look ahead. He deals with the immediate as He guides us through the minefields of life by voicing His direction through the Bible, music, sermons, and the collective wisdom of the body of Christ. But He also deals with the long-term. We are warned to be prepared for a conclusion to our world and warned concerning the consequences of not being prepared to face eternity.

The Holy Spirit is the presence of Jesus, the voice of Jesus, and the revelation of Jesus. He wants to indwell us, fill us, engage us, and empower us so that we will be fully equipped to change our world. The only thing stopping Him is us.

WALKING BY FAITH

John 16:16–18 *"In a little while you will see me no more, and then after a little while you will see me." Some of the disciples said to one another, 'What does he mean by saying, "In a little while you will see me no more, and then after a little while you will see me,' and 'Because I am going to the Father'? They kept asking, "What does he means by 'a little while'? We don't understand what he is saying."*

D o you know what it is like to have much to say and not know how to condense it into a short speech, or a short amount of time? People who are in love and have to part for a period of time certainly understand. Goodbyes linger as long as they can because separation is a pain that they don't want to have to face. This can be a problem for preachers as well, when they have a proclamation of truth they need to say, but only have a certain amount of time to get their words delivered.

That seems to be the situation that Jesus and His disciples find themselves in. Jesus had much to say to them, but they were not ready to receive what He wanted to tell them, and He was running out of time with them. The disciples wanted to understand, but they couldn't wrap their heads around everything that had come their way on that night of destiny.

For whatever reason, there appears to be times that the Lord keeps things from us, and we just have to walk by faith. The Apostle Paul understood this when he wrote, "We live by faith, not by sight" (II Corinthians 5:7), and "Now we see but a poor reflection as in a mirror; then we shall see face to face. Now I know in part; then I shall know fully, even as I am fully known" (I Corinthians 13:12). The writer of the letter to the Hebrews grasped this truth as well when he wrote, "Now faith is being sure of what we hope for and certain of what we do not see" (Hebrews 11:1). Yes, there are times when we must wait to find out all that the Lord has in store for us.

It's a reality that no one really likes. Our inquiring minds want to know, and it is especially true when it comes to the afterlife, like Jesus was talking about, but it's a reality that we can't change. There were things that even Jesus did not know, like when He would return, who would sit on His left and right in His Kingdom, etc., so there is no way that we are going to know more than He did. The faith-walk teaches patience, and we all need more of that.

"WE DON'T UNDERSTAND!"

John 16:16–18 *"In a little while you will see me no more, and then after a little while you will see me." Some of the disciples said to one another, 'What does he mean by saying, "In a little while you will see me no more, and then after a little while you will see me,' and 'Because I am going to the Father'? They kept asking, "What does he means by 'a little while'? We don't understand what he is saying."*

Sometimes the Lord tells us things specifically, just like He did His disciples, and we are too dull to grasp what He is saying. It's hard to comprehend the spiritual and eternal when we are so focused on the physical and present. The earthly kingdoms have an attraction for us because we can see them, but we will never understand divine truth until we can break free of earthly allures and their attachments. It's always easier to look backward and see history than to grasp the complex things of the future, but that's why waiting is so important.

Sometimes the Lord tells us things we don't understand, and we question each other instead of Him. I have a great admiration for the body of Christ, and I am convinced that we don't tap into the resources that are among us nearly enough, but there are times when we need to go directly to the Source instead.

We need to go to Jesus for spiritual enlightenment. As valuable as my brothers and sisters in the Lord are, when I really need to be sure of information that I need, it is important that I find myself at the feet of Jesus. The Lord will talk to us, and we need to take advantage of the opportunities that He affords us.

People who are outside the faith will think we are crazy if we say out loud that God talks to us, and I am often a bit skeptical myself when I hear certain people make such a statement. The truth of the matter though, is that Jesus does hear us when we come to Him, and He will reveal to us the truth we need to know if we will ask Him and wait for Him to respond.

However, it's important for us to listen until we know the voice of Christ. The only way that is possible is for us to spend time in His presence. It's also important for us to obey even when we don't understand why. We will understand in due time. Jesus never makes a mistake.

GOING FROM GRIEF TO JOY

John 16:19–20 *Jesus saw they wanted to ask him about this, so he said to them, "Are you asking one another what I meant when I said, 'In a little while you will see me no more, and then after a little while you will see me'? I tell you the truth, you will weep and mourn while the world rejoices. You will grieve, but your grief will turn to joy."*

Like so many people, there are things I want to ask Jesus about when we someday meet face to face. Because our eyes are blinded by the limitations we experience due to our humanity, we long to look into the mind of God and grasp the purpose and scope of His divine vision.

The disciples of Christ were likewise curious about why He was leaving them and where He was going. They loved their Lord and couldn't imagine having to go on without Him, and even though He assured them that His absence was only going to be temporary, contemplating His departure brought pain to their hearts and minds.

All of humanity can identify with the feeling of having questions we can't answer. All of humanity can also identify with the absence of the physical connection to Jesus in our world. We see the witness of His presence through the workings of His body, the Church, but even though we who are believers and followers of Jesus are comforted by the Holy Spirit, we hunger for more. We want to draw closer to Him, and we want Him to satisfy the questions of our minds.

Though we will have wait a while longer to see our joy completely fulfilled, we have confidence that we will someday see the end of our grief and trouble-filled days. The hope that we have in Christ carries us through the days of loss, of separation, and of uncertainty. We do not mourn like the world mourns, for we have His promise of life everlasting and the comfort of His Holy Spirit now.

I hope that someday, when I reach my eternal home, I will be able to play back all the events of my life and have some angel point out to me, "See there, all those hard places in your life? That's where God was working, and here is what He was doing. It was all for your good and look how it all turned out." But then again, maybe it won't really matter. By then I will be so full of joy that all grief will be forgotten. For now, I will just trust my Lord!

SADNESS THAT TURNS TO JOY

John 16:21–22 *"A woman giving birth to a child has pain because her time has come; but when her baby is born she forgets the anguish because of her joy that a child is born into the world. So with you: Now is your time of grief, but I will see you again and you will rejoice, and no one will take away your joy."*

The apostles seem to have wilted when it came to asking Jesus questions. Sometimes from fear of asking a stupid question we hesitate, but there are no stupid questions. The Lord wants to move us from an arm's length relationship into the inner circle with Him.

However, getting into the inner circle with Jesus doesn't come without a price. Jesus lets us know that for those who would follow after Him, joy cannot be found without experiencing pain. The illustration that He uses concerning the birth process is perfect because it clearly depicts the truth that great joy can only come about after great pain.

The concept of pain in childbirth is used repeatedly in the Bible. In Isaiah 42:14 we read, "For a long time I have kept silent, I have been quiet and held myself. But now like a woman in childbirth, I cry out, I gasp and pant." The prophet Hosea speaks of, "Pains as of a woman in childbirth comes to him" (Hosea 13:13). In the New Testament also it is used, "She was pregnant and cried out in pain as she was about to give birth" (Revelation 12:2).

Newness is rarely met with ease, and that's the reason people generally don't like change. However, when joy comes, it is there for keeps. This is not the same thing as happiness, for happiness can flee with the changing of the situation, but joy goes much deeper. Nehemiah said it best, "for the joy of the Lord is your strength" (Nehemiah 8:10).

Today we may face pain and sorrow. If not today, dire situations will surely meet us in the days to come. What we need to remember is that when we put our complete trust in the Lord, we can reach down to the joy He has placed within us and find strength to face whatever comes our way.

Jesus would leave His disciples for a time, and they would be distraught. Thankfully, we have His promise that He will never leave us, so we can lift up our heads and give praise to God in any and every situation.

JOY FOR THE ASKING

John 16:23–24 *"In that day you will no longer ask me anything. I tell you the truth, my Father will give you whatever you ask in my name. Until now you have not asked for anything in my name. Ask and you will receive, and your joy will be complete."*

S ometimes it's hard to grasp the concept that the Father wants to give the followers of His Son anything that they would ask of Him. There is something within our minds that often causes us to think that our needs are not worth bothering God about, or our humility causes us to think we are not important enough to catch the Father's eye.

To put this in perspective though, I think of the relationship I have with my children. Though both children are adults and have their own lives to lead, if either of them picked up the phone and called me saying, "Dad, I need your help," I would do everything in my power to come to their aid. Because we love our children, nothing that would benefit them would be off limits. As parents we are more than willing to "give until it hurts" for their sakes.

If that is the way we are as finite humans, just think of how our heavenly Father feels toward us. We may hesitate to ask because we are afraid of being rejected, but the Father rejects no one who honestly comes to Him. His heavenly storehouse is open to all who would *ask as Jesus would*. Matthew 7:7–8 reminds us, "Ask and it will be given to you, seek and you will find; knock and the door will be opened to you. For everyone who asks receives, the one who seeks finds; and to the one who knocks, the door will be opened."

Asking and receiving is the secret to joy. There are four principles given here that we as Christians need to remember. First, God wants to fill us with joy. Second, joy comes from seeing God at work. Third, asking God to work, and seeing Him do what we ask, increases our faith. And finally, the result of increased faith is joy.

The key to it all is found in our friendship with Jesus. Friends will do for friends more than they will do for strangers. Friends will trust friends more than they will trust strangers. Friends will rejoice when other friends rejoice. Jesus is our friend, and He is the Father's Son, so when we ask as He would, in His name, the Father is pleased to answer our request.

THE FATHER LOVES YOU—REALLY!

John 16:25–27 *"Though I have been speaking figuratively, a time is coming when I will no longer use this kind of language but will tell you plainly about my Father. In that day you will ask in my name. I am not saying that I will ask the Father on your behalf. No, the Father himself loves you because you have loved me and have believed that I came from God."*

One thing that is always true concerning our relationship with Jesus, is that we reach Him at different stages of our physical, educational, and spiritual development. Because we come to Him on different levels, our understanding of what He teaches may vary. It was true for His original disciples also—and they lived with Him.

These disciples must have had so many questions about Jesus. They had seen His miracles, declared His deity, watched His interactions with various people, and heard His words, but there must have always been something very mysterious about Him. It was almost as if He were not of this world.

To the uniformed, the words of Jesus are like riddles. Jesus was a master at telling stories, but the stories usually contained cloaked information. Matthew 13 contains a series of parables about the Kingdom of God that confused both the general hearers as well as the disciples, but the words of Jesus are not meant to be perceived easily. As the result, the crowds were amazed, but puzzled, and the disciples were usually just confused. Christ's words can be understood though, as revelation and thought come together, but God's word to us is not something we can grasp without an investment of time and effort.

Here we see that the Father is pleased with us because we love His Son and believe in Him. You know how it makes you feel when someone shows genuine appreciation for one of your children. Well, God is like that. Therefore, we have the privilege of approaching the Father on our own. We are allowed to use Christ's name to gain direct access to Him. The Apostle Paul would later write about "the name that is above every name," (Philippians 2:9), and we who pray to the Father in Jesus' name find power and connection with the Divine.

One of the simplest biblical truths is that God is love. He loves us because we love His Son, and because of that, we are family.

THE HOMECOMING

John 16:28 *"I came from the Father and entered the world; now I am leaving the world and going back to the Father."*

The home of Jesus is in a different location from where we inhabit. That doesn't mean He doesn't abide with us continually through His Spirit, because He certainly does, but the thing that separates our belief in Christ from many other "so called" deities of this world, is that we believe that He did not originate from this world. Jesus came from the Father and in this verse of scripture we see that He was about to go back to Him. Jesus was about to go home.

The example that Jesus shows us here is that the Father has a job for all who will choose to devote their life to Him. We are not put on this planet to simply follow our own wishes and spend time as we desire. We are to seek the Father's plan and place for our life's journey, and when the job is over it is time to take a different direction, for the Father has a way of opening doors for us at just the right time. He did it for His beloved Son, and He will do it for us as well.

The cross for Jesus was a door to another assignment. Jesus came to this world to be like us so that He could intercede for us to His Father. He couldn't be in a position to do that without the sacrifice that preceded His glory, so there may be a lesson in this for us.

Death is not our finish line, for we have a home waiting for us beyond the grave just as Jesus did. Right now, we are preparing for something bigger and better in the plan of God, for eternity will not be spent just dangling our feet in the river of life and idling away the eons. We are getting ready for the next step by what we do here. As Jesus returned to the Father to take on a new role as the glorified King, we too will report for service to God when our life here is over.

What awaits us is more than we can imagine. "No eye has seen, no ear has heard, no mind has conceived what God has prepared for those who love him" (I Corinthians 2:9). Paul continued in his second letter to the Corinthians when he wrote, "Now we know that if the earthly tent we live in is destroyed, we have a building from God, an eternal house in heaven, not built by human hands" (II Corinthians 5:1). Home with the Father awaits us.

MATURING FAITH

John 16:29–30 *Then Jesus' disciples said, "Now you are speaking clearly and without figures of speech. Now we can see that you know all things and that you do not even need to have anyone ask you questions. This makes us believe that you came from God."*

The faith that we possess is a gift that comes from God. There is no way that we can achieve it without Him. However, beginning at the point where we first believe, and reaching the point where we are mature takes a journey—and it is one that no disciple can bypass.

It takes time for faith to fully develop. The disciples had been with Jesus for three years and no doubt there had been lots of meals, campfires, worship services, and conversations about many and varying topics. They had been witnesses to all that Jesus did. Can you imagine the interactions they had after each of the miracles? What did they have to say to Him after He turned the water into wine, after the lame man was healed, after the eyes of the blind had been opened, and after the multitudes had been fed? The Bible only records bits and pieces of the actions and reactions that took place, but it's inconceivable to think that these men just took it all in stride without being stunned beyond belief.

It seems that at this point in the story they are beginning to get a glimpse into what Jesus had been trying to get them to understand for so long. It took them until the end of His life to finally grasp who He was, and to start to understand what He had been saying to them. When they said, "Now we see," I imagine Jesus must have thought, "Finally!"

Of course, we aren't much quicker than they were. Our faith also needs time to mature and process what the Bible says, and time to recognize the voice of God through His Holy Spirit. We have our "AHA!" moments along the way, but as we see through the mist and clouds of our humanity it requires us to develop eyes of faith to see things clearly. Because our walk with the Lord is a work in progress, we need to make sure that we keep our eyes wide open, and our ears tuned for messages He may send to us along the way. Our relationship with Him is not static, but dynamic. There is give and take on the journey, and we too will have questions. The important thing is for us to keep going. Light will come to us as we walk in faith.

FRAGIL FAITH

John 16:31–32 *"You believe at last!" Jesus answered. "But a time is coming, when you will be scattered, each to his own home. You will leave me all alone. Yet I am not alone, for my Father is with me."*

Even when faith has developed, error is still possible. Sometimes a paradigm shift is all that is necessary to throw us off track. Being human and being creatures of habit, we get used to doing things in a standard way and believing things that are comfortable for us to believe, but by doing so we may not see the truth Jesus wants to reveal to us.

Jesus acknowledged the faith of His disciples at this point. No doubt it brought Him joy to see the His followers were starting to get the right answers. But Jesus also acknowledged their coming failure. Before this night would pass, their world would be turned upside down. The person that they relied upon to keep them on the right path would be arrested, blasphemed, abused, tortured, and killed in the next few hours. Though they boasted and proclaimed their loyalty to Him now, in a little while they would be running like scared rabbits.

We all make mistakes, and Jesus knows that. Though He was no doubt pleased with their faith, He knew what they didn't know and what He knew had to break His heart. When we are so pious in church on Sunday, but don't represent Jesus with our actions throughout the week, He knows all about it. He wanted more than that from His first disciples, just as He does from us, but it takes time and deliberate intension for us to walk in holiness of heart and life as He did.

Our Lord shows us here that the true source of His strength and ours is in the Father. Even though Judas would betray Him, Peter would deny Him, and the other disciples would run away, He was not left by Himself. The presence of the Father was strong upon Him and that is the great example He leaves for us.

If we look to anyone but the Father as our primary source of strength, then we have settled for less that we should have. Friends will come and go, co-workers will let us down, and family may leave us, or even die. Still, the Father remains faithful and will never allow us to be tempted beyond what we are able to bear (I Corinthians 10:13). You can take that to the bank.

THE VICTORY IS
ALREADY ACHIEVED

John 16:33 *"I have told you these things, so that in me you may have peace. In this world you will have trouble. But take heart! I have overcome the world."*

Here is a lesson that we really need to remember, even if we don't remember anything else. Where there is Christ's peace, there is victory. We can face a lot of things if we have peace. We can face the loss of property, the crumbling of our health, the fickleness of friends, and the companionship loss of those we love, if we have the peace that Jesus gives. We can even face the unknown if Jesus is there with us. Life can throw some tough curves at us, but when we have His peace, we can be overcomers.

In His defeat Jesus became victorious. The cross is the ultimate paradox because there was no way that anyone of that time could see anything good coming from this prophet out of Nazareth being nailed to a tree. In the same way, when we are weak, or even defeated, we can rely on His triumph. When we go to our knees it is not a sign of weakness or surrender to our circumstances, but a sign of submission to the One who can bring out beauty from the ashes of despair.

In our weakness we rely on what Jesus did on our behalf. In the midst of conflict, we can have faith that He has already won the battle and that we will never have a challenge where Christ will leave us defenseless or alone. Through His Holy Spirit we have a constant companion.

The battles we face are the Lord's. God knows who belongs to Him even when we are weak. He gets down into our problems with us and supplies our situation with the resources we can't produce on our own. He reminds us that our victory has been bought and paid for by the blood that was shed on the cross. In our faith in Christ, we find our victory. We won't find it through our intellect, our cashflow, our talents, or our scheming, but we will find it in Jesus.

I John 5:4 reminds us, "This is the victory that has overcome the world, even our faith." His ability to overcome provides us with all that we need to conquer our greatest fears, challenges, and trials. With the Apostle Paul we can declare, "I can do all this through him who gives me strength" (Philippians 4:13). So, take heart, we are on the winning side and when the day is over and the smoke has cleared, our Lord will be standing by our side.

"THE TIME HAS COME"

John 17:1–2 *After Jesus said this, he looked toward heaven and prayed: "Father, the time has come. Glorify your Son, that your Son may glorify you. For you granted him authority over all people that he might give eternal life to all those you have given him."*

It is customary for most people to bow their heads as they pray, for in doing so we are showing reverence for the One to whom we are praying. In this account of Jesus praying, however, He lifted His head and focused on the Father, who had given Him His mission. The posture we assume in prayer is not important though, so long as we honor the Creator of all things.

This prayer acknowledges the plan and timing of the Father in the events surrounding the cross. The coming crucifixion of Jesus was not a plan that went wrong. There are those who really believe that Jesus tried to make a difference, to bring God's truth to the world, but that He was unsuccessful in His mission, and fell victim to the forces of evil in our world. Nothing could be farther from the truth. Revelation 13:8 speaks of Jesus as "the Lamb who was slain from the creation of the world." The cross was not a failure, but the key part of our salvation, which was planned for us by the Father to correct the problem of man's rebellion. Jesus carried out that divine plan to perfection.

The words Jesus uses here as He describes the coming trials are wrapped up in glory. The cross would bring glory to the Father's name. The cross would bring glory to the Son, who would endure such torture for mankind. The cross would make eternal life possible for the generations of history to come. Jesus did not see His fate as a defeat in any fashion, for He knew that everything was unfolding just as it had been ordained to happen.

Such love is indescribable! That Jesus, who was given full authority over everyone, would allow Himself to be treated in such a way that exposed mankind's deepest depravity is nearly unbelievable. Who would do such a thing? Who would allow sin's worst to be on display in this manner? Only the One who could conquer sin and bring about the victory that man needed to be set free from sin's grasp.

We owe so much to our Savior. When His time came, He was ready to die for us. When our hour of trial comes, will we live for Him?

WATCHING FROM THE FRONT ROW

John 17:3–5 *"Now this is eternal life: that they may know you, the only true God, and Jesus Christ, whom you have sent. I have brought you glory on earth by completing the work you gave me to do. And now, Father, glorify me in your presence with the glory I had with you before the world began."*

Some people spend fortunes and plot the majority of the years they live, trying to find some way to stay alive forever. Immortality to them is the holy grail that always seems to be just beyond their fingertips. Science fiction books and movies are filled with stories of people who have sought the ability to avoid death, but even in that realm the goal is rarely achieved.

Jesus made the path very clear and very simple for us all. We obtain eternal life by knowing the Father and the Son. Entering into a relationship with God by faith in the work of Christ, through the drawing power of the Holy Spirit, is the way to immorality for all who would desire it. It's not for the select few, or those who are better than anyone else, but for all who will cast their lives on the grace of Jesus.

The reason we find this way to life only through Jesus is because He is the only one who completed the work the Father gave Him to do on our behalf. He alone became sin for us and paid the price with His life so that we could be set free from its grip on us. He alone was raised from the dead to prove that He had conquered not only sin, but the grave as well. His sacrifice and His resurrection provide all who will trust in Him the pathway to live forever.

He spoke here about glory. God was glorified by Jesus, and because Jesus was willing to complete the work the Father gave Him, He was able to return to the glory He had before He came into this world as a human. Not only did Jesus rise to die no more, but He was also resurrected to the place of authority He had before His journey to the cross as a man began. Jesus always has existed and always will. The Father, the Son, and the Spirit are one from before the beginning of time and will continue forever. It's not only amazing, it's glorious!

We who put our trust in the work of Christ on our behalf have a ringside seat to see God continuing to work in our world. We see His grace extended through the ministry of Christ's body, the church, and we see Jesus continuing to be exalted as a result of lives that are being changed.

BELIEF: FINALLY!

John 17:6–8 *"I have revealed you to those whom you gave me out of the world. They were yours; you gave them to me and they have obeyed your word. Now they know that everything you have given me comes from you. For I gave them the words you gave me and they accepted them. They knew with certainty that I came from you, and they believed that you sent me."*

Reveal parties are big things today. A lot of effort, planning, and sometimes quite a bit of expense goes into the broadcasting of the gender of a baby that is coming to a couple. I'm old enough to remember when we didn't know what sex the baby would be until the time of delivery, but that's almost unheard of anymore.

What Jesus revealed to His disciples was much bigger news, for it affected the lives of every person born for generations to come. He broke the news of His divine identity to those who belonged to His inner circle, for He put His trust in them even when they didn't deserve it.

According to Jesus, these disciples were a gift to Him from the Father. It was in the Father's plan that they should come to Jesus, and when they did, they received the word of His identity revelation with sincerity. It took them a while to gain a level of understanding that would enable them to be fully capable of being Christ's representatives, but Jesus was convinced that they would be true to Him, and as usual He was right.

We are witnessing a very intimate setting here as Jesus is in prayer. He was conversing openly with His Father and though the disciples were present as He was praying, it is almost like He was talking past them and about them. He provided His followers with such an example of what prayer truly is as He was lost in conversation with the Father and seemed very comfortable in that state.

Oh, that Jesus would say such things about us. To hear Him say that we belonged to the Father, that He knows our confidence is in the Son, and that we believe whatever He tells us is a high commendation. The fact that He considered these men as family and feels the same way about us is too rich for words. Perhaps today we should strive to live up to the level of confidence that Jesus has placed upon us. Because He trusts so much in us, we should never give Him reason to regret that trust.

HE IS PRAYING FOR US

John 17:9–10 *"I pray for them. I am not praying for the world, but for those you have given me, for they are yours. All I have is yours, and all you have is mine. And glory has come to me through them."*

It is certainly a beautiful thought, that Jesus would pray to the Father on behalf of His disciples. In the same way we can expect that He continues to do that on behalf of all those who call upon His name and trust in Him for their salvation. With Jesus interceding for us to the Father, we can rest assured that we are never out of His care.

But it is also a telling factor when Jesus reveals that His disciples were put on a higher level of concern than the world in general. I don't think that means He isn't concerned for the world, for John 3:16 tell us that "God so loved *the world*" (emphasis mine) that He sent His Son for its redemption. These disciples are of major concern to Jesus though, for they were given to Him by the Father. It was the Father that put them in His path and allowed the connection for Jesus and these men.

This reminds me about just how invested God is in our lives. He not only is the Creator of all things, but He orchestrates the affairs of mankind as surely as He controls the wind and the waves. We are not puppets who are unable to make our own choices, but the Father provides what we need to live our lives pleasing in His sight if only we will not fight against Him. We belong to Him as we put our trust in His Son.

The relationship between the Father and His divine Son is symbiotic. What is good for the one is good for the other. What belongs to the one belongs to the other also. They are so interconnected that they are truly one in every way, while remaining separate persons.

This is the relationship that Jesus invites us to enter. His prayer is for His disciples, and as we follow after Him that includes us. His prayer is that we would be protected from the world and any distraction it might provide to pull us away from the closeness He desires to enjoy with us. The result of such personal interaction is that it produces glory; glory for the Father, glory for the Son, and we who join the family get to be a part of their continuing ministry and connection to our world. Service is glorious in itself, but when it makes Jesus and the Father look good, we have done our part.

AN EXAMPLE IN PRAYER

John 17:11–12 *"I will remain in the world no longer, but they are still in the world, and I am coming to you. Holy Father, protect them by the power of your name—the name you gave me—so that they may be one as we are one. While I was with them, I protected them and kept them safe by that name you gave me. None has been lost except the one doomed to destruction so that Scripture would be fulfilled."*

Jesus was about to be on the move. Though the men sitting around him were oblivious to the events that would take place over the next few hours, Jesus knew that the wheels of change were in motion and soon His address would be different. He had come from the heavenly realms, and He was about to return there when His work on the cross was over. Though I am sure there was dread concerning the pain that was about to befall Him, a part of Him was longing to go home.

But in the midst of all that was about to happen to Him, He still cared greatly for the disciples who would remain behind. They would need the protection of the Father or else they would drift away from their training and calling, just as Judas already had.

Those of us with families understand on some level just what was going through the mind of our Master. We know that our days on this planet are numbered, for we will follow Jesus to the grave eventually. A big concern on our minds is for our spouses, children, grandchildren, and others close to us who will feel the void of our absence when our time here is ended. Just as Jesus was concerned for those who would be left behind when He went home, we share in that thought for those we love.

We are given a path to follow here as we reflect on the needs of these people, and we are to do as Jesus did; we are to pray for them. I pray for my daughter, my son, my grandson, and my daughter-in-law. I pray for my wife, my sister, for my relatives, and my in-laws. I ask that the Father would provide for them, direct them, protect them, and keep them from the enemy of their souls who would destroy them. I ask the Father to give them wisdom and a heavenly blessing that would fill their lives with the Holy Spirit. I want the best for them because I care for them.

Jesus prayed for those close to Him. Can I do any less?

JOY—FULL

John 17:13 *"I am coming to you now, but I say these things while I am still in the world, so that they may have the full measure of my joy within them."*

We who have put our faith in Jesus Christ for our salvation don't speak nearly enough concerning the joy that He provides for our lives. Maybe that's because the idea of joy is so often confused with the fleeting feeling of happiness. Happiness passes as our emotions change, but joy goes so much deeper. Joy is something that Jesus places within us, and it doesn't fade when circumstances alter our lives and schedules.

Jesus realized that a very scary time was coming for His disciples. The cross loomed large before Him, and though they had been told on several occasions that it was coming, at this point His followers hadn't quite caught on to what He had been talking about.

The possibility that lay before them was that when the going would get tough, these disciples would come apart at the seams. They were a fickle bunch, and the rubber was about to meet the road in the next few hours, so they were going to need something to hold on to for the days ahead. Therefore, Jesus asked the Father to give them joy.

Did you catch what Jesus was saying? He was asking the Father that those who follow Him would have the full measure of His joy placed within their lives. Because I believe in keeping the scripture in context, I know that He was specifically referencing the eleven disciples who were in this prayer meeting. However, I also believe that Jesus was asking for all those who would follow after Him. We all need to have His fullness in our lives and such fullness always produces joy, regardless of our situation.

There is no doubt that many of our days are filled with stressful events that have the potential of stealing our joy. However, that doesn't have to be the case. Remember, Jesus prayed that the Father would give us *His* joy. Since Jesus only asked for what was in alignment with the Father's will, and since we know that the Father always responds to the requests that are asked according to His will, we can count on the joy Jesus gives to be our constant companion. The world will try to take it from us, but joy from Jesus is with us always, as long as we put our trust in Him. Because His presence in us produces this blessing, we can face whatever life throws at us with joy.

LIVING LIKE OUR MASTER

John 17:14 *"I have given them your word and the world has hated them, for they are not of the world any more than I am of the world."*

The Word of the Lord is powerful. Those who listen for the voice of Jesus and take time to reflect on the messages He gives us, find that their lives do not remain the same afterwards. That's because the Word of the Lord is not static, but dynamic and continues to check us when we are going in a direction that is contrary to His desires for us and points us in the way that leads us into productive service for His glory.

The disciples that surrounded Jesus had spent the previous three years listening to the messages from the Father that Jesus had imparted to them. It wasn't always easy to hear, and it wasn't always easy to understand the points that Jesus was relaying to them, but the more they listened and began to grasp what He meant, the more their lives would be changed.

Back in the Sermon on the Mount (Matthew 5-7) Jesus had proclaimed to them and the masses, "You have heard ... but I say until you..." He took the Law of Moses and brought it up to date so that those who truly looked to follow God would get clarity to the truths that had sometimes been clouded by man's manipulation and misunderstanding. Those who would hear Him came to realize that He was taking them to a higher standard of life in God than to just obey rules. They began to see that what He was saying was not only for the glory of God, but for their good as well.

By the time this night of destiny came to pass, the disciples would come to realize that God was always working, and the way to the cross was just another step in His divine plan. In time, they too would become martyrs for His cause because the way of righteousness and the way of sin always clashes. Just as Jesus was hated, and is hated still by many, those disciples, and we as His disciples, will face times when hatred will come our way as well.

The good news is that because of the transformation that takes place through the power of the Holy Spirit in our lives, we have opportunities to continue to be witnesses to the Word of the Lord for this day. Regardless of how the message is received by others, we are renewed daily. Thanks be to God, who continues to guide His servants every step of the way.

STAYING PUT, BUT
BEING PROTECTED

John 17:15–16 *"My prayer is not that you take them out of the world but that you protect them from the evil one. They are not of the world, even as I am not of it."*

One of the problems with the so-called, "rapture" view of what lies ahead for the church is that it is heavily weighted with an escapist view for the Christian. Nowhere in the Bible do we find that Jesus is going to take His followers out of the troubles of this world so that they can escape the path of the cross. We are called to be in the world and difference makers in the world, for the glory of God, and for the redemption of God's creation. If we are not careful, we can fall victim to the ideology of "flight," rather than "fight" the good fight of the faith.

Certainly, Jesus had no illusions of escape from the world for the followers He was praying for on that night of nights. He knew that the way of the cross was not only ahead in His path, but that it would be in the pathway of all who would take on His name and follow His example. As a result, according to church tradition, all of the original disciples except John would die a martyrs' death for the sake of Jesus. They truly were not of the world that has been so tightly wrapped by the power of sin and darkness, and they would pay for the privilege of freeing others with the Good News of the Kingdom with their lives.

Down through the centuries there have been countless others who numbered among the faithful, who have given their last measure of devotion for Jesus. Some have been famous and have become inspirational models for people like us to admire, but many more will remain nameless in this age, but will be counted great in the eternal Kingdom of God.

When Jesus prayed that His followers would be protected from the evil one, He was not saying that they would escape the enemy's influence in this world. He was praying that they would stay strong, and overcome failure while they labored here, until they were called home to their reward when their lives were over.

That's the example for us. We will be tempted, we will be tried, and we may face great persecution, but hold fast, for in the end, we win—through the power of Jesus Christ!

"Sanctify Them!"

John 17:17–19 *"Sanctify them by the truth; your word is truth. As you sent me into the world, I have sent them into the world. For them I sanctify myself, that they too may be truly sanctified."*

O h, how I love these verses! Jesus prayed that His followers would be sanctified just as He was sanctified. His prayer is that such a walk would not only be possible but expected because He asked it of the Father for us.

Sanctification has many times been misunderstood. It means to be set apart, to be purified, and enabled with divine ability to carry out the Master's will in our world. It means that self-interest has to die, that self-promotion must perish, and self-centeredness must be crucified on the altar of sacrifice. It is determining that we will follow Jesus and His teachings until our last breath, and that we will allow no earthly pleasure or distraction to move us from that commitment.

To be sanctified is not just a ritual, or a second trip to the altar, or even a strong intention to put the things of God first. To be sanctified is to experience God accepting the promises we make to Him, and then receiving the fullness of His Spirit upon our life. We commit, consecrate, and dedicate ourselves to God, but then sanctification happens as God does His part and imparts His cleansing and empowering grace in abundant measure.

Sanctification is all tied up in the idea of the cross. Jesus sanctified Himself by fulfilling the Father's plan for His life and giving His life for the ransom of all creation. If we would receive and live the sanctified life, then we too must die to all that is between us and the plan of God He has laid out for us.

This is no small matter. It means that doing the will of God must be more important than our spouse, our children, our job, our money, our health, our plans, and everything else that would call for our attention to make it first place in our life. It requires each of us to count the cost, and for us to be willing to walk in the way of being all that God wants us to be.

The act and the process of sanctification puts us in the role not only of God's servant, but also of God's steward, or manager. It's when we realize that everything we have is not ours, but belongs to God, and we just manage what is His. This costs us everything but frees us like nothing else can.

HE WAS THINKING ABOUT US

John 17:20–21 "My prayer is not for them alone. I pray also for those who will believe in me through their message, that all of them may be one, Father, just as you are in me and I am in you. May they also be in us so that the world may believe that you have sent me."

This passage of scripture may be some of most important words that Jesus records in this chapter. It is well and good that He prayed for the disciples who were gathered around Him, for their next few days were going to try their faith like nothing ever had. They needed Jesus to intercede on their behalf.

However, it is also true that we need the concern and oversight of Jesus as well. These verses remind us that we have been prayed for by Jesus specifically, because we are included in that number who would believe in Jesus through the message He had given to His disciples. Down through the years from the time of this prayer until the present, and even into the future, we can know that Jesus has presented our needs to the Father.

The purpose behind this part of His prayer was that we would not be left out of the loop when it comes to intimacy with God. Just as Jesus was one with the Father, He prayed that His disciples would be one with the Father, and He prayed that those who would be disciples after this group would also be one with the Father. That includes you and me. When we place our trust in Jesus Christ for our salvation we are connected with God in a very real way, and that connection makes oneness with the divine possible.

The Apostle Paul reminds us that the Holy Spirit makes this connection evident as He lives within us. "The Spirit himself testifies with our spirit that we are God's children. Now, if we are children, then we are heirs—heirs of God and co-heirs with Christ, if indeed we share in his sufferings in order that we may also share in his glory" (Romans 8:16–17).

Jesus prayed that we would be included in the oneness with God that He enjoyed with the Father. Though we haven't seen Him with our own eyes, we can know His closeness to us because the Spirit tells us all about it. What a privilege to be a child of God and what a blessing to have Jesus pray for us specifically that it would happen! The prayer is for those we would disciple as well, so we need to spread the word to as many as possible. They too can be one with God because Jesus has prayed for it to be so.

PRIORITY WORDS

John 17:22–23 *"I have given them the glory that you gave me, that they may be one as we are one: I in them and you in me. May they be brought to complete unity to let the world know that you sent me and have loved them even as you have loved me."*

There are three words in these verses that are closely tied together. They are "glory," "unity," and "loved." They are words used by Jesus to describe what He had done for His disciples, what He desired for His disciples, and what He expected of His disciples.

He gave glory to the His disciples that the Father had given to Him, and it was for a similar purpose. Jesus was glorified by the Father through the relationship they shared together. It was that relationship that produced the unity they enjoyed since before the beginning of time. The glory that He passed along to His disciples was also for the purpose that they would become one. After all, they had come from very diverse backgrounds, but had become family through their connection to the Christ, who was their Lord and Master.

The unity that Jesus desired for them was not yet complete, however. On this very night they would scatter and all feelings of togetherness would be broken because of the fear that would overtake them. That unity would be restored after the resurrection, but only when they truly became one with Jesus would they be able to bear witness about Him to the world, and let the world know that Jesus came from the Father.

Once the disciples were unified, they would not only tell the story of God's divine plan through Jesus the Christ, but they would also come to know the Father's love in a way they had never realized before. They would understand that just as the Father loved the Son, they were also loved in the same measure.

These words dominate God's plan for His disciples to this day. When we experience the glory of the Father it is for the purpose of our unity in His family. When we are unified, we can tell the story to others more effectively and share the Father's gift of salvation to all who will hear. The end result of our efforts and our mission is that we get to walk in love, and in harmony with the Father through His Holy Spirit. It is that love that conquers all.

SEEING THE GLORY OF JESUS

John 17:24 *"Father, I want those you have given me to be with me where I am, and to see my glory, the glory you have given me because you loved me before the creation of the world."*

To be where Jesus was at this point in the story doesn't sound like a place most of us would want to be. After all, in just a short time Judas and the soldiers would be coming, and the forces of hell would have their heyday. Jesus knew that the coming sacrifice would be the way He would be glorified, however, so He wanted to make sure that His followers would witness what He was about to face. They would need to know for sure that He had died before they could accept the truth of the coming resurrection. Glory doesn't come easy, but when it comes, it is life changing.

The glory of which Jesus was speaking was not a new thing for Him. He makes clear in this verse that He had experienced this before the foundation of the world. He reigned supreme as He created all that has been created and made even the tree that would be the instrument of His death. The most amazing thing of all time is that He was willing to lay that glory aside for a while so that He could become like us. It is beyond our understanding as to how He could stoop so low and why He would do it. The only word to describe it is love.

So many songs have been written about this love, yet it is never fully explained. So many sermons have proclaimed the love of the Father and the love of the Son for the created things that didn't deserve such consideration. So many people have experienced the change that such love brings about because they have come to receive the Holy Spirit of God into their lives. Still, with all these examples, we consider it mind-boggling to grasp the extent of such love.

The least we can do is to love our Savior back and desire to live in such a way that His glory shines out from us. We need to glorify Him to the world so that they will see His endless love for themselves. We do this by living such transformed lives that our actions and words reflect the Lord who has changed us so drastically. For us to be where Jesus is means for us to walk in holiness of heart and life, surrendering to the will of the Father in all things, even the way of the cross. This is how Jesus is glorified in us.

THE CONTINUING WORK

John 17:25–26 *"Righteous Father, though the world does not know you, I know you, and they know that you have sent me. I have made you known to them, and will continue to make you known in order that the love you have for me may be in them and that I myself may be in them."*

It is truly a sad thing that the world does not know God. It is sad because the world doesn't even realize that it was created by, and is sustained by, the unseen hand of the Almighty, even when He desires nothing but good for it always.

Jesus knew the Father on that night though. The disciples that followed after Him didn't grasp completely all that was about to transpire, but they did know that Jesus had come from God and that He was fulfilling the mission that brought Him to earth as a man. Jesus had been drilling these truths into them for over three years and slowly, but surely, they were starting to get the message.

It was for love's sake that Jesus let His disciples in on the news that would change them and all creation in the days to come. He loved them so much that He wanted them to experience that same love for each other, and for all the Father's doings.

The work that Jesus was to impart to His followers was a continuing work. He was revealing the Father to them and would do so for as long as He was with them. He does the same to us today as we draw near to Him through the agency of His Spirit. We can experience the oneness He had prayed for us to have, and we can pass that oneness along to others as we continue to walk in the revelations He puts in our path.

Having Jesus, "in us," is a thought that is hard for some people to handle. Because an x-ray or MRI can't reveal His divine presence inside our bodies, there is a faction of the world that thinks the whole concept is just a made-up religious superstition. Jesus had earlier revealed that the Father was Spirit (3:5–6), that those who worship Him must worship in spirit and in truth (4:24), and later He would remind His followers that He would be with them always (Matthew 28:20). He continues to love us and to makes the Father known to us who will look for Him. His grace knows no bounds, and today He cares for you like no one else can.

TIME TO GO...

John 18:1 *When he had finished praying, Jesus left with his disciples and crossed the Kidron Valley. On the other side there was an olive grove, and he and his disciples went into it.*

The time that Jesus spent in prayer was highly important. It was a lengthy prayer, and it covered many subjects, but it was mainly focused on His disciples and what He desired for them to experience as a result of what was about to take place, and what they would experience in the days ahead.

By this time the number leaving the upper room was twelve. Jesus, and His eleven disciples were making their way out of the city proper, to an olive grove where the time of prayer could continue in even greater earnestness. Judas was no longer with the group because he had departed from the upper room earlier to follow up on his plan to betray Jesus to the leaders of the Jews.

The Kidron Valley today lies between the eastern wall of the Old City of Jerusalem and the Mount of Olives. The valley is a twenty-mile stretch running north to south that descends 4000 feet and eventually ends at the Dead Sea. It was the same valley that King David had crossed barefoot and weeping as he ran from his son Absalom. Now, Jesus was also taking a sorrowful journey there.

It is interesting in a sense that Jesus chose an olive grove as a place to pray. To this day the olive branch is a symbol for peace and though Jesus is the Prince of Peace, the events on that night were anything but peaceful.

We can't begin to understand the depth of love that was mixed with anguish as Jesus led His band of followers there. We also can't begin to understand the confusion that must have filled the minds of the disciples who obediently made the short journey at Jesus' command. They had heard so much, but they must have had so many questions about what Jesus meant by it all. All too soon they would understand, but at this point they really didn't comprehend the words Jesus spoke to them.

There will be times when we too must walk by faith with Jesus into the unknown and sometimes frightening future. But we know He is with us and that's really all that we need.

A PLACE FOR PRAYER

John 18:2 *Now Judas, who betrayed him, knew the place, because Jesus had often met there with his disciples.*

Anyone who stumbles upon this story in the Bible for the first time might wonder just how Judas knew where to find Jesus. The chief priest, the Sadducees, and the Pharisees had been trying to find Jesus for some time, but He kept eluding them regardless of their inquiries.

Here we are told that Judas knew where Jesus would be because it wasn't the first time Jesus had taken His disciples there. The Garden of Gethsemane, as we know it today, was an olive grove that was deserted at night, so Jesus often went there for times of prayer. Apparently, the place of prayer was such a routine for Jesus that Judas just knew that is where he would find His Master on this Passover night.

This makes me wonder about the prayer habits of the church at large today as well as the prayer habits of individual Christians. Certainly, it is appropriate that the church would gather for times of prayer on a regular basis—and there is no time more appropriate than on a Sunday morning when it can collectively lift the needs of the community of faith and the unbelieving world before the Father. The time of prayer in our local services should be a high priority in the planning of our worship experience together.

However, this place and time of prayer for Jesus was outside of any public service, but it was done with such regularity that Judas and the rest of the disciples just considered it a common and regular experience. Jesus prayed often, and Jesus prayed often in the Garden of Gethsemane. We may just remember it for this final time, but it was a usual spot for Jesus.

So, here's the question. Do you have a regular place and time for prayer in your life? Is your time before the Father so regular that people close to you would know when and where it takes place? Are you so committed to this routine that to find you elsewhere and doing otherwise than being in a state of prayer would seem strange? I wonder.

Jesus considered time with the Father of utmost importance. He got His instructions from the Father, and He got His inspiration and strength from the Father. He couldn't fulfill His calling without it. Do we really think we can?

THE EFFECTS OF SIN

John 18:3 *So Judas came to the grove, guiding a detachment of soldiers and some officials from the chief priests and Pharisees. They were carrying torches, lanterns, and weapons.*

The scene changed drastically from what had been a prayer meeting. The quiet night that previously had been filled with the sound of snores from the disciples and the cries of anguish from Jesus, was broken with the marching of the temple guards. The long-awaited movement that would bring about the salvation of the world was about to begin.

Judas was carrying out his despicable deed and making good on his promise to betray Jesus to those who had already determined that He should die. Whether Judas actually realized that this is what they had in mind will always be debated, but the sin was committed, nonetheless. He would go down in the annals of history as the person who did the most corrupt thing of all time. He handed over the only pure and innocent man that ever lived to men who were not worthy of the positions they held.

The soldiers were just doing what they had been ordered to do. Because they were temple guards, they were under the command of the Jewish leaders, made up of the Sanhedrin. The Romans would be involved before the night would be over, but these men were sent from the chief priests of God's chosen people. It's the ultimate irony that the holy priesthood of God would sink so low as to do what they would do to Jesus.

How could men who were commissioned to be God's instruments sink so low? The simple answer is sin. Sin has a way of binding, blinding, and corrupting everything that it touches, and it doesn't end with the sinners because it aways affects everything around it. These men who were commissioned as soldiers are good examples of the bystanders who got caught up in the crime of the ages. The lanterns, torches, and weapons were the tools of their trade. The lights would break the darkness of the night, but not the darkness of the hour. Sin was about to have its way like it had never had before.

We feel the darkness as we read these words. We, who know the story, are saddened because we know what comes next. The King of kings was about to take center stage, and we already feel His pain.

HIS MAJESTIC PRESENCE

John 18:4–6 *Jesus, knowing all that was going to happen to him, went out and asked them, "Who is it that you want?" "Jesus of Nazareth," they replied. I am he," Jesus said. (And Judas the traitor was standing there with them.) When Jesus said, "I am he," they drew back and fell to the ground.*

This is certainly an interesting passage of scripture that includes a variety of parts to it. First, there is the omniscience of Jesus. He knew everything. He knew what was about to happen and He faced His future willingly. Second, there is the exposure of the eternal need of mankind. When Jesus asked the soldiers who it was they wanted, they said, "Jesus of Nazareth," and unwittingly gave the answer that is true for all ages. Who is it that we really want? Why, it's Jesus, of course. He alone has the words and way of life for His creation. Even when people don't realize it as they run helter-skelter through life looking for satisfaction, it is Jesus that they really want.

Another point of interest in these verses is when Jesus said, "I am he." Because this was a Jewish crowd and Jewish soldiers, the phrase, "I am," meant something very important to them. The "I AM" was the presence of God that met Moses at the burning bush (Exodus 3:14–15), where God said that this would be how He would be known throughout all generations. Because of the majesty of those words and the very presence of Almighty God in the person of Jesus, the soldiers shrank back in awe, momentarily stunned. Again, just as in the story of Moses and the burning bush, when the presence of God was revealed, they were afraid to look at Him.

All these examples point to the fact that the cross was not an accident, or a situation that just got out of control. Jesus was not thwarted in His attempt to rescue mankind and fell victim to the overpowering forces of darkness. He was in total control of all that was happening. Though the people around Him didn't recognize it at the time, the plan of the Father was being fulfilled right down to the letter, for Jesus could have changed the situation entirely if He had wanted to do so, but He allowed prophecy to be fulfilled.

Judas was listed by John here as the traitor, and certainly he was that. But the story unfolding is not about him, but Jesus, and how His majesty dominated the scene even when others thought it was an out-of-control situation. But Jesus was reigning then just as He is now, and forevermore.

SAFE IN HIS ARMS

John 18:7–9 *Again he asked them, "Who is it you want?"*
And they said, "Jesus of Nazareth." "I told you that I am he,"
Jesus answered. "If you are looking for me, then let these men
go." This happened so that the words he had spoken would
be fulfilled: "I have not lost one of those you gave me."

In the midst of what appeared to be the darkest moment of His earthly existence, Jesus never forgot about the people who were around Him. When it became clear that the mob was after Him, He drew the attention of the moment to Himself so that His followers would not be caught up in the event that was taking place. He had their backs, even though they would run away like scalded dogs from the scene. He protected them with His own life.

That's the way Jesus has always worked. He cares supremely about those who belong to Him. This is why we can go to the Father in prayer at any point in our lives and know that the Son is interceding for us to protect us and keep us from danger.

Some will say, "Well, if that is the case, why do bad things happen to good people?" It's an age-old question, but one that has a simple answer. He protects us in the way that will fulfill the Father's plan for our lives and will guarantee us an eternal dwelling with Him when our life here comes to an end. In the meantime, He is right in the midst of the tough situations we face through the presence of His Holy Spirit. As He promised His disciples earlier (John 16:7), the Spirit would be sent to them and be a constant presence with them.

He cares about us in all we go through. He cares about the crisis points in our lives that have the potential to draw us away from Him. He cares about the mother with a sick child, He cares about the family breadwinner who can't find work, and He cares about us all when we too must walk through the valley of the shadow of death. There is never a time that those who put their trust in Him for the needs of their lives and souls, that He is not watching over us and helping us. We may not always see it, but the situation is never out of His hands.

On that night of betrayal, He was watching out for His own. They were in danger, and He took that danger upon Himself. He does the same for us today as we trust Him with all we have.

DOING WHAT COMES "SUPERNATURAL"

John 18:10–11 *Then Simon Peter, who had a sword, drew it and struck the high priest's servant, cutting off his right ear. (The servant's name was Malchus.) Jesus commanded Peter, "Put your sword away! Shall I not drink the cup the Father has given me?"*

Simon Peter always seemed to be the impetuous one. We find instances where he is boastful, brash in his speech, and acting without thinking. He apparently was a doer, a fisherman who had learned that fish don't just jump into the boat. One must put out a net or a line to get them. Those patterns of behavior drove him to actions that sometimes were not in the best interest of what God had planned.

To many of us, what he did on that night seems perfectly rational. His love for Jesus and his desire to protect Him caused him to defend Him in the only way he knew how. He would fight to save his Lord. Even if no one else took up the sword, or even if he was completely outnumbered, he would stand his ground and fight to save Jesus.

Matthew 26 tells us that Jesus had asked Peter, along with James and John to go beyond the outskirts of the Garden of Gethsemane, beyond the other disciples, to pray with Him. But on two occasions Jesus came to them in the midst of His praying to find them sleeping. In fact, he even woke them up and chastised them for their sleepiness, but they just drifted off again after He went back to prayer.

It's easy to criticize Peter, but then if we were in his situation, we might not respond any better. The lesson that he would remember from all the events surrounding this arrest was the words of Jesus reminding him that the Father's plan had to be fulfilled. The soldiers were acting in accordance with the prophecies from hundreds of years before. The cup Jesus was about to drink was a bitter one, but one that He had to face.

Just as the Father had a plan for Jesus, He has one for us as well. Are we willing to drink from the cup, to walk in the plan that He has for us? We may not be asked to go to a cross, or even face hardship in the fulfillment of that plan, but we might. Can we have the attitude and mind of Christ for such an event that will bring to pass the way God has laid out for us? If we can, then we will find life and life more abundant, for the Lord always keeps His word.

ONE MAN HAD TO DIE

John 18:12–14 *Then the detachment of soldiers with its commander and the Jewish officials arrested Jesus. They bound him and brought him first to Annas, who was the father-in-law of Caiaphas, the high priest that year. Caiaphas was the one who had advised the Jews that it would be good if one man died for the people.*

We are reminded by the writer that Caiaphas, the high priest, had first been announced to the reader back in John 11:50, when he said that it was expedient that one man should die for the nation of Israel. He was right in his pronouncement then, but he had no idea that Jesus would be dying for the sake of every person ever born on this planet.

As high priest, Caiaphas presided over the Sanhedrin, that group of forty men who served as the leadership council for the nation of Israel. This council had to walk a fine line with the Romans as they did not have the freedom to do as they wished but could only go as far as the authority from Rome would allow them.

The soldiers were sent out by Caiaphas, but they brought Jesus to Annas, his father-in-law. Annas had been the high priest from A.D. 6-15, at which time the Romans had removed him from office. Even so, he still carried a lot of weight with the Sanhedrin, shown by the fact that Jesus was taken to him first before he went to the current high priest. Five of his sons would also serve in the position of high priest, but at this point in time it was his daughter's husband, Caiaphas, who held this office.

Politics can be a very dirty business, but when politics are mixed with religion it is downright nasty. We see a picture of this in Revelation 12–14 where the dragon (Satan), gives his power to the beast (the state), who in turn gives authority to a second beast (organized religion). When the people of God begin to compromise and collaborate with the power of the state, they are in great danger of being used for the purposes of the evil one. Such was the state of the high priesthood in this story.

God can work through anyone, and this scene is a good example of that. Though corrupt and self-serving, Annas and Caiaphas would start the ball rolling to bring God's plan of salvation to fulfillment. They didn't know it, but God will be glorified, and Jesus will be Lord regardless of man's actions.

LOOKING IN FROM THE OUTSIDE

John 18:15–16 *Simon Peter and another disciple were following Jesus. Because this disciple was known to the high priest, he went with Jesus into the high priest's courtyard, but Peter had to wait outside at the door. The other disciple, who was known to the high priest, came back, spoke to the girl on duty there and brought Peter in.*

We often get the idea that all the disciples ran away from the Garden of Gethsemane the night that Jesus was betrayed, but there were two of them that followed the mob to see what would happen to their Master. Apparently, John had some inside connection to the high priest that allowed him to get past the girl who was the gatekeeper that night. In any case, he was able to get himself admitted, and then later able to bring Simon Peter in as well.

It must have been a surreal feeling that came upon these two disciples as they watched in horror to what was happening to Jesus. At this point they were powerless to do anything to stop the sham of a trial that was about to unfold, and if they came out publicly in His support it would probably have put their own lives in jeopardy. In the garden they might have been able to put up a fight, even if it was a losing cause, but here they stood as helpless onlookers while the drama of the ages unfolded.

Have you ever been in a situation where all possible options were out of your control? I have experienced this a few times when I was a hospital patient before and after major surgeries, and everything surrounding me was controlled by others. To be present and aware of distressing situations, but unable to change anything to improve those circumstances is nearly maddening.

As I read this account of the first encounters of Jesus before the Jewish court, I sense the pain that John and Peter must have felt. Mobs produce fear, anxiety, and often very unfortunate results, and this mob was motivated by jealousy, hate, and greed. That combination is capable of producing a very combustible atmosphere. Things could only get worse for Jesus and most likely the apostles had a very sick and sinking feeling in their stomachs.

But though it appeared all hope was gone, actually the reason for hope was just beginning. Jesus was taking the first steps to the cross, and it was on the cross that our salvation would be purchased. Thanks be to God!

A Bitter Denial

John 18:17–18 *"You are not one of his disciples, are you?" the girl at the door asked Peter. He replied, "I am not." It was cold, and the servants and officials stood around a fire they had made to keep warm. Peter also was standing with them, warming himself.*

Here was the moment of truth. Peter had earlier declared that he would stand by Jesus to the bitter end, even being willing to go to his death if need be, for His Lord, but now his words were being put to the test.

It's really kind of strange. If John had not gone back out to get him and brought him inside the courtyard of the high priest, he would have gone unnoticed like the rest of the disciples who ran away. He could have waited outside for John to bring him news of what was happening, but that wasn't Peter's style. He had to be in on the doings himself. His was an inquiring mind that wanted to know.

It was in the middle of the night and the chill that came from the darkness caused the necessity of a fire for people to keep a degree of warmth. While trying to look innocent, Peter's own shivers drew him to the flames to get some relief from the cold. However, the girl that stood watch over the door took notice of him and suspected that he had more than just a passing interest in the events that were taking place.

"You are not one of his disciples, are you?" was a question that had to shake Peter to his core. How could he answer such a thing? Seeing how Jesus was being treated and remembering that His Lord had earlier told them that the student would be like his teacher (Luke 6:40), confessing his loyalty to Jesus would have meant danger for sure. His reply was simple and without explanation, "I am not." He was not willing to give his identity and his safety away at this point.

It's easy for us to say that we would have handled the situation differently. Perhaps we would have, but then Peter had been very adamant about his loyalty to Jesus too. We may never know how we would react to a life-or-death decision concerning whether to acknowledge Jesus or not, but many in the world over the centuries have had to do just that. Peter would later have given anything to have those words back. May we be wise and strong enough to stand the test when it is our turn to speak up.

THE OPEN GOSPEL

John 18:19–21 *Meanwhile, the high priest questioned Jesus about his disciples and his teaching. "I have spoken openly to the world," Jesus replied. "I always taught in synagogues or at the temple, where all the Jews come together. I said nothing in secret. Why question me? Ask those who heard me. Surely they know what I said."*

There were two issues that the high priest was particularly interested in. The first involved the disciples of Jesus. It was most likely providential that the majority of the apostles didn't show themselves at the proceedings that were going on during the illegal Jewish inquisition of Jesus. The Jewish leaders wanted to know how many there were, who they were, and how they could find them to make sure anything that Jesus had started could be put to an end. This line of questioning may have caused Simon Peter to realize his vulnerability, which led to his denial of Jesus.

The main focus, however, was on Jesus Himself and the doctrines He had been spreading throughout the land. The testimony here is that though there were times when He had met with His disciples alone for teaching and training purposes, His general teachings had been on public display for all to hear. The message of the Kingdom of God was not something that was ever meant to be covered up but spread and taught everywhere.

Plenty of people had gathered around Jesus when He had spoken publicly. Many times, the numbers grew large, even into the thousands, but we can be sure that among the many sincere seekers of truth, there were also many Jewish spies who were trying to trick Jesus and catch Him in some theological error so that they could accuse Him. Jesus had always been too smart for them though, and this mock trial was a last-ditch attempt to bring His ministry to an end.

I have reflected on the fact that Jesus told those questioning Him to ask the people who had heard Him as to what message He had been spreading. Surely, they would know. Or would they? I have found that after five decades of preaching that many people hear what they want to hear and don't always grasp truth when it is right in front of them. The words of Jesus were powerful and have been repeated down through the centuries. Perhaps we should read them again and really pay attention to what He said.

THE ILLEGAL TRIAL

John 18:22–24 *When Jesus said this, one of the officials nearby struck him in the face. "Is this the way you answer the high priest?" he demanded. "If I said something wrong," Jesus replied, "testify as to what is wrong. But if I spoke the truth, why did you strike me?" Then Annas sent him, still bound, to Caiaphas the high priest.*

This is one of the first indications that Jesus is in no court of law. He is not even before the current Jewish leader at this time, for the rabble that took Him prisoner took Him to Annas, the former high priest, who was the father-in-law of the current high priest, Caiaphas. Talk about a warped family affair, or a classic example of nepotism! This is a prime example.

Some people list this as the first illegal trial of the night, and certainly, slapping the defendant who is on trial would not be accepted in anything but a kangaroo court (my apology to kangaroos everywhere). Jesus was not disrespectful, nor was he untruthful, but He no doubt recognized where He was, and who He was before, and He realized that there was nothing legitimate about what was happening to Him in any way. He was slapped for sidestepping the question put to him. Attacking the helpless is the way bullies act when they don't get their way, and Jesus allowed it, though He was anything but helpless.

Most of us have been attacked at some point in our life, either verbally or physically, concerning a matter in which we were totally innocent. We were not innocent like Jesus—to the degree that we had never sinned—but when we are attacked unfairly, we know how frustrating it can be. There may be times when we feel helpless to do anything about it, and it appears that the bully is going to get away with the abuse that He or she has heaped on us.

Jesus could have caused the man who slapped Him to wither up and die as surely as he did the fig tree (Matthew 21:18–19). The one who raised the dead could just as easily taken the life of every person who oppressed Him. But what we see here is His continual love in action. He restrains Himself so that scripture would be fulfilled, our sins would be atoned for, and the Kingdom of God would be launched in earnest.

Bad guys do get their way, but only for a time. God is in charge and there will be day of reckoning, but for now, we wait, and we love, as Jesus did.

A BROKEN MAN

John 18:25–27 *As Simon Peter stood warming himself, he was asked, "You are not one of his disciples, are you?" He denied it, saying, "I am not." One of the high priest's servants, a relative of the man whose ear Peter had cut off, challenged him, "Didn't I see you with him in the olive grove?" Again Peter denied it, and at that moment a rooster began to crow.*

There was that question again. It contained the same words as the first inquiry. "You are not one of his disciples, are you?" If it wasn't for the fact that Jesus had predicted that there would be three denials, we might just assume that John was recording the same question twice. We aren't told who it was that asked Peter this time, but his answer didn't change. "I am not," came the reply. There was no way he was going to expose himself in this charged atmosphere.

But then someone came into the conversation that Peter hadn't expected. A relative of Malchus, the man Peter had attacked in the Garden of Gethsemane came forward and accused him of being with Jesus in the olive grove. Apparently, he too had been in the mob that came after Jesus. It seemed that Peter was caught red-handed in his lie.

But still Peter denied that he had been with Jesus. In Matthew 26:74 it is recorded that he not only denied Jesus, but that he called down curses on himself to prove his point. Mark 14:71 records also that he called down curses on himself, but the writer adds that Peter claimed to not even know Jesus. Luke 22:60 tells us that along with the denial, Peter said he didn't even know what the accusers were talking about. In all four gospels the denials are recorded, and that the rooster crowed after the last one, just like Jesus said it would happen. Luke adds one very poignant point though, when he records that after the rooster crowed, Jesus turned and looked Peter in the eye. What a sobering experience for this unfaithful apostle.

The result of it all was that Peter then ran away in tears. He knew he had done the unforgiveable, so he hid in shame and left the place a broken man. But what he didn't know at that time was, when we break the Lord's heart, He still forgives whenever we repent and ask for forgiveness. This is certainly a sad, sad story, but sin always leads to brokenness. But when we are broken, and realize it, Jesus can heal us if we will go to Him.

ANOTHER PHONEY TRIAL

John 18:28–29 *Then the Jews led Jesus from Caiaphas to the palace of the Roman governor. By now it was early morning, and to avoid ceremonial uncleanness the Jews did not enter the palace; they wanted to be able to eat the Passover. So Pilate came out to them and asked, "What charges are you bringing against this man?"*

There isn't much information given to us by John concerning what happened when Jesus finally stood before the high priest, Caiaphas. Verse 24 of this chapter shows Jesus being taken from the home of Annas to Caiaphas and then verse 28 tells us that Jesus was led away from Caiaphas to Pilate. That's about it. For more information on the events that surround Jesus standing on trial before Caiaphas we have to look to the other Gospel accounts. Matthew 26:57–75, Mark 14:53–72, and Luke 22:52–71 give us more about the sham proceedings to fill in the blanks of the story.

As Jesus is moved from the home of Caiaphas to the governor's palace, the Romans are brought into the story. Up to this time we have tracked the journeys of Jesus throughout Israel and have witnessed His encounters with various groups and individuals among the Jewish nation and certain Samaritan people, but Rome has been a silent witness to all that has been surrounding this Prophet from Nazareth. They no doubt have been watching to a certain degree, to make sure order could be maintained, but thus far they have not added much to the story. That was about to change.

The days of the Jewish Passover Feast was upon the land. It didn't mean much to the Romans, but it was of great significance to the Jews. This Passover, more than any other, would change the destiny of the world forever, but only Jesus knew it at this time.

It was so ironic that this murderous group of Jewish leaders would be so concerned about staying ceremonially clean that they wouldn't enter the home of a Gentile during their feast days, while their hands were literally dripping with the stains of the blood money they had paid out to get Judas to betray Jesus. Jesus had called out their previous hypocrisies many times, but this was the ultimate blatant example of their treachery.

The charges would be false, but that wouldn't make any difference in the outcome. Jesus was about to pay the price to atone for your sins and mine.

ROLE PLAYERS

John 18:30–32 *"If he were not a criminal," they replied, "we would not have handed him over to you." Pilate said, "Take him yourselves and judge him by your own law." "But we have no right to execute anyone," the Jews objected. This happened so that the words Jesus had spoken indicating the kind of death he was going to die would be fulfilled.*

Pilate had to leave the inner comforts of his palace to go outside to meet with the religious radicals who masqueraded as holy Jewish leaders. Even when he asked for the list of offenses of which they were accusing Jesus, they only brought forth generalities. They proclaimed that He was a criminal, and that He even deserved to die, but nothing material was presented at this point to back up their claims. There wasn't even any circumstantial evidence, or corroborating witnesses, to back up their charges.

It's of little wonder that Pilate pretty much blew off the whole affair. He saw this as a petty Jewish squabble among men for whom he had only distain to begin with. They were in his eyes, unruly children that needed to settle their silly differences out on their own playground and not bother the adults with their insignificant matters. The Romans would placate the Jews to a certain extent, but Pilate had no interest or desire for getting caught up in their tribal dealings, so long as unrest in the land was held to a minimum.

But when the Jewish leaders brought up the fact that this case was a matter for capital punishment, it must have gotten the governor's attention. It wasn't that he was squeamish about killing another Jew, for Galileans and Judeans had been hung on crosses by the thousands to date, and one more wouldn't make a big difference to him. However, to have the weight of the Sanhedrin itself making such a request, to kill one of their own, well, this was different.

What Pilate didn't realize and what the Jewish leaders could not imagine, was that God was at work in the entirety of the proceedings that were unfolding. The prophecies of the Old Testament Scriptures were being fulfilled, Jesus was completing the plan of the Father right down to the smallest detail, and all the anger, fears, lies, and deceit of those who thought they were bringing the Christ to an end, were just actors in the drama for the redemption of the world. Just as we know what was about to happen because of history, Jesus knew in advance, because He was God.

WHO IS ON TRIAL, ANYWAY?

John 18:33–34 *Pilate then went back inside the palace, summoned Jesus and asked him, "Are you the king of the Jews?" "Is that your own idea," Jesus asked, "or did others talk to you about me?"*

"**A**re you the king?" I can almost hear the sneer in Pilate's voice as he questioned Jesus. Here was this non-descript Jew standing in front of him, derided by his own countrymen and religious leaders, and Pilate wondered why he even had to deal with such a farcical claim.

Jesus seems to always have a question ready to answer a question. Earlier when He was asked by Annas about His teaching, Jesus sidestepped the inquiry and asked a question of Annas. Others had heard Him speak often, so why not ask them what they heard Him say? Jesus was wise and He was shrewd, and He knew how to handle the questions of men when they tried to get the better of Him.

What impresses me most about this scene is that there doesn't appear to be any sense of panic or fear in the Master. He earlier had spoken boldly to the Jewish leaders and declared His identity (Matthew 26:64), so that no one would have any question as to who He really was. Now He was before the Roman governor, the man who thought he had the authority to release Him or crucify Him, but Jesus knew who was really in charge. He was fulfilling the plan and will of the Father, and nothing that was going to happen to Him would deter Him from fulfilling all that the Father had in store for Him.

What an example for each of us today. When we are living in the center of God's will and plan for our life, when we are filled with the Spirit and have the assurance of His divine presence in our life, there is never a reason to worry, to be anxious, or fearful, regardless of what we have to face. We are precious to our Creator, and nothing can snatch us from His hand. Nothing can happen to us that will not fulfill the purpose He has for us, so long as we continue to put our trust in Him.

Jesus asked Pilate if others had been talking to him about His situation. He knew what the answer would be, and He knew what others had said. But by putting the question to Pilate, the accused moved from defendant to the role of prosecutor. In truth Jesus was not on trial here, but Pilate was. The outcome eventually was clear for all the ages to witness.

THE KING AND THE GOVERNOR

John 18:35-36 *"Am I a Jew?" Pilate replied. "It was your people and your chief priests who handed you over to me. What is it you have done?" Jesus said, "My kingdom is not of this world. If it were, my servants would fight to prevent my arrest by the Jews. But now my kingdom is from another place.*

Pilate's response appears to be a scoffing rebuke to Jesus, who had just asked the governor if his question concerning His own royalty came from his own opinion or from elsewhere. He reminded Jesus that it wasn't a Roman idea to bring Him to trial, but in fact it was the religious leaders of His own country that had turned Him in. They were the ones who had put this monkey trial into play.

It is interesting to note that at this time there had been no charges leveled against Jesus. He was declared a criminal by the chief priests, but they had offered no particular crime for which Jesus was responsible. Pilate had gone outside to meet with the Jewish leaders since they refused to darken the doorway of a Gentile during their holy feast days, but now Pilate was back inside after their meeting, and he still didn't know what Jesus was supposed to have done that got them so stirred up.

Jesus shared a truth that at this point must have caught Pilate off guard. He did not deny His divine right to royalty but informed the governor that His kingship was one that was not a part of the world ruled by Rome. The fact that He was from another place would not have been unusual for Pilate to hear, but that He was from another world was different matter altogether.

Pilate could have written Jesus off as someone who was demented and not capable of being rational. Hearing the words of Jesus speak of His Kingdom would be like someone telling us that they were originally from outer space, and that they had come to our planet as an alien being. Perhaps there were eyerolls and a smirking grin from Pilate, but in any case, he didn't know what Jesus was being accused of doing that would be worthy of death.

Jesus was an enigma to Pilate and remains a puzzle to many in our world still. That He was from another place is readily accepted by the church community, but many still don't believe He was any more than a man, if He ever existed at all. Still, whether faith in Him as Lord is there or not, He remains the Creator of the universe, and the coming triumphant King.

ALL ROADS DON'T LEAD TO GOD

John 18:37 *"You are a king then!" said Pilate. Jesus answered, "You are right in saying I am a king. In fact, for this reason I was born, and for this I came into the world, to testify to the truth. Everyone on the side of truth listens to me."*

Whether Pilate was amazed to think about being in the presence of royalty or amused at the thought of someone in Jesus' situation thinking he was a king, is hard to tell from what he says. There is little doubt though that this was unlike any case he had ever presided over before, or one he would ever see again.

Jesus had only a short time to present His case, but He did it eloquently. He affirmed His royalty and gave the explanation as to why He had come to be in this world as He was. His Kingdom has always been a Kingdom of Truth and He bore witness to it before the Roman governor.

When He stated that everyone on the side of truth listens to Him, it became a very telling commentary on the state of Israel at that time, and the state of the world today. In 2021 the world statistical charts recorded that 2.38 billion people in this world professed Christianity as their religion. Of course, that number takes in many people of varying degrees of devotion, but it is symbolic at least of the total amount of people who profess the name of Jesus as their religious focus. However, there are nearly 8 billion people on the planet, so that means the vast majority still do not subscribe to the truth but are being led astray by some form of idolatry.

All religions are not the same. All roads do not lead to the same place. All belief systems do not result in eternal life in the Kingdom of God. There are many false religions who proclaim to be the only way to God, and others who say that just believing in anything is sufficient, for it is faith itself that counts. The problem with that line of thinking is that some things are not true, and some things are just wrong. Only Jesus is "the way, the truth, and the life" (John 14:6), only Jesus is "the resurrection" (John 11:25), only Jesus has the words of eternal life (John 6:68), and only Jesus will have printed on His robe and thigh, "KING OF KINGS AND LORD OF LORDS" (Revelation 19:16), when the days of this age come to a close.

Yes, He is a King, and it is a blessed privilege to be His servant!

AN INFAMOUS CHOICE

John 18:38–40 *"What is truth?" Pilate asked. With this he went out again to the Jews and said, "I find no basis for a charge against him. But it is your custom for me to release to you one prisoner at the time of the Passover. Do you want me to release 'the king of the Jews'?" They shouted back, "No, not him! Give us Barabbas!" Now Barabbas had taken part in a rebellion.*

The world continually searches for truth. Pilate couldn't recognize it when He stood right in front of him. People today are always trying to find the difference between what is true and what is false, but unfortunately many make the wrong choice and follow a fool's journey throughout their years.

Pilate was wise enough to see through the schemes of the Jewish leaders. He could tell that the one before him was a righteous man, and he declared for all to hear that he couldn't find anything with which to charge Jesus. He had an idea for a compromise to his situation and offered them the opportunity to rethink their decision about condemning the innocent, but the Jewish leaders that had been thwarted by Jesus for so long would not accept the offer. They wanted the blood of Jesus, but they couldn't see that His blood would be the only thing that would ever be able to set them free.

Life is full of decisions. All of us make them every day from the time we get out of bed in the morning until we go back there at night. Even the routines of rising and sleeping are decisions we make. That's why we have alarm clocks to govern our bedtime hours. The decision that was made for Barabbas instead of Jesus was one of the worst decisions ever made in the history of the world, but it was made by people who had no real interest in godliness, righteousness, or truthfulness. Jesus would die. They would see to it, and nothing else would satisfy them.

The King of the Jews was the silent observer throughout this entire proceeding. Except for the few words He uttered to Pilate, He stood mute as the decision was being made concerning His freedom. He could remain calm in the midst of such a time not only because He knew the outcome, but also because He was never really alone. Though His disciples, except for John had left Him, the Father was always one with Him. He provided us with the example of how we can face our end, for we can do it with the full assurance that the Holy Spirit will be with us to the very end of our lives.

BRUTALITY AT ITS ZENITH

John 19:1–3 *Then Pilate took Jesus and had him flogged. The soldiers twisted together a crown of thorns and put it on his head. They clothed him in a purple robe and went up to him again and again, saying, "Hail, king of the Jews!" And they struck him in the face.*

If there were ever words in the Bible that were understated, these words truly are some of the guiltiest ones on that charge. Flogging brings to mind a person being whipped, but often little more. What Jesus experienced was torture. It wasn't unusually harsh compared to what others had experienced at the hands of the Romans, but truly was a crime in itself.

The whip had several thongs, and at the end of each strap there was a piece of metal or bone attached. Even after only a few strokes the human body would be reduced to a bloody pulp. The person being whipped was first stripped of his clothing, then tied to a fixed object like a pillar or post, and then whipped until his flesh hung in threads. Unlike those flogged under the Jewish Law, who were not to receive more than forty lashes, the Romans had no such rule. The scourging could go on for as long as the tormentor wished, or until the victim was dead.

After Jesus was so inhumanly treated, He was then mocked. Purple was the color of royalty, and the crown made of thorns that they pushed deep into the flesh that was left on His head, created a scene of mockery as the soldiers bowed before Him and then slapped Him across the face. We are not told how long this went on, but it is obvious that by the time the cruel abuse ended, Jesus was hanging on to life precariously.

Such a tremendous price was paid by our Lord for your sins and mine. He had done nothing even worthy of a scolding, for He lived without sin, but this portrayal of man's inhumanity to man painted a picture of just how far sin can carry a person. Except for the grace of God, all of us would be relegated to such barbarism.

When I read these words, my heart sinks. The anguish of the hour is too horrible for us to contemplate for very long, for the images are graphic and terrible. But these words also make me bow in adoration over the love that caused Jesus to endure such treatment. Though unworthy, I am eternally grateful to the Creator who cares so much for His creation.

THE MAN, THE KING, THE GOD

John 19:4–5 *Once more Pilate came out and said to the Jews, "Look, I am bringing him out to you to let you know that I find no basis for a charge against him." When Jesus came out wearing the crown of thorns and the purple robe, Pilate said to them, "Here is the man!"*

There was a purpose behind the scourging that Jesus endured. Pilate knew that Jesus was an innocent man, and it seems very clear that He didn't want to grant the Jews the crucifixion they requested. Having Jesus tortured in the way that He was and dressing Him up in purple with His crown of thorns was designed to elicit sympathy for this helpless Galilean from His accusers. Only the most hard-hearted of people could look at that pitiful remnant of a man that Jesus had become and not be stirred in his soul.

Being a bit of an American history buff, I have read many accounts of the Old West. In these stories there are accounts of the crimes against humanity that white men heaped upon Indians and like manner when the Indians retaliated against the whites. The practice of scalping, often while the victim was still alive, staking out people on anthills, impaling them, and burning their flesh slowly are not just stories from nightmarish novels. They are events that happened. Reading through these events are not pleasant, but I do so to better inform myself of historical happenings. I cringe still when I read the words though, because I can't imagine the horror the victims felt.

Often such tortures were committed to send a message to those who would find the dead remains. This is how others would be treated if the perpetrators desires were not met. It was meant to convey fear, disgust, and terror. The end desire was not just revenge, though that often played a big part of the murders, but also to cause a change of heart. Perhaps minds could be changed once such terrible things had been witnessed.

This is what appears to be in the mind of Pilate as he paraded Jesus back before the Jews. They could easily see how much He had already suffered, and there was always a chance that His accusers would be sickened by what they saw and determine that Jesus had endured enough. Sadly, that was not what happened.

Sin is a terrible taskmaster. Satan desires only to kill and destroy. Jesus took the punishment so we wouldn't have to. Such love is immeasurable!

CRUCIFY HIM!

John 19:6–7 *As soon as the chief priests and their officials saw him, they shouted, "Crucify! Crucify!" But Pilate answered, "You take him and crucify him. As for me, I find no basis for a charge against him." The Jews insisted, "We have a law, and according to that law he must die, because he claimed to be the Son of God."*

The picture before us is one of total depravity. Even though Jesus had endured the brutal torture of the Roman soldiers, even though He had been stripped publicly and humiliated, and even when they saw Him paraded like a bloodied clown before them, they still weren't satisfied. These Jewish officials had hate in their eyes and murder in their hearts. They would not be satisfied until this enemy of theirs would be further brutalized until He was dead. Then they could get back to their usual habits of greed and Jesus wouldn't be around to stop them... or so they thought.

Pilate had to have been getting His fill of these Jewish hypocrites. He wanted the whole affair behind him, and he had given these men before him every opportunity to take pity on their victim and be satisfied with what He had already endured. But it wasn't enough. Satan was having his way with them.

The ironic part of this story is that the Jews were proclaiming, "We have a law, and according to the law..." and on that they were basing their decision concerning Jesus. What hypocrites! By their actions they were breaking the first, the sixth, the ninth, and the tenth commandments (Exodus 20), but they were willing to drum up phony charges just to get Jesus out of their hair.

The people of God are often accused of being hypocrites, and sometimes that charge is legitimate, but it only happens when the relationship between God and His people break down. I have known people who wouldn't eat in the church building because they had misunderstood the Apostle Paul's words in I Corinthians 11:22 but had no problem committing adultery and taking another man's wife. Such things are not only immoral, but stupid. To strain at a religious gnat only to swallow a camel is an apt description of such actions.

Jesus claimed to be the Son of God because He was and is the Son of God. His enemies were children of the devil, and they acted just like him.

THE REAL SOURCE OF POWER

John 19:8–11 *When Pilate heard this, he was even more afraid, and he went back inside the palace. "Where do you come from?" he asked Jesus, but Jesus gave him no answer. "Do you refuse to speak to me?" Pilate said. "Don't you realize I have power either to free you or to crucify you?" Jesus answered, "You would have no power over me if it were not given to you from above. Therefore the one who handed me over to you is guilty of a greater sin."*

The writer slips in a comment here that we often pass over if we aren't careful. Pilate was afraid. This was an age of superstition, and since the Romans considered many gods to be real, the idea of possibly having one standing in his court must have concerned him greatly. The Gospel of Matthew records that Pilate's wife's words were adding fuel to his fears when she said, "Don't have anything to do with that innocent man, for I have suffered a great deal today in a dream because of him" (Matthew 27:19). When Pilate heard from the chief priests that Jesus had declared Himself to be the Son of God, he realized that he had quite a dilemma on his hands.

So, he went back to the source. He questioned Jesus, who had remained in the palace during Pilate's interaction with the Jesus, directly. He was amazed that Jesus would not answer him, and that only added to his fears. When Jesus did speak, His words were not comforting, but prophetic. His Father was in charge of all these things and Pilate was no more than a pawn who lacked the courage and integrity to do the right thing. For such people, and for those who had committed this great sin against Jesus, there was good reason for fear.

Many people want religion when they are afraid. They want Jesus to speak words of peace to them when they face life's greatest challenges, but here is an example of truth. Jesus will always be kind, but He is also just, and He knows how to call people to account for their sins. We cannot ignore His Lordship and live without fear, for someday every knee will bow before Him and we will not only confess that He is Lord, but we will also confess all the deeds that we have done against Him.

The time is now for us to make our peace with Him. Today He is our Savior, but one day He will be our Judge. Pilate found this out too late.

PILATE AT HIS CROSSROAD

John 19:12–13 *From then on, Pilate tried to set Jesus free, but the Jews kept shouting, "If you let this man go, you are no friend of Caesar. Anyone who claims to be a king opposes Caesar." When Pilate heard this, he brought Jesus out and sat down on the judge's seat at a place known as the Stone Pavement (which in Aramaic is Gabbatha).*

Poor Pilate. History reflects so badly on him. From John's account it would appear that he felt trapped between doing what he wanted to do and what he was being pressured to do. He certainly had no respect for the Jewish leaders and didn't fear their authority, but he was faced with a problem. If he crossed them in this matter with Jesus it would look bad for him politically. After all, no Roman governor would last long if word got to Rome that he was soft on insurrectionists, and that is what they were accusing Jesus of being, even though they didn't have a shred of evidence to that effect and Pilate wasn't really buying the idea either.

So many times, through the ages, people have traded what they should do for doing what was the most expedient at the moment. Pilate was just a template for multitudes who would follow after him. He is a role model for all the men and women of history that lacked the courage and grit to stand up to threats and slander in order to do the right thing.

Jesus should have been set free, for nothing had been produced as evidence against him except the cries of a frenzied mob that had been stirred up by the Jewish leaders. In any legitimate court of law, even among the Romans, he should have been released. Pilate just couldn't make that happen, however.

Today each of us stand before an Almighty God who is aware of every decision that we make. He knows when we choose boldly for righteousness and when we compromise to take an easier path. What we don't always realize is that when we go with the flow, the flow usually goes down the drain. No doubt mistakes will be made, but cowardice and self-interest rarely lead to a good result.

The Jews were guilty, Pilate was guilty, the guards who tortured Jesus were guilty, but Jesus stayed pure. He continued to follow the Father's plan and in the end was victorious. That's a pretty good lesson for us all.

NO KING BUT CAESAR

John 19:14–16 *It was the day of Preparation of Passover week, about the sixth hour. "Here is your king," Pilate said to the Jews. But they shouted, "Take him away! Take him away! Crucify him!" "Shall I crucify your king?" Pilate asked. "We have no king but Caesar," the chief priests answered. Finally Pilate handed him over to them to be crucified. So the soldiers took charge of Jesus.*

The night before, that had begun with the Last Supper, had been filled with mock trials, the torture from the Roman guards, and now an attempt by Pilate, the Roman governor, to change the mindset of the Jewish mob. It was approaching noon on Friday and finally the governor assented to the wishes of Jesus' enemies and delivered Him over to them. Darkness was reigning, and at this point in the story there was no one but Jesus Himself who could envision it ever having a happy ending.

There is a telling statement listed here from the Jews. In their zeal to murder Jesus, they were proclaiming that they had no king but Caesar. They were stating the truth, even though they most likely didn't realize fully what they were proclaiming.

It reminds me of their forefathers, who once came to the prophet and judge, Samuel. They wanted a king so badly because, "Then we will be like all the other nations, with a king to lead us and to go out before us and fight our battles" (I Samuel 8:20). The reality of their request then, and of the Jews who called for the death of Jesus, was also found again in the story of Samuel when God told him, "Listen to all that the people are saying to you; it is not you they have rejected, but they have rejected me as their king" (I Samuel 8:7).

It is true that the Jewish mob had rejected their true King at this point. Pilate, the inept Roman governor, who couldn't stand his ground in the face of possible political smears, also rejected the opportunity to do the right thing and set an innocent man free. By these actions the crowds were denying the God of their faith, the governor was capitulating to pressure, and Jesus was the recipient of their folly.

When the soldiers took charge of Jesus, they had no idea that they weren't really in charge at all. The King of kings was about to enter into His glory.

THE CRUCIFIED KING

John 19:17–18 *Carrying his own cross, he went out to the place of the Skull (which in Aramaic is called Golgotha). Here they crucified him, and with him two others—one on each side and Jesus in the middle.*

S o many songs have been written about this place called Golgotha, also known as Calvary. All four Gospel accounts speak of it, and it is most likely the most famous hill in history.

The fact that Jesus carried His own cross up the hill to where He was crucified is truly amazing. He had been beaten so badly that He was a mere shell of the person He had been just a few hours before. Regardless of how rugged and strong a man He had been, the cruelty of the Romans had taken its toll on the human frame of Jesus. No wonder Matthew, Mark, and Luke each record that Simon of Cyrene was enlisted to help Him carry the cross.

It is said so simply, "Here they crucified him." Though the ordeal would be spelled out in the following verses, this is the understatement of the ages. These four words encapsulate the horror and pain that He would go through during the hours on the cross.

The fact that two others were crucified with Him only amplifies what was happening. The Romans were masters at this task of torture, and they knew just how to inflict the necessary pain needed to make the victim endure the greatest discomfort possible. Only the Gospel of Luke records the words of the other men on the cross, and only in Luke 23:39–42 do we find the story of the thief who asks for the Master to be merciful to him. John, who was recorded to be present at the event and therefore an eyewitness, says nothing about it. We can only speculate as to the reason why.

The cross upon which Jesus died is the symbol that has gone down in history. Though today many use the symbol as a tattoo design, or a piece of jewelry to adorn their body, we who know the Savior personally understand that it was the most important piece of lumber ever created. On that cross Jesus would suffer, on that cross His blood would be poured out, on that cross forgiveness was proclaimed, and on that cross sin was defeated once and for all. As the old hymn records, "I will cling to the old rugged cross, and exchange it someday for a crown." The cross made possible our salvation and deliverance. Thanks be to God!

THE TELLTALE SIGN

John 19:19–22 *Pilate had a notice prepared and fastened to the cross. It read: JESUS OF NAZARETH, THE KING OF THE JEWS. Many of the Jews read this sign, for the place where Jesus was crucified was near the city, and the sign was written in Aramaic, Latin, and Greek. The chief priests of the Jews protested to Pilate, "Do not write 'The King of the Jews,' but that this man claimed to be king of the Jews." Pilate answered, "What I have written, I have written."*

The road passing by the hill upon which Jesus was crucified was so cosmopolitan that the charge against Him had to be written in three languages: Aramaic—the language of the Jews, Latin—the language of Rome, and Greek—the language that was predominate in a large part of the world. Crosses were stationed along busy roads with the criminal's offense written on them as sort of a public service announcement. The sign telling what the accused had done was a warning to others not to do the same thing or they would suffer a similar end. It was a powerful warning and most likely those who witnessed such a thing never forgot it.

Of course, even though the label was correct for Jesus, the Jewish mob that was responsible for the trumped-up charges didn't see it that way. They didn't want anyone to think that this is how they treated their royalty, so they protested to what Pilate had written. In most likely what was an act of disgust concerning the whole affair, Pilate stubbornly ruled that what he had instructed to be written to remain the charge.

It's hard for any feeling person to remain dispassionate as we read of these events unfolding. John would slowly walk through the story, and though the words describing it would be decades in the making before it reached the written page, such a sacrifice and all the details surrounding it would remain fresh in His mind. When one comes face to face with the cross of Jesus, that person is never the same again.

Such an impact is as true to today for us as it was for John. When we stand in the shadow of the cross, we are convicted, humbled, and remade. The sacrifice was too great for thinking people to ignore, and the change that His cross brought to our world is too tremendous to disregarded. Everyone throughout the ages has been affected by the reality of the cross of our King!

GAMBLING FOR HIS CLOTHES

> **John 19:23–24** When the soldiers crucified Jesus, they took his clothes, dividing them into four shares, one for each of them, with the undergarment remaining. This garment was seamless, woven in one piece from top to bottom. "Let's not tear it," they said to one another. "Let's decide by lot who will get it." This happened that the scripture might be fulfilled which said, "They divided my garments among them and cast lots for my clothing." So this is what the soldiers did.

It's amazing how much scripture was fulfilled by Jesus going to the cross. The quotation in this section comes from Psalm 22, where in context it reads, "I can count all my bones; people stare and gloat over me. They divide my garments among them and cast lots for my clothing" (22:17–18). As John continues to relate this story, he will use several Old Testament passages as evidence that God had been planning this for a long time. The other Gospel writers did the same.

Psalm 22 is attributed to King David, who lived about 1000 years before Jesus was put on the cross. As he wrote, he was describing his own feeling of despair when he began the psalm with "My God, my god, why have you forsaken me" (22:1). However, the psalm ends with "Posterity will serve him; future generations will be told about the Lord. They will proclaim his righteousness to a people yet unborn" (22:30–31). As the Holy Spirit inspired David's words, Jesus fit their prophetic message to the letter.

We are told here that there were four soldiers who were given the task of crucifying Jesus. They were doing what they were ordered to do and doing what they were paid to do. For them it was all part of the job as they made sure that Roman law would be upheld as assigned by their commanders. Whether or not they felt pity for the men in anguish who would suffer under their torment we are not told. We only catch a glimpse of the gambling that was taking place and the booty they could receive from their hapless victims.

There are days of evil around us still, even though Jesus crippled sin at the cross. Whenever we feel that God has forsaken us, we can remember that in spite of the agony on Golgotha, in spite of the gambling soldiers, and in spite of all that hell could throw at Jesus, He would eventually emerge triumphant. And because He did, we can too!

A MOTHER'S LOVE

John 19:25–27 *Near the cross of Jesus stood his mother, his mother's sister, Mary the wife of Clopas, and Mary Magdalene. When Jesus saw his mother there, and the disciple whom he loved standing nearby, he said to his mother, "Dear woman, here is your son," and to the disciple, "Here is your mother." From that time on, this disciple took her into his home.*

We often love stories about mothers and their sons, but the real stories of their lives usually go a lot deeper than the gifts they exchange on holidays. This is one of those stories and it comes as one of the final acts of Jesus before His death. The fact that it was a final act of love makes it all the more special and endearing, for in it we find some guiding principles that transcend the ages.

First, we find that it is part of the mother's job to love her children for as long as she lives. In doing this she teaches others about how to treat their own offspring. If we could make a list for current society, it would go something like this: 1) Don't abort them. 2) Don't neglect them. 3) Don't spoil them. 4) Tell them often that they are loved. 5) Show them they are loved by how you live. Mary was there for Jesus to the bitter end.

Second, we see an example from Jesus. Here we see that it is the child's responsibility to provide for his or her mother for as long as she lives. Whatever she did for you, you should be willing to do for her. Again, we have a short list: 1) Do clean up her messes. 2) Do provide her with a good, clean, safe place to live. 3) Do make sure she is well fed and cared for. 4) Do let her know often how thankful you are for her.

There are some don'ts as well: 1) Don't lose patience with her. 2) Don't forget she needs you. 3) Don't stop expressing your love for her. 4) Don't fail to provide for her till your last breath.

Even on the cross Jesus recognized His responsibility to the woman who brought Him into this world. His words made sure that care for Mary would be provided for as long as she lived. He didn't forsake His personal duty to her even when there were plenty of reasons for Him to be distracted. His love that showed how much He cared for Mary, extended from the cross to her as an example for us all. May God help us to be just as faithful toward our mothers for as long as He blesses us with them.

"It Is Finished!"

John 19:28–30 *Later, knowing that all was now completed, and so that the Scripture would be fulfilled, Jesus said, "I am thirsty." A jar of wine vinegar was there, so they soaked a sponge in it, put the sponge on a stalk of the hyssop plant, and lifted it to Jesus' lips. When he had received the drink, Jesus said, "It is finished." With that, he bowed his head and gave up his spirit.*

By this time Judas was dead. The disciples, except for John, were in hiding. The women that were witnessing the crucifixion were also mourning and finally the crowd had ceased their mocking. The long, painful ordeal of the Christ had finally come to an end.

Because the life of Jesus was over, it was the end of the incarnation of God in the sense that Jesus would never again have to deal with a deteriorating body that was growing older. It was also the end of His relationship with people as a mere human. After the resurrection people who met with Him would never see Him in the same light. Those who were responsible for His death would still consider Him a criminal, but one to whom they thought they had dealt the final blow. However, those who actually would see His resurrected body knew beyond any shadow of a doubt that that He truly was God in the flesh. No, people would never look at Him in the same way again. The good part of this story is that it was the end of His days of suffering. The work of salvation truly was finished!

As the disciples would eventually realize, the scriptures about Jesus were being fulfilled. The promise given in the Garden of Eden concerning the serpent (Genesis 3:15) was completed. The covenant that God made with the patriarchs concerning their offspring being a blessing to all nations (Genesis 22:18) had come to pass. The hope listed in Isaiah 9:6 of one who would be called "Wonderful Counselor, Mighty God, Everlasting Father, Prince of Peace," was fully on display. Micah's words (5:2) about the Messiah coming from Bethlehem would be completely understood.

Yes, it was finished. Jesus had broken the power of sin (I John 2:2). He had ended the reign of Satan (Ephesians 1:22), and His coming resurrection would restore the hope of mankind. The cross is the watershed mark of history. Nothing before or since will ever have the impact that it made.

A Blinding Disease

John 19:31 *Now it was the day of Preparation, and the next day was to be a special Sabbath. Because the Jews did not want the bodies left on the crosses during the Sabbath, they asked Pilate to have the legs broken and the bodies taken down.*

The day of Preparation actually began at sundown on Thursday and went until sundown on Friday. It was considered to be a time for people to get everything ready to observe the Sabbath. That means all work preparations had to be finished and everything put in order so that no labor would be done while the holy day was being observed.

We have come to know this particular day as "Good Friday." It is good because it was the time that our salvation was purchased by our Lord on the cross. Jesus was paying the price for our sins and preparing to show us the way to the resurrected life.

The Jews in the story remained hypocrites to the end. Earlier they wouldn't enter Pilate's palace because entering the home of a Gentile would have made them unclean to celebrate the Jewish Passover, but they never considered that their lies, treachery, and murder would make them truly unclean in the eyes of the only one who really counted, their Father in heaven. But they didn't want to see their handiwork hang on the crosses for too long, because that would make it a messy Sabbath day, so they opted to have the legs of the men broken so that they would die quicker, and thereby not mess up the Jews religious schedule.

Sin is such a blinding disease. It causes those who take part in it to not be able to see or understand the depth to which it takes them. Even if the three on the cross would have been the worst people on the planet, it would have been so terribly cruel to have them tortured to an even greater extent, to heap even more pain on them, just so they could hurry their murders along. The hate that possessed them must have been great indeed.

The idea of a Preparation Day is a good one because it causes people to begin getting their lives in order as they would stand before a holy God in worship. We could all use a little more time for reflection and planning to make sure all things in our lives are ready to give God the reverence He deserves. But when it's just ritual, it only adds to our hypocrisy.

DEAD AND PIERCED

John 19:32–34 *The soldiers therefore came and broke the legs of the first man who had been crucified with Jesus, and then those of the other. But when they came to Jesus and found that he was already dead, they did not break his legs. Instead, one of the soldiers pierced Jesus' side with a spear, bringing a sudden flow of blood and water.*

Jesus was dead. The person who created the world and all that is in it was as lifeless as any person could be. In days to come there would be spin-offs from the Christian faith, known as Gnostics, who would deny that Jesus was even made of flesh and blood, and therefore could not actually die as all men do. John makes a totally different claim.

The fact that Jesus didn't need His legs broken like the thieves who were crucified on each side of Him, gives evidence of His mortality. The Romans knew what they were doing when it came to torturing and killing men, and they would certainly have known if Jesus was just unconscious or pretending to be dead. To be absolutely sure, the spear in His side would leave no doubt as to His demise.

It was such a terrible price that Jesus paid to redeem the world that had turned against Him. But the price He paid made possible our freedom from the bonds of sin, and would open the door to a resurrected life when the plan of the Father brought it to pass. In this world, without His death on the cross, we would never have the power to overcome the sin that continually ensnares us, and we would have no hope beyond the grave. Jesus didn't die just so we could go to heaven, but so that when this age comes to its conclusion, our physical bodies will be resurrected just like His was, never to die again.

The work of the cross truly was a day of preparation for all that was about to happen. The crucifixion, combined with the coming resurrection, provides all who will put their trust in Jesus as their own personal Savior, a hope for life beyond the grave.

On this Friday in history, it was undoubtedly a dark day and there was no one present who could envision anything "good" about it. But it had to happen. The night needed to fall before the glorious dawn could be realized. As has been said, "It was Friday, but Sunday was coming!"

THE PRICE OF REDEMPTION

John 19:35–37 *The man who saw it has given testimony, and his testimony is true. He knows that he tells the truth, and he testifies so that you also may believe. These things happened so that the scripture would be fulfilled: "Not one of his bones will be broken," and, as another scripture says, "They will look on the one they have pierced."*

There are three verses of scripture that have a point of reference to this verse and they all have to do with the fact that Jesus didn't have any of His bones broken. In both Exodus 12:46 and Number 9:12, a reference is made to the fact that the Passover sacrifice should not only be without blemish, but also that none of the lamb's bones should be broken. Breaking them would have made the sacrifice unacceptable. The third reference here is from Psalm 34:20, where the psalmist speaks of "the righteous man," who is delivered from His troubles by the LORD, and as a result He is protected and none of His bones would be broken.

These Old Testament scriptures fit the scene of Jesus on Calvary perfectly. He truly was the unblemished Lamb of God that was offered up as a sacrifice for the sins of all people. He was also the epitome of righteousness, and His heavenly Father watched over Him to make sure that in His death not a word that was prophesied about Him would be lost.

By the time John would write these words, decades would have gone by since that day on Golgotha's hill outside of Jerusalem. But he was able to give testimony that these things were true because by the time of His writing He had witnessed the risen Christ and could see how the words of the prophets had been fulfilled in Him. Jesus was pure, righteous, and pierced, but His bones had not been broken, just like the lamb that was prescribed in the Law of Moses. John may not have understood it all on that day that these events happened, but later He would understand fully.

We may wonder today why the events surrounding the cross had to happen as they did. The plan of God to redeem the world may seem to be too complex to have been real. However, John was able to put it together once He had all the information. We walk by faith, as billions have done down through the centuries, and we know that what Jesus did changed the world. And because He did what He did, we can be what we are—redeemed!

THE COST OF BURIAL

John 19:38–39 *Later, Joseph of Arimathea asked Pilate for the body of Jesus. Now Joseph was a disciple of Jesus, but secretly because he feared the Jews. With Pilate's permission, he came and took the body away. He was accompanied by Nicodemus, the man who earlier had visited Jesus at night. Nicodemus brought a mixture of myrrh and aloes, about seventy-five pounds.*

The person we know as Joseph of Arimathea is listed in all four Gospel accounts. We see him in Matthew 27:57–60, Mark 15:43–46, Luke 23:50–55, and here in the nineteenth chapter of John. There are many legends and rumors about the man, most of which have become church lore, but cannot be proven with any actual evidence. Such tales list him as the uncle of Mary, the mother of Jesus, that he would eventually go on preaching missions for Jesus, that when Jesus was young Joseph took him on business trips to England, India, and even South America. He was said to have been among the few of the Sanhedrin who voted against the crucifixion of Jesus. Again, though, these are just points of speculation and legend.

It is a well-documented fact, however, that Britain led the world at that time in the area of tin mining, and that Joseph of Arimathea was known by the Romans as "Nobilis Decurio," or "Minister of Mines" in government circles. He was apparently a very wealthy man.

He was accompanied by Nicodemus, the man who will forever be known as the Jewish leader who came to Jesus by night. These two took on the responsibility of seeing that the body of Jesus was properly cared for after His death. That alone gives them a significant place in history.

John records an interesting fact concerning the spices that were used in the burial process. What makes it interesting is their weight. Seventy-five pounds of myrrh and aloes is a lot of myrrh and aloes. The cost of such spices at that time would be worth $150,000-$200,000 in today's market. They really had a great devotion to this man called Jesus.

Though these men may have been secret disciples, they were there for Jesus when they were needed. After the crucifixion they came out of the shadows and showed their love for their Lord. They serve as examples to us of faithfulness to Jesus even when others turned their backs on Him.

DEAD AND BURIED

John 19:40–42 *Taking Jesus' body, the two of them wrapped it, with the spices in strips of linen. This was in accordance with Jewish burial customs. At the place where Jesus was crucified, there was a garden, and in the garden a new tomb, in which no one had ever been laid. Because it was the Jewish day of Preparation and since the tomb was nearby, they laid Jesus there.*

We are told here that the body of Jesus was wrapped "in accordance with Jewish burial customs." So, just what were the Jewish customs for the dead?

Well, first the body was to be buried. The Old Testament describes the horror of leaving dead bodies unburied when it records, "They have given the dead bodies of your servants as food to the birds of the air, the flesh of your saints to the beasts of the earth. They have poured out blood like water all around Jerusalem, and there is no one to bury the dead" (Psalm 79:2-3).

The dead were to be buried fairly quickly, usually within eight hours because of the rapid deterioration of the body in a hot climate. But before the burial could happen, the body was washed, and spices were applied to it in order to preserve a sense of tolerable smell for those who may visit the remains as the body was decomposing. After the spices were applied, the body was wrapped in a shroud, then the hands and feet were tied with strips of linen, and the face was covered with a cloth. Cremations were not done among the Jews of that time because of their firm belief in the literal resurrection of the physical body.

When Jesus was placed in a tomb, it was chosen because of its proximity to Calvary. There wouldn't have been the tradition parade of wailers to mourn Him because of the circumstances surrounding His death. Matthew 27:57 tells us that the tomb belonged to Joseph of Arimathea, which had been carved out of a rock. All this was done quickly after the body was taken from the cross because the Sabbath was approaching.

Joseph and Nicodemus defiled themselves and made themselves unclean to celebrate the Passover because of their contact with a dead body. It was a sacrifice on their part, but nothing compared to what Jesus did for them. Whatever the price, they did what they could, and will receive their reward from the Father for doing so, and so will we.

WHERE DID HE GO?

> **John 20:1–2** *Early on the first day of the week, while it was still dark, Mary Magdalene went to the tomb and saw that the stone had been removed from the entrance. So she came running to Simon Peter and the other disciple, the one Jesus loved, and said, "They have taken the Lord out of the tomb, and we don't know where they have put him!"*

Sunday morning finally arrived, and the Jewish Sabbath was now over. Mary could then make the journey to the tomb without any fear of going over the half-mile limit that restricted the Jewish distance of travel. She is recorded by John as going alone to the tomb, but Matthew 28:1 records another woman named Mary accompanying her, while Mark also adds Salome, and Luke lists Mary Magdalene, Joanna, Mary the mother of James, and "others with them," who told of the resurrection to the disciples. We can't know for sure why each Gospel writer tells the story a little differently, but most likely it was to fit the writer's purpose as he best remembered the event.

It seems interesting to me that the two disciples whom Mary contacted were the last two who were seen with Jesus. John had been with her at the cross, but Peter had departed the scene after his final denial of even knowing Jesus. Maybe Mary didn't know what he had done, but she went to him anyway.

Another interesting part of the story is that when Mary found the tomb empty, she was convinced that someone had taken the body of Jesus away. It never even occurred to her that God had done what Jesus had previously said He would do. Matthew 16:21, Mark 8:31–32, and Luke 9:21–22 all specifically record Jesus telling His disciples that He would be crucified but raised from the dead on the third day. Perhaps Mary wasn't there when He related what would happen, or perhaps the terrible events surrounding the cross caused her to lose hope, but it doesn't appear that she had any understanding that Jesus would return from the dead in a living body again.

In time to come she would believe, and just like countless other disciples who have followed after Christ, she moved from thinking God was limited to understanding that He is limited by nothing. The cross had to happen so that the tomb could be empty. Because His body was raised, we have hope that our body will be also. The resurrection of Jesus changed everything!

THE FIRSTFRUITS

John 20:3–5 *So Peter and the other disciple started for the tomb. Both were running, but the other disciple outran Peter and reached the tomb first. He bent over and looked in at the strips of linen lying there but did not go in.*

Can you imagine the thoughts that were racing through these disciples' minds as they heard the news of the empty tomb? They definitely had been present on the multiple occasions when Jesus taught them about His coming death and resurrection, but they hadn't understood what He was talking about. They, like everyone else in the first century, knew that dead people didn't come back to life again. To consider it possible was more than their overworked imaginations could grasp.

Actually, Mary didn't tell them that Jesus had been raised from the dead. She had only related that the tomb was empty and wondered if someone had taken the body during the night. She perhaps thought that the body had just been moved to another location. Most likely, the idea of resurrection wasn't on her mind either.

We don't know if age or physical condition made the difference in the outcome of the race to the tomb, but John did get there first. His heart must have been pumping wildly as he saw the boulder that had been removed from the grave's entrance, and the burial cloths just lying there without a body to accompany them. He may have wanted to go in, but possibly he was afraid to do so. After all, these were primitive times and the idea of ghosts being there might have drained any thought of investigating the scene. He had seen Jesus die. He had witnessed the spear going into His side. He had watched His lifeless body being taken down from the cross and carefully, but quickly, prepared for the grave by Joseph and Nicodemus. All this had to be confusing to him to say the least.

Don't be too hard on John, for the idea of being resurrected from the dead into life is still a concept that many people have a hard time getting their heads around. To this day we believe like the people of the first century did, namely that people who die don't come back from the dead. There is no evidence of that ever happening to anyone—but Jesus.

That's what sets Him apart. He is the first fruits of the resurrection. In due time, we who believe in Him will follow His path to life everlasting.

SEEING AND BELIEVING

John 20:6–9 *Then Simon Peter, who was behind him, arrived and went into the tomb. He saw the strips of linen lying there, as well as the burial cloth that had been around Jesus' head. The cloth was folded up by itself, separate from the linen. Finally, the other disciple, who had reached the tomb first, also went inside. He saw and believed. (They still did not understand from Scripture that Jesus had to rise from the dead.)*

Faith takes time to develop and more for some people than others. One would think that after spending three years with Jesus, on a daily basis, that these disciples would have been further along in their spiritual development, but even for them, it took time.

Perhaps their inability to believe was because they had witnessed the terrible ending to Jesus' life. The mock trials and the torturous crucifixion were enough to stretch and test the faith of any thinking person. The gruesome events of the previous days still haunted their memories.

But this was a new day and everything now seemed different. The tomb in which Jesus had been placed was empty. The burial cloth that had covered His face was now folded and placed in a separate place from the shroud that had covered Him. The strips of cloth that had bound His hands and feet were no longer occupied, and there was a sense that something very different and very dramatic had happened in that tomb.

When John lists that He saw and believed, it seems contradictory to his next statement that the disciples still didn't understand the necessity of the resurrection. We don't know what exactly they were expecting, but this was explicitly what Jesus had been telling them as He tried to prepare them for the events that were unfolding before them. Perhaps it is in the word "had" to rise that is telling. The word is "dei" in the original Greek language and it has the meaning of "necessity." Perhaps they didn't understand that it was absolutely necessary for Jesus to rise from the dead.

Of course, we know it was imperative for Jesus to be raised up. The resurrection proved His power over death, hell, and the grave. The resurrection gives us the hope for the day to come when we too can be raised from our graves. The resurrection proclaims that Jesus is the victor, and that the enemy of our souls has been defeated. It says, "Jesus is Lord!"

WITNESSES TO THE RESURRECTION

> **John 20:10–12** *Then the disciples went back to their homes, but Mary stood outside the tomb crying. As she wept, she bent over to look into the tomb and saw two angels in white, seated where Jesus' body had been, one at the head and the other at the foot.*

It would sure be interesting if we had a transcript of what Peter and John said as they were returning to their homes after seeing the empty tomb. We were told in the last verse that they still didn't fully understand from the scriptures that Jesus had to rise from the dead, so they were probably confused beyond words.

Mary took a different route. Even though the two men decided that there was nothing left to see in the tomb, Mary's love for Jesus didn't allow her to depart the scene as rapidly as Peter and John. Her devotion was rewarded with a divine experience that must have left her in awe.

John specifically records two angels in white as being in the tomb when Mary looked in. They asked her one question, but there is no other commentary from them in this account. Matthew 28 records only the angel of the Lord, rolling the stone away from the tomb, and then giving direction to both Mary Magdalene and the other Mary, which sent them hurrying from the tomb to tell the disciples. Mark 16 records a young man dressed in white, who was sitting inside the tomb, who instructed the three women who were present with words similar to those which were recorded in Matthew. Luke 24 speaks of two men dressed in white who instructed multiple women concerning the resurrection of Jesus.

The details from the witnesses vary, but not the point of the passage. In each account it is clearly evidenced that Jesus is no longer dead but has been raised to life in His resurrected form. Such a staggering event may cause some confusion as to the details, but the main focus is never in question. Jesus is no longer dead, but alive!

Sometimes in our human zeal we rush to compare the accounts, and skeptics try to poke holes in the Easter story because of the varying details of the witnesses. However, the fact of the empty tomb remains and that is all that really matters. We need to follow the theme of the story and proclaim that Jesus is alive. The rest of the story will take care of itself.

"Where Is My Lord?"

John 20:13–14 *They asked her, "Woman, why are you crying?"*
"They have taken my Lord away," she said, "and I don't know where
they have put him." At this she turned around and saw Jesus
standing there, but she did not realize that it was Jesus.

Have you ever had a conversation with angels? No? Well, neither have I, at least not that I am aware. Mary Magdalene did, however, and whether she understood their identity or not, she did what many of us dream about.

The angels probably already knew why Mary was crying, but then, I am only speculating about that. Since the heavenlies are outside our preview, we can only guess about what they know and don't know.

If they did know why Mary was crying, they must have had a hard time keeping a straight face because while she was weeping about not knowing where to find Jesus, He was standing right behind her all the time. The tears that she shed would soon turn to shock, and then joy as her view of the resurrection was being able to see Jesus face to face.

There are a lot of people like Mary. They weep over their troubled situation in life and look desperately to God for some kind of answer, some sign from above to point them in the right direction. If words from the angels could be purchased with money, the billionaires of the planet would be lining up and forking over their riches gladly, because they too face eternity without hope if they are trusting in their own strength and wealth to get there.

Mary would soon find out who it was that came up behind her. Perhaps she didn't recognize Him because her eyes were filled with tears. Perhaps she didn't perceive that it could be Jesus because she had seen what the Romans had done to Him and knew that He had been as dead as any man can be. Perhaps the resurrected body of Jesus, which we know bore the nail-prints in His hands, and a wound in His side from the spear that impaled Him, was so mutilated by the abuse heaped upon Him that even people who knew Him couldn't recognize Him. However, those scars would now be medals of honor that brought glory to the plan of the Father.

Whatever the reason, she didn't know Him. But He was there for her just like He is always available to us, to the very end of the age.

HE KNOWS YOUR NAME

John 20:15–16 *"Woman," he said, "why are you crying? Who is it you are looking for?" Thinking it was the gardener, she said, "Sir, if you have carried him away, tell me where you have put him, and I will get him." Jesus said to her, "Mary." She turned toward him and cried out in Aramaic, "Rabboni!" (which means Teacher).*

We love it when we have an "AHA!" moment. It means we have witnessed something that we have never seen before. Mary was having the "AHA" moment of all "AHA" moments.

It was dark when she had first arrived at the tomb. She saw that the stone had been rolled away from the entrance and that the tomb was empty, so she ran to get Peter and John. They also had run to the tomb, but they only found what Mary had declared to them. The tomb was empty except for the burial clothes, which were folded neatly inside the cave. John professed that a spark of faith developed at this encounter, but nonetheless, he and Peter left Mary alone there and returned home.

Mary wasn't willing to leave. She was still grieving over the death of her Lord when she saw the two men in white. She conversed with them, but was unaware of Jesus coming up behind her, and even when she did acknowledge His presence, she didn't know who He was. But when He spoke her name, everything changed. Once she realized that Jesus was alive, she would never be the same again.

What can we take away from this scene? Here are three things for sure: First, when, like Mary, you look for the Lord, you will find Him. He is available to all who will call upon His name. Second, when you find Him, you will find He already knows you. After all, He is the Creator of all things, including you, and He knows you on the most intimate level. Finally, when you hear Him call your name you will recognize Him like you never have before. To know and be known by Jesus is the best thing we will ever experience.

The resurrection of Jesus brings about a renewal of our faith. It gives us hope to call out to Him, and it give us hope that we can have such a relationship with Him that He is aware of who we are. He knows you, He loves you, He died for you, He was raised to life for you, and He wants to enter into a personal relationship with you. This is the story of Easter.

EASTER EMOTIONS

John 20:17–18 *Jesus said, "Do not hold on to me, for I have not yet returned to the Father. Go instead to my brothers and tell them, "I am returning to my Father and your Father, to my God and your God." Mary Magdalene went to the disciples with the news: "I have seen the Lord!" And she told them that he had said these things to her.*

Easter has always been a vital part of my life. My first church activity was an Easter egg hunt when I was five. I have been in the plays, the programs, the pageants, the musicals, the sunrise services, and the breakfasts, but what I love most of all is, "the story."

Jesus had gone from being a hero to a heel in less than a week in the eyes of the Jewish people. What a difference between Palm Sunday and Good Friday. However, Mary Magdalene experienced a personal transformation throughout the course of these events that reveals the power of the gospel. These last few days had taken her on quite a ride of faith.

First, there was confusion. She was confused about the empty tomb and was asking questions. "Where do I find the Savior?" "Why is the tomb empty?" She didn't realize at first the extensive plan of God.

Next, there was disappointment. She had to have been disappointed in the disciples, for she learned firsthand that the followers of Christ are not perfect. She must have been disappointed in her own foolish hopes. She had come so far on shear faith in Jesus. Was it all for nothing?

She had searched blindly and earnestly for Jesus, but it wasn't until He rewarded her searching with a personal revelation that she began to realize what had taken place. This revelation of Christ caused her to bear witness of Him to the rest of the disciples, for she was obligated to share what she knew as reality. The resurrection story was too great to keep to herself.

It's sometimes hard to face the truth, but in this one truth, we find joy: Jesus is alive and wants to live in relationship with us. Mary was never the same again once she witnessed the living Lord. It is the same way for each of us when by faith we see Him for ourselves.

The mortality rate up to that time was 100%, but it would never be again. The resurrection of Jesus from death to life changed the world forever!

THE FIRST EASTER EVENING

John 20:19 *On the evening of that first day of the week, when the disciples were together, with the doors locked for fear of the Jews, Jesus came and stood among them and said, "Peace be with you!"*

The first Easter evening was even more dramatic than the morning. In the morning Jesus was missing to everyone except Mary Magdalene, to whom He appeared at the grave's entrance. In the evening He appeared inside a locked room, right in the midst of the disciples who had fled the garden on Thursday evening. The scene would have been like an episode of Star Trek, where a body materialized instantly before them as if it had been molecularly transported in science fiction fashion.

We can only imagine what a stir this sudden appearance of Jesus before this frightened group would have been like. If they were previously astounded by Jesus walking on the water, or even hearing the news from Mary that He was alive again, this would have really knocked their socks off ... if they had been wearing socks with their sandals. First, He wasn't there, and then He was there. The door didn't open, but there was Jesus right before them. They must have been scared nearly to death.

It is therefore no small thing for Jesus to say to them, "Peace be with you!" Peace was probably about as far from their emotional state as can be described. How would you react if all of a sudden, the bodily form of Jesus appeared right beside you right now? I dare say that most of us would need to be offered the gift of peace.

That's what Jesus always does for His followers though. He provides them peace. The disciples were huddled together in hiding for fear that the Jews would track them down and do to them what they had done to Jesus, and therefore they had good reason to be afraid. But when Jesus came to them, He came with peace, and with that peace an assurance that is always beyond understanding.

Jesus has a way of changing terror into tranquility. He changes bewilderment into blessing. The saints throughout the ages have testified to this fact and I have experienced it myself. He is more than just alive, for He is able through His Holy Spirit today to actively minister in our lives. Like the disciples, in the midst of confusing days we can trust Christ for peace.

NOW IT BEGINS...

John 20:20–21 *After he said this, he showed them his hands and side. The disciples were overjoyed when they saw the Lord. Again Jesus said, "Peace be with you! As the Father has sent me, I am sending you."*

In the midst of the wide spectrum of emotion that had to be present when Jesus appeared to His disciples, He quickly got to His purpose for being there. While there was no doubt an atmosphere of hilarity from His followers because of their new found awareness of His return from the dead, there was still the mission of the Kingdom for them to be about. Though seeing the scars in the hands, feet, and side of Jesus was an unforgettable experience, so too was the task to which our Lord called His disciples to take up.

We see here that bottling such emotion can be a great catalyst for action, but we also see the value of moving past the emotion of the moment and refocusing on the job to which we who are in Christ are called. Such emotion, even the powerful experience of seeing the living Christ, is not the base out of which we operate, and we cannot allow our religion or church services to be dominated by it. In the New Testament we must remember that rejoicing comes as the result of great sacrifice, not an emotional high. It was wonderful to see Jesus bodily alive again, but He had to go through the cross and the grave to get to that place. His disciples would follow the same path eventually, as most of them too would be martyred.

We are reminded that our feelings are useless without a focal point. The disciples could have shouted, "Hallelujah!" and taken to the streets right then and there, but who would have believed them? Our Lord shows us a path for doing the will of the Father, as first there is the task of planting (death and resurrection), then cultivating (transformation and training), then harvesting (being sent by the Father and experiencing His power in our labors)—and the mission doesn't spread effectively if we mess with the order.

A purpose must direct our actions. As Jesus was sent on the Father's mission, now He sends His disciples. They are to continue doing what He had been doing: preaching, teaching, and healing. They must become as Jesus was: pure, wise, humble, and strong. The resurrection didn't end the work of the Father but launched it in earnest. All disciples of Jesus are called to get to work and finish what the empty tomb started.

THE BREATH THAT
CHANGED THE WORLD

John 20:22–23 *And with that he breathed on them and said, "Receive the Holy Spirit. If you forgive anyone his sins, they are forgiven; if you do not forgive them, they are not forgiven.*

It's important for us to recognize from these verses, that the responsibility Jesus placed upon His disciples was to be about the Father's mission. He had completed His mission from the Father and now it was necessary for these disciples to receive power to accomplish their assigned tasks.

We begin by looking at the seriousness of the responsibility that Jesus places on all those who will follow His leading. We are accountable for whether people are forgiven or not. It's much like the story of Israel's watchman in Ezekiel 3:17–19, and it echoes Matthew 16:19 where Jesus gives the authority for binding and loosing in His name. We decide who will be saved through the burden we bear for our brothers and sisters in the world, and we decide who will be lost due to our lack of concern and dedication to the cause the Father has placed upon us through the command of Jesus. Think about it. Who do we give up on? Who do we say that Jesus doesn't care about? The very thought should stop us in our tracks.

But we also need to recognize the sureness of the power Jesus provides to make fulfilling His words possible. The receiving of the Holy Spirit into our lives makes the difference. It is not our power and our will and our determination here, but His power through His Spirit that wins the day. Any place where Jesus is, is a place that is being renewed. Any person in whom Jesus is working, is a person that is being made into a new creation.

Though He works now through the Holy Spirit, He stands among us now as He did on that first Easter evening. He still offers peace, purpose, and power. He is supporting us with whatever we need to make His words into a reality. Do we need peace? He is waiting and able to supply that to us. Do we need a new purpose and direction? He is more than willing to guide us. Do we need power to accomplish His plan for our lives? His resources have not dwindled by the slightest fraction since He gave these words to His followers that evening in the upper room.

Jesus wants us to realize that the resurrection power is still in effect today. He has given us our marching orders. Are we going to follow them or not?

"I Don't Believe It!"

John 20:24–25 *Now Thomas (called Didymus), one of the Twelve, was not with the disciples when Jesus came. So the other disciples told him, "We have seen the Lord!" But he said to them, "Unless I see the nail marks in his hands and put my finger where the nails were, and put my hand into his side, I will not believe."*

There were only ten disciples present when Jesus first met with them after the resurrection. Have you ever wondered why that was the case? Since He knows all things, especially after His resurrection, one might ask why it was that Jesus didn't wait until all the remaining eleven disciples were gathered before He revealed Himself to them. Some might consider it just to be coincidence, but if we read the Gospels carefully, we will discover that Jesus didn't do things by chance, but with a specific purpose in mind

One obvious, but often overlooked truth is that it's tough to believe in Jesus as Lord until we have a personal meeting with Him. Let's be honest. This whole resurrection thing is a pretty unbelievable story. At first blush it sounds like something from some tabloid, or radical news podcast. It might be easy for some folks to believe that the crucifixion happened, for Roman historians tell of many such tragedies. It might be believable to think that somehow the disciples outwitted the Roman guards at the tomb and had banded together to move the boulder that covered the cave entrance so they could quickly whisk Jesus away to some undisclosed location. But this is a pretty big stretch of one's imagination also.

The story of the resurrection tops all other scenarios, however. To think that God raised Jesus from the dead and replaced His deteriorating body with one that will last forever, takes a huge leap of faith on anyone's part. Peter and John had been to the empty tomb, but they still didn't understand what had happened, though they believed something had happened. Mary told the story of seeing the angels, but even that personal testimony wouldn't have been enough for men who had experienced the worst event of their lives. These disciples needed reassurance on the day the resurrection happened. The fact that Thomas wouldn't show up for another week didn't change the need for people to verify that Jesus was alive. Jesus told them He would be raised on the third day, and He was. They needed to see that right then, and thankfully, Jesus always provides what just we need.

TIME TO EAT CROW

John 20:26–28 *A week later his disciples were in the house again, and Thomas was with them. Though the doors were locked, Jesus came and stood among them and said, "Peace be with you." Then he said to Thomas, "Put your finger here; see my hands. Reach out your hand and put it into my side. Stop doubting and believe." Thomas said to him, "My Lord and my God!"*

Well, that was embarrassing! Like so many people who scoff at the idea of the resurrection, Thomas was put in the unenviable position of having to eat his own words right in front of all his friends. This would absolutely be a day he would never forget.

John goes into detail here to make sure that the reader understands that Jesus didn't just walk in through a door to get into the room where the disciples were waiting. As it was recorded earlier in the chapter (verse 19), we are told that the doors to the room were locked, and nothing is mentioned about Jesus having a key, or of someone opening the door and letting Him in. There was one moment when He wasn't there, and then in the next moment He was. Jesus moved from place to place without any physical hindrance or need of transportation. It's as if a door from another dimension opened and He just stepped from it into our world. It's a science fiction fan's dream come true.

This is the third time that John records the words of Jesus as being, "Peace be with you." Each time that He arrived in a place where there is someone who hadn't seen Him in His resurrected form, He gave the same greeting. To witness what these men were experiencing would surely require an extra dose of peace.

The key message here is the reaction of Thomas to the presence of Jesus before him. He found that once a person meets Jesus, it becomes impossible not to believe in Him. Hearing about Him may not produce any real faith, but once a person encounters the living Christ, His resurrection cannot be denied any longer. We can decide whether we will follow Him, but if we really meet Him, we are not going to be able to ignore Him ever again. Thomas was unconvinced until he saw Him, and then he had no choice but to believe. He got it right though, for Jesus truly is our "Lord and our God!"

"DON'T DOUBT—BELIEVE!"

John 20:29-31 *Then Jesus told him, "Because you have seen me, you have believed; blessed are those who have not seen and yet have believed." Jesus did many signs in the presence of his disciples, which are not recorded in this book. But these are written that you may believe that Jesus is the Christ, the Son of God, and that by believing you may have life in his name.*

The truth that we share in the twenty-first century is that we who have not seen Jesus in the flesh, are invited to believe in Him, and we will be blessed if we do. That's this verse in a nutshell, but John doesn't stop there. He reveals more that we need to know.

We learn here that Jesus did more miraculous signs while He was with the disciples in the locked room. At this point, we can only imagine how the men who followed after Jesus had their minds shifted into high gear. After all, Jesus had just come back from the dead, He was more alive than they had ever seen Him, and He popped in and out of rooms at will. What more could He have done that they would consider "signs?" If there were greater miracles than what they had already seen, it's impossible to imagine what they would be.

It is a bit of a shame that more information was not written down for us to read today. I know that everything had to be written by hand on parchment, or some kind of animal skin for the most part, since paper and the printing press were still many centuries in the future, but students of the Word of God always want to know more than is revealed to us. I guess John was inspired by the Holy Spirit to just give us what we need rather than what we want.

The key point of all these things though, is that we may have faith. We are able to read the Gospels, and we know that God has been at work. For this to become all that it can be in our lives, however, it must become more than an historical fact. It has to become a part of our active and daily faith system. The words were written so that we would believe, and our believing makes life, real life, possible. This is not about pie in the sky by and by, but a declaration of how our faith in the resurrection of Jesus provides life for us right now. We know eternal life is coming, but we don't have to wait for it to live. Jesus' resurrection gives us hope for today, tomorrow, and all our days ahead because He is with us always, and He is life!

DOING WHAT COMES NATURAL

John 21:1–3 *Afterward Jesus appeared again to his disciples, by the Sea of Tiberias. It happened this way: Simon Peter, Thomas (called Didymus), Nathanael from Cana in Galilee, the sons of Zebedee, and two other disciples were together. "I'm going out to fish," Simon Peter told them, and they said, "We'll go with you." So they went out and got into the boat, but that night they caught nothing.*

I've never been much of a fisherman. I guess the fish I have caught in my entire life could be counted using my fingers and toes, and still have some digits left over. I certainly have not been a night fisherman, but maybe that's when the most fish bite. I don't know because, well, I'm not a fisherman.

Simon Peter was a professional fisherman though, and he knew how and when to be about the business of catching fish, because it was how he had made his living for years. Why the six companions mentioned here went with Peter we are not told. Maybe they didn't know what to do, and this at least gave them an opportunity to possibly find some food.

Alas, it was not to be the case though. Although John doesn't record how it was that Peter began to first follow after Jesus, in chapter five of Luke's Gospel we find out how it all came about. The scene was very much like this one. Peter had fished all night and had caught nothing—just like in this story. However, when Jesus told Peter to try one more time he did so and caught an overwhelming number of fish. It was that miracle which put Peter in mind of the fact Jesus was more than just another preacher. Now, here he was again, toiling away at his nets, cast after cast, but having no fruit for his labor. There must have been something strangely familiar about it all.

The disciples were in a state of limbo at this time. They knew that their Lord had been raised from the dead, but they didn't understand what it all meant to the world, or what it meant to them personally. They were no doubt still afraid of what the Jews might do to them if they caught up with them, so perhaps fishing was a way to pass time until further direction came from Jesus, or at least a way to stay away from the Pharisees.

They were doing one thing right. When there is no clear direction from Jesus, it's best to keep on with what we are doing until His words come. If He speaks, we will know it, but until then it's best to keep to what we know.

SUCCESS FROM SCARCITY

John 21:4–6 *Early in the morning, Jesus stood on the shore, but the disciples did not realize that it was Jesus. He called out to them, "Friends, haven't you any fish?" "No," they answered. He said, "Throw your net on the right side of the boat and you will find some." When they did, they were unable to haul the net in because of the large number of fish.*

It had been a long night of labor with nothing to show for it when the dawn broke upon Simon Peter and his fishermen friends. They hadn't been doing anything wrong. They were just returning to the work they knew best while waiting to find out what Jesus had next for them. Fishing might be a relaxing pastime for some, but for these men a night of fishing that produced no fish was not only frustrating, but a cause for financial concern as well. No fish meant no money and no food, and that's always a problem.

But then Jesus came on the scene. He always seems to know just when to show up and is always able to deal with whatever situation His followers are having. But this is one more occasion that when Jesus appeared, those who were speaking to Him didn't realize who He was. Had He really changed that much? Were the scars from His crucifixion still so visible that His natural state couldn't be discerned? Couldn't they recognize His voice when He called out to them? After all, they had been with Him for over three years and had heard that voice daily. These and many other questions remain, but it could very well be that we are going to have to wait until we see Him face to face to get answers to them.

Peter had to recognize the very familiar feeling of having no fish and then being told to cast his nets on the other side of the boat to find some. It was so very similar to what Jesus had said to him as recorded in Luke 5:4. When he did as he was told and found the catch that resulted from following the instructions, I can almost see the bells start to ring in Peter's mind.

This is another good lesson in obedience for us. If we will remember that the Lord always has our best interests at heart, and we know that His way always works out best, it would be foolish for us to do anything but obey Him when He speaks. Our best laid plans don't compare to the difference Jesus can make with just a simple sentence. As we look to be productive in our lives, it's always best to just do as Jesus instructs us.

"It Is The Lord!"

John 21:7–10 *Then the disciple whom Jesus loved said to Peter, "It is the Lord!" As soon as Simon Peter heard him say, "It is the Lord," he wrapped his outer garment around him (for he had taken it off) and jumped into the water. The other disciples followed in the boat, towing the net full of fish, for they were not far from shore, about a hundred yards. When they landed, they saw a fire of burning coals there with fish on it, and some bread. Jesus said to them, "Bring some of the fish you have just caught."*

John always referred to himself as "the disciple whom Jesus loved." It's not as if he thought that he was the only one who was loved by His Lord, but it was a humble way of recording events in which he was involved without giving his name. It is most likely an act of modesty.

Simon Peter is usually depicted as a person who is the living antonym of modesty and decorum. He speaks without thinking, acts without planning, and usually ended up putting his foot in his mouth in the process. He was a creature of great emotion and impulse if he was anything.

Once again, we find Peter slow to recognize Jesus, but when John suggests that it is the Lord who is calling to them, Peter doesn't hesitate to act. He apparently had been fishing in minimal clothing, so he quickly donned his outer garment and made his move toward Jesus, swimming ahead of the boat and his companions. I can see the surprise in the eyes of his friends as Peter leaves to them the task of bringing the boat to shore, as he plunges ahead to reconnect with his Lord. After all, it was Jesus who suggested that they cast their nets to the other side of the boat in order to produce the haul of fish they would catch, so they couldn't all just leave the nets behind and rush off through the water.

When they got to shore, they found Jesus already cooking fish and bread for their breakfast. He didn't need what they were bringing to Him. He only wanted to demonstrate to them once again that He was the person in charge of all things, and to affirm their faith in who He was. It is good to note, however, that Jesus requested that they contribute to the breakfast as well. He didn't need them to give for His sake, but they needed to give in order to realize anew that His plan was going to be to work through them. He took what they had and made it better. He still does that with us today.

WHO COUNTED?

John 21:11–14 *Simon Peter climbed aboard and dragged the net ashore. It was full of large fish, 153, but even with so many the net was not torn. Jesus said to them, "Come and have some breakfast." None of the disciples dared ask him, "Who are you?" They knew it was the Lord. Jesus came, took the bread and gave it to them, and did the same with the fish. This was now the third time Jesus appeared to his disciples after he was raised from the dead.*

Can you picture what is going on in this scene in your mind? By this time all the disciples are fully aware that it is Jesus who has entered the picture and they have the opportunity to have breakfast with someone who has come back from the dead. But at some point, in the midst of this tremendous experience, somebody takes the time to count out the number of fish that they had caught. Now that is a dedicated fisherman who really wanted to be sure of his facts before he told the story of their big catch.

Though I have no idea why John lists the number of fish that were brought in, he apparently had a reason for doing so. Perhaps it was because the standard sized net wouldn't normally hold that many fish, and John wanted to emphasize just how great the miracle was, but when one has the opportunity to spend time talking with the risen Lord, counting fish seems to be totally out of place.

My views here may not be right in line with what John is trying to relate, but my mind drifts to the many times the followers of Jesus have majored on minor things when the more important thing was left unattended. We focus on how many people we can get into our church buildings, how much money comes in through our offerings, how many followers we can get on our podcasts or online church viewings, and such trivial things as to what people were wearing as they entered into worship. The list of minor things is endless. Should we have pews or chairs, should our sanctuary be a decorated temple or a plain warehouse-type setting? Is the King James Version of the Bible really the authority we must go by, or are there other translations that will tell the story of the Lord equally well?

Oh, how we love to major on minors. Apparently, someone did on that day also, but I know one thing. When I someday get the opportunity to sit at Jesus' feet, I'm not going to be counting fish.

"Do You Love Me?

John 21:15 *When they had finished eating, Jesus said to Simon Peter, "Simon, son of John, do you truly love me more than these?" "Yes, Lord," he said, "you know that I love you." Jesus said, "Feed my lambs."*

One has to wonder if Jesus confronted Peter right in front of the other disciples who were among the breakfast crew that day, or if Jesus took Peter aside to talk to him. Either way, Peter wasn't prepared for the questioning the Lord was about to put him through.

The meal had been finished and the initial hilarity of seeing the resurrected Jesus alive again had no doubt calmed down a bit because of the casual meal the friends had shared together. Perhaps it was expected that Jesus was going to begin teaching the group once again, and yet it had to have been wonderful just sitting in the presence of their Master. They must have had so many questions and they would never have another opportunity like this to find answers to those questions. There would be a lesson alright, but it wasn't the one they were expecting.

The English translation disguises the words from their original language meaning sometimes. Here is one classic example of that fact. When Jesus asked Peter if he loved Him, the Greek word He used was a form of "agape," which is a pure God-given, deep devotion love. The word Peter used in response was a form of "phileo," a term for friendship, or family love. The two words have two entirely different meanings, so in essence Peter was sidestepping the question that Jesus asked. It's as if Jesus asked, "Do you love me?" and Peter answered, "I am your friend."

It's a painful feeling to express love for a person and that love not to be reciprocated. To be told that you are a friend, even a best friend, doesn't carry the same meaning as being told you are loved. Every person who has ever been on a date understands that fact. Whether Peter misunderstood the question or didn't know exactly how he felt is not clear here, but the question and answer doesn't fit together well.

It makes one wonder how many people have a friendship with Jesus, but not a loving relationship. If we were asked the same question, how would we answer? Would we consider Jesus a good friend, or would we express devotion to Him as the love of our life? Our answer says it all.

"I AM YOUR FRIEND!"

John 21:16 *Again Jesus said, "Simon son of John, do you truly love me?" He answered, "Yes, Lord, you know that I love you." Jesus said, "Take care of my sheep."*

Since Simon Peter didn't really answer Jesus the first time He questioned him, Jesus tried again, and once again He used a form of the Greek word "agape" for "love." It's almost as if Jesus was giving Peter the benefit of the doubt in case he didn't understand the question the first time.

When Peter responded he went right back to the same answer he gave the first time, using a form of the Greek word, "phileo." Jesus was asking if Peter really loved him, and the answer was, "Well, you are my friend."

Of course, there is no way to get into Peter's mind at this point. Jesus was not being vague or unclear since He had phrased His words very specifically. Strange as it may be, Peter was either not willing to make the verbal commitment or was still not grasping what direction Jesus was going with this conversation.

This was the second time that Jesus had instructed Peter to feed His sheep. He was literally saying to him that he was to shepherd the flock of Christ. This echoes the instruction that Jesus gave Peter back in Luke 22:32 where He told him, "And when you have turned back, strengthen your brothers." Jesus had a special role for this big fisherman.

We can gain comfort in the fact that Jesus always knows our capabilities. Before Peter denied his Lord on the night before the cross, Jesus knew that he would do so. But He also knew that Peter possessed a quality of leadership that would prove indispensable to the church in the early days of its existence. Peter might have been outspoken, braggadocios, ego-centered, and slow to catch on, but he was a leader and Jesus was putting a lot of stock in that fact.

Like Peter, many of us have messed up at many points in our lives. We haven't always been the sharpest with the facts, or the most faithful in our service, but the good news is that Jesus knows us intimately, and still has a purpose for us in His Kingdom. We can trust in the fact that He is still waiting for our response to His love, so He can make us the best we can be.

HOW MUCH DO WE LOVE?

John 21:17 *The third time he said to him, "Simon son of John, do you love me?" Peter was hurt because Jesus asked him the third time, "Do you love me?" He said, "Lord, you know all things; you know that I love you." Jesus said, "Feed my sheep."*

The light bulb was finally beginning to glow above Simon Peter's head. Though his previous answers to this question didn't produce the response that Jesus was looking for, it seems that Peter was starting to understand.

Love causes us to face facts. When Jesus first asked, "Do you really love me more than these?" what was He asking? Was He talking about the boats, the men, the fish? Maybe Peter didn't understand the question. When Jesus asked, "Do you really love me?" Peter's answer was similar to many people today, "You know I do, Lord, but I've got a life to live." When Jesus said, "Simon, son of John, do you love me?" Peter had to begin remembering all that Jesus had done for him and had allowed him to experience. The walking on the sea, the healings, the Transfiguration, the Garden of Gethsemane, the resurrection; these events could not be ignored.

Love causes us to get specific. How much do we love? Though Jesus used a form of the word "agape" in the first two questions, the third time He used the word Peter had been using to answer Him, "phileo." "Do you love me like a friend?" When Peter grasped what Jesus was asking, it grieved him to his core.

Much has been made of the fact that Peter had denied Jesus three times, so now Jesus was asking the question of his commitment three times. Peter was going to be a leader in Christ's church and his devotion needed to be complete, for love also requires us to be responsible. Only if Peter loved Jesus more than all other things could he love, feed, guard, and shepherd the flock of faith.

Many of us, like Peter, have had our love stretched and our hearts broken. Sometimes we feel like Paul felt in II Corinthians 4:8–9, "We are hard pressed on every side, but not crushed; perplexed, but not in despair; persecuted, but not abandoned; struck down, but not destroyed." But love causes us to venture on, however. Will we love Him enough to be filled with His agape love? He is waiting to place that love within us.

"Follow Me!"

John 21:18–19 *"I tell you the truth, when you were younger you dressed yourself and went where you wanted; but when you are old you will stretch out your hands, and someone else will dress you and lead you where you do not want to go." Jesus said this to indicate the kind of death by which Peter would glorify God. Then he said to him, "Follow me!"*

When Jesus said, "I tell you the truth," He wasn't kidding. Even though Peter had no idea at this point in time what fate would await him in Rome many years later, the words of His Master were prophetic. According to church tradition Peter died as a Christian martyr in Rome under a command from Emperor Nero. Again, according to some traditional thinking, he was crucified like Jesus, only hanging upside down—at his choice—because he didn't feel worthy of dying as Jesus did. The exact manner of his death can't be completely verified, but it is widely considered that he died in Rome somewhere around A.D. 67-68.

The end for Peter would be much more dramatic than many of us face today, but there are some similarities. It is not uncommon for people as they get into their latter years, to be unable to dress themselves or bath themselves, have to be led where they go, and are many times put in situations that they would rather not be in. A time of infirmity will come to us all if we live long enough.

The point that Jesus was making to Peter, however, was that regardless of how he would end up, it was important that Peter made firm his commitment to follow Jesus wherever He would lead. The "Follow me," command is the most important one that Jesus ever gave. It was necessary for Peter to settle the question of his loyalty, and it is necessary for us to do the same. Three times in a row Peter had denied his Lord and Jesus wanted to make sure that he realized the importance of being grounded in his servant's role once and for all.

The command is for us as well. We too are called to follow Jesus wherever He would choose to lead us. It may be in places of sunshine and glory, or it may be in places where there is great despair and grief. It may not be where we want to go, but if He calls us there, He will provide grace for the mission, for following Jesus is the most important thing we will ever do.

"WHAT ABOUT HIM?"

John 21:20–22 *Peter turned and saw that the disciple whom Jesus loved was following them. (This was the one who had leaned back against Jesus at the supper and had said, "Lord who is going to betray you?") When Peter saw him, he asked, "Lord, what about him?" Jesus answered, "If I want him to remain alive until I return, what is that to you? You must follow me."*

"Lord, what about him?" Now, there is a question that people have asked Jesus down through the centuries. Sometimes it is asked in the context of great personal pain. "What about him? He has so much ease in his life, and I have such sorrow and misery? What about that, Lord?" Sometimes it is asked concerning what we have or don't have. "Lord, why do they get to have children and we have been unable to carry a child to term?" Or it could be, "Lord, why am I working so hard behind the scenes, and others are getting all the credit and get to take the public bows?" Questions like these could go on all day.

We aren't told why Peter turned to John when he asked the question. After all, earlier in this chapter we were told that there were multiple disciples present during the fishing trip and breakfast afterwards. Perhaps John was just nearby, or maybe John wrote this down because Peter pointed him out before the other men. We don't know, but to Jesus it really didn't matter who Peter was talking about.

When we come to Jesus and make the decision to be His servant and devoted follower, at that point we give up all our rights to Him. We don't get to pick and choose our assignments, or our lot in life. We may make plans and try to bend the circumstances to favor our journey a bit, but the bottom line is that Jesus has the same command for all of us: "Follow me!" Following is just that. We are not leaders in His Kingdom. At best we are just under-shepherds. The Good and Great Shepherd remains at the head of the flock, and we are to do and experience what best fits into His plan for us.

This brings us back to the necessity of total surrender at the feet of Jesus. We can call it consecration, heart holiness, entire sanctification, perfect love, or a variety of other titles, but they all mean the same thing. Jesus is Lord and we are not. Jesus commands us, and we are to respond in agreement and accordance with those commands. It's His way or the highway!

IT DOESN'T MATTER
WHAT OTHERS DO

John 21:22–23 *Jesus answered, "If I want him to remain alive until I return, what is that to you? You must follow me." Because of this, the rumor spread among the brothers that this disciple would not die. But Jesus did not say he would not die; he only said, "If I want him to remain alive until I return, what is that to you?"*

Society and the church alike both have active rumor mills. Whether it is intentional gossip or just information that gets garbled with the repeated telling, it doesn't take long for a message that means one thing to be distorted to the point that what is spread is actually the complete opposite of the original intent.

This appears to be the situation with these verses. Jesus was making a strong point to Simon Peter. He was insisting that Peter get his eyes off John and other people and focus on what he was being told by his Master. The message was that the highest priority of being a servant of the King was following the King's commands as they are given, not watching for others to show the way.

Jesus was calling Peter to be a leader, a trend-setter if you will. It didn't matter what John did or didn't do, and it didn't matter what the whole world did or didn't do. The command was for Peter to follow Jesus even if he were to be the only one on earth who did so. This was not an optional suggestion. If he truly loved Jesus and really wanted to be the servant who would feed the Master's flock, he had to do as he was told—and he was told to follow— period. No questions, no arguments, and no opinion polls needed to be consulted. The word of Jesus was definite and firm.

This is where we as followers of Jesus often have trouble. We like to consult authorities, look for precedents, and get the opinions of our family and friends before we make our decisions. Though there can be some value in the counsel of men, the main focus of the disciple's life is to find the will of the Lord and follow it.

We used to use a term around the church that isn't heard much anymore. We spoke about "praying through." It means praying until we touch the throne of God and get our orders directly from on high. Unless we do just that we will always be in doubt as to whether our path is the right one.

THE BEST SELLER OF ALL TIME

John 21:24–25 *This is the disciple who testifies to these things and who wrote them down. We know that his testimony is true. Jesus did many other things as well. If every one of them were written down, I suppose that even the whole world would not have room for the books that would be written.*

We now come to the close of this Gospel account and John gives us a summary of what he has written. He uses his own standing as a disciple of the Lord as proof of the validity concerning what he has recorded. It is commonly accepted, though not without doubters, that the person who wrote these words was actually one of the original twelve disciples whom Jesus hand-picked. We can be sure, however, that whether he was one of the original apostles or not, he truly was a disciple and follower of Jesus Christ.

We are left to speculate as to what other things Jesus did as the God-man who walked among us. The Bible records His birth, but nothing else about His childhood, for the next time we see Him is at twelve years of age when he was separated from His parents at the temple in Jerusalem, as recorded in Luke 2:41-52. We have nothing recorded about His teenage years or even His early adult life until He reaches the age of thirty (Luke 3:23), when He began His public ministry.

There have been over 15,000 books written about Abraham Lincoln, and he holds the record as the second most popular person to ever be written about. You know who holds first place? It's Jesus, the Nazarene from Bethlehem. Still, all we know about Him is collected from those two events of His early life and the three years of public ministry that is recorded in the Bible. That's a lot of popularity for someone who never went to college, never held a public office, and never wrote a book.

John is so correct though when said that the "other things" Jesus did would fill up the world if books were to be written about all His exploits. John gives many proofs of His divinity in this account, but Jesus, the Son of the Living God, did much more than is recorded, and could have done much more than that if He would have desired to do so. The rest of His story will be told when He returns. Through the power of His Spirit, He continues to empower His church, transform lives, and build His Kingdom. Someday He is coming back for us. Until then, we wait, work, and believe until He calls us home.

Printed in the United States
by Baker & Taylor Publisher Services

Printed in the United States
by Baker & Taylor Publisher Services